THE PRIVATE LIFE
OF LOUIS XV

LOUIS XV, KING OF FRANCE
From an engraving by J. Houbraken after J. G. Heilman

THE PRIVATE LIFE
OF LOUIS XV

BY MOUFFLE D'ANGERVILLE
ANNOTATED AND AMPLIFIED BY QUOTATIONS
FROM ORIGINAL & UNPUBLISHED DOCUMENTS
BY ALBERT MEYRAC TRANSLATED
FROM THE FRENCH BY H. S. MINGARD

NEW YORK: BONI AND LIVERIGHT: 1924

PRINTED IN GREAT BRITAIN BY MORRISON AND GIBB LTD., EDINBURGH

A BRIEF FOREWORD

THERE is the less occasion for a long preface to this work as very little is known of the life of Mouffle d'Angerville. We know, and we know little else about him, that he was an advocate in the reign of Louis XVI and that he died about 1794, perhaps on the scaffold, for he proclaimed, always very openly, his anti-revolutionary convictions.

He was a collaborator in the celebrated compilation known as the *Mémoires de Bachaumont*, and, in conjunction with the pamphleteer Pidanzat de Mairobert, he wrote the seven duodecimo volumes, dated Amsterdam, 1774–1776, and entitled *Journal historique de la Révolution opérée dans la Constitution et la Monarchie française*, by the Chevalier de Maupeou ; and with Rochon, *Mémoires pour servir à l'Histoire*. These works are long since forgotten and slumber undisturbed upon their shelves.

But his principal work, the work that preserves his name from oblivion, is the *Vie privée de Louis XV, ou principaux évènements, particularités et anecdotes de son règne,* 4 vols. crown 8vo, published in London in 1781 ; and thereafter, in the same year, and also in 1788, appeared in four duodecimo volumes two new editions " augmented from the author's MSS."

From these most curious and certainly most veracious

Mémoires on which the purveyors of anecdotes and droll stories have so often drawn—albeit without acknowledgment—for their most suggestive incidents, we have extracted these piquant pages, which we might call " The Love Affairs of Louis XV," supplementing, completing and correcting them in the light of contemporary memoirs, and certain pamphlets and satirical songs of the day.

A. M.

Stryienski's *Le XVIIIe siècle*, which is frequently quoted in M. Meyrac's footnotes, forms vol. iv of " The National History of France," and I have availed myself of the English translation by H. N. Dickinson (London : Heinemann, 1916).—Trans.

CONTENTS

vii

CONTENTS

LIST OF ILLUSTRATIONS

The Publishers' thanks are due to Messrs. Suckling & Co. of Garrick Street, who kindly lent several of the engravings which are reproduced in this work.

THE PRIVATE LIFE
OF LOUIS XV

THE PRIVATE LIFE OF
LOUIS XV

CHAPTER I

EARLY DAYS OF THE REIGN

THE difficulties of writing the history of a reign that has just drawn to a close are too formidable to permit us to make the attempt in the case of Louis XV (1715–1774). Over and above the necessity we should be under of securing access to the Government archives, which would probably be denied us on the ground that current events were too closely bound up with those of the immediate past, we should have need of a similar privilege in respect of the other chancelleries of Europe, where the difficulties to be overcome would doubtless be more numerous still. If, on the other hand, we decided to disregard those original sources of information, our history would run the risk of exhibiting those defects of incompleteness and partiality that are the greatest blemishes from which a work of this nature can suffer.

It is quite otherwise with a monarch's private life. It would, of course, be dangerous to write, under his very eyes, a sort of day-to-day record of it and to run the risk of wounding his vanity—and so incurring his wrathful displeasure ; but, as soon as he has breathed his last, the intending chronicler cannot be too prompt in collecting

1

the multitudinous facts that make up his story—facts which, in many cases, are only preserved from oblivion by oral tradition, and of which the fleeting traces grow dim, and sometimes disappear altogether, with the lives of the original witnesses.

We shall not stay to demonstrate the useful purposes that are served by private memoirs. Our generation is too philosophical not to appreciate their value, and the large number of such productions to which it has given birth, and which have achieved such striking popularity, show how greatly they are preferred to the historical treatises of a more solid and weighty description. Indeed, if the attraction of a story depends on our secretly putting ourselves in the position of the hero, what interest can possibly be excited by the narrative of the good and evil fortunes of a prince whose lot the reader can never share, and whose glory he can never hope to rival? If, on the other hand, we divest him of the appurtenances of his dignity and grandeur and show but the man, then all readers, whatever their social status, will take an eager interest in his domestic trials and felicities, deploring the former and rejoicing at the latter. They will all be brought home to them, so to speak, by the possibility of their undergoing similar experiences themselves. If, however, the merit of such anecdotal memoirs is undeniable when they are compiled with care and discrimination, it is in the case of Louis XV that the general truth of this statement is most conspicuously manifested. It is well known how greatly that prince was enamoured of privacy. People will remember with what reluctance he emerged from it to tread the public stage, and with what eagerness he withdrew to his inner apartments as soon as his rôle was finished. Who among us has not heard his servants, his intimates, his ministers say, " If only the King had been born one of us, he would be the kindest friend, the best husband, the best father and the most worthy man in his kingdom " ? [1]

These oft-repeated statements can only have the effect of accentuating the desire to behold Louis XV in these several capacities, and we shall lose no time in satisfying the impatience of our readers.

In his last will and testament, Louis XIV had appointed the Maréchal de Villeroi guardian to the young monarch, the Duchesse de Ventadour his governess, the Bishop of Fréjus his tutor, and Father le Tellier his confessor. The sole modification that took place in this arrangement was the dismissal of the Jesuit.

Madame de Ventadour [2] was the only one of them all who was able to take up the active performance of her duties.

[1] There is no doubt that Louis XV was an excellent father ; his daughters adored him. Throughout all his childhood the Dauphin was for him an object of real interest, and he only drew away from him when he thought it evident that he was putting himself at the head of a jealous opposition ; and even then his paternal feelings regained the upper hand when the Dauphin fell sick. " You are a kind papa," Dr. Ponce is reported to have said to him, " and I am glad to see it. Take courage, your son will be restored to you." His kindness and amiability as a monarch were, like his religion, a mask adopted for appearance' sake. He was anxious to appear moved by the distress with which, during his reign, his people were afflicted. He caused bread to be distributed in years of famine ; he gave money to people whose homes had been destroyed by fire, pensioned retired officers and indigent noblemen out of his privy purse, and found husbands for dowerless girls. Some people looked upon him as the most gentle and affable of masters. At heart, however, he was a downright egoist who could not bear the recital of ills that he deemed himself unable to remove, and was incapable of any of those remedial acts which do more than all the almsgiving in the world to bring consolation to the suffering. He remained quite unmoved by the death of those who had served him. Cf. Carré, *La France sous Louis XV*, ch. i. pp. 5–8.

[2] The Duchesse de Ventadour was a demoiselle of the House of La Mothe Houdancourt. See A. Meyrac, *Louis XIV, sa cour et ses maîtresses. II., A. Michel.* Saint-Simon hints that she was not entirely free from reproach. " Madame de Maintenon," he writes, " used to declare that she had a greater affection for women who had erred and repented than for those who had never wrought anything to repent of. She lived a long time

This princess of the illustrious House of Rohan, which has since given many another governess to the royal children of France, was pre-eminently endowed with fitting attributes for her task. She combined in a marked degree the qualities of gentleness and dignity ; she was passionately devoted to her royal charge, and the care she lavished on him was more that of a loving mother than an ambitious stranger. Current events and the circumstances of the case only served to augment her vigilance. She was well acquainted with the horrible suspicions by which all anxious hearts were visited. What deep misgivings must have been hers when she beheld the guardianship of Louis XV entrusted to the heir-presumptive to the throne. She redoubled her watchful solicitude and never relaxed

apart from her husband, who was deformed and very ugly. The satirists did not spare her.

> La femme par prudence
> L'a quitté depuis vingt ans ;
> N'a souffert pas trop longtemps
> Son importune présence :
> Je n'en dirai pas le nom
> Elle a soin des fils de France.

(His wife out of prudence left him twenty years ago; she could not endure over long his disagreeable presence. I will not tell her name—she has charge of the Princes of France.)

And with great care did she fulfil her charge. In the play entitled *Les présages de la religion*, written on the occasion of the King's complete restoration, 1721, we read :

> . . . de la piété j'implorai le secours ;
> Elle vint sous les traits d'une illustre mortelle,
> Et pour lui, chaque instant, renouvela son zèle.
> Occupée à sa garde, elle sent tour à tour
> Et la crainte et l'espoir et la joie et l'amour,
> La mère pour son fils a bien moins de tendresse.

(. . . of piety I implored her aid. She came to me in the guise of an illustrious woman, and, for him, every moment she renewed her zeal. Keeping watch over him, she feels alternately fear and hope, joy and love. A mother for her own son displays less tenderness.)

her vigilance for an instant during the whole period—nearly eighteen months—of her attendance on the King.

One remarkable circumstance occurred during this governess's period of office, whereby she received a distinction that had been vouchsafed to none of her predecessors. Louis XV came to Parliament to hold his first Bed of Justice on the 12th September, in order to confirm the decision pronounced by that court in favour of the Regent. The Duchesse de Ventadour represented the Queen Mother and Regent on this occasion, acting in every respect as she would have done, save that she did not take her seat on the throne but took her part in the proceedings sitting at the King's feet. However, she spoke in his name. She was then about forty years of age and still beautiful, and the grave dignity of her demeanour eminently befitted her to play so exalted a part. "Messieurs," she said, "the King has bidden you to assemble together in order to make known to you his wishes : his Chancellor will explain them."

Sinister were the auspices under which Louis XV, who was nearing his majority, began a reign which was fated to conclude amid clouds more sombre still. At that age, however, none could impute to him responsibility for the calamities of the State. Indeed, the Prince's natural characteristics seemed of happy augury for his times. Although the delicacy of his constitution forbade the prosecution of those studies that call for great concentration of mind, there appeared, as early as 1718, a book entitled *Cours des principaux fleuves de l'Europe*, which was printed in his name, as being his own composition. Fifty copies were issued and the courtiers tumbled one over another in their eagerness to possess one. It is said that M. Delisle, his preceptor in this department of knowledge, had given him much assistance. Evidently, however, the pupil must have played some part in the work in order that his flatterers might have an opportunity for thus ministering to his vanity. M. de Voltaire indeed observes, in the course of his commendatory notice, that the King's taste in this direction enabled him to acquire a considerable acquaintance with astronomy and natural history.[1]

He also developed the physical graces, and, when only ten years old, danced with several young noblemen of the Court in the comedy *l'Inconnu*, his performance being much admired.[2]

He distinguished himself still more in an exercise worthier of his royal dignity. In order to give concrete effect to the lessons in military art that he was receiving, a camp was formed six miles from Versailles, and there a fort was besieged and an engagement fought, exactly as

---

[1] Louis XV's exercise books, corrected by Fleury, are preserved in the Bibliothèque Nationale. Every day he had lessons in writing, Latin and French history. Three times a week he had lessons in geography, which he liked very much, and in astronomy, which he liked still more, as well as in mathematics and botany. Later on, we find him sending strawberry seeds " to the very celebrated and very noble M. Linnæus." In all these studies, says Buvat, he made great progress, adding, however, that he had the advantage of being instructed " by skilful preceptors : Guillaume Delisle, the best geographer of his day, Chevalier, the eminent mathematician," Puységur the Lieutenant-General, and Hermann the engineer were his professors in the military art. He had a particularly good memory and great mental alertness.

[2] Louis XV at this time was an attractive and pretty child, though the selfishness of his character was already revealing itself. He had no love for anybody but Madame de Ventadour, whom he called " his dear Mamma." His health was delicate and sickly. It was dangerous to thwart him ; he was allowed to do as he pleased, and the result was that he was very much spoilt and was rebellious, stubborn and proud, only emerging from the obstinate silence that was habitual with him, to deliver himself of some pert and stinging remark. The Bishop of Metz, Monseigneur de Coislin, came to do homage. " Oh, what an ugly man ! " exclaimed the little King. " What a badly brought up little boy," said the Bishop, turning on his heel. *Vide* Stryienski, *Le XVIIIe siècle*, pp. 8–13 (Paris, Hachette), and pp. 16–17, the amusing scene that took place when Mohammed Effendi, the ambassador of the Sublime Porte, was presented to Louis XV. " May God Almighty, who created so fair a child, grant him His blessing," said the Turk as he took his leave.

in real war. The King was immensely delighted. Not content with playing the part of a mere spectator, he put himself at the head of the attacking party, and the ardour with which he bore himself justified the expectation that he was destined to prove a warlike monarch.

In due course, he proceeded to display the majesty of his kingly office in an audience which he granted to Mohammed Effendi, the Turkish ambassador, whose appearance was well calculated to contribute to the royal child's amusement. It was no doubt with this object in view that the audience was arranged, rather than for the reason publicly announced which, so it was given out, was to assure the King that, out of regard for him, the Sultan was about to take under his protection the monks at Jerusalem, and that he had given orders for the restoration of the monastery and church of the Holy Sepulchre. His Majesty was much less impressed by these assurances than by the pearls and other precious gems that scintillated on every part of the person of his Turkish guest.

It is well known that Louis' judgment never misled him, and it speaks volumes for his tact that, when in 1720 he began to take part in the Regency Council, he had the prudence and good sense to hold his tongue. It was not until the following year that he spoke for the first time. M. d'Armenonville had just read over to him a letter from the King of Spain containing the news that that monarch agreed to the proposal that his daughter the Infanta should wed Louis XV of France. The Regent informed His Majesty that it was necessary for him to make a reply. The King answered that he gave his consent with pleasure, and that the marriage was eminently agreeable to him.

But, even when he maintained silence, that silence itself was eloquent. When His Royal Highness the Regent brought word to the King that M. d'Armenonville had resigned office for the second time, and introduced his successor to the Seals, the mournful air with which the King regarded them made it perfectly evident that the change was distasteful to him.

The answer he made to the Regent on the day he attained his majority equally displayed his reluctance to accept the inevitable responsibility that was now to fall upon him. His Royal Highness in handing over the reins of government and the destinies of his kingdom, which was now in happy plight and free from the ravages of the plague,[1] inquired what commands it pleased His Majesty to give in respect of divers matters and especially in regard to those of his subjects who had been exiled as a result of ecclesiastical dissensions. His Majesty replied that he had sent no one into exile. Nevertheless the fact that the system of *lettres de cachet* became more prevalent than ever and endured throughout the whole of his reign, would rather lend colour to the belief that this was a pretence. He also displayed much emotion on the occasion of the downfall of his tutor, Maréchal the Duc de Villeroi. Six months before the King attained his majority, the Regent had publicly declared that it was time for His Majesty to be instructed in the affairs and secrets of his realm, and that he himself would undertake this duty. He spoke with the King's tutor in private on the matter and announced that he himself would work with the young monarch every morning. On the 10th of August the Regent begged His Majesty to come with him into his cabinet. Maréchal de Villeroi made as if to follow his royal pupil, stating that he could not lose sight of so sacred a charge. The Regent

---

[1] A merchant ship which arrived at Marseilles from Sidon in 1720 had introduced the plague into France. For nearly two years its ravages were exceedingly great. Cordons had been drawn round the frontiers of several provinces in order to hinder the spread of the disease. At the end of the year 1722 they had just been raised. This plague of Marseilles is celebrated in history, as also is the heroic devotion displayed by the Bishop, Monseigneur de Belzunce.

was so incensed at the mistrust thus displayed, that he sent the Maréchal into exile and put in his place the Duc de Charost, whom the King had asked for since he was not allowed to retain the other.

The Regent's action was the more high-handed in that the Maréchal de Villeroi had a precedent for his action in what had occurred to his own father who, in his day, had been tutor to Louis XIV. It happened that one day Anne of Austria, the Queen Regent, had something of a private nature to impart to the young King; the old Marshal was fain respectfully to withdraw during the colloquy. "Nay, do not go away, monsieur," said Her Majesty; "since I have entrusted you with the upbringing of the King my son, there is nothing that we wish to keep from you, and you must never lose sight of his person." The Regent's conduct was therefore enough to revive those terrible suspicions that had so often been spread abroad concerning His Royal Highness. The hasty and voluntary resignation of the ex-Bishop of Fréjus which occurred on the same day was also attributed to the Regent. The King wept and was so completely beside himself that he broke the windows of his apartment, refusing either to eat or sleep, so great was his grief at being bereft of two persons with whom he had become familiar. It was this which decided the Duc d'Orléans not to pursue his resentment against the latter, whose flight (for flight it seemed) made matters look suspicious. He therefore ordered him to return at once and resume his duties. This he did, and by so doing it would appear that he built up the large fortune to which he ultimately attained.[1]

---

[1] François de Neuville, Duc de Villeroi, Marshal of France (1644–1730), was brought up with Louis XIV and always proved himself an amiable courtier. He was a man of great personal courage but an indifferent soldier, and the fortunes of war were invariably against him. After the signal defeat he sustained at Ramillies, in the Low Countries, in the year 1703, he never reappeared at the head of the army, but he still remained in the

The young Prince's character underwent no further development until the ceremony of his coronation, the vain pomp of which we shall forbear to describe. We will merely record, as a circumstance hitherto unique in our history, that the six lay Peers of France were represented on this occasion by six Princes of the Blood.

The coronation took place at Rheims. On the morning of the ceremony, which was very long and fatiguing, the young monarch was offered, in accordance with a time-honoured usage doubtless authorized by a Papal dispensation, a bowl of broth, notwithstanding the fact that he was to receive Holy Communion, which the Church enjoins should be taken fasting. He refused to touch it in spite of urgent persuasion and the example set him by his predecessors. He said that he would rather have it recorded in history that he had refused to take any food before drawing near to the Holy Table. This circumstance reveals how, even in those days, he was animated to a much greater extent by the consideration of earthly things than

favour of Louis XIV, who said to him genially : "People of our age never have any luck, Monsieur le Maréchal." We should add that this mot is apparently quite apocryphal, and seems to have been invented by Voltaire. Few Generals have been more mercilessly lampooned on account of their incapacity. The following epigram, which has been frequently quoted, was uttered in 1702 when the Imperialists carried out a raid and kidnapped him at Cremona, where he had just arrived. They were, however, unable to take the town itself.

> Français rendez grace à Bellone,
> Votre bonheur est sans égal,
> Vous avez conservé Crémone
> Et perdu votre général.

(Frenchmen, give thanks to Bellona, your good fortune has no equal; you have preserved Cremona and lost your General.)

Arrogant and hot-tempered, he yet showed himself servile in the presence of Louis XV. "Sire," he said to him one day, pointing to the crowd that had gathered beneath the windows of the Tuileries, "all that belongs to you." He finished by falling out with the Regent, who sent him to live in exile at Lyons. In 1724, however, he returned to Court.

by the true spirit of religion. On this same occasion,
when they had placed the crown on His Majesty's head,
he removed it and laid it on the altar. It was pointed out
to him that he ought to wear it during the ceremony,
but he replied that he would rather offer it as a tribute to
Him to whom he owed it. He was no doubt already
imbued with the doctrine—which he subsequently defined
so vigorously before Parliament on the 3rd March 1766—
that he held his crown from God alone.

In the course of his journey home from Rheims, the
King stayed for a while at Villers Cotterets, where the
Duc d'Orléans gave a splendid fête in his honour. All
His Majesty's retinue were entertained on a scale of great
magnificence, and this hospitality was extended also to
the crowds of sightseers who flocked thither in large
numbers. His Royal Highness even went so far as to
have all who were unable to find quarters at the château
entertained at his own expense at the inns and hostelries
of the neighbourhood.

It next fell to the Duc de Bourbon to perform the
honours on a like scale at Chantilly, where, by reason of
the beauties of the setting, the festivities were more
brilliant still. Whereupon some one spitefully observed
that " the Mississippi must have flowed through the place."

It was at these fêtes that Louis XV first conceived that
passion for the chase which afterwards became such an
obsession with him that even advancing years did not avail
to cool his ardour.

On the 16th February, 1723, the King having entered
upon his fourteenth year, the Duc d'Orléans attended his
levée in order to pay his respects and to ask his commands
for the conduct of State affairs.

This ceremony was followed by another of a more
impressive character. This was the Bed of Justice held
on the 22nd February following, at which His Majesty

declared his majority and stated that, in accordance with the regulations of the State, he had come to his Parliament to announce to it that from that day forth it was his intention to assume the direction of the Government. To the Duc d'Orléans, who was present, His Majesty expressed his thanks for all the care he had devoted to affairs of State, begging that he would continue so to do and lend his aid in all important matters connected with the government of the country. At the same time His Majesty confirmed Cardinal Dubois in the office of Prime Minister. Then, having done more than was necessary to add the purple to his Archbishopric of Cambrai,[1] he obtained at the same time, to help him support his new dignity, the Abbey of Cercamp and the Superintendentship of Posts, shortly afterwards entering the Council. One of the prerogatives to which the Princes of the Church lay claim is that of occupying stalls immediately behind the Princes of the Blood, in front of all the other members, not excepting the Chancellor himself. Cardinal de Rohan had just set the example, but the complaints and expostulations were far more vigorous in the case of Dubois, whose birth did not lend him the same confidence. The complainants went the length of staying away from the Council on that day and, when the meeting was over, Cardinal de Noailles, who had little love for his new Eminence, seeing the regrettable false step into which he had been led by him, paid him the following compliment : " This day will be a famous one in history, monsieur. People will not

---

[1] He was enthroned, but only after innumerable hesitations and refusals by Pope Innocent XIII, whose election he had supported at Rome. The occasion brought forth a very torrent of epigrams and epitaphs, among others the following :

> Rome rougit d'avoir rougi
> Le maquereau qui gît ici.

(Rome blushes scarlet for conferring the scarlet on the parasite who lies here below.)

forget to put it on record that your entry into the Council caused all the great ones of the realm to desert it."

The absence of a few of these gentry would not have been unwelcome to the Duc d'Orléans and his favourite, but their general defection was highly vexatious to them. It was in vain that they essayed to arrive at some arrangement whereby the claims of each should be respected. Not one would be persuaded. This terrible etiquette must needs possess an importance that is hidden from the majority of men, since the gravest counsellors, men whose every action one would expect to be guided by principle, subjected themselves to its decrees and sacrificed everything to it.

Thus, on this occasion, the Maréchal Duc de Villeroi, who shortly afterwards suffered exile and the loss of his post as tutor to His Majesty, because he would not leave him to discuss affairs of State in a *tête-à-tête* with the Regent, had no compunction in remitting his duties and abandoning his sacred charge rather than yield precedence to the Cardinals. Thus, too, the Chancellor, after signing all manner of things against the Parliament to which he owed his fortunes, and against his conscience which prompted the reverse course of conduct, fearing lest he should be compelled to return a second time to France, nevertheless preferred to proceed thither on this occasion rather than submit to any derogation of the rights and dignities appertaining to his office.

Parisians, and particularly the Jansenists, did not regard the step from the same point of view. They considered it highly patriotic. They looked on him as a glorious exile and did not diminish their respect for him. Cardinal de Bissy, being on his way to spend Easter in his bishopric of Meaux, deemed it his duty to inquire of Cardinal Dubois whether His Royal Highness would take it ill of him if he paid a visit to the chief magistrate. " Far from it," was the reply; "on the contrary, His Royal Highness would be very pleased and, if I myself were less occupied with affairs, I should have much pleasure in bearing you company to Fresnes."

At the Palais Royal the matter was spoken of less seriously; they cracked jokes about it. At one of the Regent's elegant supper-parties, to which his favourites were admitted and where they had full liberty to deliver themselves of any sallies their merry mood might prompt, even on the gravest matters, it chanced that the conversation fell upon this topic, and a certain noble, after bewailing the vicissitudes of human greatness, took as his text these coveted Seals of State and their passing, turn and turn about, from the Chancellor to the merest pettyfogging attorney, exclaimed that "'twere a hundred times better to be a beadle, for the same man had been in the service of Messieurs de Ponchartrain, Voisin, d'Aguesseau and d'Argenson, and was now with their successor, and that if he followed the magistracy, he would aim no higher than that." Whereat the Regent burst out laughing and capped the quip with others more extravagant.

The Seals were bestowed upon M. d'Armenonville,[1] a man of gentle and pliant disposition, who gave rise to no

---

[1] Joseph J.-B. Fleuriau d'Armenonville, born 1660, died 1728 at the Château de Madrid. His ancestors, the Bonneaus, Bouchauds, and Fleuriaus, were merchants of Touraine. D'Armenonville, who was at first Intendant, became Director of Finance, and subsequently Keeper of the Seals in succession to D'Argenson. He had so embellished the Château de Rambouillet that Louis XIV purchased it from him for the Comte de Toulouse, granting him in exchange the usufruct of the Château de la Muette and of the Bois de Boulogne. The following is the " portrait " of D'Armenonville in the *Mémoires secrets pour servir à l'Histoire de Perse* (Persia, *i.e.* France), a book in which the appreciations and portraits of people who are referred to by borrowed names are for the most part sincere. " Daracha (D'Argenson) was succeeded by Fazel (D'Armenonville), the grandson of a merchant who had waxed rich in trade. He had grown grey in divers departments connected with finance. He was of too limited a

fear that he would kick over the traces. He took his seat
without a murmur behind the Cardinals. As for the
Dukes and Peers and the Marshals of France, they could
be dispensed with. One and all they were forbidden to
attend and their names were forthwith struck off the
pension list.

The aged Maréchal de Villeroi expressed himself with
much indiscretion concerning the Chancellor's dismissal
and said that, if he were still alive when His Majesty
attained his majority, he would make so bold as to call his
attention to this act of injustice. The new Keeper of the
Seals having come to greet him, he replied for all to hear :
" I offer you no congratulations, for I know full well how
pained you must be at being called to fill the place of such
a man as Monsieur d'Aguesseau."

All this contributed not a little to whet the Regent's
resentment towards him, and he seized the occasion to rid
himself of so severe and inconvenient a censor.

As for the general public, they were little pleased with
the appointment of M. d'Armenonville, whose ability
they held in small esteem. But to the Duc d'Orléans
and his favourite nothing was less necessary than a man of
ability. Both alike were only on the look out for such as
would readily do their bidding, and both were sufficiently
endowed with brains and knowledge to supply the de-

capacity to become a Minister of State, and professed the opinions that were
dictated to him. For such consideration as he enjoyed, he was indebted to
his son Abdoul (Ch. Fleuriau, Comte de Morville, Minister of Marine in
1722, and afterwards Secretary of State for Foreign Affairs). The Seal of
the Sophi having been taken away from his father, whom he supported by his
merit and reputation, he, the son, was so overcome by this piece of ill-
fortune, that he committed the folly of resigning his post of Chief Secretary
of State. From that day forth, both father and son were forgotten of all
men (a mischance that frequently befalls one at Court), and they were
reduced to passing their days in a solitude which weighed the more heavily
upon them that in former days they had moved amid so brilliant and
numerous a throng. Heaviness of spirit fell upon both, and in no long
time brought them to the grave."

ficiencies of those who worked for them. Moreover, it was the design of His Royal Highness to appoint Cardinal Dubois to the office of Prime Minister, whereof he already wielded nearly all the power ; but ere he did so, he aimed at making him *persona grata* both at home and abroad. For example, the marriage of the Infanta of Spain, which had been arranged for the King, had won him the good graces and support of His Most Catholic Majesty who, in exchange, asked that Mademoiselle de Montpensier, the Regent's daughter, should wed the Prince of Asturias.[1]

[1] The *Journal de Barbier* should be consulted for a description of the triumphal reception and magnificent discourses accorded and delivered to this " Infanta," who was five or six years old when she came to France. She was already referred to as " Her Majesty " and " the Queen." " This marriage," the Duc de Noailles took occasion ro remark, " will end like Law's system." Exile was his reward for the prophecy, but nevertheless it was fulfilled. The poor little Infanta was bundled off home again, and the fat was nearly in the fire with Spain. All they told the child was that " Papa wanted to see her again." What a host of intrigues it cost to send her packing ! The Prince de Bourbon had refused to tolerate that the crown of Spain should become the appanage of a rival family. Meantime, Philip V having abdicated on the 17th January, 1724, the Prince of Asturias, his son, became King under the title of Louis I, and, in consequence, Louise Elizabeth, his wife, the Regent's daughter, became Queen. Six months later, King Louis was in his grave.

Madame d'Orléans, the Princess Palatine and mother of the Regent, writes as follows concerning her granddaughter : " One could not say that Mademoiselle de Montpensier (Louise Elizabeth) was ugly ; her eyes are fine, her skin white and delicate, her nose well turned, though a little thin, and her mouth very tiny. Notwithstanding all that, she is the most disagreeable person I ever met in my life. In everything she does, whether she be talking, eating or drinking, she is unbearable. Not a single tear did she shed when she left us ; she scarcely said good-bye." The granddaughter's conduct in Spain justified the grandmother's somewhat severe verdict. She carried her wayward sullenness so far as to refuse to show herself at the fêtes given in her honour. When she became queen she remained in the seclusion of her own apartments wholly wrapped up in her young maids of honour. The King, her husband, deemed there was scandal in this association and he drove these maids of honour (?) from the Court, and shut up his wife in the Château of Buen Retiro. Subsequently they made it up. When she became a widow, she returned to France, " white-haired, fat, but with about as much determination as a child of seven," says Barbier. In 1727 she retired to a convent with a lady-in-waiting, a dog and a couple of cats. Vide *Correspondance de Madame*, pp. 355-56, vol. ii. (Brunet).

This double marriage had been brought about by the Jesuit d'Aubenton, the King of Spain's confessor, who in return had demanded that his Society should be reinstated at the French Court in its prerogative of furnishing the King's confessor. And it so happened that the Abbé de Fleury, having asked to be relieved of that duty, was replaced by Father de Linières. He had for some years been confessor to Madame, to whom he had been commended by Father de la Chaise. His quiet disposition and mediocre intellectual equipment seem to have been the determining factors in bringing about his appointment, which, without giving rise to any apprehension, gave satisfaction alike at Madrid and Rome. At the same time it offended the Jansenist faction, who were always active, despite all attempts at conciliation. They regarded this as one of the most grievous blows that could have been dealt them, and Cardinal de Noailles gave vent to his ill-humour in the most immoderate fashion. Father de Linières, as was his duty, came to pay his respects to His Eminence and to ask for his authority. "You want your authority, mon Père," he said as soon as the Jesuit came in sight; "well, I cannot give it you, and I am glad to be able to inform you in person that I forbid you to confess the King. There are plenty of reasons I could give you for my refusal, but at present I have too bad a cold."

The Maréchale de Noailles, his sister-in-law, who had no suspicion of a cold, took up the harangue and rated the Jesuit with all the harshness that an angry woman is capable of expressing. The prelate persisted in his refusal even to the Regent and the King, explaining his reasons in a letter wherein he set out to show that his own conscience would not suffer him to endure that a son of Ignatius should have charge of the conscience of his King. Nevertheless, by one of those inconsequences so common among those who are swayed by party spirit, he suffered without

2

protest the Duc d'Orléans and Madame to have Jesuit confessors. Father de Linières was consequently obliged to go and live at Pontoise, which was in the diocese of Rouen, and the young monarch went to Saint Cyr, which was under the episcopal jurisdiction of Chartres, and there the Jesuit administered to him the sacrament of penance. Soon afterwards a brief was obtained from the Pope allowing the King to choose a confessor approved by the ordinary, and declaring that His Majesty belonged to no diocese in particular. When His Eminence saw that he was no longer needed, he acquiesced in whatever was asked of him.

It must be acknowledged that the presence of this Jesuit at Court gave umbrage to many, even to some who were not Jansenists. The Princesse de Conti, the first dowager of the realm, gave him a very chilly reception. The Abbess of Chelles,[1] after listening to his long-winded

---

[1] Louise Adelaide, Abbess of Chelles, who died in 1743, was the Regent's third daughter. She was remarkably learned, a theologian, a musician and an artist " to the finger-tips." The *chroniques scandaleuses* of the day, for she had to endure something more than mere satire in some of the couplets about her, hint that, like her sister the Duchesse de Berry, she was by way of being the mistress of her own father. Her Abbey was a palace of delight. " In the Abbey where Venus dwells :

> Pour tout office
> On goute tous les jours
> Mille délices
> Qu'assaisonne l'Amour ;
> Chaque instant sur les cœurs
> Il répand ses faveurs.
> A ce Dieu si propice
> Elles livrent leurs cœurs,
> Pour tout office.

(their sole office is day by day to taste a thousand delights to which Love gives zest ; every moment o'er their hearts he sheds his favours. To this propitious deity they surrender their hearts, 'tis their sole office.)

See the *Correspondance de Madame*, to which we have already referred, for some very interesting letters in which the grandmother speaks in great detail about her granddaughter : her portrait ; why she became a nun ;

address, answered : " Since the King had of necessity to have a confessor of your cloth, I would as soon see you as any one else in that position ; but I cannot conceal from you that I am vexed to see a Jesuit there at all, for you must be aware that I do not like your Society, of which I am, indeed, somewhat afraid. You will observe that I am a good Frenchwoman."

The Jesuits, for all their triumphs, were unable to obtain one thing for which they hankered no less than for the post of royal confessor, and that was to be included on the list of benefices, without which the post is merely an honorary one, like that of Chancellor without the Seals.

In vain did they intrigue to enlist the aid of the Spanish monarch to this end, on the pretext that the appellant party, despite all endeavours to secure its overthrow, was still extremely powerful ; that the principal means of destroying it was to keep the benefices out of the hands of seditious or suspected ecclesiastics ; that to compass this required as much knowledge of persons as zeal ; that no single individual could rival a Jesuit in the former since the Order had its observers and correspondents all over the realm, and that none could harbour any doubts about the latter, whereof the Society had given such numerous and conspicuous proofs.

The activities of the Jesuits were powerfully supported by the Nuncio ; but neither the Regent nor Cardinal

---

her quarrel with her mother ; her confession ; the ceremony of her installation. In the convent she was known as Sœur Bathilde. Racine the younger wrote a poem on her taking the veil :

> Plaisir, beauté, jeunesse, honneur, gloire, puissance,
> Ambitieux espoirs que promet la naissance,
> Tout au pied de l'Agneau fut par elle immolé.

(Pleasure, beauty, youth, honour, glory, power, ambitious hopes held out by noble birth, all at the feet of the Lamb she offered in sacrifice.)

But there were other poets who sang of her in a very different fashion !

Dubois was at all disposed to acquiesce in claims so excessive. Their view of the situation was that it would be desirable to render the Jansenists powerless for action but not to crush them or to destroy the balance of power by allowing too great a predominance to their enemies. It was in these circumstances and with a view to increasing his prestige, that on the 22nd August His Royal Highness deemed the time had come to declare Cardinal Dubois Prime Minister.

Among the congratulations that His Eminence received on this occasion, those of his brother the Abbé Dubois, a Canon of Saint-Honoré, excited particular remark. He wrote telling the Cardinal that the new dignity to which he was promoted obliged him to redouble his prayers to God that by His grace he might use the power that had just been granted to him for no other purpose than the welfare of the State and the advancement of religion.

The most curious anecdote concerning this elevation, and one most suitable to supply food for reflection to the philosophic reader as well as to reveal the character of the favourite and his master, is the story of what took place at one of the Regent's supper-parties. The guests were indulging in much mockery at the expense of the new prime minister, but the Duc de Noailles it was who permitted himself the bitterest jest : " Your Royal Highness," he said, " may make him what you like, but you'll never make an honest man of him." The next day he was sent into exile. In vain the Comtesse du Tort reproached the Regent with his weakness, the *lettre de cachet* held good, and it was not until the Cardinal's death that the Duc d'Orléans wrote to the Comte to come back. The letter was a strange production and fully in keeping with the rest of the story : " Dead men don't bite," it ran. " I shall expect you to-night for supper at the Palais Royal."

Dubois had long been a sufferer from some bladder trouble which was generally ascribed to his excesses and debaucheries. He had to undergo a horribly painful operation and his spirit quailed at the sight of the instruments. It fell to the Duc d'Orléans to screw the patient's courage to the sticking-point.[1] Dubois died the next day, which was the 10th August, at the age of sixty-six.

One day, or it may have been two, before his death, the Cardinal made his confession to a Franciscan. The ceremony only lasted a little over five minutes, which made it seem as though he only wanted to satisfy convention and to show a last mark of deference to the Duc d'Orléans, who had always impressed upon him how important it was for the reputation of both of them to keep up appearances. One proof of his disregard of spiritual succour was afforded by the fact that he did not receive viaticum because of the ceremonial that has to be observed in

---

[1] The tremendous efforts he had to make, on the occasion of a review, to keep himself in the saddle, are said to have brought about the bursting of an abscess due to some venereal complaint.

Ci-gît que Vénus eleva
Et que Vénus terrassa.

(Here he lies whom Venus raised and whom Venus laid low.)

Ci-gît le Cardinal de Brive-la-Gaillarde.
Eh! Cadédis, qui l'a mis là ?
C'est son humeur paillarde.

(Here lies the Cardinal de Brive-la-Gaillarde. Eh! Cadédis, what put him under ? Why, what but his lecherous instincts !)

Le ciseau de La Peyronie
Vient donc de délivrer l'Etat
De ce ministre scélérat.

(The knife of La Peyronie has just rid the State of this scoundrelly minister.)

Dubois died on the 10th August, 1723, the day after La Peyronie had operated on him, amputating his reproductive organs, which were all gangrenous.

administering it to a Cardinal, or if not that, then it shows the importance attached to the observance of etiquette since a Prince of the Church was apparently willing to jeopardize his salvation because of it.   The last and least equivocal sentiment that he evinced was his never-failing attachment to the House of Orléans.   Whatever pangs it may have cost him to bid adieu to life, he protested that he would have departed content if he had been able to crush (such were his own words) the enemies of His Royal Highness.

We have noted the various stages by which Cardinal Dubois mounted the successive rungs of the ladder till he attained the highest honours in Church and State.   He was also anxious to shine as an intellectual luminary and procured his election to the Académie française.   It was within the walls of that august institution that the voice of Fontenelle, to whom, as director, it fell to pronounce the address of welcome on that occasion, declared to him that in view of the number of potentates who had canvassed his election to the Cardinalate " he was a prelate of every Catholic country and a minister of every Court."   And he added on another occasion : " You remember that I desired to have you here long before you could bring so many titles to the distinction.   None knew better than I that you would have come armed with those titles that we value above all others."

Dubois, who in everything followed closely in the footsteps of Mazarin, had a shrewd eye to his private affairs and would have amassed a very considerable fortune if time had allowed.   As it was, he left his heirs about two million *livres* in hard cash.   We are not quite sure whether it was some similar piece of scrupulosity which was at the bottom of his desire to make the Regent his residuary legatee.   However this may have been, the Regent would not permit it.   He would only accept the service of gold

Rigaud, Pinxt.   *Jouannin, Sculpt.*

CARDINAL DUBOIS

plate that the Cardinal had ordered to be made for State occasions.[1]

He was given a magnificent funeral. They even struck a medal in his honour. On one side was his effigy, and on the other a tree blown down by the storm, with the following inscription round the edge : *Visa est dum stetit minor.* The licentious invented a very different and very coarse epitaph, and he thoroughly deserved them both.

We have only to bear in mind the means by which he rose to prominence in order to realize how contemptible and ignoble was his character. When, however, we have regard to the talents that he manifested in his high position, it must be allowed that he displayed the attributes of a real statesman. The Regent could find no worthier successor to carry on his duties than himself, and this sets the seal on his eulogy of the dead Cardinal.[2]

[1] The sale of the furniture produced about 800,000 *livres*, which Dubois' nephew, the Canon of Saint-Honoré, divided among the hospitals of Brive la Gaillarde and the hospital of Paris. The library, with the exception of a small portion bestowed on the Collège de Brive, was sold in Holland. Of Dubois we possess a portrait painted by Rigaud, and engraved by Drevet with the arms of the Cardinal statesman.

[2] Dubois' career was certainly no ordinary one. He was the son of a little apothecary at Brive la Gaillarde. He succeeded in becoming tutor, an easy-going tutor, to the Duc de Chartres, the future Regent. " I will do him justice," was the comment of the Prince's mother, " he has plenty of ability ; he talks well, he is very good company, but he is as double-faced and as selfish as the devil himself. He is like a young fox ; you can read deceitfulness in his eyes." Saint Simon's verdict is still more severe : " He looked like a ferret and a prig. Duplicity was writ large on his face. He made no attempt to cover up the looseness of his conduct, and he indulged in such wild excesses that you might have thought he was mad. He made no secret of his contempt for religion ; he scouted such things as honest dealing or keeping one's word. He ever treated life as a huge mockery and jest, and was as sensual as he was ambitious. He was mealy-mouthed, a cringing flatterer, readily adopting any tone or playing any part to gain the various ends he set out to attain."

Ordained to the priesthood so that he might get himself appointed Archbishop of Cambrai—as successor to Fénelon !—a member of the Académie française, prime minister, Cardinal almost despite Innocent XIII, after having enlisted the support, in order to gain the purple, of England, Spain, Austria, the Oratorians and the Molinists—that is to say, after focusing on the same object the most irreconcilable foes and spending eight millions, which were paid by France. Nevertheless it would be unjust merely to view Dubois in the light of the licentious satires of the day. He was something more than the "Regent's pimp," as he was currently nicknamed, something more than the mass of gangrene, the sceptical and blasphemous prelate. He was undoubtedly a great politician. He triumphantly championed the interests of France against England and Spain; he reorganized the country's finances after the downfall of Law; planted nearly all our roads with trees, carried out a land valuation in order to introduce a more equitable method of taxation, as an outcome of the inquiry he was instructed to conduct into the condition of the provinces; he further ordered the occupation of the Ile de France, the fortification of the Ile Royale, and was responsible for many other important acts.

The Regency, personified by Dubois and the Duc d'Orléans, is too commonly judged by the supper parties, masquerades and balls at the Opera, and the incredible laxity of morals that characterized the period. It is no more than just to set some limit to the notions rendered current concerning Dubois and the Regent by the lampoons, calumnies, ribald songs and tittle-tattle of the day.

CHAPTER II

THE REGENT AND DUBOIS

SINCE the crash brought about by the failure of Law's system,[1] all the machinery of taxation was placed under Government control. It was transferred in the month of October to the jurisdiction of a specially selected board of assessors, who made it an obligation to hand over to the King every year a sum of fifty-five million *livres*. The fund thus created at present amounts to more than one hundred and sixty millions.

This was the last public act of the Regent who, although his constitution was of the strongest, could not long sustain the crushing burden of work which, especially since the death of Cardinal Dubois, he had been compelled to undertake. He needed a second self to help him in his labours, and that second self had been snatched away

---

[1] There being no funds in the Exchequer, which had been depleted by the wars of Louis XIV, the Regent lent a favourable ear to the counsels of the Scotchman Law who, with a view to increasing the public revenue, put into circulation a quantity of paper money in the form of bank notes, thus getting possession of the coinage for the purpose of exploiting the problematic natural resources of Louisiana. But Law issued these bank notes in such large numbers that the people began to get anxious. They next tried to exchange their notes for gold, and riotous scenes were enacted in the Rue Quincampoix, where the head office of the bank was situated, when it became evident that the metal reserves were insufficient to cover the paper issue. Panic and disaster followed as a matter of course. In spite of this, the National Debt had diminished. Commerce, industry and shipping had developed on an unprecedented scale. This was the happiest outcome of a system which had ruined the fortunes and exhausted the savings of countless private individuals, by the speculative operations in the rise and fall of the Company's shares to which it inevitably gave rise.

from him by death. Of all the persons who at that time filled the various government offices, none could boast of more than second-rate abilities, so that the Regent was constantly obliged to supplement and direct their work. The Keeper of the Seals, though he had usefully filled a gap, was but a cipher, without a will of his own, incapable of taking a line or following it up, or of combining, as his position demanded, an absolute deference to the orders of the Court, with that inflexible steadfastness of purpose in the face of parliamentary and clerical opposition which was necessary to ensure their execution. The Comte de Morville, his son, who had come from the Admiralty to take charge of the Department of Foreign Affairs, though possessed of great abilities, was not sufficiently familiar with the duties of his office to take up the various threads, or to handle them with the coolness and dexterity that the circumstances of the time demanded. Dodun, the Comptroller General, who had been recruited from the Parliament in the hope that that body would show more alacrity in adopting the measures he proposed, displayed such an ignorance of finance as must have cured the Government of any temptation to repeat their error. As for M. de Breteuil, the Secretary for War, he was accounted as highly fitted for this post in time of peace. The Comte de Saint Florentin and the Comte de Maurepas were still very young and had only just entered this department. The whole burden therefore fell on the Duc d'Orléans. He had, however, found a man for his needs, to wit the second son of the late Keeper of the Seals, since known under the style of the Comte d'Argenson. The Prince had tested him by putting him through his paces as Lieutenant of Police, and the result left him in no doubt as to his capacity or devotion. He had just appointed him his Chancellor and Keeper of the Seals, as well as his chief Counsellor and Comptroller of his Household and accounts,

In announcing this appointment he congratulated himself on his choice and exclaimed : " People will never be able to say that my Chancellor was not a man of breeding and ability." His purpose was to appoint him Comptroller General of Finance. But this time did not permit.

On the 2nd December, the Prince had just given an audience. As he was returning to his closet, he fell in with the Duchesse de Phalaris, his mistress. " Come in," he said; " I am mighty pleased to see you. You will beguile me with your tales ; for my head is very heavy." Scarcely were they alone, when he fainted and lay motionless and unconscious. The frightened lady called for assistance, but he was beyond the reach of human succour. He died in her arms, a circumstance which provoked a foreign gazette maliciously to report that the Duc d'Orléans had died in the presence of his Confessor-in-Ordinary.[1]

Such was the end of a prince whose conduct of the Regency will be for ever memorable, seeing that, in circumstances which held as it were in embryo every species of social disorder, which ever multiply with unhappy fecundity amid perpetually agitated and stormy minorities, he was nevertheless able to repress and stifle them by the mere force of his genius. To Parliament he restored the freedom of discussion and remonstrance. But in thus allowing it to resume its pristine lustre, he retained the power to restrain it and prevent it from abusing a freedom not unfraught with danger.

If he was not able completely to allay the ferment occasioned by the famous Bull, he at all events succeeded in preventing the religious disputes from having the sinister results which in previous centuries had characterized quarrels of this nature. He so contrived that they found expression in mere appeals or pastoral proclamations, or

[1] For full details of this death-scene, here very accurately summed up, see the Memoirs of Saint-Simon and Duclos.

at the most in a few explosions of ecclesiastical thunder followed by fires that were extinguished before they were well alight. He repressed the extravagant ambitions of the legitimized princes and gave due and formal recognition to the constitution of the nation and, in this way, settled a domestic dispute which had arisen among the members of the royal family. But notwithstanding his *de facto* recognition of the claims of the princes and even of the nobles, he maintained to the full the authority entrusted to him and repelled with equal severity such encroachments on these various estates as might have tended to bring about delicate and difficult situations. He faced with courage the violent storm that Spain directed against him, and by the bold decision of his policy and actions not only disconcerted the manœuvres of that Power, but, instead of a war which bade fair to be one of extraordinary ferocity and duration and to degenerate into a civil conflict, he brought about a durable and glorious peace, cemented a friendship between the two royal houses, a friendship which had been interrupted rather than violated, and finally secured a throne for two of his daughters. Worthy of admiration as is the art with which he conducted these negotiations, in what terms shall we describe the skill with which he won over the support of England and Holland ? When Louis XIV died, the kingdom was left without allies. The same feelings of hatred, jealousy and fear that had united the whole of Europe in a common league against the late King were still in being. In London the authors of the last peace were being aimed at, the safety of France was being menaced. The powers were not unmindful of many bitter humiliations and the cruel dilemma in which they had been placed when they were forced to choose between becoming the prey of an arrogant victor and being submerged beneath the flood. It was to be feared that these natural enemies, still incompletely reconciled and still smarting from the indignity of having been made the sport of Court intrigues, might avail themselves of the favourable opportunity now offered by the isolation of France, to destroy her power for harm for ever.

It was at this critical moment in his country's destinies that the Regent conceived and carried out the bold scheme of uniting them in a triple alliance with France in opposition to Spain, whose power he personally regarded with the greatest apprehension. We shall not here stay to inquire whether, in taking this step, he was actuated more by private interest than by solicitude for his country's welfare; suffice it to say that the nation derived benefit from his policy and that history should therefore account it to his credit.

The lamentable condition into which the country's finances were plunged was also a cause of discontent which clamoured for a remedy. Doubtless the measures he saw fit to employ were harsh and drastic and fraught with dangers of which he was not fully cognizant. But from this crisis also he emerged victorious, and the power and prestige of the body politic were sensibly augmented in consequence.

An administration which, carried on through eight perilous years, was uniformly and universally crowned with success, cannot but be regarded as the sure index of eminent qualities of statecraft, and the Regent will assuredly be ranked by posterity among the foremost of those rulers to whom the destinies of France have been committed.[1]

---

[1] These encomiums will perhaps strike the reader as excessive; nevertheless, as we observed concerning Dubois, we must not allow our estimate of these personages to suffer undue refraction by judging them in the light of the frivolous, dissolute and licentious habits of the time. "The Regency," writes Michelet, "is a whole century compressed into eight years. It brought with it these things at one and the same time; a revelation, a revolution, a creation. It was the sudden revelation of a world which had been held in restraint and concealed beneath a mask for a period of fifty years. The King's death was a dramatic climax. Things were turned

Furthermore, the Regent had an aptitude for detail which is not the invariable concomitant of genius and which in fact either stifles it or is disdained by it.   The first six months of his Regency were marked by a spirit of wisdom, equity and pacific moderation for whose counterpart we must look to the government of the Cardinal de Fleury, his successor.   He suppressed a number of the unnecessary taxes and burdens under which the people groaned ; while the armed forces of the nation were reduced to a figure proportionate to its needs.   He adopted the scheme of M. de Vauban and gave instructions for experimental measures to be taken with the object of creating a Crown revenue, to which the King's subjects should contribute voluntarily and which should be paid over in its entirety to the Royal Treasury.   The repeopling of the provinces, increased land cultivation, the restoration of trade, were also matters that engaged his attention ; but, as there is nothing perfect in this world, he is reproached with exhibiting two vices of cardinal importance in a ruler, two

topsy-turvy.   The roof was torn off, and the whole contents of the fabric laid bare.   Never was a society revealed with such a flood of light.   Not only was it the light that returned, but movement also.   The Regency was a social and economic revolution, and the greatest that had befallen us prior to 1789.   It appeared to have been abortive, yet it bore fruit none the less. The Regency saw the creation of countless innovations ; public highways, facilities for communication between province and province, free education, the science and practice of accountancy.   Gracious and charming arts were brought to birth ; all things which contribute to the ease and amenities of the home.   But, greatest of all, a new spirit began to make headway against the uncouth spirit of barbarism, the narrow inquisitorial spirit of the preceding reign ; a broad and humanistic spirit.   The foe was the Past, the barbarous Middle Ages ; the friend was the Future with its promise of progress and a new intellectual outlook.   It was the Revolution of which the Regency was, so to speak, the first act.   Such is the character, such the " note " of the Regency as revealed in its leading actors.   Through and beyond their shortcomings, the Regent, Noailles, Law and, above all, Dubois, on one side or other of their nature belong to the party of the Future—hence a great apparent fluctuation in the history of the Regency, and the more accurate and true its historian, the more improbable seems the narrative he presents to us.

defects which furnished material for the numberless satires directed against his administration. The first was that he derogated from the maxim that the word of a king is sacred, a maxim of which Louis XIV had never lost sight, even in the most critical and calamitous periods of his reign. The Regent, on the other hand, is charged with having adopted as a principle of government the fraudulent conduct of those unscrupulous merchants who repay the too easy confidence of their creditors by shamefully evading their liabilities and enrich themselves by a series of bankruptcies which, in justice, should have brought them not wealth but a prison.

The second charge has relation to the moral corruption of which he made a sort of parade and which is described, with unhappily too much truth, in those famous Philippics whose author, in a style less delicate but more forcible than that of Petronius, gives us a swift but faithful picture of the Regent's Court, a picture which possesses the greater value for posterity in that no allegorical veil conceals the identity of the actors. From it we perceive that he made light even of the crime of incest. In fact, if his guilty love for the Abbess of Chelles, his daughter, is not completely established, it is difficult to withhold belief from the stories of his passion for the Duchesse de Berry, whose hands, the loveliest ever possessed by mortal woman, had exercised a peculiar thraldom over him.[1] His grief for her death was less suggestive of a bereaved parent than of a lover plunged in the depths of despair.

[1] Collectors set high store on a caricature which this occasion called forth. It is something of a curiosity and merits description. It is in the style of those picturesque rebuses with which the Jesuits are accustomed to entertain their pupils at certain seasons of the year. The Regent is shown toying with his daughter, and with particular eagerness kissing her divine hands, which the princess places upon his eyes to prevent him from seeing what takes place. Meanwhile the Comte de Riom, who is behind her, raises Her Royal Highness's petticoats and with a gesture of ungovernable desire, proceeds to wreak his will upon her. In a far corner, half concealed

Howbeit, if Malice in the hideous portraits of the
Prince which are scattered up and down in scores of
pamphlets has forgotten certain lineaments, the epitaph
that was composed for His Royal Highness's mother—
but which was less appropriate to that lady than to her
son—would give expression to them all : " Here lieth
Indolence."

Whatever the spirit of the law which declared the
Kings of France to have attained their majority so soon
as they had completed their thirteenth year, it could not
hasten the processes of nature and render their reasoning
faculties more precocious than those of the generality of
their fellow-men. The wisest monarch at this age is he
who shows the greatest willingness to follow the recommendations of his counsellors. Such was Louis XV. Since
the hour when he was solemnly invested with the royal
prerogative, he refrained from manifesting his will save
in such personal matters as did not affect his people as a
whole. It was thus that he caused the bed of his tutor
to be removed from his room, declaring nevertheless that
he deemed it fitting that the Duc de Charost, or in his
absence his deputy, should sleep for three years in his
chamber in the same manner as had been followed when
Louis XIV came to his majority. Every evening, therefore,
a tent was erected in the royal bedchamber which was
taken down again in the morning.

A more difficult situation arose when death deprived
Louis XV of his Prime Minister, the Duc d'Orléans, and
the young King was obliged to decide on a course of action.

in the shadow is seen the Abbé Dubois, who is noting, with a smile, all that
is passing. Beneath is the following Latin inscription : *Regius stultus,
Abbas ridet, rideamus quoque,* which is intended to signify : A foolish Regent
at whom the Abbess is laughing ; let us join in the laughter. The picture
atones for whatever may be lacking in the inscription, and the meaning of
the scene is quite obvious.

It is well known that the Comte de Riom, who was the Princess's lover,
subsequently passed for her husband.

Deeming himself too young to take the management of affairs into his own hands, he appointed as his successor the head of the House of Condé.[1]

In making the choice, which no doubt was not the best he might have made, owing to the fact that he lacked the necessary experience not only of men but of himself, he nevertheless acted in strict accordance with the rules of etiquette. He deemed it his duty to confer the post, which was the most important in the kingdom, upon a prince of the royal house. As they were all young men, he appointed the eldest, who, however, was but thirty-one years old. The manner in which His Royal Highness had managed his own revenues, and had added to them, despite his youth (that being a period when a man's thoughts are

[1] This was Louis Henri de Bourbon, Prince de Condé, and more commonly called Monsieur le Duc. He was born at Versailles in 1692, and died at Chantilly in 1740. Being appointed by the Regent Chief of the Regency Council, he took advantage of his position to enrich himself by means of Law's system. An incompetent statesman, he was harsh and sombre in manner, and almost entirely discredited with the King. He was moderately good-looking as a young man, but being over-tall, he afterwards began to stoop, and became " as thin and dry as a chip of wood." He was disfigured by an accident which befell him while hunting, when the Duc de Berry put out one of his eyes.

" His stork legs ill support the weight of his body, and his eyes are so red that you can hardly distinguish the good one from the bad." Numerous lampoons ridiculed his incapacity, and alluded to the fortune he had so rapidly acquired.

> Prince, dites-nous vos exploits ;
> Que faites vous pour votre gloire ?
> Taisez-vous, sots ! Lisez l'histoire
> De la rue Quincampoix.

(Prince, tell us your exploits ; what do you to win your glory ? Silence, fools ! Go read the story of the rue Quincampoix.)

> Grand Condé, ton petit-fils
> Déshonore ta mémoire ;
> Jamais son nom dans l'Histoire
> N'y sera qu' avec mépris.

(Great Condé, your grandson does dishonour to your memory ; never will he be named in History save with contempt.)

wont to be exclusively centred upon pleasure) was a strong
presumption that he would prove a capable public administrator, and the fact that he was already rich led people
to imagine that he would not trouble his head about adding
to his fortune. Finance, indeed, was the most important
department of public affairs at that time. What France
needed was a government which would pursue a policy of
peace, conciliation and retrenchment, and avail itself of the
tranquil condition of Europe in order to bring about by
trade, industry and the gradual restoration of the metal
reserve, a recovery from the state of exhaustion into which
the country had fallen. No one, however, failed to
appreciate how immensely inferior in talent the Duke was
to the Regent. The following is a portrait of the former
contained in a work whose author, although enshrouding
his characters in a veil of mystery, is nevertheless more
prone to adulation than to satire : [1]

" Inferior to his predecessor in ability but no less
addicted than he to habits of debauchery, he was tall, thin
and unattractive of feature. His manner was harsh and
unaccommodating ; he was a collector, with an ardent taste
for rare and precious objects ; he was the possessor of a
very beautiful wife whom, however, he did not value at
her full worth,[2] seeking elsewhere for pleasures he was

---

[1] The work in question is *Les Mémoires secrets pour servir à l'Histoire de
Perse*. The book has been reprinted by Plon under the following title :
Toussaint, *Anecdotes curieuses de la Cour de France sous Louis XV*, with
comments and explanatory notes by Paul Fould.

[2] Very pretty she was indeed, but not so pretty as her mother, Made-
moiselle de Nantes, the legitimized daughter of Louis XIV and Madame de
Montespan. She was eleven when she was married to the Duc de Bourbon,
Louis III, grandson of the great Condé and a pupil of La Bruyère. See
Allaire's scholarly work *La Bruyère dans la maison de Condé* (Didot. 2 vols.).
" Her extraordinary gaiety amused the King. She was full of talent,
humorous, given to raillery and no respecter of persons. She would go
wild with delight at a mere nothing, anything would please her. She would
dress up her knee like a doll when she had nothing to do "—*Mémoires de
Choisy*. Saint-Simon speaks in several places of her graces, her good qualities

ill befitted to enjoy, squandering his wealth in great style." Truly we shall look in vain among these divers attributes for one that would denote the statesman.

and her defects. She was born and legitimized in 1673, died in 1743, and was left a widow when she was thirty-six, but she was not inconsolable, which is the less surprising since the *chroniques scandaleuses* of the day give us to understand that her conjugal fidelity was probably not without a blemish. After all, and not to mention that he was " not quite the sort of man to inspire affection," did not the Duc de Bourbon live openly with Madame de Prie, one of the Regent's numerous ex-mistresses ?

CHAPTER III

THE KING'S MARRIAGE—FLEURY—THE DUC
DE BOURBON

THE sending home of the Spanish Infanta by the Duc de Bourbon's government was an act which cannot be regarded with approval. The slight thus put upon a sovereign, and he the King's uncle, just when the circumstances of the time imperiously demanded that he should be tactfully dealt with, was the more gratuitous since it had for its object the union of the King with the daughter of a prince who had lost his throne. In vain was it given out that the little princess, who was then scarcely seven years old, was too young ; that she could not marry for several years, and that something had to be done to satisfy the wishes of the people who were impatient that the King should be provided with heirs to the throne. Not only were the people innocent of the impatience ascribed to them, but they had already become used to the sight of their future Queen growing to womanhood beneath their eyes. They were beginning to take an interest in her and they looked on her departure with sorrow. They regarded with high disfavour the policy of forming an alliance which could not be profitable and might become burdensome. Certainly when, Stanislas having chosen Weissenburg in French Alsace as his place of refuge, the Regent bade M. Sum, who had been sent by King Augustus to protest, tell his royal master that France had ever afforded asylum to princes in misfortune, he never expected that the daughter

of that same Stanislas would bring about the dismissal of
the Infanta, whose marriage he had arranged, and come to
seat herself in her place. Nor, we imagine, did Stanislas,
when after his flight from Poland he found his daughter
lost and abandoned in the manger of a village hostelry,
entertain such high hopes for her future. The more we
study history, the more is the conviction forced upon us
that we are a race of blind men led by a destiny blinder
even than ourselves. Here, nevertheless, are the hidden
and incredible machinations with which this intrigue was
carried out.

King Stanislas in his retreat at Weissenburg was
living there, as is clear from the terms of the Regent's
reply, under the protection of France ; and as a mark of
respect, a few regiments were quartered in the place, the
officers of which composed his Court so to speak. Among
them happened to be the Comte, who afterwards became
Maréchal, d'Estrées. He was young, handsome, well
proportioned, active and well adapted to find favour in
women's eyes. Stanislas noticed that his daughter had
taken a liking to him. One day he took him aside, broached
the matter to him and declared that although he had no
hopes of ever regaining the throne of Poland, he doubted
not that justice would be done to him and that he would
recover the property that belonged to him in that kingdom.
This, he added, would enable him to give a rich dowry to
his daughter, and even to wed her to the sovereign of some
minor state ; but that he nevertheless valued the happiness
of his beloved child at a far higher figure than any ambitious
considerations of that sort ; that he had observed the
favourable effect he had produced on her, and that he
was not indisposed to give her to him in marriage if, in
addition to his illustrious birth, he, on his side, were able
to bring some dignity that would distinguish his posterity,
such, for example, as a dukedom.

D'Estrées was ardent and eager to make his way.   After replying in the first instance with becoming modesty, he confessed that though his breast was warmed with a tender and respectful passion for the princess, he would never have dared to cast his eyes so high ; but that now, encouraged by His Majesty's kind condescension, he would use his best endeavours to render himself worthy of so great an honour.   He accordingly set out for the Court and besought the Regent to confer upon him the required title. His Royal Highness, however, had no liking for the Louvois, and threw abundance of cold water on any such proposals by alleging that D'Estrées was not befitted to wed the daughter of a sovereign, elective and throneless though he were.

M. le Duc having come to visit His Royal Highness shortly after this interview with D'Estrées, the Regent, still amazed at the young colonel's audacity, spoke to him thereon, and in the course of conversation hinted to him that he would do well to think of the match for himself, adding that such an alliance would be eminently suitable for him, especially in view of the possessions which Stanislas would in all likelihood recover.   The Duke had a great love of money and was far from disdaining the proposal, but before taking any conclusive step, he thought he would wait and see how matters went with the royal fugitive. Moreover, he was then in the toils of his mistress the Marquise de Prie,[1] who, with the object of retaining

[1] Agnès Berthelot de Pléneuf married in 1718 the Marquis de Prie, who was appointed ambassador at Turin.   The beauty of her person won her an extreme ascendancy over the Duc de Bourbon, in whose name, from 1723 to 1726, she governed the country.   Being exiled to Normandy, she there took poison, in 1727.   According to President Hénault, she was of a slender figure and above the usual height.   She had the face and bearing of a nymph, delicate features and pretty cheeks, a well-shaped nose and rather shadowy hair, eyes somewhat slanting but bright and frolicsome ; in a word, a lively and distinguished physiognomy.   With all those talents that coquetry knows how to employ, Nature had endowed her.   There is

her hold on her illustrious slave, used every means she could devise to prevent his approaching the hymeneal altar.

Meanwhile the Regent dies and M. le Duc is appointed Prime Minister. This additional grandeur still further excited the ambition of the Marquise, who realized quite well that she was about to hold the reins of government behind his mask. The King's youth and his timid disposition permitted the hope that the arrangement would last some time. But an ambitious woman is ever anxious and on the alert. Madame de Prie feared that the marriage of Louis XV with the Infanta would rob the Duke of his influence, or at all events necessitate its being shared with others : she therefore conceived the idea of sending the princess home to Spain, and the better to persuade the Minister to take this course, she proposed that the King should be married to one of his sisters,[1] a course which would make his office secure against attack and give him a permanent influence over both their Majesties. The Duke was

extant a portrait of the Marquise painted by Vanloo. She is holding a captive bird :

> In your fair hand that prisoner enchanted
> Disdaining to attempt to wing his way to freedom,
> Content to sport and sing the livelong day,
> In order to be happy of freedom hath no need.

[1] The sister in question was Mademoiselle de Vermandois, at that time in a convent at Fontevrault. See the *Mémoires de Richelieu*—edited by Soulavie—for a quite imaginary account of a visit paid to Mademoiselle de Vermandois by Madame de Prie, disguised so as not to be recognized, and by the Dowager Duchesse de Bourbon. The conversation begins ; mention is made of the Marquise de Prie, about whom Mademoiselle lets her tongue run away with her : " Never was there a more wicked and despicable woman." When she came out of the convent, Madame de Prie, who, especially after this onslaught, had taken care not to reveal her identity, is said to have exclaimed : " You ! you will never be Queen of France." The whole thing is pure romance. See also the *Mémoires du Président Hénault*.

greatly taken with the plan, but before putting it into execution, he thought he would like to consult his mother, who was possessed of greater acumen than he. He was, moreover, in hopes that, as this piece of advice, which was intended to advance the fortunes of his house, came from Madame de Prie, his mother, who could not endure the lady, might at length be disposed in her favour.

The Duchesse de Bourbon, who also had a taste for dominion, far from disapproving the proposal, warmly embraced it, but twitted her son for owing it to a woman instead of being able to devise from his own resources so sound a scheme for his own advancement. However, she promised to adopt a more conciliatory attitude towards Madame de Prie and to receive her with less asperity. Her object was to bring her son up to the first hurdle, which was the breaking off of the match with the Infanta. When she saw that this project had finally gone by the board, she resumed her old attitude of hauteur and disdain towards the Marquise. The latter, driven to bay, vowed she would have her revenge, and this is how she went about it.

" Monsieur le Duc," said she to him in one of those intimate conversations in which they weighed the destinies of France, " our whole scheme was a blunder. To marry your sister to the King is doubtless a good thing for your house, but it is a bad thing for you. You have a mother who will most assuredly exercise a predominating influence over the future queen if she is her daughter. You cannot possibly have any doubts about that, knowing full well how she endeavours to dictate to you and what trouble you have to shake off her control. My opinion is that if you want to maintain your influence, you must give up the notion of this glorious match and simply give the young monarch a princess without connexions who, since she will owe her fortune to you, will show you lasting gratitude." [1]

This, of course, was obviously indicating the daughter of King Stanislas, and the wily lady thus thought to fulfil her double aim. First and foremost she would bring mortification to the heart of Madame la Duchesse de Bourbon and upset all her ambitious calculations; next, she would be consolidating and perpetuating her own dominion by thrusting aside the matrimonial projects of her lover. M. le Duc at once realized whom she had in mind, but only read into her proposal an excess of zeal to preserve to him in all its plenitude the power he wielded as Prime Minister. The scheme commended itself to him the more because the princess, who was kindly, gentle and not very clever, was very agreeable to him. He brought the proposal before the Council and obtained the consent

[1] A list of all the eligible princesses of Europe had been drawn up for Louis XV to choose a wife from. There were ninety-nine candidates. A process of elimination reduced them to seventeen, then to five, and the fifth was Marie, daughter of the exiled King of Poland, Stanislas Leczynska. This was the queen that the Marquise de Prie wished for and mentioned. "Poor and unassuming," thought she, "she will never forget that she owes it to me that she is Queen of France, and then, through her, I shall retain my influence." See Stryienski, *Le XVIIIe siècle*; P. de Nolhac, *Louis XV et Marie Leczinska*, ch. i., and especially Thirion, *Madame de Prie*; Marquis des Réault, *Le Roi Stanislas*; Henri Gauthier-Villars, *Le Mariage de Louis XV*.

A marriage beyond all expectations, to be sure! Queen Marie herself used to tell the story of how she learned of this extraordinary event in her career. She was in a room at Weissenburg, she and her mother, busy about their works of charity. They were talking over the news from Poland, which seemed more disheartening than ever, since King Augustus had just finally refused to give back to Stanislas any part of his patrimonial property. Into the room where the two women were holding converse there entered the exiled King, his face radiant with an expression of unwonted happiness and bearing a letter in his hand. "Ah, my daughter," he exclaimed, "let us fall on our knees and give thanks to God!" "What, father, have you been recalled to the throne?" "Nay, Heaven has vouchsafed us a still greater boon; my daughter, you are Queen of France!" Father and daughter embraced with tears, and then knelt down to utter a prayer of thanksgiving for the tidings that put an end to so many sorrowful anxieties. Cf. P. de Nolhac, *Louis XV et Marie Leczinska*, pp. 36–37.

of the King. There is reason to believe that His Majesty, already secretly guided by the ex-Bishop of Fréjus, only gave his consent at the suggestion of that prelate who, more clever than the Duke, was planning a long way ahead to supplant him, and only let his rival have his way because he believed he saw therein a means of strengthening his own authority. Thus it came about that Marie, who at one time was proposed as the bride of a mere army colonel, was taken up by a prince of the blood royal and ended by becoming, on the 4th September, Queen of the fairest realm in Christendom.

The reader will see as he progresses in these memoirs that, by reason of the fate that ruled over the destinies of mankind, this marriage turned out to be the most fortunate that Louis XV could possibly have contracted. That, however, was a result that human prescience could never have foreseen. In fact, if the interests of the State had alone been consulted, everything should have dissuaded the Prime Minister from lending his countenance to the match. The very schemes that he and his mistress had devised to push on their own fortunes went awry, and the storm fell upon them from a quarter whence they least expected it.

At this point begins the second epoch of Louis XV's reign, the ministry of M. le Duc having merely been a sort of continuation of the Regency. In view of the King's extreme youth, its duration is regarded as having extended to the ministry of Cardinal de Fleury, because he had the exclusive direction of affairs, even before he was appointed Prime Minister.

After the unrest and uncertainty of an unhappy regency, the era of peace and prosperity that followed offers a more agreeable and welcome spectacle. France, who had been so feared and hated during the previous reign, who had suffered such bitter humiliation towards its close, now

MARIE LECZINSKA, QUEEN OF FRANCE
From an engraving by Delpech after Belliard

emerges as the arbiter of European affairs and wins the
affection and admiration of the world by reason of the
fairness and moderation that guided all her actions.
Frenchmen beheld their King playing the part of trustee
for the interests of his rivals, and gaining for these rivals,
almost in their own despite, a peace which brought happiness and prosperity to the subjects of his own realm.
Scarcely had the Cardinal assumed the reins of government,
when a conspicuous transformation took place in the internal
condition of the country. The exhaustion to which it
had been reduced by Law's banking scheme, the general
lack of confidence that had continually grown more
accentuated under the *régime* of M. le Duc, the corn
famine which occurred in the year that preceded his
dismissal,[1] the hunger and sickness that are the inevitable
consequences of a famine, the continual fluctuations in
the value of the currency, the chaos that prevailed
throughout the kingdom, particularly in the department
of finance—all these evils disappeared. Credit was restored
within and without the kingdom, trade revived and
increased by leaps and bounds, and the provinces, which
a few months earlier resembled a war-stricken area, grew
before long richer than they had ever been before. Such
was the flourishing condition of France when the election
of the King of Poland came to disturb the general harmony.
That event compelled France to enter a war in the course
of which the King's forces, nearly everywhere victorious,
gained the kingdoms of Naples and Sicily for a prince of the
House of Bourbon, and added to the crown of France what
Louis XIV had never succeeded in winning for it, to wit
the duchies of Lorraine and Bar.[2]

[1] In 1725 the harvest was ruined by incessant rains.
[2] This eulogy is exaggerated. Fleury's administration, which was as
honest as any administration under Louis XV, derives considerable advantage
from the fact that it follows that of the Duc de Bourbon. If the latter
persecuted the Protestants, Fleury showed no mercy to the Jansenists.

Such, in broad outline, was the general effect of the splendid administration of Cardinal de Fleury. It is for the historians to complete it in all its details. For ourselves, having reached the period when Louis XV, arrived at man's estate, is about to occupy our particular attention, we shall merely refer to it in brief, and only so far as the facts enter into our plan, which is to portray the character, genius and conduct of a prince who provides an invaluable subject of study not only for his fellow-princes, but for the world in general. Louis XV,[1] when he decided to free himself from the tutelage of M. le Duc, was entering upon the threshold of manhood, being about seventeen years of age. We learn from contemporary testimony that he was good-looking, well set up, had shapely legs, a

True, the great Jansenists of the seventeenth century were no more, and Jansenism had become a mere matter of politics. At home, Fleury's *régime* was capable though not brilliant; abroad it was disastrous. Avarice led him to leave the body politic to get better of its own accord, as you might leave a strong man to recover from an illness, with the result that France was humiliated and her frontiers endangered.

[1] " Cha-Séphi (Louis XV) when he was sixteen or seventeen years of age was handsome and well set up. He had a perfectly formed leg, a noble mien, big eyes, an expression in which gentleness was more apparent than hauteur, dark eyebrows and a delicate constitution which, however, gained strength as he grew older, so that in the end he was able to endure the greatest fatigues. His education having been neglected, he boasted few intellectual adornments. He had a shy and gentle disposition, and an unconquerable aversion for business, the very mention of which he could not endure. Hunting was his staple occupation ; he spoke little save when he was in the company of his intimates and favourites, and out of earshot of the courtiers. At first he was indifferent to women and the pleasures of the table, to which, however, he afterwards became greatly addicted. The sultana, his queen, was older than he [*Louis was born in* 1710 *and Marie in* 1703]. Her face and figure were but moderately attractive, with little nobility of physiognomy and mien. Her disposition was kind and gentle. She had a good heart and sufficient good sense to hold aloof from all Court intrigues. She was endowed richly with virtue and common sense. Left too often to herself, she was clever enough not to show that she was conscious of this lack of attention and regard. It will be readily understood that, with such characteristics, and being dependent on a Minister who had the upper hand of her husband, she enjoyed but little or no credit "—*Mémoires secrets pour servir à l'Histoire de Perse.*

high-bred mien, big eyes, an expression gentle rather than proud, dark eyebrows, his whole appearance suggesting that delicate constitution which, however, he so strengthened by dint of exercise, that in the end he became capable of enduring the greatest fatigues. It is unquestionably due to the tardy development of his nature that we must ascribe the quiescence of those passions that are usually so active in normal individuals, particularly in young men of princely rank, among whom everything contributes to their early awakening. In his early days, women, gaming and the pleasures of the table (to which he afterwards became so addicted) had few attractions for him. The chase was his sole pleasure, whether it was a natural instinct that predisposed him towards this salutary recreation or whether it was that, having much time on his hands, he was fearful of falling a victim to that ennui which was already beginning to eat like a canker into his brightest hours, for his education had been much neglected for fear of overhardening his childish faculties. The result was that he had few intellectual attainments, and had not acquired that taste for study which is so invaluable a resource at all times and in every rank. He had an invincible dislike for business, the very mention of which was repugnant to him. Unambitious of renown, he lacked that energy which, in his great forerunner, counterbalanced a defective upbringing and made up for the lack of knowledge. To sum up, his disposition was easy-going, indolent and timid; and he was therefore fated to come under the sway of the first who should establish an ascendancy over him. This the young prince's tutor had not been slow to perceive, and he availed himself of it in laying the foundations of his power.

In many respects there was a close similarity of character between the tutor and his pupil. Hence arose that mutual sympathy which was so potent in making the one so loyal to the interests of his royal charge and the other so obedient to the counsels of his preceptor. Simplicity, modesty, wisdom and circumspection acted, so to speak, as a check upon the ambitions of the former Bishop of Fréjus. In his case, ambition was subtly interfused with his virtues; it made its way by patient and insinuating methods, and exhibited nothing of the turbulent and tumultuous activity that is its conspicuous characteristic in the majority of men. The Bishop had doubtless made much headway, but it had been gradual and "without observation." He was seventy-three when he was appointed to assume the reins of office. Born in a southern province of France, his family, if not exactly obscure, was at all events but little known, and he was thus destined for the Church. He received due instruction in the departments of knowledge suitable to this profession, which he embraced at an early age, and which is the most fitting vocation for all whose birth is not sufficiently exalted to mark them out for high office of State.

The Abbé de Fleury [1] had an ardent desire to play a part at Court, convinced that his youth and comely appearance would work wonders for him. He intrigued to such good purpose that he came to Court with powerful recommendations which he reinforced by his influence, of which, however, he availed himself with that sedate reserve which characterized all his actions and which had, up to then, successfully resisted all encroachments. He obtained an

---

[1] Fleury (André Hercule, Cardinal de), born at Lodève in 1653, died in Paris in 1743. Chaplain to Queen Marie Thérèse, he was appointed by Louis XIV to the see of Fréjus in 1698, and in 1715 he became tutor to the future Louis XV. He was seventy-three years of age when, in 1726, he succeeded the Duc de Bourbon as Prime Minister. He then received a Cardinal's hat. Though a member of three Academies, he left no literary remains behind him save his pastoral letters.

"Despite his advanced age (he was seventy when he took the helm of State), Ismaël Bey was still a fine figure of a man. He had a fresh complexion, keen eyes, a penetrating glance, a lofty brow, a shapely nose and ruddy lips. He was above the medium height, upright, easy in his carriage, with a well-turned leg, firm and upright in his gait, possessing a mobile mind, animated by high ambitions and endowed, more richly than the most accom-

ANDRÉ HERCULE CARDINAL DE FLEURY
From an engraving by J. C. Philips after J. Dassier

appointment as chaplain and a few years later a bishopric. Thus he found himself relegated once more to the provinces and far removed from the great stage on which he had made so brief an appearance. Hypocrisy, however, was destined to be the mainspring of his elevation. His conscientious attention to duty attracted the notice of Louis XIV and won him his appointment as tutor to the royal heir. He deemed that he was soon to realize in his person the lofty predictions of the astrologers, in whom he reposed great confidence, for, great as were his mental attributes, he lacked that genius which, rising superior to events, feels itself capable of moulding them to its will and of shaping its own destiny. This weakness, however, was not without its compensations, since, by relying on these happy prognostications, he readily grew accustomed to his exalted position, which he filled without any awkwardness; and this belief in his star, though it never made him over-bold, imparted to him that perseverance which takes the place of energy and emboldened him to map out for himself a career which otherwise he would never have dared to conceive. The ascendancy which he realized he possessed over his pupil, in proportion as it increased his qualities of heart and mind, convinced him that he had only to bide his time to achieve all his aims; and the Regent's death seemed to lay open the widest field for his ambition.

plished courtier, with the art of ingratiating himself at Court. Knowing when to yield to the force of circumstances and how to profit by them, he presented a modest exterior, and displayed an air of candour well calculated to deceive. He spoke with effect even on trivial matters, and was a great man with the ladies, over whom he was said to exercise considerable influence, and through whose agency he was reputed to have risen to power. A voluptuary by inclination, he kept himself well within bounds. He was a redoubtable antagonist and an indifferent friend, with a wide and varied knowledge, but too little elevation of mind to guide the destinies of a great kingdom. Always irresolute, he was slow in the dispatch of affairs. He knew neither when to make war nor when to conclude peace. Of the former he was profoundly ignorant, and he kept an indescribably jealous guard over the contents of the royal treasury"—*Mémoires secrets pour servir à l'Histoire de Perse.*

CHAPTER IV

MOLINISTS AND JANSENISTS—THE " CONVULSIONNAIRES " —DEACON PÂRIS—BIRTH OF THE DAUPHIN

IF the Molinists [1] went out of their way to abuse their access to government quarters in order to embroil the public services and kindle the fires of discord, the better to torment their adversaries the Jansenists, the latter retaliated by methods which, though more amusing, were, owing to the unrest they

[1] The Molinist doctrine is explained and set forth by the Spanish Jesuit, Molina (1535–1601), in his work entitled *Accord du libre arbitre avec les dons de la grace, la prescience divine, la Providence, la prédestination et la réprobation, 1588*. This doctrine may be summarized as follows : God recognizes in advance, from all eternity, the just and the reprobate; He nevertheless bestows upon all the gifts of grace necessary for salvation, which are efficacious for some, inefficacious for others. Furthermore, man is free and responsible for his acts, and therefore capable of meriting eternal reward or eternal punishment. How are these two ideas to be reconciled. Grace *per se* and in its nature Molina concluded to be efficacious. If it has ceased to be so, it is because man, instead of acting with it, acts against it. Thus God, who reads the future as accurately as He reads the present, sees from all eternity the use that each one will make of His grace.

The Jansenist doctrine is set forth in the *Augustinus* of Jansen, Bishop of Ypres (1585–1638). It is as follows : Man is never free, within himself, because his will is subjected sometimes to concupiscence, sometimes to grace. If God always gave us grace we should never sin ; but sometimes He withholds it from us, and allows free play to concupiscence which leads us into evil. The grace of salvation is granted only to the elect, and Jesus Christ died for them alone.

All that is directly opposed to the teaching of the Catholic Church, which says, " Jesus died for all, grace is for all ; and if we lose our souls, it is because we choose evil instead of good."

It is all very subtle and, above all, very much out of date in these days. Between Molinists and Jansenists purely theological polemics quickly degenerated into political polemics. Religion, supplanted by questions of government, was thrust into the background.

occasioned, no less dangerous, and which, seeing how this unrest was mixed up with matters of religion, were in danger of culminating in the most violent disorders.

There was in the parish of Saint-Médard a certain deacon named Pâris. He came of a good family, his father being a counsel in the High Court, his brother a counsellor in the Court of Inquiry. He was withal a simple, modest man, one of those saint-like simpletons that all the sects have need of to impress the foolish and the credulous, since fanaticism can mould them as it wills. In the month of May, 1727, an historian no less simple than himself, and no less zealous a champion of Jansenism, wrote an account of his life, wherein, among other edifying particulars, it was recorded that sometimes for two years together he would neglect to perform his Easter duties; that in a codicil executed shortly before his death, he had bequeathed his property to certain poor priests to relieve them from the temptation of saying many Masses; that when he was a child he had taken a delight in thrusting lighted straw up one of the chimneys in order to set fire to the College of Nanterre; that when he was ten years old he began sorely to try his masters, who soothed their patience by trying their pupil's; that he was subsequently twice turned out of his father's house, and thereafter partly disinherited; that he had learned how to make stockings on a knitting frame; that he had held aloof from the altar and from every kind of ecclesiastical ministration; that all he had done had been to teach little children their catechism and lecture to young candidates for orders; and especially that he entertained a cordial detestation of the Jesuits, and that, a little while before his death, he had delivered himself of the following prophetic words: " They cannot be too thoroughly exposed."

Such was the new candidate for canonization, and as miracles are the touchstone of sanctity, no time was lost

4

in making him perform some and in printing a list of them.
A celebrated magistrate who belonged to the party, M.
Carré de Montgéron, a member of the parliamentary
council, himself presented to the King a volume in which
was set forth all the testimony that tended to demonstrate the considerable certainty of these prodigies. He
was shortly afterwards imprisoned for this extravagance.
This did not deter twenty-three Paris curés from presenting two memoranda to M. de Vintimille certifying several
others. M. de Colbert, Bishop of Montpellier, and M. de
Caylus, Bishop of Auxerre, solemnly made public the
details of two miraculous cures that had been effected by
the same intercession, and, before them, Cardinal de Noailles
had recorded several others on the authority of duly sworn
testimony.

It is true that the miracles of M. Pâris [1] were of a very
special nature. Those who invoked him at his tomb were
tormented by horrible convulsions, worse than the maladies
whereof they prayed to be healed. Thus it came about
that people who suffered in the manner described above
were called " convulsionnaires." All this would have been
of no great account if the cures had been genuine ; but
there were not wanting adverse critics who contested them
and even went so far as to utter bitter jests on this latter-
day thaumaturge. Here, they said, we have the case of a
girl healed of a kind of dropsy, which the elapse of nine
months would have brought away in the ordinary course
of nature, without any recourse to the miraculous. Here,
again, was a case of cataract which was cured, but with the

---

[1] The deacon François de Pâris, a Jansenist, died in 1727, in a modest
house in the Faubourg St. Marcel, where he passed the last years of his life
distributing his goods to the poor. He was buried in the little cemetery of
Saint-Médard. The Jansenists conceived the idea of exploiting the veneration
in which he was held for the support of their tottering sect, and recounted
a host of miracles which they said had been performed at his tomb. See,
in the *Receuil* Clairambault-Maurepas, v. pp. 255–265, *Le tombeau du
diacre Pâris ; Les Miracles du diacre Pâris.*

loss of the other eye. Or again, some impotent old canon, who could now do anything, except say his prayers. Then some bungling swindler went to the miraculous tomb lame in one leg, and returned from it lame in both. Finally the much-talked-of cure does not even admit of discussion. The story of her illness and cure, as it was drawn up, was solemnly denied by the girl's aunt, brother, sister and even by her mother; as well as by the two surgeons who had been in charge of her case, by thirty-four witnesses, and by the affidavits of two doctors and three sworn surgeons who had examined the case and denied its authenticity. The woman was publicly banned by the Archbishop of Paris, who observed, in the course of his charge, that popular credulity was obviously being abused. The woman was, in consequence, obliged to make an appeal.

Mankind is so attracted by the marvellous that soon vast crowds began to flock to the tomb of M. Pâris; for nearly five years they continued to throng the place in ever-increasing numbers. That was the greatest as it was the solitary miracle enacted there. Can one form an idea of the stupidity of the spectators who, rejecting proofs of fraud, quackery and gross deception, which were incessantly being brought before their eyes, complacently continued to cling to a belief the falsity of which was being demonstrated every day by the evidence of their senses? Still more difficult is it to conceive how there came to be, even amongst people with brains, and among trained theologians, two parties violently opposed to each other, concerning either the matter as a whole or the various details of it, and that this controversy was responsible for the production of upwards of fourteen quarto volumes, containing the arguments for and against; that all, or nearly all, these writers were in agreement as to the truth of the alleged facts; and that only a mere handful ascribed the phenomena to nature and her undiscovered operations, thus affording a striking contrast to the doctors of our faith who to a man believed them due to a supernatural agency, differing only as to its character. Some plainly recognized the hand of God, others the finger of the devil. People nowadays would never credit the business, were it not for the tangible proof afforded by these rhapsodical documents. Such a pitch did the delirium attain that in July, 1731,[1] M. de Vintimille forbade the invocation of M. Pâris, he being as yet not canonized ; that an appeal was lodged against the archiepiscopal mandate; that four eminent counsel signed the memorandum; and that Parliament did not disallow the appeal which was supposed to remain pending.

The authorities were obliged to come to the support of the prelate and to prevent his mandate being flouted, and also to put a stop to the scandal brought about at the tomb, by reason of the crowds that gathered there and the robberies and licentious scenes that took place—at least according to the reports based on the evidence of the " convulsionnaires." The King issued an edict, dated 27th January, 1732, which enacted that the gate of the little cemetery of Saint-Médard should be shut and remain shut except for the purposes of burial, and forbade all persons, whatever might be their rank and condition, to meet together in the neighbouring streets and houses, under the severest penalties. We shall see in due course what were the effects of this injunction. Here we will merely observe that, on the day following the closing of the

---

[1] " The Archbishop's mandate against the miracles of the Blessed Pâris has been issued ; but it is only so much powder wasted. The crowds are bigger than ever. People are incensed that the Archbishop should have attached two medical reports to his mandate giving a clear and plain-spoken explanation of the menstrual function. Women complain that he ought not to have told all this ; that it shows a want of consideration "—*Correspondance de Marais.*

cemetery, the following Jansenist quip was found affixed
to the gates :

> De par le Roi défense à Dieu,
> De faire miracle en ce lieu.[1]

We are now drawing near the period when, dealing more
especially with the King and his private life, we shall see
how there commenced to germinate in his mind those
passions which, fomented by unscrupulous courtiers,
played havoc with his heart and brought disorder into the
affairs of the kingdom. He was at that attractive age
when the fancy is taken by the very novelty of things and
when sights and spectacles, childish though they be, have
unfailing power to charm. It afforded great entertainment
to His Majesty to invest M. Morosini, the Venetian
Ambassador, with the insignia of knighthood, to give him
the accolade in accordance with ancient custom, and to
present him with a very costly sword with a belt of cloth
of gold, whereas the other senators' belts were merely of
some dark-hued cloth.

But nothing could approach his joy at the Queen's
pregnancy and his delight at being a father. It was
doubtless not so excessive on the first two occasions when
he bestowed the paternal kiss on two princesses. Both he
and his august consort fell to importuning Heaven with
prayers to grant them a son. On the 8th December, 1728,
both entreated Him in a special manner with their prayers,
as did the people, and, as the Queen has since oft-times
declared, they communicated with this intention. Nor
evidently was this all they did, for, at the end of nine
months, Her Majesty was delivered of the late Dauphin.
This auspicious event was hailed with delight by a people
accustomed to idolize their rulers. A solemn thanksgiving
service was held. The King was present at the *Te Deum*

---

[1] By the King's command, God is forbidden to work any miracles in
this place.

that was sung in Paris, and afterwards supped at the
Hôtel de Ville with the Princes of the Blood and numerous
nobles. The Provost of the Merchants, Turgot, waited
on the King, and the sheriffs and other officers on the
Princes. When, on her recovery, the Queen went to
fulfil a vow she had made for her safe delivery, and in her
turn came to render thanks to God—which did not prevent
her from going to Notre-Dame de Chartres some years
later to consecrate to the Blessed Virgin the young Prince
whom she regarded as her special gift—the capital gave the
most brilliant public fêtes and was imitated by all the towns
throughout the kingdom. The joy felt in France spread
to other countries, for the birth of this Prince was an
assurance of peace and tranquillity for Europe. The States-
General presented a gold medal of a hundred ducats to
the courier whom M. Van Hoey, their ambassador, sent
to the Hague. A medal was struck in Paris on which were
effigies of the King and Queen. On the reverse were a
goddess sitting on a globe with the Dauphin in her arms,
and this inscription : *Vota orbis* (The vows of the universe).

CHAPTER V

EARLY MISTRESSES AND COURTESANS

SINCE Cardinal Fleury had brought about the downfall of M. le Duc, certain of the royal princes then at Court had been causing him some uneasiness. To begin with, there was the Comte de Charolais, who was equally notorious for the truculence of his behaviour and the breadth of his knowledge.[1] The Prince de Conti, extremely witty, amiable, insinuating, brave, fond of campaigning, alert, was jealous of his rank and a terrible spendthrift; it was this Prince, who, on his equerry coming to him to report that there was no more fodder in his stables, called for his steward, who excused himself on the ground that there was no more money in the treasury, adding that the tradespeople would give him no more credit : " All refuse save only the landlord of the cookshop." " Very well," said the Prince, " let my horses have fat pullets ! " Lastly, there was the Duc du Maine, whose ability, avarice and servile uxoriousness were notorious, and who had given umbrage to the Regent himself.

Fortunately the King's tastes inclined him to attach

---

[1] It is a notorious fact that in his youth this Prince killed a man with every circumstance of savage cruelty, just as children delight in squashing a fly—and when he himself came to crave mercy, the murder he had committed was alleged to have been either the result of an unfortunate nerve storm or a necessary act of self-defence. The day came when, granting mercy, the King said to him : " Here is my pardon ; but I would have you to know at the same time that whoso kills you has my pardon in advance."

himself to the Comte de Clermont,[1] who was nearly the same age as His Majesty, with whom he had been brought up—a dull and narrow-minded Prince, whose sole thoughts were of pleasures and women ; and also to the Comte de Toulouse, who, though not very brilliant, was a man of refined tastes and strict morals—he was unmoved by any strong passions, moreover he was cautious and too ashamed of his ill-assorted union not to cultivate the good graces of the all-powerful Cardinal.

The Princesses, who at that epoch had a right to aspire to the Monarch's affections, occasioned the Minister no apprehensions. First and foremost was the Queen. She was complete mistress of her royal husband's heart : she alone could minister to his sensual appetites, and to do so was her sole aim and desire. She was already given to religious devotion, but it was a devotion unmingled with fanaticism, and because of that the clergy, who would fain have used her as an instrument for their intrigues, exercised no influence upon her mind. Moreover, her spiritual director was a Jesuit, a member of an Order devoted to the Cardinal, who gave free rein to his hatred of the Jansenists.

[1] Charles de Bourbon-Condé, Comte de Charolais, and brother of the ex-Prime Minister, the Duc de Bourbon, died suddenly in 1760, in his *petite maison* in Montmartre. At this epoch a " little house " was a " discreet shelter " furnished as delicately and as luxuriously as possible. " Orcan (the Comte de Charolais) had spent an extremely irregular youth ; the most extravagant debauchery had long been the mainspring of his actions ; he was handsome, gifted with a great genius, and in the end, growing wise with increasing years, atoned for the errors of his youth. His brother, who was called Wiram (the Comte de Clermont), was also handsome, though his figure was a trifle heavy. Of limited intelligence, he was given to extravagance, and caused women to be collected from every part to stock his harem. Fluttering from one to the other, without always giving the preference to the one who deserved it, he was capable of sacrificing his entire fortune to gratify the whim of the moment "—*Mémoires secrets pour servir à l'Histoire de Perse.*

Louis de Bourbon-Condé, Comte de Clermont. The lavishness with which he squandered money upon Camargo and Leduc, both dancers at the Opera, was the talk of Paris. Mademoiselle Leduc used to go to church, covered with diamonds, in a coach-and-six.

Louis XV was still enjoying the delights of an affectionate intimacy with Mademoiselle de Charolais and the Comtesse de Toulouse. Although she was the daughter of the Grand Duchess, and the sister of M. le Duc, Mademoiselle de Charolais [1] played no part in their intrigues.

[1] Mademoiselle de Charolais (Louise de Bourbon-Condé), born at Versailles on the 23rd June, 1695. " Fatmé (Mademoiselle de Charolais), sister of Mirza-Haddi (the Duc de Bourbon), extremely beautiful, possessing all the charms, a refined and dainty mind, and of an amiable commerce ; she was an affectionate and faithful friend, extremely sensitive to delicate attentions, losing her friends only through their own fault and with regret ; she was proud yet gentle, melancholy yet sprightly, insouciant and lively, sometimes whimsical, tenacious of her rank, fond of pleasure, turning day into night, and night into day "—*Mémoires secrets pour servir à l'Histoire de Perse.*

There is no proof to support Soulavie's statement that she initiated the King into the ways of adultery. Her intimacy with the Duc de Richelieu created a great scandal. She was jealous of the Regent's daughter, Mademoiselle de Valois, who was also Richelieu's mistress. They composed their quarrel when their lover was shut up in the Bastille, where they both went together to visit him. For an account of this interesting episode, see *Richelieu's Memoirs*, edited by Soulavie. Richelieu's perverted sexual instincts led him to dress his mistresses as nuns, and this is why these verses remain famous :

" On Mademoiselle de Charolais painted in the Habit of a
Franciscan Friar."

By a strange freak,
The angelic brother of Charolais
To the girdle of Saint Francis,
 Tirra-lirra,
Unites the zone of Venus.
Robin, tirra-lirra, lirra.

A big and fat Franciscan friar,
Admiring this figure,
Said with a sigh : Alas !
 Tirra-lirra.
Why art thou but a picture ?
Robin, tirra-lirra, lirra.

All the convent's novices,
In very humble attitude,
Will offer to the fair young boy,
 Tirra-lirra,
All the pleasure he requires,
Robin, tirra-lirra, lirra.

From her youth onwards her beauty and her charm foredestined her to a life of pleasure. She was endowed with a nature of extreme sensitiveness which made her, soul and body, the votary of love. She had had a host of lovers, and children nearly every year, making scarcely more attempts at concealment than a common opera girl. Yet, for decency's sake, they gave out, about six weeks before the event, that she was indisposed, and the Court, who were in the secret, used to send to inquire for her. Once she had a Swiss lacquey who was unversed in these manœuvres. With disconcerting frankness he would say to the callers : " The Princess is doing as well as can be expected, and so is the child."

Nor did the Prince's sisters display any greater restraint. Mademoiselle de Sens' principal lover was M. de Maulevrier Langeron and Mademoiselle de Clermont's, M. de Melun. The latter was gored to death by a savage stag while hunting in the Bois du Boulogne. As she was a very languid sort of person, the Grand Duchess inquired if the news had caused her any emotion.

Mademoiselle de Charolais was said to have secretly married a leader of the nobility of Dombes, from whom,

And it was for Mademoiselle de Charolais, too, that this song which still retains its popularity was written :

> The eyes of my Iris
> Are like courtyard gates,
> Whereon you see written :
> Here you may make love
> By day or night.

The Comte de Toulouse was the son of Louise XIV and Madame de Montespan. The Comtesse de Toulouse, like Mademoiselle de Charolais, was reputed to have been the initiatrice, or at least " one of the initiatrices," of Louis XV into the art of love.

The ambition and the absorbing aim of these two women was jointly to minister to the King's pleasure by the various distractions they could offer him, and so to monopolize his favours, sharing the credit amicably between them. Is it not, therefore, a remarkable thing that Louis XV should have remained so long a faithful spouse ?

however, she had not yet obtained permission openly to claim him as her husband because of the etiquette which even the most exalted are so strictly compelled to obey. The Cardinal had thus a hold on both, and the hope with which he inspired them of gaining His Majesty's consent necessarily made them his partisans.

Mademoiselle de Charolais was on terms of great intimacy with the Comtesse de Toulouse, whose marriage, whereof no secret was made, was calculated to bring about the recognition of her own, which it resembled in many respects ; or if not that, at least to secure its toleration, should considerations of policy render its open avowal inexpedient. Although they differed in many things, since the former was a woman of the world with a taste for excitement and for sumptuous and noisy festivities, and the latter a devotee who loved the country, retirement and tranquil pleasures, they agreed on many others.

Besides, interest which moulds and maintains so many unions incited Mademoiselle de Charolais to foster her friendship with the Comtesse, since it enabled her to obtain from the King all the favours she solicited for herself and her followers.

This Prince often hunted at Rambouillet with the Comte de Toulouse, who, since his marriage, spent most of the year there. Here he liked to seek repose from the wearisome round of Court. Its grandeurs weighed heavily upon him, and it was a relief to him sometimes to forget his kingly state. In a word, it was just one good friend paying a visit to another for a few days spent in the most charming intimacy. Only a few specially favoured ladies and courtiers accompanied him and enjoyed this intimacy. During the day, they would be ceaselessly engaged in hunting the wild creatures with which the vast domain abounded. This violent exercise, which was at first a simple passion with Louis XV, gradually became essential

to his health, and necessary for the distraction of his
mind, which was naturally disposed to melancholy. In the
evening he sought relaxation in play, and repaired his
forces at the table, of the pleasures of which he had grown
more appreciative. In these surroundings he was content
because he was free. He was gay, amiable, enlivened the
conversation, willingly lent himself to the sprightliness of
Mademoiselle de Charolais, delighted in the witty and
delicate sallies of the Comtesse de Toulouse, who had been
like a mother to him and had in some measure introduced
him into the world. She helped him to overcome his
shyness, taught him to speak and to speak well. He was
careful to address himself to every one; in a word, he tried
to please the various guests as much as they pleased him.

To give an idea of the intimacy of this society, we will
cite one fact. One of the ladies, who was pregnant,
suddenly felt the preliminary pains of her approaching
confinement. Every one was alarmed, and, as it was
impossible to remove the lady to Paris, they sent by stage-
coach for an accoucheur. The King was greatly troubled.
"But," said His Majesty, "if the operation becomes urgent,
who will take charge of it?" M. de La Peyronie, the
chief chirurgeon, answered, "I myself, Sire, have delivered
women in my time." "Yes," said Mademoiselle de
Charolais, "but it is a matter that requires practice and
perhaps you have somewhat lost the art." "Have no
fear, Mademoiselle," said he, a trifle offended at the doubt
thus cast upon his skill, "one can no more forget how to
get them out than how to put them in." Furious, Her
Highness blushed scarlet and, so as not to give vent to her
indignation in the presence of the King, left the room.
The chirurgeon, realizing the unseemliness, or rather the
shamelessness of his words, in spite of his aplomb felt
very much embarrassed; but glancing timidly at the
Monarch, he saw him laughing and was reassured. Soon

Mademoiselle de Sens was brought to follow His Majesty's example.[1]

The Cardinal's mind was quite at ease when he knew that the King was in the surroundings of which we have been speaking. His feeling of security was such that, although he was a particular friend of the Comte de Toulouse, he refused to be one of his guests, excusing himself on the ground of his age and the diet which he was compelled to follow. Though, however, he was not present at these gatherings he knew everything that happened. He was not unaware that during these visits, the Princesses, taking advantage of their influence, obtained whatever favours they solicited from His Majesty ; yet they urged their requests with discretion. Not a single favour was granted but the Cardinal was cognizant of it, and so he even directed the bestowal of the King's favours without the Monarch's suspecting it.

[1] Elisabeth Alexandrine de Bourbon Condé (Mademoiselle de Sens). We know that the Duc de Bourbon would have liked to marry his sister, Mademoiselle de Vermandois, to Louis XV.

> If I dared I would offer
> My young sister Vermandois to you ;
> Better than any other
> She will sing
> HALLELUJAH !

We know how the marriage failed. The Duc de Bourbon must, it appears, then have thought of his other sister, Mademoiselle de Sens.

" It is said that M. le Duc's tactics go so far as to marry the King to his sister, Mademoiselle de Sens. This Princess is beautiful, but she is twenty years of age, and so too old for the King. Perhaps this marriage has been thought of in view of M. le Duc's interests, because he would become the King's brother-in-law, and, through it, would keep his post as Prime Minister and maintain his ascendancy over the Duc d'Orléans, now out of favour and shorn of his authority "—*Journal de Barbier.*

" Gemel (Mademoiselle de Sens) was twenty-one years old. She was very fascinating ; her complexion was milky-white, her eyes extremely soft, her features of surpassing loveliness, and there were certain charms about her that one could feel but not express. She was kind and good-natured, yet she had a certain air of haughtiness, which often made it difficult to believe in her kindness "—*Mémoires secrets pour servir à l'Histoire de Perse.*

CHAPTER VI

THE BOTANICAL GARDENS—EXPLORERS—A SCIENTIFIC MOVEMENT

IN 1721 the King had given orders for ten French youths to be brought up at his expense at the Jesuit College, where they were to study Latin and Oriental languages, so that his consuls might employ them as dragomans and interpreters in the Levantine Ports. Before the appearance of these young students, popularly called "Armenians," the Ministers and the subjects of His Majesty had been the victims of the ignorance, the dishonesty and perfidy of foreign interpreters. The Cardinal gave this purely political establishment a literary character. He founded a college in Constantinople and imposed upon these students the task of translating the native books of the country. Subsequently these translations, together with the originals, were placed in the King's library. In 1729 the Abbé Surin had been sent to Constantinople to purchase all the manuscripts—Greek, Turkish, Arabic or Persian—on which he could lay hands. Thus, in 1732 the library was enriched by the addition of a priceless treasure in the shape of ten thousand manuscripts, and a special medal was struck to commemorate the circumstance. In addition, six learned scholars or distinguished men of letters were attached to the staff in order to pursue an uninterrupted search for books suitable to add to the library, each working in his own department.

The King's Garden, now so famous, also engaged the attention of the Cardinal, who persuaded His Majesty to make it an object of special interest, and for that purpose to include it in the department of his Secretary of State, and to place the management of it in the hands of M. Dufay, a man of great learning and distinction and a member of the Academy of Sciences. Hitherto neglected, the garden now began to blossom apace. Great expense was incurred in collecting from all parts a large stock of simples, plants and foreign shrubs, and in the erection of hothouses necessary for their preservation. No long time after, a splendid natural history cabinet and two of the most complete herbariums in Europe were displayed to the public admiration. Every year, for those who were anxious to increase their knowledge, a series of lectures on botany, chemistry and anatomy were delivered entirely free of charge. To this school it was that the many illustrious men who have adorned and enriched these sciences in France were indebted for their early training.

But what will make M. Dufay's administration for ever famous in the history of science, was the execution of the daring scheme determining the configuration of the earth, a piece of knowledge so important for navigation. To carry this into effect it was necessary to measure one degree of longitude beneath the Pole, and another beneath the Equator. The Minister did not spare any expense to that effect ; he readily fell in with the suggestion of the Comte de Maurepas, then Secretary of State to the Admiralty, who gave him to understand that such a project could never be undertaken in more favourable circumstances, and that it was realizable only under a prince who, to power and an influence with other sovereigns, united a love of science and a solicitude for the security of trade.

The three astronomers who were destined for the south were MM. Bouguer, Godin and de la Condamine, and they left first in 1733 ; MM. de Maupertuis, Clairault, Camus and le Monnier were sent north. They started off in 1736 and returned in 1737 after erecting, with the King of Sweden's permission, a pyramid at Tornea, on the borders of Lapland, to commemorate their glorious work. Twelve months were sufficient to enable them to carry out their observations, but another whole year was spent in travelling and in the inevitable conflict with nature in those desert climes.

First they endeavoured to find a place suitable for their operations on the Gulf of Bothnia, but without success. They were compelled to penetrate deeper into the heart of the country and ascend the river of Tornea, from the town of Torno, situated north of the bay, to Mount Kiltes beyond the Arctic Circle.

They had to protect themselves against those dangerous flies so dreaded by the Laplanders, which draw blood when they sting and can kill a man when they attack in large numbers. These flies poisoned their food; and the birds of prey, very numerous and very bold in those climates, would sometimes carry off the meat prepared for our academicians. They were like Æneas among the harpies.

They had to cross rapids and hack their way through a vast forest which obstructed their route and interfered with their operations. They had to climb mountain after mountain and clear their summits of birch trees, pine trees and of all the other trees that obstructed their view. They had to erect at the top of the eight highest mountains signal posts which could be seen miles away and which would enable them to take the necessary sights. Then again they had to establish an observation base on a frozen river, covered to a depth of several feet by a fine and powdery snow like sand, which afforded but a slippery foothold and concealed the most dangerous crevasses down which they might have been precipitated.

They had to endure so rigorous and frigid a temperature that even the inhabitants who were used to it sometimes lost a leg or an arm from frostbite. Brandy was the only liquor that did not freeze. If one put one's lips close to the flask they stuck to it and had to be torn away.

But nothing availed to daunt our academicians. Each one made his own observations separately. They then collated their results, which, being in perfect agreement, proved the accuracy of their labours. Then, finally, after all their toil and trouble, they were wrecked in the Gulf of Bothnia and came within an ace of losing not only their lives but the hard-won fruits of their long and arduous enterprise.

The academicians who went to Peru had even worse obstacles to encounter. They expected to be away four years, but it was ten years before they got home again. Nature seemed to have been in league with the natives to baffle and torment them. They were accompanied by M. de Jussieu, a botanist; M. Seniergues, a surgeon; M. Hugo, a clockmaker, engineer and specialist in mathematical instruments; M. Verguin, a cartographer; and M. de Morainville, a natural history draughtsman.

They had letters of introduction from the King to various foreign governors, and passports from the King of Spain. They had money and bills of exchange; in a word, all that could make their journey easy, useful and comfortable had been thought of and provided for.

After a long, laborious and perilous journey, M. de la Condamine was the first, so to speak, to take possession of the country in the name of Science. He engraved in Latin on the rock of Palmar: " We have ascertained by astronomical calculations that this promontory is situated below the Equator."

Unfortunately, after this auspicious *début* they met with such terrible hardships on their way to Quito that the reader is daunted by the mere recital of them, while, as for the mere fatigues they had to endure, they were equalled only by the patience with which they bore them.

The academicians for lack of money were obliged to sell their clothes, they were accused of smuggling because they sold their shirts, and an action was brought against them. At last they succeeded in erecting their signal posts on the summit or the slope of thirty-nine mountains along a line two hundred and forty miles in length, beginning a little above the Equator and finishing three degrees below it.

Their triangles extended from Cabaraurou, north of Quito, to Chinan, south of Cuença.

Their work was not yet finished when, attending a bull fight in the latter town, the mob, roused to fury, rushed upon them, threatening them with death. Seniergues, the only one who understood the reason of this riot, stood upon his defence ; for a while he overawed these savages and kept them at bay, but at length, while still bravely keeping up the fight, he fell, pierced through and through, at the feet of the academicians who carried him away, covered with blood, shielding themselves as best they could against this unlooked-for onset.

A love affair was at the bottom of this attempted massacre. A Peruvian, jealous of Seniergues, had decided to have him assassinated ; and he succeeded only too well. Seniergues died in M. de la Condamine's arms, charging him to avenge his death.

Thus the academicians were compelled to bring the assassin to trial in the Court of Justice. The case dragged on for three years. The murderer was condemned to exile, but he did not quit the country, and eventually became a priest.

Before leaving they were involved in a third lawsuit. It was about two pyramids that they desired to erect in connection with their observations. These pyramids were

to afford an easy and accurate means of verifying their
calculations. Obviously these pyramids were designed
for use rather than as a monument to their achievement.
Some Spanish officers, however, took fright at the inscription,
in which the King of France was mentioned, and opposed
the erection of the pyramids. M. de la Condamine, who
conducted the case for his colleagues, won it, and the two
pyramids were erected. They were, however, demolished
after the departure of the academicians.[1]

[1] The names of all the great men mentioned in this chapter are too well
known and too popular to render a biographical note necessary.

By a decree of January 1626, registered in Parliament in July of the same
year, Louis XIII founded the Royal Botanical Garden, and entrusted its
management to the Chief Physician. It was created a separate office by an
edict of 31st March, 1718. See the work of M. Gudin, entitled *Aux Mânes
de Louis XV*.

CHAPTER VII

THE QUEEN—MEN AND WOMEN CORRUPTERS—MADAME DE MAILLY—MADAME DE VINTIMILLE—THE LITTLE APARTMENTS

CARDINAL DE FLEURY'S eagerness for power was well known, and men whose sole claim to consistency lay in the determination with which they pursued their careers of licentiousness and debauchery, pandered to this foible of his in order to attain their ends. The Cardinal's mistress was the Princesse de Carignan.[1] That is to say, he was ruled by her, told her all his State secrets, and never took a decision without her advice. This was what the word "mistress" connoted in his case, and it was frequently employed at Court with this acceptation. Such was the only possible signification the word could have in connexion with a woman of forty-five and an old man verging on ninety for whom the pleasures of sensual love must have long since passed into the domain of reminiscence. The satisfaction of ruling the Minister who himself held the Monarch in leading strings was the Princess's most thrilling delight, albeit her ascendancy hung by a thread.

[1] In the *Couplets sur les Mœurs du temps*, we read :

> Que l'Hypocrite Carignan
> Soit avare et voluptueuse,
> Quand dans l'esprit de bien des gens
> Elle passe pour vertueuse.

"She pretends to be devout and makes money out of the transactions she engineers at Court through the Cardinal, with whom she is on good terms "—*Journal de Barbier*.

Constant until now in his love for his royal spouse, the King had turned a deaf ear to those who had endeavoured to seduce him from the path of conjugal fidelity. Whenever an artful attempt was made to awaken his interest in some fascinating creature, the King would coldly answer, " I think the Queen is more beautiful." [1] Yet it was thought he might come to tire of her. The many children she had presented him with were perhaps calculated to hasten the fatal moment. But what a formidable sequel such a transference of the royal affections might involve. The only way to avoid disagreeable consequences was to take the initiative and to introduce as a partner of the royal couch some dependable enchantress who would be sufficiently absorbed by the pleasures of the flesh to leave politics and affairs of State to His Eminence.

They broached the matter to the Princesse de Polignac, who, in turn, passed the word to the Cardinal, and in due course they hatched a plot in which Wisdom itself would have been ensnared. To begin with, they enlisted the good offices of the Queen's father confessor. In pious terms this holy man hinted to Her Majesty that, having fulfilled her duty by bringing forth an heir to the throne and princesses to adorn it, she would now be doing the most agreeable thing in God's eyes if she pursued a life of chastity, the greatest of all the virtues, and abstained from those periodic indulgences in carnal pleasures which were ever calculated to drag our souls into the mire instead of

---

[1] These words, when he uttered them, were sincere, but how soon they were to be forgotten! His enthusiasm was but instinctive gratitude to one to whom he was indebted for his initiation into a life he had never dreamed of before. But the daughter of Stanislas was unwitting how to profit either by circumstances or by the King's sentiments towards her. Then again Louis XV was naturally shy, selfish and fickle ; moreover, it was soon to be impressed upon him that he had only to express a wish for it to be granted without opposition. " Sire," the Maréchal de Villars declared to him one day, " 'twere preposterous that a King of France should be sad and weary at twenty-five ! "

raising them up to heaven, our real home. Doubtless, if Marie's nature had been a sensual one, such advice would have been barren of effect, but the little passion that she had was cramped and repressed by religious devotion.[1]

One day, as her husband had succeeded in sharing the Queen's bed, heated as he was with wine and consequently ill-prepared for amorous dalliance, the Queen made no secret of her disgust, and rejected his caresses with such evident repugnance that the Monarch felt his pride had had a fall. He swore on his oath that such an insult should not be offered him again, and he kept his word ! [2]

[1] The Queen was neither pretty nor elegant. She feigned a sort of prudery although her language was graphic enough. At certain dates, vigils, feasts and days consecrated to the memory of illustrious saints, she demanded—well, let us call it a " respite " from the King's attentions. But gradually new saints of minor importance were invoked, and Louis XV became impatient. He did not chafe at the great elect, but he drew the line at all these petty saintlings. At first he was content with such a device as breathing on a mirror and writing on the fleeting mist, " Your Majesty is a proud minx " ; but one night, pleading that it was a saint's day, the Queen refused to admit him to her bedchamber. " Madame," he shouted at her, " you shall pay for this," and immediately commanded Lebel to go and fetch a woman, no matter whom. Lebel sped away, and soon returned with an amiable and tantalizing maid of the Princesse de Rohan, who undertook these supplementary duties with the most charming alacrity. She had to be provided with a husband a few months later—the case was urgent—and she shortly afterwards gave birth to " Dovigny le Dauphin," who as a dealer in mirrors became famous in the world of commerce, and was credited with the authorship of a play called The Loser Pays, which took Paris by storm, and in which the famous actor Volange, nicknamed Jeannot, scored a notable triumph.

Jean de Bourgogne adds that Dovigny, this pseudo-scion of the royal house of France, owed his birth to Marie Leczinska's untactful conduct. This adventure has always been slurred over, in order that Louis XV's emancipation from the conjugal bonds may be taken to date from his liaison with Madame de Mailly.

[2] The story is in the highest degree improbable. The rupture came naturally, of its own accord. Marie Leczinska's charms had no longer sufficient novelty and fascination about them to maintain their hold on Louis XV. Her exaggerated piety, her offended dignity, and her weariness of perpetually bearing children, combined to hasten this separation. In 1734, however, the royal spouse was not yet the object of neglect ; the Monarch still received Holy Communion and was still listening to the violent exhortations of Father Teinturier, who chose as the subject of his Lenten

The corrupters had an easy game to play. They had merely to overcome the King's bashfulness, startled by a change to which he was not accustomed and increased again by a timidity which was the basis of his character. The Comtesse de Mailly, a Lady-in-Waiting of the Queen's, was recognized to be the most suitable to play the part. She was more or less like a widow, without children, straightforward and devoid of ambition. She was a friend of the Comtesse de Toulouse and incapable of abusing the advantages of her situation or of giving the least umbrage to the Cardinal; besides, she was of an affectionate disposition, and well primed with all the artifices necessary to subdue this modern Hippolyte to her will. She was neither young

sermons "The Luxurious Life." In 1737 a seventh child was born, a girl, Marie Louise de France, who was destined to die a Carmelite nun. With rough irony her father called her Princess Final. It was then plain enough that a rupture was at hand. When it actually occurred, the problem was to explain it.

La Vie Privée de Louis XV and the *Mémoires de Richelieu* give the same version. According to D'Argenson, the Queen foolishly imagined that her health was endangered since Madame de Mailly had been on intimate terms with the libertines of the Court . . . and so, one night, the King spent four hours in the Queen's bed, she firmly refusing to comply with his desires. The King left her at three o'clock in the morning, saying, " 'Tis the last time that I will essay this adventure." Next day the plotters played their trump card. Madame de Mailly crept stealthily into the "little apartments," to spend the night there, and Bachelier pulled aside her hood, as by mistake, so as to let her be seen. Cf. Fleury, *Louis XV intime et les petites maîtresses.*

It must be mentioned that P. de Nolhac in his interesting work, *Louis XV et Marie Leczinska*, absolutely denies that the King ever nicknamed his daughter "Madame Dernière." "The truth," he says, "is quite otherwise." It was on the 26th July, 1737, the King had remained at the Queen's side during her pains, and had kissed the hand she had extended to him. Immediately after her delivery, and knowing it was a girl, the Queen begged the King to come near and said to him, "I would willingly go through all this again to give you a Duc d'Anjou." The King exhorted her to keep calm. This tender appeal from his spouse, so moving and sincere, was heard by the Duchesse de Luynes, a Lady-in-Waiting, who never left the Queen's bedside. The desire to replace his lost son had never forsaken her, and up to the final abandonment, she yearned with all her soul for another Duc d'Anjou. It cannot therefore be maintained that the Queen made any attempt to evade her wifely duty or that she ever wearied of bearing children.

nor beautiful, she was not even pretty. She was thirty-five years of age, and there was nothing very remarkable in her face save two big, dark eyes, well set in her head, and very bright. Their expression, though usually somewhat hard, grew soft as she looked upon the King, retaining only that shade of boldness which tells of passionate desire and is well calculated to stimulate the neophyte to try his fortune in the lists of love. Her voice was loud and tended to confirm the impression which was still further heightened by her slow and lascivious gait. In the circumstances, such an exterior provided charms by far more potent than the loveliest of necks, the most shapely arms, or even the high lineage, the graces and manifold attractions of a hundred other Court beauties. Moreover, she surpassed them all in an art which compensates for the absence of many charms—to wit, the art of dressing. This she possessed in the highest degree, and in it she exhibited an exquisite taste which her rivals attempted in vain to imitate. In a word, nature had endowed her with such admirable qualities of heart and mind as richly to compensate for whatever she had denied her in the domain of physical attractions. She was entertaining, sprightly, good-tempered, a trusty friend, liberal, compassionate, and ready to help. Unfortunately, even after her promotion, she was compelled to employ indirect methods in all she did, lest by acting independently she should forfeit the favours she enjoyed and the affection of the royal personage to whom she was indebted for them, particularly the protection of the Cardinal, who had given her the preference over all other candidates, on the understanding that her part was to be a purely passive one.[1]

[1] Louise Julie de Mailly Nesle, born the 16th March, 1710, married the Comte de Mailly, her first cousin, on the 31st May, 1726. She was then succeeding her mother, Armande Felicité de la Porte Mazarin, as Lady-in-Waiting to the Queen. The above description of Madame de Mailly is very true to life. If she had fine legs—we shall shortly see what part these legs were destined to play—her throat and arms were rather unattractive,

When the preliminaries had been arranged the Prime Minister entrusted the Duc de Richelieu with the delicate mission of broaching the matter of Madame de Mailly to the King. This skilful and seductive courtier had insinuated himself into the King's good graces and enjoyed his full confidence. The Cardinal had no doubt that whatever the object to which he directed his talents, the Duc de Richelieu would not fail, and that, whether it was an affair of State or an affair of the heart that was involved, his charm and tact would prove equally successful. And so, taking advantage of the familiar terms on which he stood with Louis XV, he adroitly cast blame upon the Queen for the void she left in his heart, and brought him to agree that it was necessary to find another to take her place. He showed that love is a consolation to all men, especially to great princes who are bound to seek some relief from the burden of State affairs. He thus brought the King to have an interview with Madame de Mailly, but in spite of the ardour natural to his age, in spite of the impetuosity of his nature, in spite of his prolonged abstinence, the meeting was fruitless. Timidity so chilled his desires that the disconsolate Comtesse bewailed the insignificant impression she had made. It was with difficulty that she was persuaded to consent to another *tête-à-tête*. It was enjoined upon her that she must forget the monarch, and only remember the man. The docility with which the young prince came back to her was a

and her mouth somewhat large. "One day," says D'Argenson, "the favourite received a petition from the Comte de Luc, which terminated as follows : ' A word from the beautiful mouth of such a beautiful lady as you will settle the matter.' The mistress showed the petition to the King, who said bluntly : ' Beautiful mouth, eh ? I should hardly think you can flatter yourself on that score ! '" Her forehead was large and high, her cheeks flat, her complexion rather dark, but on the whole there was undeniable charm about her. Madame de Mailly had been somewhat neglected by her husband, and was said to have had intimate relations with the Marquis de Puysieux before she became the King's mistress.

wonderful encouragement and convinced her that to triumph she had only to open the attack. She allowed herself to employ the shameless artifices of the most unblushing courtesans—her fondlings and caresses acted like magic, and the lover, entering at once into the full exercise of his rights, gave rein to a passion which was the more vehement for having been so long restrained. When this love passage came to an end, Madame de Mailly, highly delighted with herself, and still flushed and disordered from the amorous encounter, went out in this condition to display herself to those who had set her on and were waiting to know what had happened. All she said to them was, " Just look what this rake has made of me ! " [1]

Now that the ice had been broken, the King felt no further compunction. Without any qualms of conscience he gave himself up to this double adultery. For a time, however, the meetings still took place in secret ; but soon he shook off this reserve and made no mystery whatever about his conquest. The courtiers began to talk ; the Queen herself got to know of it, and instead of attempting to exert her old influence over her husband, and so secure his return to the nuptial couch, she contented herself with lamentations before the altar.

The Comte de Mailly, who had hitherto taken but scant notice of his wife, suddenly took it into his head to

[1] Thus described in *Richelieu's Memoirs* : " At the time, the King, who was still timid and devout, would have made no advances to any woman if she had not made advances to him. Waiting for the moment to come, Madame de Mailly reclined on a sofa in an attitude of voluptuous abandon, showing the most beautiful leg to be seen at Court, with the garter becoming undone. This pose rather repelled the young Monarch. Bachelier tried to excite his interest in the lady's attractions, but the King, who was either indifferent or ashamed, did not take any notice. Seeing that unless some prompt and decisive actions were taken all would be lost, Bachelier took the King under the arms and forced him. . . . The King, who used to play at ' Saddle my nag ' with Bachelier and Lebel, and sometimes with the Cardinal in the privacy of his apartments, made no objection to being thrown on Madame de Mailly by his valet."

complain of her infidelity. For his pains he was told to have no further connexion with her. The Marquis de Nesles, the favourite's father, who came of one of the most illustrious families in the kingdom, was also inclined to criticize her conduct. His animadversions, however, were thought to be inspired by pecuniary motives, for his affairs had gone awry and he was in sore need of funds. Money was therefore given him in plenty, to keep his mouth shut.

The personage who showed the most embarrassment at the beginning of the King's love affairs was the Cardinal. With the sole idea of impressing the people he, who was indirectly responsible for his royal pupil's misconduct, pushed his hypocrisy so far as to give utterance to a few remonstrances. " I have conferred upon you the conduct of my kingdom," said His Majesty; " I hope you will leave me to mind my own." Despite their sharpness, these words were not displeasing to the Cardinal. One can imagine how the Parisians talked. People in general, and the French people in particular, like things to change because they hope they will improve. They indulged in the expectation that a mistress would bring about some great transformation ; when, however, they perceived that she only served to increase the rigour of the Chief Minister's authority, those who clapped their hands at the King's peccadilloes now took a totally different view of the situation. The royal irregularities were said to have a most disastrous influence, and it was proclaimed that the vengeance of Heaven would assuredly descend upon the kingdom. The royal lovers were freely lampooned in satire and song.

What excuses the rôle played by Madame de Mailly, a rôle to which she was quite unaccustomed and which she was doubtless enacting for the first time, infamous and abominable as it would have been in any other case, is the fact that her heart was genuinely engaged—that it was the man rather than the monarch that attracted her, that she really loved Louis XV, that she asked no favours for herself or her relations, that she was never a burden to the State, and that she quitted the Court as poor as she entered it. After the manner of Madame de la Vallière she thought that none was worthy to take the place of her earthly love save God, and it was with tears and ceaseless penances that she continued until her death to expiate the scandal she had caused, and to atone for the one crime that ever incurs condemnation, the crime of soiling the marriage bed.[1]

Alas, long before that, at the zenith of enjoyment, she was to find her punishment in the passion she had excited ! More than once she repented of having deprived the King of the bridle to his passions ; that Prince, who admired rather than loved her, was restrained by no sense of shame and gave full rein to all his desires : even incest did not scare him.

[1] " Lest Cha-Séphi (Louis XV) should be prompted merely by his eyes and heart to elevate to the rank of favourite some young and beautiful woman, who might perhaps be ambitious and capable of governing, it was thought by Fleury and his party that the best thing to do in the interests the common weal was to direct his affections to Rétima (Madame de Mailly), who had none of the characteristics they apprehended. She was a trust-worthy woman and they were careful to extract from her a promise that she would seek no other honour than the King's love and that she would never attempt to influence the actions of Séphi (the Monarch) save with the approval and co-operation of those who, to her knowledge, enjoyed his confidence and esteem. It was a queer sort of arrangement this, and by it Rétima paid dearly for the semblance of credit and honour involved in the permission to appear side by side with Cha-Séphi at those gatherings to which only his favourites were admitted. But she continued loyal to the agreement so long as she remained in favour.

" Her good faith is deserving of praise, more especially as she was doubtless aware that there are moments of triumph when a favourite may dare and demand anything from a sovereign, even the least suscept-ible, particularly when she happens to be his first love. But apparently Rétima's passions were all genuinely of the heart, and she sought not so much the Monarch as the lover, to whom she might attach herself with sincere affection. She was really in love "—*Mémoires secrets pour servir à l'Histoire de Perse.*

MADAME DE MAILLY

The favourite's sister was Madame de Vintimille,[1] who had only been married a short time. She too was tall, and she had this advantage over her sister : she was young.

But she was even more witty, and she soon made use of her gifts to supplant Madame de Mailly and to ensnare the King. All who knew her feared her power—she was haughty and intriguing, envious and vindictive, fond of ruling and of being feared, having only a few friends and little capacity for making any, merely thinking of her own interests, possessing no other aim than that of taking advantage of the weakness of the man she had enslaved. Success would have been hers had not death intervened to put an end to her career at its outset. She died in child-bed and a suspicion arose that she had been poisoned. Her loss caused the King to shed tears for a few days. Her sister, whom the King had retained as a go-between in arranging their clandestine assignations, mingled her tears with his and sincerely mourned her rival. Madame de Vintimille left a son, the Comte du Luc, who was the living image of His Majesty. Madame de Mailly loved him tenderly and he was known at Court as the demi-Louis, to perpetuate the memory of his origin.[2]

[1] Pauline Félicité de Mailly, known as Mademoiselle de Nesle (1712–1741) before her marriage (in 1739) to J.-B. Félix Hubert de Vintimille du Luc. Unsuspectingly her sister, Madame de Mailly, introduced her to the King. "Zacchi (Madame de Vintimille) was tall, and no more attractive than Rétima (Madame de Mailly), but younger; she was exceedingly witty, haughty, intriguing, envious, vindictive, fond of ruling and of being feared, not possessing many friends and little capable of making any ; thinking only of her own interest and having no other aim than to profit by the favour in which she was held. She would have succeeded if death had not cut short her career at the beginning. She would have been a dangerous favourite." —*Mémoires secrets pour servir à l'Histoire de Perse.*

[2] Pauline Félicité was an inmate of Port Royal and had sworn to be the King's mistress and to rule France through him. But death cut short that ambitious design. She died in child-bed in the apartments of the Cardinal de Rohan, at Versailles. As a dead body was never left in the Palace, the corpse was taken next day to the Hôtel de Villeroy, in the parish of Notre Dame, and finally to the Recollets, where she was buried in

Happily the sensitiveness of His Majesty, usually at its height at his age, was already deadened. The King merely felt that sort of transient grief which is every one's experience when they hear of some one's death, because they realize that sooner or later the same destiny must inevitably overtake them also. Interrupted for a time, the round of pleasures soon resumed its normal course : the distractions of the chase, the ceaseless journeyings whereof the Monarch was always in need to shake off the depression that was apt to hang upon him, and which were now more necessary than ever in order to make him forget Madame de Vintimille. The first favourite regained her position and accompanied him everywhere. Mademoiselle de Charolais and the Comtesse de Toulouse supported her. They, it was, who were responsible for those delightful supper-parties in lovely retreats to which only the King's most intimate companions were admitted, and which were therefore known as " les petits appartements." Such were the chambers of secret retirement Louis XV caused to be fitted up in his divers palaces. Although not entirely shut off from the State rooms, there was no other com-

the Chapel of Saint Louis. Her child bore such a striking resemblance to his father, Louis XV, that the people called him " le demi-Louis."

This " demi-Louis " was the Comte de Luc. Madame de Pompadour, for a brief period, thought of marrying him to her daughter, Alexandrine. In 1780 he became Field Marshal of the King's armies, and he died in Naples in 1810. See his biography in Fleury, *Louis intime et les petites maîtresses*.

D'Argenson writes : " The people came up and seized it (the corpse of Madame de Vintimille) ; they offered all manner of indignities to her unprepossessing body, which had been left uncovered, a barbarous act that implied scant respect for the King." The procession was the occasion of much popular derision, and we shall see that later on the obsequies of Madame de Châteauroux took place at night, " to avoid the fury of the mob."

The people of Versailles made merry at her death, " the death of this ugly beast, whereas la Mailly was such a good woman." The King's grief was almost excessive. He talked of living with Madame de Mailly as a *friend only*, and one day, as he was suffering from an attack of rheumatism, he said to the courtiers around him : " I am not sorry to suffer this ; if you knew the reason you would approve, for I suffer in expiation of my sins " ; but pleasure soon resumed its customary sway.

munication between them than was necessary for the access of servants to wait upon the revellers. A secret door in His Majesty's bedroom enabled him to pass through unnoticed with his chosen guests whenever he so desired. Artists had lavished all their skill in designing and in furnishing the rooms with that sumptuous elegance appropriate to scenes of gallantry and intrigue. The following is a description contained in *Les Anecdotes de Perse*, whose author, in order to put his readers off the scent, declared he copied from another source :

" 'Twas a little temple within which nocturnal festivities in honour of Venus and Bacchus were secretly celebrated— the Sophi was the grand master—Rétima the high priestess— the rest of the hallowed company consisted of fair women and gay courtiers worthy of being initiated into these mysteries. There, by generous libations of the most exquisite wine and by divers hymns sung to the glory of Bacchus, they were fain to secure his favourable intercession with the goddess of Cythera, to whom they made from time to time generous offerings. The rarest wines were used for these libations, the most exquisite meats represented the sacrificial victims. Often, on days of particular solemnity, these meats were prepared by the High Priest. Comus was the Master of the Ceremonies, and Momus the President. No servant was allowed to disturb these sacred rites nor to enter the temple except when, priests and priestesses being overwhelmed at last with the divine favours, had fallen prone in utter ecstasy, thus demonstrating the fullness of their zeal and the presence of the gods. They then entered to shut the temple doors. There were some days in the year when Bacchus only was celebrated and Comus always presided. Those days, known as the minor feasts, were those to which the High Priests admitted within the precincts of the temple Sévagi, Fatmé, Zélide and a few others before whom, as being the profane, only the lesser mysteries were celebrated. Far from deserving to be included among the fortunate ones, to whom the full and inmost mysteries of the cult were unveiled, they were scarcely held to merit the partial initiation vouchsafed them."

From this mysterious narrative, whereof the truth is vouched for by nobles still living who bore a part in the scenes to which it alludes, and in which Louis XV is named "Sophi" and his favourite "Rétima," it appears that the *petits appartements* were equally intended for the pleasures of feasting and of love. To the greater mysteries admission was only granted to the courtiers who were sufficiently corrupt to take an active part in the King's debauches or debased enough to remain as spectators. The others belonged to a less vicious and less exclusive circle. The Comte and Comtesse de Toulouse, and Mademoiselle de Charolais, nicknamed by the hieroglyphic writer "Sévagi," "Zélide" and "Fatmé," were the principal actors among them. All that happened at these gatherings was decent and of good report ; if they warmed themselves with wine it was only to provoke flashes of merriment and sallies of wit, to impart a keener edge to their irony when, under the guise of a frivolous gaiety, the La Trémoilles, the d'Ayens, the Maurepas, the Coignys, the Souvrés, told the King a few useful truths whereby unfortunately he failed to profit. When the princesses had retired, or during their absence, these orgies became truly bacchanalian. Madame de Mailly, who ought to have been born fifty years earlier, was fond of champagne and gave the King a fondness for it. They revived the drinking bouts of bygone days, when one would vie with another in the attempt to put his adversary under the table, and when, after a protracted trial of strength, the trusty serving-men had to come and carry away all the guests, both victors and vanquished.

It is a stain on the Comtesse's memory that she should have enticed her lover into taking part in these disgusting orgies, which, it would appear, were far from exciting his repulsion. We are forced to this conclusion by another circumstance—Louis XV was fond of cooking; he liked concocting little stews.[1] This ignoble pastime was, if not in itself to be condemned, at all events very regrettable, since it betrayed a mind unaccustomed to occupy itself with great and sublime ideas, such as those of a Sovereign ought habitually to be. It was not in this manner that the Cardinal wished to see the King divert himself; as for the favourite, she simply followed the plan laid out for her. The time had not yet come for the *petits appartements* to be the centre of political negotiations, yet the Court was not immune from storms or intrigues.

[1] The Queen, His Majesty's lawful spouse, was a gross, a very gross, eater. "The King used often to descend to Madame Adélaïde's chamber by a private staircase; he brought down coffee made with his own hands and took it with her; he was fond also of cooking dishes he had prepared, aud on days of high festival he used to go and inspect the head cooks and supervise the roast"—Stryienski, *Le XVIIIe siècle*, pp. 114–115.

CHAPTER VIII

FLEURY'S ADMINISTRATION—HOW THE KING OCCUPIED
   HIS TIME — THE FAVOURITE'S QUARTERS — THE
   THEATRE AT CHOISY — A GOOD FATHER — THE
   DAUPHIN

THE administration of Cardinal Fleury passed by
without a cloud and ended as peacefully as his
long career. The more his royal ward increased
in years, the more submissive he became. Save
for the pomp and circumstance that surrounded the
throne one might have mistaken him for the Cardinal's
chief subject. His Eminence in turn was governed by
two very humble men—one was the Abbé Couturier,
superior of the Seminary of Saint Sulpice, who, though
not the titular confessor of the ruling Minister, largely
directed his conscience and, though he derived no pecuniary
advantage from his position, was at the head of all ecclesiastical affairs. The man was rough and uneducated, but
despite his boorish air he had been skilful enough to mani-
pulate and act upon the conscience of his penitent so as
to make himself, under him, the dispenser of all the favours
the Church had to bestow. In his antechamber he used
to receive the noblest lords of the kingdom with an
enormous hat upon his head, the brims of which shadowed
his broad shoulders ; he wore a baize cassock and white
neck-bands. His house became the nursery-garden of all
the abbés of rank who wanted to become bishops, and, as
he was a partisan of the Jesuits, he made it a hotbed
of Molinistic teaching, with which it is still infected. The

other was Barjac, the Cardinal's valet and consequently the minister of his pleasures and confidant of his sorrows. He had a marvellous insight into the weak points of his master's character, knew how to handle them, and titillated them very adroitly. He it was who, shortly before the death of his nonagenarian master, conceived the delicate courtesy of causing him to sit down to supper one Twelfth Night with twelve guests of the Court, men and women, all older than he, so that, being the youngest, he had to cut the cake. Endowed with such tact, Barjac could not help being far advanced in the Cardinal's favours. He was the dispenser of all the household favours, chiefly the pecuniary ones, whereof a considerable portion flowed into his own pockets, and so, when his protector died, he found himself immensely rich. Such were the two men, without real character, who wielded the most influence since the downfall of M. Chauvelin.[1] Yet a spirit of equity and moderation impelled the Cardinal to leave the distribution of the posts to each State Secretary, in his own department. But as they themselves depended upon His Eminence, they showed great consideration for his favourites.

As for the King, confined in a round of occupations and amusements of his own, the only really essential duty of his

[1] Germain Louis Chauvelin (1685–1762) was Chief Justice when he was appointed Keeper of the Seals. The First President of the Chamber of Accounts, when offering him his congratulations, remarked: "Monsieur le Président Chauvelin, you are rising early, there is no knowing whether you will sit very late."

"He was," says a writer of his time, "a great politician, gifted with superior genius, but a man to be feared. Amiable and easily accessible, he possessed a refined and delicate mind. He was a charming companion and a most fascinating conversationalist." "He was," says D'Argenson, "a very upright man and a great citizen, with the manners of a swindler." It is undeniable that he showed great ability in the Polish War of Succession; it is to him we are indebted for everything advantageous in the Treaty of Vienna. It was in 1737 that Fleury deprived him of the Seals, because he had been given to understand that he intended to supplant him. M. de Jumilhac was commanded to conduct him to his property at Grobois with his wife, née Fontaine des Nonces; he was a rich tradesman of Orleans.

royal office that he performed, and that only because he could not help it, was to be present at the important deliberations concerning the conduct of the State. It was then that he first began to manifest that delicate judgment which, however, was not quite so apparent as it might have been, because, since the Council was composed of Ministers of probity and experience, his advice was somewhat obscured, so to speak, by that of the others, while his modesty, praiseworthy as it was, caused him to defer to the Cardinal, whose advanced age and commanding nature overawed him. But the accuracy, judgment and delicate insight of the young King could not have escaped his preceptor, whose failure to encourage and develop these qualities constituted an inexcusable fault in the eyes of the nation.

What a happy thing it would have been for France if the Cardinal had encouraged in his royal ward these valuable characteristics. If he had urged him to overcome indolence by setting before him the great motives of duty and public service, or, if these had failed, with the lure of glory ; if he had accustomed him early to regular and industrious habits, work would have been a pastime to him. But it was not to be. His education was a failure. The Cardinal had so besotted the young Prince at the age when activity and energy should be most in evidence, that enlightened minds foresaw only too clearly the disastrous results that would inevitably follow throughout his entire reign. The King [1] was engrossed in the sanguinary exercises of the chase. He ruined his health by his excesses at table, and graduated in lechery with Madame de Mailly. As he could not completely escape the operation of the law

---

[1] Nothing could be more exact. The life of Louis XV was one of complete idleness. Hunting and the pleasures of the table continued to be his two principal occupations. Fleury, the Cardinal Minister, encouraged this idleness. He only consulted the Monarch as a matter of form, and out of

that compels all men to occupy themselves with some business or another, the King, as we have seen, took up the culinary art. He also worked at the lathe.

In 1739 he set a new fashion in New Year's gifts, a sort of snuff-box of his own design. It was a piece of round log, covered with its own bark, hollowed out inside and so roughly made that a craftsman would have been ashamed to show it. He made several of these and gave them to his courtiers, who all wanted to have one. The King was for ever asking questions, which shows that he was eager to learn. Unfortunately his questions were often futile or irrelevant to the subject of kingcraft. He talked a lot about physics, astronomy and botany. When he could get hold of some prelate or abbé, he insisted on talking to him about Latin or the Liturgy, subjects of which he seemed to possess a wide knowledge. This was a result of the education given him by his tutor, who considered religion as a salutary restraint upon Kings, but in the spirit of his own order ; that is to say, as a means of stopping any inroads a Sovereign might make, not upon the tranquillity, properties or liberties of his subjects, but against the rights, privileges, liberties or alleged immunities of the Church. The Cardinal had inspired the King with a host of ideas of that kind ; he had made him pay more heed to the letter than to the spirit. Therefore Louis XV was always a punctilious observer of outward forms and

useless deference. He knew that in that state of mind the King was, in advance, of necessity doomed to fall a prey to all the snares set by his courtiers.

> Vive Louis le chasseur !
> Vive Fleury son précepteur !
> France, bénis leur entreprise,
> L'un dépeuple l'Église
> Et l'autre les forêts.

(Long live Louis the hunter ! Long live Fleury his tutor ! Oh, France, bless their venture ; one strips the Church, the other the forests.)

practices. Even in the most vicious and disorderly periods of his career, he never missed saying his prayers, morning and night ; he used to attend mass regularly every day, and he had a prayer-book from which he did not raise his eyes, the motion of his lips showing that he was murmuring the words. He was always present at vespers, at the sermon, at benediction. Full of veneration for the ministers of religion, he insisted that they should be respected. He held the irreligious in abomination, and this is why, in spite of all the eulogies showered upon him by Voltaire, he was never able to endure him.

It was probably the religious spirit of the young King that caused him to perform two conspicuous acts of devotion during the period we are now reviewing. On 1st September, 1736, he went to Saint-Denis and attended the solemn service in memory of Louis XIV. It was the only time that the King had ever fulfilled this pious duty towards his great-grandfather, a duty the legitimized princes had never failed to perform. The superior of the Benedictines, who preached to him, did not fail to proclaim that, in accordance with God's promise, he would be rewarded with a long life and a prosperous reign. But this prediction was not more happy than that of the Tsar, and it proves that the monk could read the future no better than the heretic prince.

The year 1738 was the hundredth since Louis XIII made the vow to which he deemed he owed the birth of Louis XIV. The latter's grandson now gave orders that the annual procession instituted in Paris in Notre Dame on the day of Assumption, should take place with greater pomp than usual. The superstitious monarch flattered himself that he would thus appease the wrath of Heaven and atone by these outward acts of devotion for his adulterous and incestuous misdeeds.

Since the death of the Comte de Toulouse, Louis XV, being a slave to habit, continued for two years to pay visits to Rambouillet. He would have extended the period still longer if the Abbé de Saluberri, chief counsellor of the Comtesse de Toulouse, her director and the absolute master of her household affairs, had not, by his stinginess towards the King's attendants, alienated His Majesty's principal officers, who prevailed upon him gradually to relinquish his visits. Moreover, he purchased the Château de Choisy from the Duc de la Vallière. This residence pleased him, and he was at great pains to make it worthy of his royal person.

Louis XV began by enlarging the building, which was not spacious enough for his requirements. Soon there appeared, amongst other things, a delightful little suite contrived over the King's apartments, and communicating with them by a secret staircase. These were the quarters of the royal favourite. " The delicate carving, the gold and azure, the well-chosen furniture, and the wealth of beautiful mirrors, gave it an atmosphere of elegant simplicity and striking fascination. Art had done its utmost to render it convenient for affairs of gallantry." Such is the description of a contemporary writer. We quote it word for word in order that the reader may form an estimate of the progress made in a few years in the way of luxurious building and furnishing. If the author,[1] who was held to be one of the most intelligent and refined courtiers attached to Louis XV, was filled with such amazement, what must have been his feelings later on when he beheld the master-pieces that owed their existence to those modern Circes, la Pompadour and la Dubarry ! Nevertheless, such was the palace destined to conceal the Monarch from the evil curiosity of the courtiers and, particularly, from malicious gossip or the importunate complaints of the people. It

[1] The *Anecdotes de Perse* were said to have been written by the Duc de Nivernois, but this he always refused to acknowledge, says the author of *La Vie Privée de Louis XV*. *Les Mémoires secrets pour servir à l'Histoire de Perse* were by Toussaint; see the edition published by Plon, 1908, with Notes by Fould.

was there that he was to hold his secret orgies with his
mistress and his favourites; consequently he entrusted the
management of it to one of the latter, to wit, the son of
Maréchal Duc de Coigny. Thither he betook himself at
frequent intervals, discarding the private apartments at
Versailles, where Argus with his hundred eyes was too much
in evidence. Moreover, the situation of Choisy was
infinitely more agreeable to him. On the banks of the
Seine, fronting a wood, its rural and solitary aspect was
well suited to the taste and pastimes of Louis XV, who
never wearied of it or ceased to add to its amenities. He
created "le petit château" the most secret sanctuary,
where you may behold that marvel of mechanical genius,
since brought to perfection by the famous Loriot, and
used as a model for all others of its kind, the little table,
known as a *confidente*. It was a table that could be made
to ascend or descend as the guests desired.[1]

Thus, while a tedious and elaborate luxury was depriving
our festive gatherings of the merriment and freedom our
ancestors enjoyed, by introducing a host of serving-men,
who are nature's own spies, the mode of ridding oneself
of these continual eavesdroppers by waiting on oneself
was beginning to find favour at Court.

There was also a theatre at Choisy,[2] small but elegant.
On one occasion the piece presented was *Ésope à la Cour*.
The King considered that this play, by Boursault, was
ugly and indecent, and forbade that it should be performed
in his presence in future. It should be recalled that in

[1] A series of small tables placed near the guests at intervals, on which
were placed the meats and the wines. Each table was provided with cards
and a pencil for the guests to write what they desired (Contemporary note).

[2] It was at Choisy-le-Roi, in the district of Sceaux, that Mansart, in 1653,
built a château for Mademoiselle de Montpensier, a cousin of Louis XIV.
It subsequently passed to Louis XV, who had it almost entirely rebuilt.
Hard by it he had another château erected for Madame de Pompadour.
Both were destroyed during the Revolution. It was at Choisy that Rouget
de l'Isle died, and there is a statue of him there.

this comedy, which is a perfectly moral one, there is a scene in which the Prince asks his courtiers to name his faults. They all with one accord overwhelm him with adulation; only one has the courage to reproach him with being too fond of wine and with drinking himself tipsy, a dangerous vice in any man and especially in a sovereign. Madame de Mailly had given Louis XV the habit of drinking; he thought that the Queen, to teach him a lesson, had had *Æsop at Court* purposely added to the repertory; he made a heated complaint to the Chamberlain, demonstrating only too clearly that he was afraid of the truth.

We would here remark, to the honour of Louis XVI, that he personally requested that this play, which had been banned by his grandfather, should be given in his presence. He considered it admirable, full of good sense, and so well adapted to kingly ears that he gave orders for its frequent repetition.

The King was a good father; he loved his children with a sort of homely kindness that is rare in princes. As may be readily assumed the Dauphin [1] was very dear to him. He went to see him, or had him brought to him frequently. Those who have favours to ask are generally sufficiently astute in selecting the right means to obtain them. The following device was not lacking in ingenuity. One day Louis XV found in the baby prince's quarters the following somewhat indifferent composition in verse :

> If the son of the King, our master,
> Could through his influence
> Restore my full pension,
> A consummation devoutly to be wished,
> I should chant like Arion :
> " A Dauphin (dolphin) has saved my life."

---

[1] Louis, born at Versailles in 1729, died at Fontainebleau in 1765. On the 23rd February, 1745, he married Marie Thérèse, daughter of Philippe V, King of Spain, by whom, in 1746, he had a daughter, Marie Thérèse, who died at the age of two. By his second wife, Marie Josèphe de Saxe, he had eight children, amongst whom were Louis XVI, Louis XVIII and Charles X.

The request had been presented by a poor officer whose pension had been reduced. The King put his signature to it, and the pension was restored.

Another time the unfortunate wife of a man who was imprisoned for debt conceived the idea of petitioning the heir-apparent for his release. The difficulty was to get him to accept her plea and to stir his imagination sufficiently to make him pay attention to it, he was so young! She put a garland of flowers round the sheet of paper and waved it in front of him while he was taking a walk in the gardens at Versailles. The child noticed it and beckoned for it to be brought to him. He turned it about in all directions and, when he got home, showed it to the King. His Majesty was struck with the woman's ingenuity and granted her request.

Although it was the custom to leave the princes in feminine hands up to the age of seven, the Dauphin's progress was so rapid that he was handed over to the men before he reached that age. No one can overlook the importance that is attached to the choice of teachers, even for private children; how much more care is necessary in the selection of tutors for a boy on whom the fate of twenty millions of his subjects will one day depend? It does not appear at this juncture that Louis XV gave evidence of that enlightened interest in the discussion which is characteristic of genuine fatherly affection. The Comte, afterwards created Duc de Châtillon,[1] was appointed

---

[1] Alexis Madeleine Rosalie de Bois Rogues, Duc de Châtillon, 1690-1754. He distinguished himself at the battle of Guastalla (1734); appointed the Dauphin's governor in 1735, he took the young Prince to Metz when Louis XV was ill there. His son, the last of the male issue, died in 1760, leaving two daughters, the Duchesse d'Alzès and the Duchesse de la Trémoille. He is the Mirza of the *Histoire de Perse*. "Tall and lean, with a rather unattractive countenance, he is quick-tempered and not accommodating, of a curious turn of mind, fond of rare and precious things, has a very beautiful wife whom he does not fully appreciate, seeking elsewhere the pleasures he is hardly fit to enjoy; he is a great squanderer of money." Hardly a desirable tutor, it would seem!

governor; the Comte de Polastron and the Comte de Muy, deputy-governors; the Bishop of Mirepoix, tutor; the Abbé of Saint-Cyr, assistant tutor; the Marquis de Puy Guyon and the Chevalier de Créqui, gentlemen-in-waiting. None of these people possessed the signal merit that their positions demanded, and many of them had no merit at all. We are far from accepting, indeed we utterly reject, the vile theory held by certain people of the time who gave it out that the King was anxious to make sure that his son should never be greater than himself. In the first place, if his feelings towards the Dauphin subsequently grew colder, for reasons we will mention, he loved him tenderly then, and such jealousy is quite out of harmony with human nature. Secondly, such dark and deliberate dissimulation is scarcely a typical characteristic of frank and uncalculating youth. Thirdly, with the best will in the world, we may ask whether Louis XV, at twenty-five years of age, was the sort of person to make so cunning, so well planned and so delicate a selection? Is it not much more probable that in this case, as in everything else, he referred the matter to Cardinal de Fleury? It is certain, anyhow, that the Jesuits played an important part in these appointments; and their unhappy results, since they involved other appointments no less disastrous, are still felt to this day.

It is the more regrettable that the choice of persons to be entrusted with the young Prince's upbringing should have been so unhappy, seeing that the King, whose attitude in this matter was the same as that which he adopted in regard to the administration of his kingdom, always fell in with the plans and proposals of the people he had made the trustees of his authority. He merely went so far as to solicit a few favours for his son, without insisting on them, and without taking it amiss that they were not granted, if it was pointed out that it would be inexpedient to do so.

He liked to make his son tell of his little troubles; these were generally the outcome of a haughtiness of disposition which had been early developed by the consciousness of his rank, and the outward marks of deference lavished on royal children by their entourage, from which even their tutors are not exempt. It was, indeed, a contradiction which upset all his ideas that, notwithstanding the general attitude of submissive respect adopted by nearly every one about him, there should yet be a few people who assumed a dictatorial tone towards him, claimed to lay down the law, or thwarted his dearest inclinations. "Monsieur de Saint-Cyr," said he one day to the King, "is a man who will not listen to reason." "I can well imagine," answered His Majesty, "that your reason and his do not completely coincide, but they may in time; when they will live at peace."

Such was the intimate and friendly tone of the royal father's conversations with his son. He was never so flattered as when some witty saying of his son's was reported to him.

One day, the Cardinal de Fleury, who was dining at the Prince's table, thought he would inculcate the principles of moderation, or rather, of complete submission, by bringing home to him how powerless and possessionless he really was. He therefore began by referring to everything about him, adding after each article: "This, sir, belongs to the King; this is from His Majesty; none of these things belongs to you." The Dauphin listened to the lesson very impatiently, and at last, unable to contain himself any longer, exclaimed sharply: "Well, if the King is the owner of everything else, at all events my heart and my mind are my own."

But if the King, realizing all that depended on the Dauphin, his sole male heir, cherished him mainly on account of the importance of the rôle he was destined to play, it must be confessed that his parental affections seemed rather to be centred on his daughters, and especially on "Madame Première."[1] He was happy to give her the hope of a dominion by marrying her to Don Philip, the heir-apparent to the throne of Spain. It was a hope that consoled him for the pain it caused him to part with her. The people approved of the match because it removed the last traces of the bitterness that had been caused by the dismissal of the Infanta and lent additional strength to the bonds that united the two Courts. The marriage was celebrated with every circumstance of pomp and splendour. There was a long succession of joyous festivities and magnificent spectacles. There were triumphal arches adorned with divers devices and a series of the most sumptuous banquets. For several days the celebrations afforded entertainment to Court and City and were the marvel of the foreign visitors who had hastened from all quarters to behold them. The firework display that was given

---

[1] Marie Louise Elisabeth (1727–1759). She married Philippe de Bourbon, son of Philippe V, King of Spain, when she was twelve. " Her departure was a very sad event for the Royal Family, although the match was a valuable safeguard for the maintenance of good relations between the two royal houses. It was a very ill-assorted union. The Infante Don Philippe was of mediocre intelligence, without any will or initiative of his own, and kept in leading strings by his mother, an ambitious and jealous woman. Husband and wife were merely the Duke and Duchess of Parma, and all the eager life of Louise Elisabeth was utterly consumed in hopes that were never realized, in journeyings from Madrid to Versailles, and from Versailles back again to Parma, or in presenting frenzied petitions on behalf of herself, her husband and her children, for something better than " such a hole as Parma." She had made up her mind that at any rate her son Ferdinand should have a brilliant reign as well as her two daughters, one of whom became Archduchess of Austria, and the other Queen of Spain. Her unenviable life was one of ceaseless struggle. " It is possible," says M. Stryienski, op. cit., " that Louise Elisabeth's example discouraged Louis, and that the hard struggles of the eldest condemned her five sisters to celibacy." In spite of her great misfortunes, she nevertheless remained the idol of the Court, famed for her gallantry and beauty. When she reappeared in Versailles in 1748, her sisters, in comparison with her, " had quite a middle-class appearance."

on the Seine between the Pont Neuf and the Pont Royal, afforded, by reason of its position, so magnificent a spectacle that the wonder of it still lives on, nor has there been anything to rival it since. It will render the name of Turgot for ever memorable in connexion with diversions of this nature, though his tenure of office was distinguished by memorials of a more useful and lasting character.

The Princess was only thirteen; she was very amiable, had an extremely delicate complexion; to a gentleness of manner which won all hearts, she united a dignity that commanded universal respect. She became the idol of the Spaniards as she had been of the French. The Infante was twenty years of age, and neither in physical attractions nor in qualities of heart and mind did he yield aught to his royal spouse.

The Cardinal de Fleury was perhaps the only man in France who did not rejoice at a match which brought about a closer union between the two royal houses. He foresaw with regret that it would inevitably involve France in the conflict that had for long been brewing betwixt Spain and England. Up to now he had succeeded in preventing a complete rupture between the two Powers. As far back as 1735, he had successfully interposed the King's mediation between Spain and Portugal. Egged on by the English, and backed with a powerful fleet under the British Admiral Norris, Portugal stood by her Ambassador, who had gravely flouted the majesty of the law in Madrid. The careless insolence with which this officer had borne himself, the sabre rattling in which he had indulged, had been more productive of fear than of confidence, and by giving out that his sole mission was to protect the Brazilian fleet, which was conveying considerable sums of money belonging to his Britannic Majesty's subjects, he had increased rather than quenched the hostility of the Spaniards.

CHAPTER IX

DEATH OF FLEURY — CARDINAL DE TENCIN AND HIS
SISTER—SAMUEL BERNARD—THE EMBASSY OF ZAÏD
EFFENDI—DEATH OF THE QUEEN MOTHER OF SPAIN
—MADAME DE LA TOURNELLE—THE FIVE SISTERS—
DISGRACE OF MADAME DE MAILLY

THE health of Cardinal Fleury [1] failed from day
to day and though, in childish sycophancy,
particulars of centenarians (mostly imaginary)
were published and wonderful tales were spread
of marvellous elixirs for prolonging life, he could not fail to
see that his days were numbered. He had frequent attacks
of illness, heralds of approaching dissolution. His doctors
having insisted on his ceasing, *for a while*, all attention to
business, he took the smallest possible share in the deliberations of the Council, and spent most of his time at Issy,
a country seat six miles from Paris; but he still retained
the semblance of authority. The ministers waited on him
daily to report and to take his instructions. One morning

[1] For what has been said (including our own notes) regarding Fleury
and his ministry, see, *passim*, the foregoing chapters. We would, however,
add that Fleury did not live to see the end of the European religious and
parliamentary troubles; he left a difficult situation behind him. If the
finances were in a fairly satisfactory condition as a consequence of the prelate's proverbial parsimony, it was at the expense of the navy and of commerce, both of which had been sadly neglected since the death of Louis XIV.
" For private reasons, which he only disclosed to the King," said Maurepas,
" Fleury was unwilling to push the development of our naval forces, fearing,
it appears, to displease the English," who, immediately upon his death,
threw down their challenge and demonstrated in terrible fashion how blind
had been the confidence of their ally. Voltaire has left us a neat and mordant
portrait of the Cardinal, whom he shows as hating all system, " for his mind
was happily limited; totally incapable of understanding finance, he only
required of his under-secretaries the most rigorous economy; he would have
failed as a clerk in an office, but he was able to govern the State."

Monsieur de Breteuil, Secretary of State for War, after several hours' work with His Eminence, was taken so ill on leaving that he was thought to be dead. The Cardinal's people, fearing the effect that such a shock might have upon their master, did not render help, but, eager to be rid of the minister, bundled him into his carriage. He died on reaching Paris. Such excessive caution, or rather such abominable inhumanity, while it evoked general reprobation and cost the Marquis de Breteuil his life, only prolonged that of Fleury by a few days. The end came on the 29th January.

He suffered long and courageously, retaining his wonted lucidity till the end. The King visited him twice during his illness, and witnessed his last moments. He led the Dauphin into the death-chamber and, as the young Prince was being kept at a distance from his bed, the Cardinal begged that he should come nearer. "It is well," said the dying man, "for him to get used to such sights." This was, indeed, a philosophical utterance, but too uncourtier-like to have been permitted earlier expression ; it was a certain sign that the Cardinal realized his position. They were his last words.

It is alleged that during these interviews, at which he reported to His Majesty on the condition of the realm and gave his advice regarding the European situation, he warned him against Cardinal de Tencin,[1] a man of much

---

[1] Pierre Guérin de Tencin, Archbishop of Embrun and of Lyons, Cardinal Minister. Born at Grenoble, 1679 ; died at Lyons, 1758. He made his political début by converting Law.

> Tencin devint un magnifique
>   Agioteur
> Et fit de Law un catholique
>   Plein de ferveur ;
> Law eut toute la piété
>   D'un bon apôtre ;
> Tencin vit son bien augmenté
>   Par les débris du nôtre.

(Tencin became a splendid stock-jobber, and made of Law a fervent Catholic ; Law had all the piety of a good apostle, and Tencin's estate increased at the expense of ours.)

wit who seemed to possess his esteem and confidence, who had just become a member of the Council, and whom he had even encouraged to hope to succeed him ; moreover, he was a prelate, and a faithful disciple of the Molinists and Jesuits. This duplicity can only be attributed to the dying man's fear that such a minister would too quickly

It was, however, through his young and depraved sister Claudine, who arranged for the Regent that "Greek fête" which has remained famous in the annals of debauchery, that he made his way. She had, by the Chevalier Destouches, a child which she left on the steps of the Church of St. Jean le Rond. That child was d'Alembert. As letter-writer and novelist, Madame de Tencin is now forgotten, but in her later days her salon was much frequented by all the celebrities of the day. See Maurice Masson's *Madame de Tencin* (Paris, Hachette), 1909.

To push her brother it was said she would even stoop to crime ; at any rate, such was the opinion at the time.

> Tencin, ce fourbe si parfait,
> Comme tout le monde le sait,
> Vise toujours au grand objet.
> Sa sœur infernale
> Avec sa cabale
> L'y conduira par un forfait.

(Tencin, that perfect rogue, always keeps his goal in view. His damnable sister and her gang will commit any crime to help him reach it.)

And, when he attained his object—the Cardinal's hat—many were the epigrams that went the round concerning him !

> Jours y a qu'ouvrant ma fenêtre
> Je vis le diable ; il était accoutré
> D'un manteau long et d'un bonnet carré.
> Oh ! qu'est ceci ? Satanas s'est fait prêtre !
> Prêtre, dit-il, ah ! oui-dà, je le crois,
> Je suis prélat, regarde cette croix ;
> A damner l'univers elle devient utile,
> Oh ! l'heureux temps, ou le bien sert au mal !
> Estime, honneur, savoir, rien ne m'échappe,
> Rome me vient de nommer cardinal,
> Et tu verras lorsque je serai pape !

(The other day I was looking out of my window and saw the devil, clad in long cloak and square hat. "Whatever's this ; Satan turned priest ? " " A priest, yes indeed, I believe you ; I am a prelate,—see this cross with which I can damn the universe. Oh, happy day, when good ministers to evil ! Esteem, honour, know-

7

cause him to be forgotten.   Moreover, it had its origin
in his outlook on things, and this leads us to modify or to

> ledge, I lack none of them.   Rome has just made me a cardinal, and
> you shall see me Pope.")

* * *

> Enfin te voilà revêtu
> De cette dignité si longtemps poursuivie ;
> Tu l'as, dis-tu, conquise en dépit de l'envie ;
> C'est en dépit de la vertu !

> (Here you are at last invested with the honour you have sought
> so long.   You say its receipt outraged your own desire ; rather it
> outraged virtue.)

* * *

> On dit que sous la Régence
> De ce grand opérateur,
> De Rome viendra la dispense
> Pour coucher avec sa sœur,
> En sûreté de conscience
> A l'exemple du pasteur.

> (It is said that during the regency of that arch-schemer, Rome
> sent a dispensation permitting him to lie with his sister without
> qualms of conscience,—like the pastor.)

" Muzaim (*Cardinal Guérin*)—de Tencin was the name of a small
family estate—was sixty years of age, thin, of medium height, with a keen
eye, a shrewd countenance, a seductive tongue.   He was endowed with
great powers of persuasion ; his life was full of intrigues.   Some of them
left a very bad impression behind, which still persisted in certain quarters.
Naturally, he was not without enemies, whether at home or abroad.   He was
specially feared by the Japanese and the English.   He was not devoid of
ambition, and in many directions would have held his own in politics "
—*Mémoires secrets pour servir à l'Histoire de Perse*.   His contemporary,
President Hénault, did not treat him so tenderly.   " He was a downright
ignoramus, devoid of taste and wit.   He was reputed to be a wonderful
fellow in an intrigue with a chambermaid.   He was mild, insinuating,
false as a brass shilling, ignorant as a preaching friar, knowing naught of
our history and placing Paraguay on the Coromandel Coast "—*Mémoires
du Président Hénault*.

It has been said by many, including Saint-Simon, that the Cardinal
sprang from a " family of paupers," " of first-rate adventurers," but this is
quite inaccurate.   It has now been proved beyond doubt that the brother
and sister were the ultimate and brilliant manifestation of a race which
grew slowly and progressed steadily, rising a step with each generation.
Cf. Marquis de Ségur, " *Les Etapes d'une Famille*," pp. 101–117 in *Silhouettes
Historiques* (Paris, Calmann Lévy), 1911,

alter in part our whole-hearted condemnation of such egoism, which at first blush appears revolting and abominable. He feared to have men of profound and energetic genius in high places ; the plans of the former and the restlessness of the latter inspired him with apprehension. He did not regard such men as at all indispensable, and indeed believed they often did more harm than good. He looked on the administration of the country as similar to that of a family estate ; and he had observed that in the affairs of life it was not the most gifted men who governed their own households the best. Order, economy, gentleness, patience, simplicity, the appearance of frankness and good faith—these, according to him, were the real elements of good government, and it scarcely mattered who was employed so long as his failings were not the antithesis of these virtues. If the instance of the Regent had been urged against his views he would have retorted by adducing his own case ; and his own experience was a much more real thing to him than all the examples in the world. If he had possessed more philosophy and a wider outlook, he would have observed that Philippe was the right man for the minority of Louis XV and Fleury for the period after the Regency. On the death of Louis XIV, when the authority that had so long reposed in one person came to be divided among several, there was need for a firm hand to connect and tighten all the links ; of a leader who would be able to impose his authority by his birth, his courage, the possession of enterprising, bold genius which could carry out unlooked-for reforms, taking such quick, decisive and extreme measures as the situation might demand. France was in the position of a very sick person, who had been given up by the doctors and abandoned to the desperate experiments of a quack physician. In 1726 it was only a case of a healthy person slightly out of sorts and merely needing to be put on diet. This was the very accurate comparison the Cardinal made himself in reply to a proposal to alter the financial system. He thus indicated his policy at the outset, a policy which bore throughout the impress of his mild, tranquil nature. All the political errors and administrative failings with which he is reproached proceeded from it. If he neglected the navy, it was to secure peace with the English. If he employed *lettres de cachet* without stint, it was to secure peace in the Church. If he trusted too much to the farmers-general, if he fastened those leeches firmly to the bosom of the country, it was to avoid the disturbances that would be entailed by changes and apparent improvements. In a word, he never sought to be great, but always to be useful.

He was moderate throughout his life—at all ages, in all circumstances. His moderation even controlled his passions and, curiously enough, was the foundation of his advancement. For a long while, Louis XIV refused him a bishopric ; he waited with calm resignation. This pleased the King, who eventually appointed him to the see of Fréjus, when he had ceased to expect it. His Majesty said, " I have made you wait a while because too many of your friends were canvassing on your behalf, and I wished to have the satisfaction of seeing you indebted to me alone."

It was his moderation that led him to resign his bishopric as soon as he saw hopes of a place at Court. He pleaded that the state of his health prevented his accepting the archbishopric of Rheims, which the Duc d'Orléans offered him ; and, when the Maréchal de Villars urged him not to refuse, he replied that it would scarcely befit him to be strong enough to govern so important a diocese after being too ill to live at Fréjus. The fact is that, as he aspired to higher posts, he was unwilling to leave Versailles. He had his ambition well under control and did not show too much eagerness for honours. He worked his way to them by means of mildness and flexibility, preferring not to attract attention. He wrote as follows to Cardinal Quirini, when he was appointed tutor to the young Dauphin : " I have often regretted the solitude of Fréjus. When I arrived I learned that the King was *in extremis* and that he had done me the honour of appointing me his grandson's tutor. Had he been in a condition to listen, I should have begged him to relieve me of a burden which made me tremble; but after his death no one would listen to me. It has made me ill, and I am inconsolable at the loss of my freedom." As a matter of fact he was already seeking consolation by pulling strings to secure the Roman purple.

His even and affable temperament made of the Abbé de Fleury one of the most amiable persons at the Court. Once there, he was bound to succeed, a fact he quickly apprehended. When he had to go away he found residence at Fréjus very distasteful. He said jocularly that as soon as he saw his bride he was disgusted with his marriage, and he signed a letter, written in the same caustic tone, " Fleury, by the wrath of God, Bishop of Fréjus."

His attractive person and manner fascinated women ; his lack of ostentation commended him to men, as did his frankness, which was sometimes more apparent than real. There was, however, nothing low or despicable about his hypocrisy. Other men not only suppressed their real character but assumed a strange one. In him hypocrisy was but the natural outcome of partial self-revelation, of showing only that side of himself which he desired to reveal, and that only in the most attractive and favourable light.

By thus always appearing the same, while constantly changing, he accomplished all his aims. In 1728 he captivated the congress of Soissons by his very presence. Like another Nestor, he soon won over all his hearers by the honey that flowed from his lips. The plenipotentiaries looked up to him as to a father. Several princes of the Empire, and even the Emperor Charles VI, sometimes addressed him thus in their letters. When the Polish throne fell vacant, the Grand Chancellor presumed on the Cardinal's reputation as a man of peace, and urged the most determined opposition to Stanislas, which he said the Cardinal would tolerate. But, so far from tolerating it, Fleury took vigorous action and terminated the war much more favourably than even he had hoped. He would have died without witnessing a single French reverse during his ministry had he not been dragged into the war of 1741, which, though starting brilliantly, was thereafter attended by constant reverses until the end of his career. One of the great calamities for which it was responsible was the *dixième*, or tithe. This tax was first imposed in 1710 by Louis XIV, after ten most disastrous years of war, carried on against the whole of Europe, and after the terrible winter of 1709, a disaster unparalleled in the history of the kingdom. The most absolute of absolute monarchs was himself horrified at this terrible levy, and exclaimed, when it was suggested to him, " But I have no right to do it!" It was reimposed in 1733 and discontinued three years later. Now it was instituted before hostilities commenced, and the Cardinal soon perceived that it was destined to remain.

The war blazed up instead of dying down, and would have disturbed his hitherto unfailing tranquillity if age had not deadened his feelings, which, indeed, had never been very sensitive even to pleasure. Though a voluptuary by nature, he was sober and restrained by reason ; and his moderation contributed to the length and success of his life. He reached the age of ninety without illness, and with all his mental faculties unimpaired, still capable alike of pleasure and of work. His heart was weakened but his digestion was excellent. He always drank iced beverages, even in the depth of winter.

The Cardinal was possessed of a lively and delicate wit, a ready tongue; his conversation was amusing and was illustrated with interesting stories. He was ready and brilliant in repartee, a subtle joker with the rare gift of never giving offence. On the contrary, he used his wit to please others, by paying them clever compliments. He was an excellent speaker and writer. His last letters have been preserved and they show that he retained his felicity of style to the end. He was fond of literature and possessed taste and sound judgment. An instance that redounds greatly to his credit is that, despite the bigots that surrounded him, he had the courage to approve the famous tragedy *Le Fanatisme*,[1] in which he forestalled the judgment of a great Pope. It was played under his auspices a few months before he died. Unfortunately, however, he had not the courage to support it to the end against the very fanaticism it pilloried. Whilst not banning it he advised the author to withdraw it. All the same, it is manifest that Voltaire never forgot his goodwill, which he repaid with consistently favourable treatment from his pen.

Bearing in mind the Cardinal's well-known frugality, a quality which usually grows with age and even degenerates into miserliness, it would be natural to expect him to leave a substantial fortune, but he left nothing. He had spent what little came from his family. The revenue of 60,000 *livres* from his two benefices, the 20,000 *livres* that his seat on the Council brought him, and the 15,000 *livres* he derived from the postal service, of which he was super-

---

[1] As the clergy took offence at this title, *Le Fanatisme* (Fanaticism) was subsequently known as *Mahomet*. In 1745 Voltaire managed to procure a brief of approval from Benedict XIV. Louis XV, on the advice of the Comte d'Argenson, finally ordered the piece to be played in 1751, and it has remained ever since (unused) in the repertory of the Comédie française.

intendent, composed his total income and died with him.
The whole did not amount to 100,000 *livres*, and it is not
surprising that the Prime Minister spent it all. To-day
we may see many a senior clerk at Versailles disposing of
at least as much. Voltaire assures us that his furniture
was not worth 2000 *écus*. That is more difficult to believe,
for any artisan would be better off.

It must be admitted that, if his family got nothing
from his estate, he had provided well for them in other
ways. For a long time he resisted the temptation to
ennoble it, but finally he yielded to importunity and dealt
handsomely by his relatives, that was the most honourable
way of making their fortune. He made one of his nephews
a duke and peer, governor of Lorraine and a gentleman of
the bedchamber. The other gentlemen regarded him as
unworthy to be given a position which should only be held
by men of the highest birth. He had to exert the whole
weight of his authority, but even so could not shield the
newcomer from all the humiliations his colleagues inflicted
upon him whenever they had the opportunity.

With the exception of his servants, relatives and
protégés, the King was perhaps the only man in the whole
country to mourn for the Cardinal. In his overwhelming
gratitude he not only forthwith ordered a memorial service
to be held at Notre Dame (an honour previously reserved
for crowned heads), at which the greatest orator of the day,
the Jesuit, la Neuville, was to pronounce a funeral oration,
but he sought to extend his recognition to the Cardinal's
most remote posterity by ordering the erection of a
mausoleum in the Church of St. Louis du Louvre. His
feelings cooled later, with the result that the monument
would have remained unfinished in the sculptor's studio
had not Fleury's family paid for its completion.

The people, who (and usually with reason) regard themselves as delivered from a scourge when a minister dies,

not remembering that it is by the eventual results of his works that their joy or grief should be governed, rejoiced at the death of the Cardinal before they knew who was to succeed him. They were ignorant of the fact that the period of his administration, imperfect though it was, would one day be appreciated by historians as heaven-sent, as the " golden age of France " ; [1] that this golden age, ending with him, would be followed by a silver age, which would soon change into an iron age. [2]

A death that greatly affected the Cardinal, and of which he could not be kept in ignorance, occurred shortly before he passed away—that of Samuel Bernard, a man of almost his own age. This Jew, sprung from a race that was

[1] This was the actual expression used by the writer of the *Journal Historique de Louis XV surnommé le Bien-Aimé*, who wrote in most fulsome manner, with permission and privilege, before the disastrous end of the reign.

[2] Verses, flattering and unflattering, regarding Fleury exist in abundance. We need only refer the reader to the *Récueil* Maurepas-Clairambault, vols. v. and vi. of the Raunié edition in 10 volumes, or to the de Leyde edition in 6 volumes. We may quote as an example, *Les talents du Cardinal Fleury* :

> Un envieux m'ayant mis en malaise
> En m'ayant exilé
> De mon réduit, trop heureux et trop aise.
> Un roi m'a rappelé,
> Et j'ai chassé qui m'a donné la chasse,
> Car j'ai pris sa place,
> Moi,
> Car j'ai pris sa place.
>
> Loin de la cour j'ai su bannir le crime
> En chassant les putains ;
> Par ce grand coup j'ai mérité l'estime
> Des doux et des mutins.
> Comme jadis une habile éminence
> Je conduis la France.

(A jealous fellow had annoyed me by getting me turned out of my snug, happy retreat. A king recalled me, and I sent away him who had exiled me, for I took his place, yes, I took his place. Far from the Court I drove wickedness by banishing the harlots. So

persecuted in France and excluded from all corporate
bodies, had reached the highest position attainable by

striking an act earned for me the commendation of gentle and
headstrong alike.   I governed France like a certain skilful Cardinal
who had preceded me.)

Again, let us quote *l'Histoire véridique du Cardinal Fleury* :

Il possédait l'art de la cour.
Ou vérité brille en son jour ;
Divinement hypocrisa.

A la buvette il prit le roi
Lui dit ne vous fiez qu'à moi ;
Ailleurs on vous abusera.

Il s'avisa de guerroyer
Et puis de tout pacifier,
Sur l'un et l'autre on le siffla.

(He had all the arts of the Court.   Where truth at times shines
bright he was the sublime hypocrite.   He caught the King as he
drank and said, " Trust only me or you will be deceived."   He
decided to go to war, and then to make general peace ; in both
rôles he was hissed.)

Here are a few epigrams :

J'ai de Dubois la naissance,
Des Jésuites la manigance,
Des bigots le grave maintien !
Ah ! Fleury, je vous connais bien.

(I have Dubois' birth, the Jesuits' trickery, the grave bearing
of the bigots !   Ah ! Fleury, I know you well.)

* *
*

Confondant du passé le faible souvenir,
Ebloui du présent sans parer l'avenir,
Et dans l'art de régner, décrépit et novice,
Punissant la vertu, récompensant le vice,
Fourbe dans le petit et dupe dans le grand,
Tel est ce cardinal, accablé de son rang.

(Confused in his poor memory of the past, dazzled by the
present without preparing for the future, feeble and a novice in the
art of governing, punishing virtue, rewarding vice, crafty in little
things, a dupe in big,—such is the Cardinal in the pride of his
greatness.)

* *
*

great wealth. Of his three children [1] one had become
President of the Parliament, one Master of Petitions, and
his daughter had been married to Molé, who was subsequently appointed First President.   He was banker to the

> Quitte la vie et retourne en Provence ;
> Aux maux présents donne quelque répit,
> Vaut mieux encore, en pareille démence,
> Laisser régner l'imbécile Louis.

(Begone, return to Provence ; give us some respite from our
present woes. 'Twere better in such mad times that even the
imbecile Louis should reign.)

* * *

> Et allons donc, vieille éminence,
> Et allons donc, décampez donc !
> Tout périra dans la France
> Si votre règne est plus long.

(Begone, old Cardinal, begone, clear out ! All France will
perish if you remain in power.)

* * *

Fleury died in harness at the age of ninety.

[1] Our author is in error.   By his first marriage with Madeleine Clergeot,
" heiress of the best patch-seller in Paris," Samuel Bernard had three children
—a daughter who married Mansart de Sagonne ; a son, Samuel Jacques,
who was Comte de Coubert, President of the Paris Parliament, and announced
himself as Comte de Rieux.   It was through his second marriage, with
Mademoiselle de Saint Chamans, that was born a daughter, Bonne Félicité,
when he was sixty-five.   She was not particularly beautiful, but brought
her sixteen summers and 800,000 *livres* to her husband, Président Molé.

> O temps ! O mœurs ! O siècle déréglé !
> On voit se dégrader les plus nobles familles !
> Lamoignon, Mirepoix, Molé !
> De Bernard épousent les filles,
> Et sont les receleurs du bien qu'il a volé !

(*O tempera !* *O mores !* O disordered times ! The noblest
families are degraded ! Lamoignon, Mirepoix, Molé, marry
Bernard's daughters and become receivers of the property he has
stolen !)

M. de Lamoignon, Chief Justice, and the Marquis de Mirepoix had
married the two daughters of Président Bernard de Rieux.

Court, which transferred to him its burdens by making him accept bankruptcy on its behalf. He pointed out only too clearly to people like himself the road to fortune by way of profitable ignominy, for he left an estate of thirty-three millions. We must honour him in that he did not forsake the God of his fathers in order to become eligible for honours that his money might then have purchased, and in that he constantly used his wealth in the performance of good deeds and for the assistance of the unfortunate. Furthermore, he showed at times a nobility and steadfastness of mind that seemed to raise him above all the grandees who paid him court. When Chauvelin, Keeper of the Seals, was dismissed, the Cardinal, the more incensed against this would-be supplanter because he had given him his full confidence, was seeking evidence that would damn him. He sent Hérault, Lieutenant of Police, to ask suggestive questions of Samuel Bernard regarding certain funds that had passed through his hands. The banker refused to answer such a catechism unless full authority was produced by that officer, who had to go empty away.

Bernard was possessed of the Cardinal's spirit of moderation and regularity, and, like the Cardinal, he reaped the reward of long life and sound health. In the midst of his luxury (which did not, of course, approach that of the financiers of to-day) he behaved with a sort of modesty which made him acceptable and prevented his being hated.[1]

[1] This was not, however, the opinion of the lawyer Barbier, whose precious *Journal* reflects the general opinion, the opinion of the " man in the street " of his day. He concludes his description of a magnificent fête given by the financier as follows : " All this display and extravagance naturally offended the public. Even royal marriages were not so splendid. Indeed, it was maliciously said that a sketch of the room had been kept so that it might be used in due course for the Dauphin's wedding. Such magnificence was manifestly an outrage on the part of the thrice-bankrupt son of a painter "—*Journal de Barbier.*

His house, which still stands in the Place des Victoires, would not satisfy the humblest farmer-general of to-day; it has not even a courtyard. Tradition has handed down to us several of his eccentricities, some of which related to his household arrangements. From the moment he rose till he went to bed, one of his carriages, all ready with a coachman on the box, had to stand waiting at the door. The porter, ever listening for the slightest sound, had to open the gate before he arrived, so that his carriage might drive straight in. When he came home from his business the soup must be set on the table immediately; he then sat down and his guests took their places around him.

Samuel Bernard was very fond of *brélan*; he constantly plunged and was surprised when he lost. One night when a man had won a large sum from him, he was so furious that, without waiting till the morrow, or even giving his adversary the opportunity of arranging for the removal of such a sum, he had the bags of money carried to his door, where he was left alone with them, greatly embarrassed and expecting to have his throat cut by the first passer-by whose cupidity should tempt him.

He was superstitious, like all his race. He possessed a black hen with which he believed his fate was bound up. He caused the greatest care to be taken of it, and, as a matter of fact, the loss of the fowl occurred at the time of his own demise, in January 1739.[1]

---

[1] This story of the black hen is perfectly true. Samuel Bernard (1655–1739), the lavish millionaire banker, was excessively superstitious. His morality was suspect, and he made and lost money with equal self-possession. His operations frequently verged on the doubtful, and he made a habit of bankruptcy. He was frequently called a rogue, but that left him unmoved. Was not his salon frequented by the best society of Paris? The great men of the law, the sword and the Church foregathered there. It is true he was always open-handed, and lent to all comers—to the King and to the Government. He even posed as a patron of the arts. His collection was worth more than a million and " he kept open table at a cost of 150,000 *livres* a year." At his death there were owing to him small sums, lent to

In 1741 Zaïd Effendi came on a mission to Louis XV.
The courtiers did not fail to liken this visit to that paid by
the Queen of Sheba to Jerusalem to behold for herself
the wisdom of Solomon. Twenty years earlier the childhood of the King had been distracted by a similar event;
now it served to amuse the second childhood of His
Eminence. It was a compliment arranged for him by
Monsieur de Villeneuve, French Ambassador at the Sublime
Porte, and was a small token of gratitude for having been
raised from the position of lieutenant-general of the
seneschalship of Marseilles to so exalted a post. The
dullards who do not understand the procedure of courts,
who do not know that great ends are often achieved by
insignificant means, suggested that all this pomp and
circumstance were to furnish an opportunity for negotiations, whereas they were merely the occasion for a treaty
of commerce. The Ottoman grandee brought a great
train, worthy of his Asiatic splendour, and made a brilliant
entry. Maréchal de Noailles, brother of the Comtesse
de Toulouse, was detailed to accompany him. He was
past middle age, of medium height and undistinguished
appearance, possessed of a grave demeanour which was
relieved by bright, intelligent eyes. To a degree of intellect
unusual in his race was added wide knowledge. He was
affable and gracious, with a natural gift for appreciating

people in need, amounting to at least five millions. Cf. Thirion, *Vie privée
des financiers au XVIIIe siècle* (Paris, Plon), 1895.

His mansion in the Place des Victoires was famous. Soon nothing will
be left of those fine Mansard mansions and Prévôt façades, notwithstanding
the regulations of 1685, which provided that, for the future, " the occupiers
shall be bound to maintain the façades in their present condition, without
in any way altering them." All the splendid houses of this Place, and of
the Place Vendôme, were then occupied by the farmers-general, the *traitants*
as they were called—Crozat, Hénault, Etienne Cornet, Bourvalais, Samuel
Bernard, and many others. The common saying of the day was : " Henri
IV on the Pont Neuf in the midst of his people ; Louis XIII in the Place
Royale surrounded by his nobility ; Louis XIV in the Place des Victoires
among his tax-gatherers."

France, his delight in that country increasing the more he became acquainted with it.

Although it was bitterly cold on the day of his arrival, an enormous crowd braved the weather out of curiosity. The large number of slaves in the Ambassador's train wore their native costume. In other words, they were almost naked and, notwithstanding the climate, they had to remain for hours exposed to the rigours of the weather. The crowd also suffered from the cold, but almost unconsciously. This was specially the case with the women, who were greatly attracted by the appearance of these proud Mohammedans, so renowned in the lists of love. They were not content merely to look, and the sojourn of these people in the capital led to many amorous adventures, beginning with the chief himself. He was discreet and secret, and his love affairs made no stir ; but some of his suite caused so much scandal that he had to exercise restraint over them.

It was the custom for France to pay for the entertainment of Turkish ambassadors ; but Zaïd Effendi desired to make his own disbursements, and it was accordingly arranged to hand him a daily allowance. He was credited with a wish to make a profit out of this, which may easily have been true, for generosity was by no means his chief characteristic. He enjoyed all the pleasures of life in Paris, and people went to see him at meals as though he were the King. It was remarked that he was a " philosophic Mussalman," that is to say, that he did not adhere too strictly to his religion. He neglected some of its observances, drinking wine like a good Christian. His people followed his example and sometimes caused disorder in our taverns. After a sojourn of more than a year he left the capital with regret. The King loaded him with presents for his master the Emperor, presents richer even than the splendid gifts he had brought. He also received presents for himself and his suite in keeping with the magnificence of his great master.[1]

During his stay in Paris, Zaïd Effendi witnessed one of those spectacles that humanity constantly offers, but not often with such ceremony as to merit the attention of so exalted a visitor. The Dowager Queen of Spain died at the Luxembourg, where she had resided during her retirement. This unhappy Princess had ascended the throne when only fifteen and had to surrender it a year later. Retaining only its gloomy ceremonial she expiated in ennui the ambition of her illustrious father. She lived in this palace, which had been the scene of the fêtes and pleasures of her sister the Duchesse de Berry, and of the grief, remorse and premature demise that had followed the fleeting enjoyment and criminal debauchery of that Princess.

[1] The real name of the Ambassador was Mohammed Pasha, son of Mohammed Effendi, who, as already mentioned, came to France in 1721. As a "pasha with three tails," he was entitled to a triple suite, consisting of one hundred and eighty-three persons, including a "consulting theologian."

"This ambassador was named Horeb. He was past middle age, of medium height and undistinguished appearance, possessed of a grave demeanour which was relieved by a bright, intelligent eye. To great intellect was joined wide knowledge. He was affable and gracious, and enjoyed his stay in Paris. He was credited with several love affairs which were carried on discreetly; but those of some of the principal members of his staff made such a stir that he had to control them. It was the custom for France to pay for the entertainment of Turkish ambassadors, but he wished to make his own disbursements, and asked that the daily allowance should be handed to him. He was credited with the desire to make a profit out of this, which was probably true, for generosity was by no means his chief characteristic. He enjoyed all the pleasures of life in Paris, and when he took his departure, Cha-Séphi (Louis XV) loaded him with rich presents"—*Mémoires secrets pour servir à l'Histoire de Perse.*

Among these presents were silver candlesticks made by Ballin, the King's goldsmith; a round table for twelve persons with a great central vase to hold forty bowls of various foods; a ewer and basin by Germain; two great mirrors fifteen feet high; Savonnerie tapestries; a large organ; a suite of furniture in marquetry of Indian woods; a microscope by Lebas.

Further details regarding these festivities and this mission, which are highly interesting, but too long to be given here, will be found in the *Mercure de France* of June 1742.

These later recollections, which were more in keeping with the Queen's temperament, had greatly impressed her, leading her to excessive devotion which, while not less conducive to happiness, was less likely to poison her life and hasten her end.[1]

If such pious tastes seemed remarkable in a daughter of the Regent, they seemed still more so in his son, who might well have been styled " the Devout." [2] Disagreements had caused him to retire from the Council, although he was its chief. His views were always ignored, and he saw that such contempt would only increase and that he would become a mere cypher. This seemed to him to be inevitable in a reign in which women were to govern. He was most anxious that the country should not attribute to him any share in so scandalous an administration, and, so as to divest himself of even an appearance of responsibility in the eyes of the people, he renounced all participation in public affairs. This was just at the time when Madame de Mailly had been deposed from her position of favourite, being replaced by one of her sisters who was not less ambitious than Madame de Vintimille. This pushful and greedy woman took advantage of her position to give all the rein possible to her two consuming passions. She became the soul of all the intrigues that followed the death of the Cardinal, and gave the first impulse to all that ensued.

[1] Louise Elisabeth, usually known as Mademoiselle de Montpensier. We referred to her at length in an earlier chapter.

[2] Louis, Duc de Chartres, died at the Abbey of Sainte Geneviève in 1752 ; he was a cultured, even learned, man, particularly in theology, and was devout to excess. He left many folio works of casuistry, to-day quite forgotten. So that he might the better understand the Bible, he learned Hebrew, Greek, Syriac and Chaldæan. A contemporary said, " A verse of a psalm inspired him to write a dissertation of a hundred pages, of which he left more than a thousand to the Dominicans. He had become so holy that Jomard, the curé of Versailles, who had confessed him, contemplated publishing his confessions, asserting that he had never found him guilty of one solitary trifling sin."

The new mistress was Madame la Marquise de la Tournelle,[1] of that house of Nesle whose daughters, although without inheritance, seemed to be born with the special prerogative of sharing the royal couch. At any rate here was the fourth to enjoy that honour, and Louis XV, who had a special taste for the breed, would gladly have seen them all pass the same way.[2]

[1] Marie Anne de Mailly de Nesle, born 1717, married 1734 to J.-B. Louis, Marquis de la Tournelle, a captain in the "Royal Etranger," who died in 1740, aged twenty-three. It was in October 1743 that Madame de la Tournelle (who died in December 1744) was made Duchesse de Châteauroux.

> Grand roi, vous avez de l'esprit
> D'avoir renvoyé Mailly !
> Quelle haridelle avez-vous là !
> Alléluia.
>
> Vous serez cent fois mieux monté
> Sur la Tournelle que vous prenez.
> Si la canaille ose crier
> De voir trois sœurs se relayer,
> Au grand Tencin, envoyez-la,
> Alléluia !

(Great King, it was clever of you to dismiss Mailly ! What jade have you there ?
> Hallelujah !

You will have a mount a hundred times better in La Tournelle whom you are now taking. If the mob should make a fuss at seeing three sisters take turns, send them to the great Tencin.
> Hallelujah !)

" Of the two other sisters of Rétima (Mme de Mailly), one, named Euxica (Mme de la Tournelle), without being of the highest class, held her own at Court. Euxica was tall, well-built, and of pleasing countenance. The other was Doghdon (Mme de Lauraguais). She was the youngest, big, heavy, massive ; her face calls for no comment"—*Mémoires secrets pour servir à l'Histoire de Perse.*

[2]   Les cinq sœurs

> Chantons une ritournelle
> Sur la belle de la Tournelle
> Que la Mailly débusqua,
> Ramonez-ci, Ramonez-là
> La la la
> Ramonez-là du haut en bas.

One resisted, thanks to the firmness of her husband, Monsieur de Flavacourt, who threatened to leave nothing undone to wash any insult out in blood. Her beauty was

La charmante Vintimille
Tata peu de la béquille;
La mort trop tôt l'enleva;
A présent c'est la Tournelle,
Qui ne fut jamais cruelle,
Que Louis chatouillera.

Attendez même fortune,
Flavacourt, charmante brune,
Votre tour viendra.
Reste encore une fillette
Qui vraiment n'est pas mal faite,
Comme aux autres on lui fera.

Amateur de la famille,
Maitre Louis de sa béquille
Toutes les sœurs honorera.
Cependant Monsieur leur père
Reste toujours en fourrière,
Avec tous ces honneurs-là.

Et l'on voit son Eminence
Le grand soutien de la France
Qui se fout de tout cela,
Ramonez-ci, Ramonez-là!

(Let us sing a song of the beauty La Tournelle, whom the Mailly drove out; sweep this way, sweep that way, sweep well up and down.

The charming Vintimille enjoyed the royal embraces but little— she died too soon; now it is La Tournelle, never very cruel, whom Louis is to gratify.

Await the same good fortune, charming brunette Flavacourt, your turn will come.* There remains a younger sister, not too badly made,† who will be treated like the others.

---

* We know now that her turn never came.
† The "younger sister not too badly made" was that one of the five sisters who married the Duc de Lauraguais in January 1744. "She was young and bold, and boasted of having carefully preserved a jewel while living with Madame de Lesdiguières, who had brought her up in her own home. The King, surprised at the 'jewel' of Mademoiselle de Mont- carvel, as the third of the Mailly de Nesle sisters was called, robbed her of

tender and artless, and the courtiers mockingly dubbed her " the hen." Her behaviour was in keeping with her appearance, and gave not the slightest occasion for gossip. Madame de Mailly, although knowing by experience the danger of introducing her sisters to the King, needed her help in the heavy task of amusing him—the most amiable but the most bored man in his kingdom.   Furthermore, whereas Madame de Vintimille had been guilty of the cruellest perfidy, she had recently had cause for gratification with the Duchesse de Lauraguais, her youngest sister. According to those who knew the King's secret pleasures, one of those refinements of depravity that are not wholly confined to the exalted led him to covet a place between the two sisters, whose bodies, like their minds, offered so complete a contrast.   We have already painted a portrait of Madame de Mailly.   The Duchess was tall, heavy, badly proportioned, but of a plumpness that invited fondling.   Her bust was firm and elastic, and her hips were well rounded.   For the rest, she was commonplace, coarse, boisterous, devoid of grace and charm ; so that, if at night she gave the King pleasures that he could not procure from her skinny sister, the latter came into her own during the day ; and even Louis soon tired of merely physical gratification.

> Amateur of the family, Master Louis will treat all the sisters alike.
> But the father * still remains impounded, notwithstanding all these
> honours.
>
> We see, too, His Eminence,† the great prop of France, who
> cares not a jot about all this.)

---

it, and then married her to the Duc de Lauraguais, whom he promoted to Lieutenant-General "—*Richelieu's Memoirs*.   The reign of Mme de Lauraguais was neither long nor brilliant, for she never secured a great hold on the mind or heart of the King.

 * M. de Nesle, father of the favourites, was being sued by his creditors, and talked to everybody about his " wretched lawsuit."   He hoped the King would pay.

 † Cardinal Fleury.

Very different was the Marquise de la Tournelle, with her dazzlingly clear complexion, her beautiful face, her elegant figure and her stately bearing. Her piquant glance struck the King, and she found means of completing the conquest. Although she had not attracted much attention since the death of her husband, she did not go to Court without ambitions.[1] She was a woman capable of making better use of her charms than her sisters, and of learning from their mistakes. Furthermore, she enjoyed the advice of the Duc de Richelieu, who was said to have enjoyed her favours and, when he had had enough of her, to find this means of ridding himself of her and of making the King pay for his pleasures. Moreover, he was beginning to have ambitions, and was among those who aspired to

[1] LE ROI ET MADAME DE LA TOURNELLE

> Et allons, dame la Tournelle,
> Et allons donc, rendez-vous donc.
> Quand votre roi vous appelle,
> Vous faites trop de façon ;
> Et allons donc, Mademoiselle,
> Et allons donc, rendez-vous donc.
>
> Encor si vous étiez pucelle
> Vous le pardonnerait-on ;
> Si vous vous donnez pour telle
> Toute la cour dira non.
>
> De faire ainsi la cruelle,
> Ma foi, c'est hors de saison.
> Dans la sang de la de Nesle
> En a-t-on jamais vu ? Non !
> Et allons donc, Mademoiselle,
> Et allons donc, rendez-vous donc !

(Come now, Mistress La Tournelle, come, surrender. You make too much fuss when your King calls you. Come now, Miss, come, surrender.

Even if you were still a virgin, people would forgive you ; but if you posed as one, the whole Court would cry " No ! "

Such cruelty would indeed be unseasonable, and has never been found in the blood of the De Nesles ; good heavens, no ! Come now, Miss, come, surrender.)

succeed the Cardinal in the control of His Majesty. As he was not yet so secure of the royal favour as to be able to rout his rivals single-handed, he felt that the support of the favourite would help him. Madame de Mailly's personality was quite unsympathetic to him, whereas her sister's was far more compatible. He thus became her confidential guide and counsellor in all her schemes. Having planted her dart in the King's heart, she kept him at a distance in order to increase his pangs until she had made her bargain with him on her own terms.[1] The first condition was that Madame de Mailly should be publicly dismissed ; the second that her name of Marquise de la Tournelle should be changed to Duchesse de Châteauroux, with the full prerogatives of that rank ; the third that she should have an establishment consistent with her position, and property sufficient to enable her to face all contingencies. In the time of Louis XIV there had been only one instance of such a favour. Louis XV was so infatuated that he granted everything, and the new favourite's sway so developed that she promised entirely to govern her royal slave. There was no gallantry that he did not think of. It was for her sake that artists exhausted their imagination in devising charming retreats for the pleasures of the happy pair. It was for her that wonderful carriages were contrived,

[1] " One night the King, disguised in a long coat and a square wig, went in a blue chair to see her. His Majesty remained till four in the morning bargaining with the charmer. Having been well coached, and with all the coolness of an experienced harlot, she stipulated that she should be publicly recognized as the King's mistress, on the same footing as Madame de Montespan had been. She demanded that she should be well lodged in a manner befitting her position, and should not be expected, like her sister, to go furtively to the private apartments to sup and sleep. She demanded that the King should come publicly and hold his Court in her apartments, and sup there openly. She demanded that when she wanted money, she should be able to draw on the royal purse ; that at the end of a year she should receive letters of nobility, duly confirmed by the Parliament, as a duchess ; that if she became enceinte there should be no secrecy about it, and that her children should be legitimized "—D'Argenson's Memoirs, entry for 5th November, 1742.

for her use when her lover thought she needed special attention.

Madame de Mailly was heart-broken when she learned of her disgrace.[1] As she had really loved the King, the blow was the heavier. Religion was her sole consolation. Father Renaud, of the Oratory, was a famous preacher of the day, and, to fill the void created by the loss of her lover, she turned to religion. She went to hear this good-looking orator with his attractive voice and powerful but persuasive eloquence. He greatly appealed to her, and she sought an interview. He poured balm into her wounded heart and succeeded in calming her. Her frequent interviews with so soothing a spiritual director restored peace of mind to this Court Magdalen, and showed her the right path. This woman, formerly magnificently dressed, wallowing in enjoyment and given up wholly to pleasure, now frequented churches, simply clad and mixing with the

[1]
>Madame Olympe est toute en pleurs,
>Voilà ce que c'est d'avoir des sœurs !
>L'une jadis lui fit grand peur
>Mais, chose nouvelle,
>On prend la plus belle ;
>Ma foi, c'est jouer de malheur,
>Voilà ce que c'est d'avoir des sœurs !
>
>La Mailly est en désarroi,
>Voilà ce que c'est d'aimer le roi !
>Sa sœur cadette a son emploi,
>Et la Vintimille
>Par goût de famille,
>Avait subi la même loi.
>Voilà ce que c'est d'aimer le roi !

(Madame Olympia is all in tears ; see what it is to have sisters ! Yesterday one gave her a fright ; to-day it is the turn of the most beautiful. Upon my word, it's a great pity ; see what it is to have sisters !

La Mailly is all upset ; see what it is to love the King ! Her younger sister has the job, after La Vintimille, following the family tradition, had passed the same way. See what it is to love the King !)

rest [1] whom she resembled in her piety, her modesty, her
tears, and in the patience with which she bore the hoots
and insults of the insolent mob, who regarded her as the
author of all public calamities. On one occasion Madame
de Mailly went to hear Father Renaud, whom she followed
assiduously. As the preacher was already in the pulpit
and had commenced, some little disturbance was caused
by her being conducted to her pew. An ill-natured man
called out, "What a hubbub for a strumpet!" "Since
you know her," replied Madame de Mailly, "pray for her."
Thoughtful people regarded her with more respect and
admiration in the day of her humiliation than when she
had been at the height of her splendour. [2]

One thing that redounded infinitely to the honour of
the Comtesse de Toulouse, who had in a way introduced

---

[1] "Madame de Mailly is poorer than ever, according to what I am told
by a man who knows her well. Her chemises are frayed and in holes, and
her servant is shabby—evidences of real poverty. The other day she had
not five *écus* with which to pay her losses at quadrille "—*D'Argenson's
Memoirs*.

[2] On the 27th November, 1742, D'Argenson wrote: "Madame de Mailly
has been dismissed rather more summarily than an opera dancer. On
Saturday the King told her at dinner that he did not wish her to sleep that
night at Versailles, but she might return on Monday. There was much
letter-writing that day. Madame de la Tournelle sought to insist absolutely that her sister should never return to Versailles so long as she should
be the King's mistress, and the affair was only brought to accomplishment
on the Wednesday night "—*D'Argenson's Memoirs*.

A week after learning of her dismissal, Madame de Mailly sought an
interview with the King. "No document or letter records what happened ;
but she emerged from the King's cabinet agitated, panting and despondent.
The King followed her, fearing some violent manifestation of her terrible
grief. He spoke to her kindly and gently in the presence of the courtiers.
He said to Madame de Mailly, with his wonted duplicity in such circumstances, 'I shall see you at Choisy on Monday, Countess; I hope you will
not keep me waiting.' On Monday the King was to sleep at Choisy, but
with Madame de la Tournelle, in the very bed of blue silk that the unhappy
deserted mistress had been so many years spinning for the King and herself "
—*Richelieu's Memoirs*. But that evening Madame de la Tournelle would
not receive the King. She let him scratch at her door in vain, thinking
that the longer she put off her "defeat" the more eager and deep-rooted
would be his love.

Madame de Mailly to Court, was that she remained her steadfast friend during her banishment ; she took the exile in and lodged her in her own palace for a year. By so doing she incurred the King's displeasure, but she had too much authority for him to venture on any action, and the same baseness that permitted the King to dismiss his mistress so cruelly prevented him from showing his annoyance with the Comtesse de Toulouse, whose behaviour to the outcast was an indirect but clear reflection on his own.

It was only later that Louis XV settled an income of 40,000 *livres* on Madame de Mailly, presented her with a mansion in the Rue St-Thomas du Louvre, and arranged for the payment of her debts. These amounted to some 765,000 *livres*, a sum which, while burdensome to the State, which ought not to have been called upon to face such a liability, appears by no means extravagant if we remember that she had never profited by her position and that her yearly allowance had been only 25,000 *livres*, an amount quite inadequate for the state she had to maintain at the Court. This payment of 765,000 *livres* was charged on the farm-tax, but, notwithstanding the King's orders, those responsible for the settlement not only kept the creditors waiting but even cheated them of the greater part of the money.

With the King's favour the mistress also lost that of his wife, for she was dismissed from her post of lady-in-waiting to the Queen. In other words, she was driven away from Her Majesty just when she became worthy, by her repentance, her regular behaviour, and her exemplary piety, which were in keeping with the Queen's own conduct and tastes, to approach her.[1] The Marquise de la Tournelle

[1] " Of all the King's mistresses, Madame de Mailly alone was disliked by the Queen, for it was she whom she accused of having won her husband's affections. She could only show her contempt and loathing by black looks, and dignity even forbade them. She is credited with an offensive reply, with double meaning, when her lady-in-waiting asked her leave of absence

succeeded her sister as lady-in-waiting in accordance with
the hateful custom introduced by Louis XV, so that he
might the more conveniently have the objects of his passion
close to him at Court. This practice, designed to avoid
public scandal, only increased it. What could be more
abominable than to force his august consort to have constantly in her presence the object of her contempt and
indignation and to become in a way the protectress of her
husband's pleasures and the accomplice of his vices ?

The great changes just detailed increased the anxiety
of Court, people and, indeed, of all Europe, as to what
would happen when the King obtained his independence
through the death of the Cardinal. It was remembered
that, when Mazarin died, Louis XIV commenced that
reign which was so glorious until his tired hands surrendered
the helm to a woman. But the circumstances and, even
more, the characters of the two men, were very different.
The former was only twenty-two years old, already burning
with the lust for fame that consumed him till his dying day.
For long he consulted his oracles ; in secret he tested his
capacity for government. Finally he sought instruction,
and his impatient energy would have wrought the change
of itself if it had not come about otherwise. The other
had already reached the age of thirty-three and was devoid

on the occasion of one of the Court journeys—'By all means, madame ; you
are the mistress.' It is scarcely likely that the Queen would have used
such a phrase then, but she was constantly on the watch to see who were the
lady's associates, and, as she had a ready tongue and a spiteful wit, she could
not resist flinging at her some stinging retort. Her servants always knew,
from the Queen's continued irritability, the weeks when Madame de Mailly
was on duty, and Her Majesty had to suffer her offending presence all day
long. The torture must indeed have been very bitter to affect, even
momentarily, her placid and kindly nature "—Nolhac, *Louis XV et Marie
Leczinska*, pp. 205–209.

At the time of her death Madame de Mailly was occupying a house in
the Rue St-Thomas du Louvre, which ran from the Tuileries to the Rue
St-Honoré, and disappeared in 1849 when the approaches to the Palais
Royal were enlarged.

of strong passions. The splendour of the throne was a
nuisance to him ; he sought only obscurity and repose.
Long inaction had rendered him useless in business, and
his lethargy, so far from breaking his fetters, led him to
forge others. His first act of sovereignty was an act of
servitude, inspired by Madame de la Tournelle. This
second Agnes Sorel [1] told him that it was time for him to
become master, and at least appear to govern. She it was
who tore him from the luxury of his palace to lead his
armies in Flanders. She it was who made him traverse
his realm from end to end, and dragged him to Alsace to
stop the enemy's advance. She it was who, when driven
from the King's presence, won for him that surname of
" Well-Beloved," prematurely accorded, it is true, and
which it were better for his memory had he never borne.
It is impossible to say to what lengths she would have led
her royal slave if she had not carried the glory he seemed
to have resumed for a moment to her early grave.[2]

[1] This story of Agnes Sorel galvanizing Charles VII, awakening his
warlike spirit, was originated by François I to excuse his openly consorting
with mistresses. There had been no recognized royal favourite since the
time of Charles VII, and certainly not at the chaste Court of Louis XIII.
François I asked whether a mistress could not be an excellent counsellor
for a king. Numa, King of Rome, had indeed had his nymph Egeria !

[2] Madame de la Tournelle, Duchesse de Châteauroux, objected to
any other influence about her. She nicknamed Fleury " the old rascal "
and Maurepas " the plague." Urged on by the party of Richelieu,
Tencin and Noailles, she endeavoured to awaken the conscience of Louis
XV ; she bustled him mercilessly, for she wished to teach him his duty as
a king. Constantly stretched on a couch, and only taking the air about
eight or nine o'clock in the evening, she none the less permeated everything
with her energy and her passion for control. The King heard of nothing
but ministers and parliaments, peace and war, interests of nations, the
importance of the State. Surprised and dazed, like a man passing from
darkness into a blaze of light, he complained in comical dismay, "You are
killing me, Madame ! " and Madame de la Tournelle (she was not yet
Duchesse de Châteauroux) retorted pitilessly, " So much the better, Sire ;
we must call to life a King ! " Not content with sending him to the Army,
she followed herself, making the campaigns of Flanders and Lorraine,
heedless of the soldiers' jests. Cf. Carré, *Louis XV*, vol. viii. part I. ;
Histoire de France (Lavisse).

We are about to plunge into the war of the Austrian Succession (1740–1748), in which we fought against Maria Theresa on the side of the German princes who would not recognize her as Empress of Austria, although she was the daughter of Charles VI, but sought to partition her States. We were the allies of Frederic II, the veritable " great " King of Prussia, and the real founder of the Prussian monarchy, in a war which did not concern us in the least. On the other hand, the English profited from our chivalrous entanglements on the Continent by robbing us of Canada and, which was still more cruel, of our Indian possessions, thus rendering vain the expending of Dupleix' genius and Labourdonnais' valour.

CHAPTER X

THE DUCHESSE DE CHÂTEAUROUX—THE FLANDERS CAM-PAIGN—THE KING ILL AT METZ—THE DISMISSAL OF MADAME DE CHÂTEAUROUX—POPULAR ENTHUSIASM

MADAME DE LA TOURNELLE, now Duchesse de Châteauroux,[1] by which title we shall call her in future, had, in concert with the Comte d'Argenson, persuaded the King to place himself at the head of his troops. Both were urged on by their ardent personal ambitions. The

[1] As we have said, it was in October 1743 that Madame de la Tournelle was created Duchesse de Châteauroux. " Louis, by the grace of God . . . considering that *Our very dear and well-beloved cousin*, Marianne de Mailly, widow of the Marquis de la Tournelle, has sprung from one of the greatest families of Our realm, allied to Our own and to the oldest of Europe ; that for centuries her ancestors have rendered great and *important services to Our Crown* ; that she is attached to *Our dear consort the Queen* as lady-in-waiting, and that she joins to these endowments *all the virtues and the most excellent qualities of heart and mind,* which have won for her universal esteem, We have thought it proper to grant her, by Our patent of 21st October last, the duchy-peerage of Châteauroux . . . by virtue of which patent *Our said cousin* has taken the title of Duchesse de Châteauroux and enjoys at *Our Court* the honours attaching thereto, and desiring that the grant made by Us to Our said cousin should have the most solid, honourable and authentic form," etc.

In connection with this patent, Maurepas wrote : " I had to draw up the documents for the elevation to a duchy of the Châteauroux estate, and the King laughed heartily when he read their phraseology."

> Incestueuse La Tournelle,
> Qui des trois est la plus belle,
> Ce tabouret tant souhaité
> A de quoi vous rendre très fière ;
> Votre devant, en vérité,
> Sert bien votre gentil derrière.

(Incestuous La Tournelle, fairest of the three, you may indeed be proud of this coveted footstool ; the charms you have in front well serve the charms behind.)

one already regarded herself as more sovereign than the
Queen. She anticipated that, by this lofty inspiration,
she would win the favour of the nation, the esteem of the
army and the admiration of other countries. In her
soaring imagination she saw her lover as a young hero,
with herself as partner in his victories,[1] riding in his
triumphal car and redeeming with glory the shame of her
position. The other, without dreaming such brilliant
dreams, pursued his own ends—of insinuating himself more
and more into the good graces and favour of his master, of
increasing his own influence, of finding more opportunities
to gain satellites, of making his ministry more acceptable,
and finally of getting credit for all the successes to which
he could appear to have contributed by his presence, the
wisdom of his counsels, or the promptness of his orders.

Both feared that the generals, having little fancy for the
King's presence, and still less for theirs, would dissuade
him from his project, as the Maréchal de Noailles had done
the year before. They therefore bound His Majesty to
secrecy, and then considered in which direction he should
go. They thought that the campaign in Flanders, where
everything was ready for an offensive in the Austrian
Netherlands, would be more brilliant than those in Alsace
and the Rhine country, where France would remain on
the defensive. It was accordingly decided that the King
should go to Lille, but not before observing the formalities
that were customary among civilized nations. On the
26th April he published his declaration of war against the
Queen of Hungary, about the same time as the King of
Naples and the King of Sardinia issued theirs.

[1] At first the campaign was fortunate. The Duchesse de Châteauroux
was full of enthusiasm, and wrote to Duverney : " You hear the guns of the
Bastille, the chimes of La Samaritaine, the great bell of Notre Dame, and
you think they celebrate something superb ; but you really cannot imagine
the extent of the Army's success. The King is delighted, *and I am almost
mad with joy. I feel it is I who have won these battles.*"

Then Louis XV disclosed his heroic resolve; he announced it without ceremony, but with the simplicity that characterized all his actions. The nation was delighted and touched; its enthusiasm and affection for the King were doubled. The Dauphin, who was only fourteen, begged his august father to permit him to accompany him, but the King felt it to be his duty to refuse his consent, as the Prince, his only son, was not to be married till the following winter. He consoled the Dauphin by promising that they should make his first campaign together.

Over and above the reasons of State that rendered it undesirable for two lives so precious and without successors to be risked at the same time, decency was also against the lad's going. As has already been stated, the Duchesse de Châteauroux was to join the King. So far from her duty being to follow the Army, where, indeed, everything forbade her presence, it should have kept her at Versailles with the Queen, whose lady-in-waiting she was. The adulterous intercourse would have furnished a baneful spectacle for the young Dauphin, intensified by the mystery with which it was surrounded in order to avoid scandal. The Duchess did not share the King's quarters, but confidential orders were given to all the municipal authorities to arrange a lodging for her in a house adjoining that occupied by His Majesty and to open a secret passage between the two. Workmen publicly proceeded to pierce the walls, and the whole town knew for what purpose.[1]

[1] Braving the Queen, the Court and Maurepas, the Duchesse de Châteauroux joined the King, who was awaiting her. She travelled in the same coach as her sister, the Duchesse de Lauraguais. Ribald songs, epigrams and even hoots accompanied them all along the route, whereas the King had been acclaimed everywhere with cries of " Long live the King ! At last we have a King ! " Besenval wrote : " He attracted all eyes. That handsome, noble countenance, with its proud but gentle gaze, was rendered by the occasion even more impressive than at Versailles." The reception organized by the Maréchal de Saxe for the King at Lille was a veritable triumph.

The King left on 3rd May with his confidential Ministers. He had kept the Ministry for Foreign Affairs in his own hands, and had arranged for M. Dutheil, the chief official, to accompany him with his staff. The Comte de Saint-Florentin was authorized to deal with the correspondence and with any urgent domestic business that might arise during the King's absence.

The King arrived at Lille on 12th May. After visiting the most important frontier posts and giving his orders for their defence, he reviewed his army and promulgated a code of disciplinary rules, the observance of which was very difficult, although they were obeyed at any rate in his presence. His *aides-de-camp* were Messieurs de Meuse, de Richelieu, de Luxembourg, de Boufflers, d'Aumont, d'Ayen, de Soubise, de Pecquigny. His generals were the Maréchal de Noailles, who commanded 80,000 men, and the Maréchal de Saxe, who had an independent command of 40,000. The situation was very different from that prevailing a year previously when Cardinal de Fleury died, for then the English had secured the advantage of penetrating within the King's dominions. Now, when they sought to do so, they had missed their opportunity. The Dutch, who had hesitated to effect a junction with them earlier, had eventually done so—but too late. They soon regretted their delay, and, on 8th May, having learned of the King's progress, and of the movements of his troops, the States General, fearing for their own country, sent

---

At Metz the Duchess lodged in the Abbey of St. Arnould. A wooden corridor was contrived between her room and the King's, much to the astonishment and indignation of the people, who were told that it was for the King's convenience in going to Mass. In the evening they sang under the favourite's window :

> Belle Châteauroux,
> Je deviendrai fou
> Si je ne vous baise.

(Fair Châteauroux, I shall go mad if I don't kiss you.)

the Count of Wassenaar as an envoy to His Majesty. They deemed him the most suitable representative to send, as he combined with the frankness of his own race the urbanity of the French and had, moreover, lived at Louis' Court, where he had made many friends. He was instructed to approach His Majesty on their behalf and to procure a suspension of the French advance. The King replied : "The States General's choice of you is the more agreeable to me because of my appreciation of your qualities, Monsieur. My whole behaviour towards your Republic, since my advent to the throne, must have shown how zealously I sought to maintain sincere friendship and good relations with it. I have long shown my desire for peace, but the longer I postponed declaring war the less am I able to control its consequences. My Ministers will report to me on your mission and, after I have conferred with my allies, I will acquaint your masters with my decision."

Doubtless inspired by his religious feelings, and in order to invoke the light of Heaven on his Council and the blessing of God on his arms, His Majesty, before commencing operations, caused a Mass of the Holy Ghost to be celebrated, and held at the Abbey of Cisoing a chapter of the Order at which the Marquis de Billy was the only one to be knighted. It was in recognition of his great deeds in Italy, at the Pass of Villefranche and at Monte Grosse, a rocky height on which he fought for seven hours and captured the Marquis of Suza, a natural brother of the King of Sardinia. Two days later Courtrai was taken. The next day the Dutch envoy witnessed the investment of Menin, one of the barrier fortresses, defended by the troops of the Republic. Voltaire tells us that the King showed great personal courage, reconnoitring the position and approaching within pistol-shot of the defences, with the Maréchal de Noailles, the Comte d'Argenson and the whole Court ; that he encouraged the workmen with gratuities,

and hastened the capture of the town, which surrendered
after seven days of sapping. This was the first capture
in the King's presence. He was unwilling to spare the
place, and ordered that the fortifications (one of Vauban's
masterpieces) should be demolished. He wished both to
take his revenge on the States General by destroying one
of their defences, and to show his moderation by putting
it out of his power to use it in turn against them.

The King did not neglect to thank God for his victory ;
he attended a *Te Deum* at Lille, such as the district had
never beheld. Three royal princesses, whose husbands,
brothers, sons or sons-in-law, were fighting for the King
in various places, were the singular ornaments of the
ceremony. The Duchess of Modena had come to
Flanders with her nephew, the Duc de Chartres, and her
prospective son-in-law, the Duc de Penthièvre, while her
husband, the Duke of Modena, was leading the Spaniards
in Italy. The Duchesse de Chartres had come with her
husband ; and the Princesse de Conti, whose son was in
the Alps and whose daughter was married to the Duc de
Chartres, had accompanied these two princesses.

Notwithstanding these events, Ypres was invested.
This siege was remarkable in that the principal assaults
were carried out by the Prince de Clermont, who, with the
permission of the Holy Father, continued to steep his
hands in blood, a strange occupation for a servant of the
Church. Brigadier-General the Marquis de Beauvau fell
before Ypres, mourned by officers, soldiers and by scholars.
He was one of the most singular antiquaries in Europe,
for he had formed a collection of rare medals and was at
the time the only man of his condition to interest himself
in such records. Ypres soon capitulated, and Knocke
and Furnes followed.

The King reached Metz on 4th August, where he
received Baron Schmettau, plenipotentiary of the King

of Prussia, who came to announce the invasion of Bohemia by that new ally. The dispatches from Italy were most favourable, and things looked hopeful in every direction, when a misfortune of the most appalling character spread consternation from one end of the kingdom to the other.

The King, whose exercise had acted like a tonic, appeared to be in the most robust health, but the strongest men are sometimes smitten with illness that is the more violent because of their very strength. His Majesty had impoverished his blood by the abuse of wine and spirits; and his excesses in other directions had only increased the trouble. The fatigues of the campaign and the blazing sun which had poured on him during the march, making his legs give under him, had combined with these things to aggravate the fever that attacked him on 8th August and became both malignant and putrid.[1] By the evening of the 14th, the King was *in extremis*. It was not till that day that the Queen received a message from the Duc de Gesvres advising her of her royal husband's dangerous condition. She would have started off immediately had it not been necessary first to go for money to M. de Villemur, receiver-general of the Paris funds, who furnished her with a thousand *livres*. Her hasty departure furnished corroboration of the news that had been received in private letters. Grief was universal, the concern of the French for so cherished a life crowding out all other interests. Love for this prince and the legitimate fear of losing him, especially in such a crisis, brought everything to a standstill, and the commanders thought only of entrenching them-

---

[1] This is no slander; the causes of the illness are beyond question. "On 8th August the King woke up with a fever, owing to the fatigue of the journey, the excessive heat, or the too generous libations of the night before. The malady grew worse, and on the 11th he was given up for lost. At his bedside were the Duchesses de Châteauroux and de Lauraguais, who took it upon themselves to impose silence on every one, and jealously guarded the entrance to the royal chamber"—Stryienski, *Le XVIIIᵉ siècle*.

selves so that the enemy might not take advantage of the
general despair and of the threatened calamity. The
King was regarded as doomed, there being no room for
hope, seeing that it had been decided to administer the
last sacraments and to urge him to send away the Duchesse
de Châteauroux. It was the Duc de Chartres, son of the
Regent, who, forcing the King's door as first Prince of the
Blood, informed him of his serious condition, and suggested
the performance of these religious duties.[1] The Duc de
Richelieu, gentleman of the bedchamber in attendance,
had taken care not to speak in such terms to his master,
as to have done so would have offended both the royal
invalid and the favourite. His lucky star led him to take
a more prudent course. The King might, by some such
miracle of nature as was not without precedent, eventually
recover ; and he foresaw how his pride would be wounded.
Richelieu was unwilling to risk the King's displeasure and,
still more, that of a disgraced mistress. On the other
hand, if the King should not recover, he had little to expect
from his successor. He therefore strongly supported the
Duchesse and objected as vehemently as he could to alarm-
ing the dying man by terrifying his conscience. He dared
to oppose the Duc de Chartres for a time, and only yielded
out of deference to the rank of a prince who was next in
succession to the Dauphin. Indeed, if we are to believe
private journals, the Duc de Chartres had to use high

---

[1] Reference should be made to *Richelieu's Memoirs* for his graphic
and dramatic description of the whole episode, including the hesitation
of the King's confessor, the Jesuit Pérussot. " I know," said Madame de
Châteauroux, " that you are at the head of a party which will not recognize
that here I am in my proper place. I appeal to your conscience. Can you
possibly drive me away ? " " I am not concerned with politics or love,"
replied the Jesuit, " but I am bound to recommend the King to do his
duty." " I own to you, Père Pérussot, that I have sinned with the King
freely ; is that a reason for banishing me ? " The confessor was silent,
torn between his duty as a priest and his prudent desire not to incur the
displeasure of Madame de Châteauroux."

words and even violence. " What," said he threateningly, " a servant like you dares to refuse admittance to your master's nearest relative ! " and with a kick he burst open the door. When the King asked for an explanation of the hubbub, His Highness, still enraged, complained of the insolence of Richelieu, who was ordered to depart. His temporary disgrace was soon exchanged for high favour.

The Duchesse de Châteauroux had not left the King's bedside since the first day of his illness ; her lover, still intoxicated with passion, vowed that he only regretted her and his subjects. The arrival of the Bishop of Soissons,[1] His Majesty's Grand Almoner, in company with the Duc de Chartres, persuaded the favourite that her reign was at an end. She withdrew, and the prelate administered the rites with the fullest ceremony. He insisted that the King, before receiving the viaticum, should not only send away the being who was so dear to him, but should atone for the public scandal by craving the pardon of God in the presence of the princes, courtiers and people. The penitent, who was naturally frightened in circumstances that affect the most courageous, was smitten with religious terror and followed in its entirety the course laid down for him. The Comte d'Argenson, who only cultivated the favourite as a matter of policy and really hated her (henceforth without fear !), was charged with the duty of apprising her of her dismissal, a duty he performed with great harshness. The Duchesse, who showed more greatness at this moment than her lover, accepted her disgrace without flinching, but she did not yet know what she was to go through on the road. She got into her coach, accompanied by her sister the Duchesse de Lauraguais, and departed.

[1] Fitz-James (1709–1764), son of Berwick, Marshal of France, bastard of James II of England, who was killed at the siege of Philipsbourg. The Bishop spoke boldly and clearly, insisting on the immediate departure of the mistress, and uttering the mediæval threat of interdicting the city, and closing all its churches.

She had not even left the city before the mob, who had learned of her banishment, hooted her, revealing the sovereign contempt with which excited people always overwhelm those who have improperly demanded their deference. Moreover, they regarded her as responsible for the King's illness and for the threatened loss of a monarch who was at the moment the nation's idol and the object of its grief. Horrible curses, frightful threats were shrieked at her. In the country the peasants followed her as far as they could, and then passed on their work of execration and insult. She had a hundred miraculous escapes from being torn in pieces, and had to take an infinity of precautions. When her carriage approached a small town the Duchess stopped it a mile away, sent one of her attendants to procure relays and to spy out the bypaths so that she might evade the fury of the people. In such mortal anxiety she covered more than eighty leagues before reaching Paris. When she arrived, the public dismay became even greater, if that were possible. Her reception by the people of the capital would have been like that she had experienced in the country, had they not been too deeply preoccupied with their grief. They only left the churches, where they had been praying for the King's preservation, to run to the post, to the palace, to the mansions of the nobles, to learn whether their petitions were being answered, and, on receiving bad news, they rushed back to the churches to weary Heaven with the fervour of their importunities.

The Dauphin had just departed; [1] the Royal Family and all the princes were with the King. Paris, thus deprived of its lord and of all the pillars of the throne, felt deserted

---

[1] The King would not agree to the Queen's following him on account of the " great expense." To the fifteen-year-old Dauphin, who wished to win his spurs, he had replied, " I applaud your desire ; but your person is too dear to the State to be risked before the succession to the Crown is assured by your marriage."

and empty as never before. Only the Duc d'Orléans
remained. He retired to Sainte Geneviève, there to pray
earnestly to the patron saint of the city. He lauded the
pious resolution of his son, to which he had exhorted
him by his letter. Mingling with the throng around the
shrine, he was only distinguishable by the special bitterness
of his tears and the violence of his sobs. It was here,
before the remains of Sainte Geneviève, that suddenly and
spontaneously Louis XV was proclaimed "Louis the
Well-Beloved." [1] There was no flattery about this; it
was not Court sycophancy but the spontaneous expression
of the people. It did not occur to them that the dying
monarch would even come to know of this title, which they
awarded as it were to his shade, thus giving vent to their
gratitude. No citizen spoke to another in the street except
of the calamity, and, when they parted, both said, " If he
dies it will be in consequence of having marched to our
aid ! " The Dauphin, even at an age when a young and
splendid prince may find easy consolation in the prospect of
wearing so glorious a crown, was only concerned with the
loss of his father and the misfortune of the people. He
cried pathetically, " Ah, you poor people, what will become
of you ? What is left to you ? Only I, a child ! O
Lord, have pity on this realm ; Lord, have mercy upon
us ! " [2]

[1] This name was bestowed upon him when he made his triumphal entry
into Paris after his recovery. Joy succeeded alarm ; the crowd embraced
the very horse of the messenger who brought news of his convalescence, and
a wretched poet named Vadé, whose least obscure work is *La Pipe cassée*,
could truly say, " C'est Louis le bien-aimé," an expression which was sincere
enough at the time, and has been consecrated by history.

[2] " Every day, night and morning, the post office was filled and besieged
by crowds whom the clerks could not satisfy. In the evenings arrived
messengers who said that the King was better ; and to meet the public
excitement, it was decided to display bulletins in the courtyard of the Post
Office, and on the doors of the various Ministries. Never, indeed, had there
been such enthusiasm and vivid demonstration of the people's love for the
King "—*Journal de Barbier*.

The Queen, whose feelings were harrowed to the last, was met at St. Didier by her father, King Stanislas of Poland. He had come straight from the sick-room, where every one was in despair. When she reached Metz, however, on the 17th, a fortunate purging had brought about a change. Her Majesty profited by the work of the Bishop of Soissons, and, although her trouble and grief, added to her loss of youth, made her less attractive than ever, her attentions, her assiduity, her caresses so affected the King that, in the first impulse of his good nature and gratitude, he vowed that she alone should have his love in future.[1]

It was different with the Dauphin, for whom the King's affection began to decrease. On hearing of his departure he ordered him to return to Versailles. Concern for the Prince's health was the ostensible ground for this command, but the real cause was his unwillingness to see the arrival of his successor. The Dauphin had already reached Verdun when he met the officer bearing the King's instructions. In other circumstances he would have obeyed them ; but he brushed them aside, consulting his heart rather than his adviser, and feeling that, in the circumstances, his love might be allowed to prevail over his duty of obedience. Furthermore, he was very near his father, who completely occupied his thoughts. He did not think of him as his King and could not bring himself to return without seeing him. His tutor, the Duc de

---

[1] " It was eleven at night when the Queen reached Metz. She went straight to his room. The previous night had been the worst of all, and every one present expected it to be the last. The fever had, however, abated during the day, and the King, surrounded by the whole anxious faculty, had begun to doze. When he opened his eyes he was advised of the Queen's presence, and, without hesitation, asked to see her alone, so that he might embrace her. His first words were a prayer. ' Madame, I have caused you much undeserved grief, and I beg you to forgive me.' ' Ah, Sire, do you not know that you have never needed my forgiveness ? It is God alone that you have offended, and I beg you only to concern yourself with Him.' The Queen wept abundantly as she uttered these words " —P. de Nolhac, *Louis XV et Marie Leczinska*, pp. 299-300.

Châtillon, followed rather than led him. On his arrival at Metz, the father was revealed in turn and the disobedience of the subject was ignored ; but, as there was much illness abroad and the Dauphin already had a slight attack of fever when he arrived, he was sent home a few days later. The King vented his displeasure on the tutor, who was banished to his estate before the Monarch's return. His wife shared his disgrace, and they had only a few hours in which to prepare for departure. The real motive of this exile, concerning which such diverse tales have been told, was made clear in a conversation Louis XV had later with a lord who kept a diary of what took place at Court. The King asked whether he remembered what had happened exactly four years previously. The courtier's memory failed him. " Consult your journal," said the King, " you will find the disgrace of the Duc de Châtillon. Really he already imagined himself the first officer of State ! " It is, in fact, said that, in anticipation of the death of Louis XV, the Duke had prostrated himself before the Dauphin, saluting him as his king.[1]

The intensity of the grief into which the people had been plunged by the King's danger was equalled, or, rather, more than equalled, by the public joy at his re- covery. Paris went mad. The first courier to bring the glad tidings of the crisis that had saved the King was surrounded, caressed and almost suffocated by the mob. They kissed his horse and even his boots as they led him in triumph. Strangers called to each other from afar, " The

[1] " When the King's recovery was complete, two matters demanded con- sideration : the disgrace of the Duc de Châtillon, who had loudly approved the departure of the favourite, and had delivered a moral lecture thereon for the edification of his pupil ; and the disgrace of M. Balleroy, who was private secretary of the Duc de Chartres and related to the family of Fitz- James. His fault was that he belonged to the religious party who had so strenuously urged the public dismissal of Madame de Châteauroux. These two had been singled out because the striker had not dared to aim higher " —Stryienski, *Le XVIII*ᵉ *siècle.*

King is cured!" They congratulated and embraced
each other. All the orders of the State vied with each
other in manifesting their gratitude to Heaven. There
was not a workmen's society but ordered a *Te Deum*,[1]
and France was given up for more than two months to
rejoicings and festivals. These occasioned great expense
to which some limit should have been put. Of all the
provinces Brittany showed its thankfulness in the most

---

[1] " A *Te Deum* was sung at Notre Dame for the restoration of the King's
health. There was a firework display in the Place de Grève carried out
in the most splendid and varied manner by Italian workmen. The streets
of Paris were brilliantly illuminated, many private citizens spending great
sums of money in addition to that lavished on the mansions of the princes,
nobles and courtiers, which were decorated with frameworks or hoardings
hung with specially constructed lustres and with lamps. On the Pont
Neuf, in the public squares, and elsewhere, there were hogsheads of wine,
which was distributed with polonies and bread. In front of each of these
distributing centres was a platform for five or six musicians who discoursed
music "—*Journal de Barbier*.

LA CONVALESCENCE DU ROI

Grand Roi, que tu nous es cher !
Que tu nous as causé d'alarmes !
Mon homme a le cœur de fer :
Mais cette fois j'ons vu ses larmes,
Et pendant que Louis souffrait,
Jusqu'à nos enfants, tout pleurait.

Changeons nos cris en chansons,
Et notre douleur en noce ;
Pour que ce soit tout de bon,
Ce soir je veux devenir grosse
Et le fruit de mon amour
A lui seul devra le jour.

(THE CONVALESCENCE OF THE KING

Great King, how dear thou art to us ! What a fright hast
thou caused us ! My husband has a heart of iron, but on this
occasion I saw his tears ; and, while Louis suffered, all wept—
even the children.

Let us change lamentations for songs, and grief for festivity. As
a climax to-night I would like to become pregnant so that the fruit
of my love should really owe the day to him.)

sensible manner, the most worthy of the occasion and the most enduring. The States decreed the erection in the capital of a bronze monument celebrating the event. This monument was executed by the famous Le Moine and set up at Rennes in 1754. Poets and orators rivalled each other in celebrating the supreme moment in the life of Louis XV, that novel triumph, worthy of Trajan and Antoninus, and in handing down its memory to the remotest posterity. It is difficult to imagine the lengths to which the writers allowed the delirium of their compositions and their patriotic exaltation to carry them. One of them, relying on the resources of his genius and on the fact that in connexion with such a subject every detail was of interest, went so far as to depict the salutary crisis that had saved the King's life, in its utmost physical details, even apostrophizing the first discharges ! It is almost incredible, but people tumbled over each other for this production, the disgusting title of which would of itself have caused it, in other times, to be flung away, but which the poet, accustomed to treating all sorts of subjects and to overcoming difficulties and extravagances, had succeeded in elevating and even making sublime in parts. This is perhaps the less surprising when we learn that the poet was Piron.

When the King heard of the people's enthusiasm, he uttered an exclamation that made him seem more worthy of it : " How sweet it is to be so loved ! What have I done to deserve it ? " It was said that, while on the point of death, at that last moment when the dream of glory and all illusions fade, the King spoke in a fashion that revealed less sentiment but more heroism, and showed that, impressed with the demands of duty, he had not forgotten the interests of the State. His intention when he left Flanders was to attack Prince Charles ; but the troops had been delayed, making it impossible for him to do so in person.

Noailles, who as senior Marshal had accompanied the King, assumed the command-in-chief of the Army of Alsace. His Majesty, on learning this, said to the Comte d'Argenson, who had remained at his bedside from the beginning of his illness, " Write for me to the Maréchal de Noailles that, while Louis XIII was being carried to his grave, the Prince de Condé won a victory." Unfortunately Noailles was not a Condé, and he had to face a more formidable opponent than the Spanish general.[1]

[1] All historians agree that the dying Louis XIII had a wonderful vision of the victory of Rocroy which he foretold, and described in the delirium that preceded his death. " Prince Charles had already crossed before they learned of his passage, or rather before the Maréchal de Noailles attacked. This crossing brought much obloquy upon Noailles, who, the gossips said, was afraid of the guns. It is recorded that, one night, a wooden sword was hung before the door of his house "—*Journal de Barbier.*

> Ce n'est point la cotte de maille
> Ni le casque de Du Guesclin
> Qu'il faut donner à Noailles !
> Pour coiffure et pour casaquin.
>
> C'est une chape de moine,
> Ou l'aumusse d'un chanoine
> Dont il faut revêtir son corps
> Pour rendre son esprit plus tranquille et plus fort.
>
> Excepté que pour bigarrure
> Selon la commune voix
> On lui laisse pour armure
> Au lieu de fer l'épée de bois !

(It is not fitting to equip Noailles with the coat of mail and the helmet of Du Guesclin.

Give him rather the vestments of a monk or of a canon with which to clothe his body and to calm and fortify his spirit.

But, as an oddity, the gossips say that he was given for weapon, instead of steel, a sword of wood.)

CHAPTER XI

TRIUMPHAL RETURN TO PARIS—RICHELIEU—THE KING
REGRETS HIS MISTRESS—RECONCILIATION—REVENGE
—DEATH OF THE DUCHESSE

A T last, in November 1744, the King put an end
to the impatience of the Parisians by returning
to the capital. His entry was a triumph,[1]
which the joy, the cheers and the transports of
his people made the more affecting because it was not
attended by any brilliant and impressive ceremonial.
Rather the people, still shaken by their fear of losing him,
seemed, in their eagerness, to seek assurance of the real
existence of their resuscitated monarch. They were not
so much surrounding the chariot of a conqueror as em-
bracing the knees of a tender father.

[1] When Louis XV returned to Paris, his path was a succession of triumphal
arches, and these not merely stage properties, but permanent monuments.
The great Louis XIV at the zenith of his career had not witnessed such
transports of delirium when he returned from the wars. Every tree on the
road bowed beneath the weight of spectators. When he reached Paris, the
King entered the coronation coach drawn by eight horses which carried
their heads high, not, as it was said, because they knew they were drawing
a victorious monarch, but because they belonged to the royal stables and
had long been trained to bear themselves proudly. The King was handsome, and it was then really believed that this handsome King had just
saved France. Louis XIV had been compared to Jupiter, and Louis XV
was likened to Apollo. A rich noble of his suite, affected by such worship,
scattered handfuls of money, but none stooped to pick it up. All the crowd
wanted was to salute the King, who was actually addressed by the "ladies
of the fishmarket." In the midst of this delirious throng, a simply clad
woman sought to avoid recognition, although she felt that the King would
return to her just as he was returning to his people. It was Madame de
Châteauroux, who wrote to Richelieu : "His Majesty stopped for three
minutes just where I was. My eye caught his, and I there beheld his surprise
and joy. I can scarcely tell you what I felt at that moment."

His Majesty stayed three days at the Tuileries, showing himself as much as possible and allowing people to approach him freely. He dined at the Hôtel de Ville, thus manifesting to their municipal representatives his gratitude to the people. In accordance with custom they had the honour of waiting on him, the Provost of the Merchants standing behind the King, and the senior alderman behind the Dauphin. In connection with this celebration, Voltaire criticizes, and with reason, the public inscriptions and mottoes which, following a ridiculous custom, were in Latin and, instead of expressing the feelings of a nation that neither speaks nor understands that language, only reproduced the puerilities of pedantic minds.

All these fêtes and all this outpouring of the emotions of the French people did not, however, fully satisfy the King. The image of the Duchesse de Châteauroux haunted him more than ever; it was she to whom his illness had been fatal. Condemned by her lover himself to live in tearful retirement she could have no part in the general rejoicings. He, for his part, reproached himself for having banished her, and was wroth with the Bishop who had insisted on such a course. He would have liked to make amends for the harshness with which his orders had been carried out, by recalling her with such public honour as would make her forget the humiliation of her dismissal; but he was restrained by other considerations. Fear of public opinion, that tyrant even of kings, held him back. He had just received from the Queen signs of the tenderest attachment, in return for which she only asked to be restored to her rights. Alas, his feelings were in opposition to his duty, and, on the plea that it was necessary to restore his strength, which had been exhausted by his illness and the remedies prescribed, he postponed the satisfaction of her desires. Those who appreciated the strength of passion speedily foresaw what would happen. The Duc de

Richelieu, who had been restored to the King's favour, after having been clever enough to get into trouble on account of his zeal for the favourite at the most critical moment, was eager to reap his reward through her recall. As this noble will henceforth play an important rôle it will be well to give more particulars concerning him.

Born at the end of the previous century, he was nearly fifty years of age. He was a tall, handsome man, with a pleasant face, extremely gallant and inheriting both the chivalrous taste of the old *régime* and the corruption of the Regency.[1] Pleasure still had the strongest attraction

[1] Louis Armand de Vignerod du Plessis, Duc de Richelieu (1696–1788), Marshal of France, Ambassador to Austria, Governor of Languedoc, where his administration was not always above suspicion. He was brave, contributed to the victory of Fontenoy, and relieved Genoa; captured Port Mahon and oppressed Hanover, which he treated as conquered territory, allowing it to be stripped by his pillaging troops. He was the most famous lady-killer of the eighteenth century, some of his affairs causing scandals. He was the man by whom women actually boasted of being " dishonoured " (the current expression), from the proudest princesses, like the daughters of the Regent, Mademoiselle de Charolais, the Princesse de Polignac, and many others, to the poorest chambermaid provided she was pretty. He was thrice confined in the Bastille, as much on account of his love affairs as of his complicity in the Cellamare conspiracy. He was a member of the French Academy, although he could not spell; a member of the Academy of Inscriptions and Belles-Lettres, although the most ignorant man of his day. He was married three times, the last only two years before his death, when he was a feeble dotard. He was a supple courtier, at times obsequious, knowing how to keep on good terms with all the favourites, although his relations with Madame de Pompadour were clouded through his declining for his son, the Duc de Fronsac, the hand of her daughter Alexandrine. " Azamuth (the Duc de Richelieu, grandnephew of the Cardinal) was a tall, well-built man with an attractive face, extremely gallant and very fond of pleasure, the excessive indulgence in which caused premature age and feebleness. He had greatly loved the ladies, who were reputed to have been very kind to him; his amorous adventures made a great stir, and led him into several scrapes from which he always managed to extricate himself with honour. He was witty, gay, amusing, very rich, but a bad economist. He held high position at the Court, and succeeded in winning the good graces of Cha-Séphi (Louis XV). He was ambitious and, after the death of Ismaël Bey (Fleury), was credited with aspiring to the ministry, a position for which, notwithstanding all his talents, it may fairly be said that his voluptuousness, his indolence of mind, and his somewhat dissipated bearing, did not fit him "—*Mémoires secrets pour servir à l'Histoire de Perse.*

for him, although excessive indulgence had already enfeebled and prematurely aged him.   Passionately fond of women and very kindly treated by them, he liked to advertise his conquests.   Some of them occasioned great commotion and led him into awkward scrapes, from which he managed to extricate himself satisfactorily, for there was courage behind his audacity and shamelessness in these matters.   He was witty and gay, wealthy but extravagant.   Indeed, his prodigality made him very anxious for ｜favour, so that he might repair the inroads that his pleasures constantly made into his fortune.   Always lucky, he succeeded in everything he undertook.   Although far beneath her in birth, he had married a princess of the House of Lorraine.   It is true this marriage gave rise to a dispute, but that only served to add lustre to his fame through a duel in which he was victorious. Appointed to the command of Languedoc, with the rank of lieutenant-general, he persuaded the States at the beginning of the war to promise the King that they would raise, clothe, arm, equip, mount and maintain, throughout its duration, a regiment of dragoons called "Septimanie."   His Majesty, who was pleased with this promise, rewarded the father's services by appointing the son, the Duc de Fronsac, colonel of the regiment, and also attached the Duc de Richelieu more closely to himself by appointing him First Gentleman of the Bedchamber, in succession to the Duc de Rochechouart, who had fallen at the Battle of Dettingen.

This courtier, whose heart, open to all passions, was also devoured by a thirst for honours, saw a prospect of further advancement, to attain which the best means was to get the Duchesse de Châteauroux back at Court.[1]

[1] Had he not said at Metz, " Go at once, but be sure the King will return to you ! "   With reference to this, the following song was written :

SANS LE SAVOIR

Ce messager toujours fidèle
Mercure, qui près d'une belle   (Richelieu)

LOUIS FRANÇOIS ARMAND DU PLESSIS, DUKE AND MARSHAL DE
RICHELIEU

He dispelled the King's scruples. He arranged hunting parties at which he secretly contrived opportunities for

> Sait si bien faire son devoir,
> Sous le manteau qui le déguise
> N'ose paraître que le soir.
> Aurait-il fait quelque sottise
>   Sans le savoir ?

> Enfin, je divine l'affaire ;
> Le meilleur suppôt de Cythère   (le Roi)
> Veut se soustraire à son pouvoir ;
> Un déserteur de cette espèce
> Peut exciter son désespoir,
> Causerait-il tant de tristesse,
>   Sans le savoir ?

> Mais quoi ! à la fleur de son âge
> Veut-il reprendre l'esclavage
> Que l'usage appelle devoir ?
> Amour, redoutez peu ses chaînes ;
> Ouvrez votre cœur à l'espoir,
> Il rentrera dans vos domaines
>   Sans le savoir !

> Châteauroux, cette chaste veuve
> Aux revers d'amour presque neuve
> Affecte un tendre désespoir ;
> Richelieu lui dit ; tais-toi, folle,
> On est maître de se revoir
> Quand on a donné sa parole
>   Sans le savoir !

(ALL UNAWARE

Mercury, the ever-faithful messenger [Richelieu], who, in presence of the fair knows so well how to do his duty, only dared to appear at night, wrapped in a mantle. Had he done something stupid, all unaware ?

At last, I understand, the great functionary of Cythera [the King] wishes to escape from her toils. Such a deserter may drive her to despair. Can he cause so much sadness, all unaware ?

What! in the prime of life does he wish to resume the captivity that custom calls duty ? Love, fear not such chains nor close your heart to hope. He will come back to your realm, all unaware !

Châteauroux, that chaste widow, after so brief a love appears in trembling despair. Richelieu says, "Be silent, fool, there is no reason forbidding reconciliation if the promise was given all unaware ! ")

10

the deserted mistress to see the King and regain her influence. At length Louis, weary of self-denial, complained openly that advantage had been taken of his condition to besmirch his honour by forcing him to treat unworthily a woman whose only fault was that she had so greatly loved him. He determined to restore her to her position, her titles, and her honours. He prepared her triumph by giving her satisfaction against the Bishop of Soissons, who was ordered to retire to his diocese, and against the Comte d'Argenson,[1] who, having been the person to communicate to her the order for her departure, was now instructed to tell her of her recall. He asked her, on behalf of the King, for a list of those whom she wished to have punished. It is stated that Maurepas' own name headed the list, and that the Minister, seeing that he could not hope to be received back into her favour, adopted the only alternative, of deciding to clear the situation promptly by getting rid of any need for reconciliation once and for all. No crime can be imagined more easy to talk and write about and more difficult to commit. It is much more likely that the excess of joy caused a sudden shock to the Duchesse, which

---

[1] It was Maurepas, and not D'Argenson, as is erroneously stated by our author. Madame de Châteauroux and the King met at night, and the whole programme of her sensational return was arranged. "All that remained was for her to fix the hour. On the 25th November, Maurepas (this was his only punishment) brought her a letter, which became public property the next day, begging her to return to Court. The Duchess was in bed, with a touch of fever, and the Minister felt some embarrassment on being introduced into her presence. He handed her the letter, gave her time to peruse its contents, and then sought to plead his own cause. "The Plague" was permitted to kiss a disdainful hand, which indicated that his humiliation was regarded as sufficient punishment for so paltry an adversary. . . . Dumb consternation prevailed around the Queen, and loud rejoicing among her opponents. . . . Madame de Châteauroux wrote several letters. . . . To Madame de Boufflers she said, "The King has just sent me word by M. de Maurepas, that he was very sorry for all that happened at Metz and for the shameful manner in which I was treated, that he begged me to forget it, and that, to show I had done so, he hoped we might return to our apartments at Versailles"—Cf. Nolhac, *Louis XV et Marie Leczinska.*

proved fatal. Some doctors say that the shock was caused by her eagerness to receive the impatient King's embraces, which led her to undress, bath and perfume herself when she was not well. Whatever may be the truth of the matter, the following epitaph was written, an epitaph which would have been more justified, in such circumstances, if applied to Madame de Mailly, who really was capable of such generous thoughts:

> Sans relever l'éclat de mon illustre sang,
> Ce trait seul fera vivre à jamais ma mémoire:
> Mon roi revit le jour pour me rendre mon rang,
> Et je meurs sans regret pour lui rendre sa gloire.[1]

(Apart from any reference to my illustrious birth, this one thing will suffice to keep my memory green: my King came back to life to restore me to my place; I die without regret to restore to him his fame.)

This loss, striking in the time and circumstances of its occurrence, plunged Louis XV into a profound melancholy; if his despondency was as violent as had been his passion, it must have been extreme. The Duchess had so com-

---

[1] Later on, when " the Well-Beloved " was no longer the well-beloved, this epitaph would seem too modest for the mistress and too flattering for the King. " Worse or more obscure lines could not be written. What is the meaning of ' I die to restore to him his fame ' ? Is it not rather a fact that, like another Agnes Sorel, she had roused the King from his lethargy? Would the King have ceased to merit his glorious title if Madame de Châteauroux had not been poisoned? Her death was apparently a mere act of vengeance, and added nothing to the reputation of the King, who soon bound himself with fresh fetters, for he could not exist without them " —*Anecdotes secrètes*. The suggestion is that if Madame de Châteauroux had reigned longer she would have exercised a greater influence on the period, such, for example, as the Marquise de Pompadour exercised soon after.

It seems that this tradition of Agnes Sorel stimulating the courage of Charles VII had been invented by François I as an excuse for his own mistresses. At the time the rôle of Joan of Arc was scarcely appreciated (it was only in the middle of the nineteenth century that her wonderful services were properly comprehended), and in the days of François I they talked only of the " Lady of Beauty."

pletely regained her sway over her august lover that she had a second time dictated terms. In addition to the conditions already mentioned, which were designed to repair the insult in the eyes of all Europe of her ignominious dismissal, she had insisted on the official and not less striking satisfaction of being appointed Mistress of the Household to Madame, the prospective wife of the Dauphin, and the King was so infatuated as to agree. By giving her this post of confidence and dignity, which presupposed the possession of reserve and propriety, an incorruptible heart, irreproachable behaviour and an unblemished reputation, he advertised scandal, enthroned vice, and offended morality, public decency and the Court of Spain, the austerity of which would have been outraged by such an infamous choice. Death anticipated all these evils, and such violence to all shame was not perpetrated ; but the reconciliation of the King with Madame de Châteauroux had a most unfortunate effect on the people, and materially lessened their affection for him. Who does not remember the cry of the fishwives, whose cries are always echoed by the public : " Since he has taken back his whore, he shall not find another prayer for him in all Paris." [1]

[1] The Duchesse de Châteauroux did not die of poison any more than she died, as is narrated in *Richelieu's Memoirs,* of "immoderate and violent indulgence" after the reconciliation. She was feverish when Maurepas came to her, and the fever did not decrease the following day. Rather her mingled emotions, added to the fact that she was suffering from a trouble of her sex, increased it. This illness seemed to the King to be a judgment from Heaven. He broke down, discontinued dining in public, and refused to leave the private apartments. Madame de Flavacourt watched by the bedside. Madame de Mailly came to see her sister, but no one cared to ask the delirious woman if she would receive her, and Madame de Mailly was only admitted to kneel and weep before the dead body.

CHAPTER XII

THE DAUPHIN'S FIRST MARRIAGE—THE WEDDING FESTIVI-
TIES—WHO WILL BE THE NEW MISTRESS?—THE
BEAUTIFUL HUNTRESS—MADAME POISSON AND MAD-
AME D'ÉTIOLES—"THE HANDKERCHIEF IS THROWN!"
—A ROYAL MORSEL—DEATH OF MADAME POISSON

AT that time Versailles was adorned by a bevy
of young princesses who had been assembled as
companions for the Dauphin's future consort.[1]
They were to supply her with company and
amusement, as she was not yet of an age for her tastes to
be in keeping with the old Court. The Duc de Chartres
had married the sister of the Prince de Conti. She was
eighteen or nineteen years old, beautiful, of good figure,
charming and lively, enthusiastic for pleasure, fond of
fêtes and magnificence, endowed with a pleasing character
and a refined mind. She had already become generally
liked through the affability and popularity that always
seemed to be prominent characteristics of her stock. Her
husband was also kindly and humane and very likeable ; he
was handsome, and his excessive fatness was redeemed by
his activity. His temperament, however, scarcely suited
that of the Duchess, for he had not the bent for pleasure
and luxury that she would have liked to see in him. His
mind and intellect had promised well in childhood, and
would probably have been well developed if his second

---

[1] Maria Theresa, daughter of Philip V of Spain. She had a daughter,
Marie Thérèse, known as "Madame," who was born in 1746, and died in
1748, by which time the widowed Dauphin was married again (in 1747)
to Marie Josèphe of Saxony, daughter of Frederic Augustus III.

governor had followed the same lines as the first. This
governor was banished, at about the same time as the Duc
de Châtillon, which was the more surprising as he was
closely related to the D'Argenson family, who had introduced him and thus far protected him ; but he had made
himself so little liked that scarcely any one was moved by his
downfall. It does not appear that even his illustrious
pupil troubled about it.

The Comtesse de Toulouse had more recently married
her son, the Duc de Penthièvre, to the Princess of Modena,
whose father, a sovereign without a realm through his
attachment to France, was reduced to commanding the
troops of the King of Spain. She was a few months
younger than the Duchesse de Chartres, beautiful, less
attractive on the surface and less lively, but perhaps more
capable of ensuring the happiness of her husband. The
Duchess her mother, sister of the Duc d'Orléans, daughter
of the Regent, had at one time hoped to marry her daughter
to her nephew, and had secured the advantage over the
Princesse de Conti, who, however, not less vigorous, stubborn
or resourceful, had successfully pulled other strings. The
Duke of Modena's poverty was the real cause of the change
in the marriage scheme ; had circumstances been different,
no doubt his daughter would have been preferred, but,
however right and proper it may be, an alliance with the
unfortunate is not attractive. The Princess of Modena
was thus reduced to marrying a legitimated prince. It is
true that, on the occasion of this marriage, the Comtesse de
Toulouse had a fleeting hope that the King would restore
to her son, and consequently to the sons of the Duchesse
du Maine, the Prince de Dombes and the Comte d'Eu,
all the honours, rank, rights and prerogatives that Louis
XIV had solemnly accorded to his children, but which,
as we have seen, were officially withdrawn from them
during the Regency and later on definitely and finally

cancelled so far as their posterity was concerned. The curious thing is that these proceedings were instigated by the very sister of the Duc du Maine and the Comte de Toulouse, the Duchesse de Bourbon, who, legitimated as they were, could not degrade them without degrading herself. This is surely a proof that, among the highly placed, blood counts for nothing and the call of nature cannot prevail against the envious passion of ambition. Jealous of the favour shown by the late King to her brothers, she had incited her son, the Duc de Bourbon, to move in the matter, and, with hideous treachery, had forced him to take the first steps while he was actually a member of a house-party at Rambouillet, the home of the Comte de Toulouse, his uncle.

Eventually His Majesty granted to the children of the Duc du Maine and of the Comte de Toulouse the same honours as their fathers had enjoyed, but by a personal warrant, and only for life. It was a poor enough thing, which could only satisfy their vanity within their own palaces or at Versailles. The princes of the blood, the peers, the Parliament and the nation had not concurred in these distinctions. The House of Este desired that, in honour of their alliance, the King should grant special favours and utilize the whole machinery of sovereign power in order to give them the necessary confirmation. This was precisely what so many illustrious personages, jealous of handing down to their descendants their rank and privileges unimpaired, were concerned to prevent. This affair caused great agitation at Court. The more prudent among the courtiers acted silently; the less circumspect made an uproar and were punished by exile. Some, although but recently loaded with favours by the King, did not allow their gratitude to outweigh the importance of etiquette, for it was scarcely possible to alter the articles of succession to the Crown or the absolute prerogatives of the

princes of the blood. Louis XV did not imagine that he
could restore the work of Louis XIV, and even if he had
wished to do so such a vigorous step would have been
beyond his strength. Furthermore, it would have been
the more dangerous for him to attempt it, as he himself,
following in the gallant footsteps of his ancestor, might
some day experience the tender feelings of blind paternity.
He therefore stopped short at the personal warrants, and
the claimants, despite the marks of the King's displeasure,
did not refrain from protests and other usual defensive
actions.

It was in such circumstances that the Dauphine arrived.
The French Ambassador having made the usual demand
eight days previously, the marriage of the Infanta Maria
Theresa was celebrated in Madrid, on 18th December, by
the Patriarch of the Indies. The Prince of the Asturias
acted as proxy for the Dauphin. Three weeks later she
was delivered by the officers of the King of Spain, on the
Ile des Faisans, to the Duc de Lauraguais, who was appointed
to receive her. Here again we see the power of the Duchesse
de Châteauroux who had procured this honour for her
brother-in-law, securing also the appointment of her sister,
the Duchesse de Lauraguais, as lady of the bedchamber to
the Dauphine and of the Duchesse de Brancas, her mother,
as lady-in-waiting, by reason of her age and dignity. It
was only on the 23rd February, 1745, that the Infanta
reached Versailles, where she received the marriage blessing
a second time, at the hands of Cardinal de Rohan, the
Grand Almoner. This Princess, although her face was
quite unattractive, won the Dauphin's love. Whether it
was the effect of some secret sympathy or of the burning
ardour of a young prince experiencing transports to which
he had hitherto been a stranger, he was enchanted with
her, and the love that first impressions had kindled was
intensified by her personal qualities, The Princess was

endowed with loftiness of feeling, sweetness and amiability of character, a taste for meditation and devotion which conformed admirably with the Dauphin's upbringing. On the other hand, it was evident that her august bridegroom, notwithstanding the brilliance of his youth and rank, and the similarity of their minds, did not inspire reciprocal feelings. Possibly a longer intimacy might have brought that about, but Heaven only gave the nation a glimpse of the Dauphine. That was quite sufficient to make her carry with her the most sincere regrets when she died.[1]

Notwithstanding the disasters of the war, the most brilliant festivities took place throughout the kingdom,

[1] In 1745 the Dauphin was slim and graceful, as he is represented by Latour in the Louvre pastel. He was like his mother, and the good Queen's subtle and refined smile was reproduced on the face of this lad of sixteen. The Dauphine, the Infanta Maria Theresa Raphaëlla, was four years older than her husband. She was ugly, red-haired and austere, but she inspired the Dauphin with deep love. The son of Louis XV was married for reasons of State, to assure the succession, and for family reasons; to cement the reconciliation of the two crowns. At the same time he was made happy, a rare event in marriages of diplomacy. His happiness only lasted two years, for, as we have just said, the Dauphine died in 1746, after giving birth to a daughter who only lived about eighteen months.

Regarding the death of the Dauphine, see the long poem, *La Mort de la Dauphine* in the *Recueil* Clairambault-Maurepas, Raunié edition, vii. p. 67.

> Muses qui consacrez les vertus magnanimes,
> Sur l'immortel airain de vos fastes sublimes,
> Inspirez-moi des vers lugubres et touchants :
> Accordez vos soupirs à mes plaintes funèbres
> Et prêtez à ma voix, pour ces mânes célèbres,
>   Toute la douceur de vos chants.
>
> O vous, Peuple français, et vous, tristes Ibères,
> Donnez un libre cours à vos larmes sincères ;
> Déplorez tous ensemble un sort si rigoureux !
> Candeur, douce innocence, accourez sur ces rives,
> Secondez nos regrets, et vous, grâces plaintives,
>   Elevez des cris douloureux.

(Ye Muses who consecrate the generous virtues on the imperishable bronze of your sublime tablets, inspire me with sad, affecting

and the wedding of the Heir Apparent was celebrated magnificently, even lavishly. Paris, infinitely ahead of all other capitals in splendour and wealth, also sought to surpass them in manifestations of zeal and affection for the Royal Family. Its head was no longer Turgot, so renowned for his magnificence; the Provost of the Merchants was now M. Bernage, a mediocre person, little suited to so great an occasion. All the same he possessed, or rather borrowed, a happy idea. As it was winter, and the cold, rain and frost might have interfered with the festivities, or even have rendered them impossible, he caused to be erected in the twelve finest sites of the city green arbours which, by recalling spring to the eyes, would drive from the mind the wretched weather that was actually prevailing. Into these spacious enclosures, with entrances on all sides, crowded indiscriminately rich and poor, whose mingling is always the first medium of rejoicing in such revelries. Unlimited refreshments were provided, the best musicians were ordered to attend, and the sound of their playing and of a thousand tuneful voices, accompanied by the murmur of a thousand fountains which ran with wine, intensified the delirium of the countless throngs. Foreigners who came from the most distant countries to participate in the celebrations could not realize that a war, as ruinous as it

lines; add your sighs to my funereal lamentations, and lend to my voice, on the occasion of this royal mourning, all the sweetness of your songs.

Ye people of France, ye mourners of Spain, give free course to your hearts' tears; mingle your weeping over so cruel a doom! Candour, sweet innocence, come hither and join in our grief; and ye, O mourning Graces, raise your sorrowful cries.)

See also the notes of D'Argenson: " The loss was great; she would have been very fruitful, a prime quality in women of her rank,—indeed all that is demanded of them. . . . Inwardly she possessed the Spanish pride that ill consorts with the French spirit. . . . To reconcile the Dauphin to her death, her faults, real or imaginary, were constantly pointed out to him."

was bloody, was desolating France. Had they not been told, they would have imagined the country to be enjoying the most profound and happy peace.

Those who incited Paris to indulge in these wonderful demonstrations not only sought to show to Europe the love the French people had for their masters, but also to distract Louis XV. Since the death of the last favourite all the most beautiful women of the Court (and, encouraged by the earlier choices, even those who were not excessively beautiful) unsuccessfully presented themselves as candidates.[1] Among them was specially noticeable the Duchesse de Rochechouart, who had been a widow for a year—a charming creature if ever there was one, a veritable Hebe. Brought up with the King, with whom she had been on a sort of familiarity at Rambouillet, she had done all she could to attract a prince who was fascinating even then, before he became King, but ever without success. By a forcible comparison, which was perhaps too close by reason of the dubious image it suggests, it was said that she was like the horses of the *petite écurie*, always offered, never accepted. In vexation she took a second husband, the Comte de Brionne, and died eighteen months later. It was thought that among the lesser dames, or among the women of Paris, who could thus be quietly submitted to the King,

[1] " All the fair women of Paris took the field and presented themselves as candidates. Their number was considerable, and they availed themselves of every device of nature and art to attract the opposite sex. Every one was busy—dressmakers, hairdressers, trimming-makers worked day and night. It was as though all women were widows preparing for a second marriage. Never were such sales of materials, of ribbons, laces and trimmings. They bathed and perfumed themselves in readiness for any eventuality. From finery they passed to other means of attracting. Before they heard of the favourite's death, the women of Paris enjoyed good health. Now they found themselves afflicted with terrible headaches, and most of them went to Versailles for a change of air. The chief thing was to be seen by the King and to speak to him. The usual resource of writing was not neglected, for that had succeeded during the previous reign. Innumerable *billets-doux* were written to the Prince "—*L'Espion Chinois.*

Cupid might find a fresh opportunity of fettering the
royal slave. With this intent a ball was held at the Hôtel
de Ville, which the newly married pair and the King were
to honour with their presence. In order to further the
purpose of the fête every one was to be masked. Louis
and all his Court went in fantastic but elegant disguises.
He was agreeably surprised at the assemblage of beauty.
Here were no painted allurements, no charms sustained
and intensified by art, such as he was accustomed to see
at the palace, but Nature herself who seemed to have
chosen that day to expose to his gaze her most perfect
handiwork. Enchanted by so brilliant a sight, the King
lingered before each object of which it was composed
without fixing his choice, when a young blonde, slender and
beautifully formed, arrested his attention. She was dressed
as a huntress, with bow and quiver on her shoulders ; her
flowing curls were spangled with jewels, and her half-bared
bosom excited his desire. " Fair Huntress," said His
Majesty, " happy are those who are pierced by your darts ;
their wounds are mortal." [1]

[1] It was at this masked ball, given at Versailles on 25th February, 1745,
and immortalized by Cochin's engraving, that Louis XV noticed a young
lady of whom he had already caught several glimpses at the hunting-parties
in the forest of Sénart. This lady, elegant, graceful, and very pretty, was
Antoinette Poisson, wife of Le Normand d'Étioles, the Director of Public
Works. She was to become, by the King's favour, Duchesse de Pompadour.
She was then radiant in all the charm of her twenty-four summers. Madame
de Châteauroux was already forgotten, and the obscure citizeness was about to
enter upon twenty years of absolute power. Cf. Stryienski, *Le XVIIIe siècle*.

> Notre pauvre roi Louis
> Dans de nouveaux feux s'engage ;
> C'est aux noces de son fils
> Qu'il adoucit son veuvage.
> Aie ! aie ! Jeannette ! Aie ! aie !
>
> Les bourgeoises de Paris
> Au bal ont eu l'avantage ;
> Il a pour vis-à-vis
> Choisi femme de son âge ;
> Aie ! aie ! Jeannette ! Aie ! aie !

Here was the golden opportunity to plant one of her arrows in the King's heart, but, whether she did not know who was speaking to her; or, already smitten elsewhere, was little impressed by the conquest she had made; or whether, which was more likely, her excited vanity made her lose her head, her self-possession so failed her that, without replying, she fled and mingled with the crowd of revellers, so that he did not discover who the beauty was. An English quadrille, then much in fashion, executed by a score of young girls whose sprightly freshness made them resemble celestial houris, quickly effaced the impression caused by the modern Diana. The fire of love coursed through his veins. In his uncertainty he would gladly have possessed them all, and, as they were masked, his embarrassment could only be ended by one of them uncovering. Since he had seen the first his heart, which only yearned to be occupied, had promptly been impressed by her image. Having waited in vain, he went to the end of the hall, where the ladies of lesser importance stood on steps arranged in an amphitheatre. They yielded nothing in attire to the ladies of higher degree, and had the advantage of that cheerful countenance which is the sign of happiness and is more frequently seen among the less distinguished. Such were the thoughts that passed through the King's mind as he gazed upon them, envying

> Le roi, dit-on à la cour,
> Entre donc dans la finance,
> De faire fortune un jour
> Le voilà dans l'espérance;
> Aie! aie! Jeannette! Aie! aie!

(Our poor King Louis is scorched by a new flame. It was at his son's wedding that he consoled his widowhood. Oh dear! Jeannette! Oh dear!

The bourgeoises of Paris profited by the ball; he chose for partner a lady of his own age. Oh dear! Jeannette! Oh dear!

The King, said the Court, is going in for finance; see him hoping to make his fortune in a day. Oh dear! Jeannette! Oh dear!)

their lot. He was awakened by a mask who came and plagued him ; it was the charming Madame d'Étioles. Sprung from the humbler class, she was the daughter of one Poisson,[1] a low, coarse, dissipated fellow, not, however, devoid of a certain caustic wit which he even directed against himself. He was butcher to the Invalides, a position that brought him considerable wealth. His wife was one of the most depraved women imaginable, entirely unbridled and shameless. After having trafficked in her own charms she reckoned on those of her daughter and, through telling her that she was a morsel fit for a king,[2]

[1] Jeanne Antoinette Poisson, Marquise de Pompadour (1721-1764), daughter of François Poisson, equerry to the Duc d'Orléans, and of Louise Madeleine de la Motte. She was brought up in genteel fashion by an unscrupulous mother and a father who was convicted of fraud. She married, in March 1741, Charles Guillaume Le Normand d'Étioles, son of a treasurer-general of the French mints.

Madame Poisson's potent charms won the hearts of Le Blanc, Secretary of State, and of Paris, Montmartel and Duverney. Le Normand de Tourneheim, an extravagant but very wealthy farmer-general, who left twenty millions at his death, was to bear the yoke in his turn. He became a familiar of the Poisson household, and his financial help was never lacking. When Antoinette was nearly eighteen, Tourneheim, who was a bachelor, induced Le Normand d'Étioles, his nephew and heir, to marry her. On their wedding day he gave the young couple his château of Étioles, forty thousand *livres* a year, and all their expenses in Paris. It was a surprising and splendid situation, but Madame Le Normand d'Étioles looked for something even better, and with reason. Cf. Thirion, *Vie Privée des financiers au XVIII* *siècle*, pp. 150-170 (Paris : Plon). In the account of Madame de Pompadour's expenditure, published by J. A. Le Roy, we find " 600 *livres* to Mme Lebon for having predicted, when she was only nine, that she would one day be mistress to Louis XV."

[2] Madame Le Normand d'Étioles was just a beautiful woman if she so desired, or beautiful and vivacious, together or separately, having acquired these arts from the lessons her mother had procured for her from actors, famous courtesans, preachers and lawyers. This diabolical woman had gone to all the professions that call for subtle and varied expressions for private instruction, in order to make her daughter really " a morsel for a king."

" She could weep—like an actress. She could be at will superb, imperious, calm, roguish, a tease, judicious, curious, attentive, by altering the expression of her eyes, her lips, her fine brow. In fact, without moving her body, her mischievous face made of her a veritable Proteus.

" Unfortunately her lips were pale and withered ; she had so habitually bitten them that she had severed the tiny blood-vessels, thus causing the

inspired her with the desire to become the King's mistress. This desire had so developed that she had neglected no opportunity to bring about its fulfilment, devoting herself to it more assiduously after the death of the Duchesse de Châteauroux. She attended all the royal hunts ; she sought every opportunity of attracting attention ; she used all the resources of dress ; and she had no intention of missing her chances at the ball. After exciting the King's curiosity by her allurements and witty remarks, she yielded to his importunities and unmasked. By a refinement of coquetry, she immediately mingled in the crowd, but without leaving the King's sight. She had a handkerchief in her hand and, by accident or design, she dropped it. Louis eagerly picked it up, and, being too far away to hand it to her, tossed it to her as politely as he could. Such was the first victory of Madame d'Étioles. A vague murmur arose in the room, " The handkerchief is thrown ! " and all the other aspirants were in despair. The King, who had recognized in this beauty the woman he had already noticed at the hunt, was now really enamoured of her. Two subordinates—Monsieur Binet, one of His Majesty's confidential valets, who was a cousin of Madame d'Étioles ; and Monsieur de Bridge, one of his grooms, who was a friend of the lady's, skilfully fanned the flame. The attractive qualities of her mind completed the conquest of her royal lover, who was smitten to the extent of seeking solitude—and a confidant. The Duc de Richelieu, who continued to enjoy more and more the confidence of his master, was ever at hand. He had seen all. He knew all that was going on, and, when the King opened his heart

dirty yellow colour they bore, except when recently bitten "—*Richelieu's Memoirs* ; Soulavie's *Historical Memoirs* ; also the interesting work by Jean Hervez, *Les Maîtresses de Louis XV* (Paris : Bibl. des Curieux).

With reference to the match-maker Binet and the first interview, see the scholarly and interesting book, *Louis XV et Madame de Pompadour*, by Nolhac (Paris : Calmann Lévy).

to him, he undertook to bring about the promptest alleviation of His Majesty's torture. Madame d'Étioles was too obscure a person to be able to lay down conditions like the ladies of high degree who had preceded her ; to make her way she had to submit to all the monarch's wishes. All the same she yielded in such a way as to maintain and even increase her sway. Furthermore, she possessed mental accomplishments and talents that were calculated to retain her lover even after physical passion was satisfied. She soon conquered the mind of the King by her wonderful faculty of amusing him, and accomplished her purpose of being declared the absolute and recognized mistress. It was decided that she should accompany her royal lover during the campaign he was contemplating that year, but in a sort of incognito.

Madame Poisson was very ill at the time of her daughter's interview with the King. The glad tidings prolonged her life ; but, when she was sure of the good fortune of Madame d'Étioles and that she was the official favourite, she said she had nothing more to desire, and passed away.[1]

---

[1] LA MORT DE MADAME POISSON

En France on prend le plus grand deuil,
La Poisson est au cercueil ;
　　Se peut-il que la mort
　　　Moissonnière,
　　Se peut-il que la mort
　　Termine ainsi son sort ?

La Marquise dit au roi :
Je suis toute en désarroi,
Je perds chère maman
　　　Poissonnière
Qui m'aimait si tendrement.

De sa bonne instruction
Vient mon illustration,
J'ai touché votre cœur,
　　Mon beau sire,
　　Est-il un plus grand bonheur ?

As to the husband, he was too fond of his charming wife, whom he had possessed for so brief a time, not to be greatly affected by her desertion. The hope of favours did not extinguish his love, and he could not regard anything as compensation for the loss of one so dear to his heart. Plunged in anger, fury and despair, he gave vent to tears, reproaches and imprecations. As his faithless wife feared that in the excess of his frenzy her husband might be guilty

> Ce galant royal amant
> Qu'on connait compatissant
> Lui jure de nouveau
> Sa tendresse,
> De l'aimer jusqu'au tombeau.
>
> Et lui tient ce beau propos :
> Tous mes sujets sont égaux,
> Ainsi, par conséquent,
> Ma bergère,
> Vous touchez au plus haut rang.

THE DEATH OF MADAME POISSON

(All Paris is in deepest mourning, for the Poisson is in her coffin ; is it possible that Death the reaper, is it possible that Death can thus end her fortunes ?

The Marquise [de Pompadour] says to the King, " I am all upset, I am losing my dear mama Poisson, who loved me so tenderly.

"It is through her good training that my celebrity has been won. I have touched your heart, oh splendid Sire ; can there be greater good fortune ? "

The gallant royal lover, with his well-known compassion, swears to her again the greatest tenderness, and vows to love her till death.

And he makes this fine speech to her : "All my subjects are equal, and so you, my shepherdess, attain the highest rank.")

" Madame Poisson died suddenly on the 24th December, 1745, scarcely forty-six years old. She had been one of the most beautiful women in the country, and very clever "—*Journal de Barbier*. D'Argenson is particularly hard on her : " She was a well-known prostitute of the Palais Royal, who had destined her daughter for a high position in that profession. She secured the daughter's marriage to a farmer-general, but even then her ambition was not satisfied. She witnessed her daughter's triumph and then died of a pox "—*Mémoires de d'Argenson*.

of some extravagance, the first use she made of her influence was to get him exiled. This overwhelming cruelty made him so seriously ill that he came nigh death, but it also had the fortunate result of opening his eyes, and he recovered both bodily health and peace of mind. Such were the events and intrigues within the Palace of Versailles during the winter, whilst politics gave rise to others.

CHAPTER XIII

THE MARÉCHAL DE SAXE—FONTENOY—MILITARY GLORY OF FRANCE

THE Maréchal de Saxe commanded the army;[1] his talents had already won for him the complete confidence of the nation, but he was now in a decline and almost dying. When he left Paris he said, in answer to a question as to what he could do in

[1] We are still in the thick of the War of the Austrian Succession. After the King's illness at Metz and his return to Paris, the Maréchal de Saxe invaded Belgium with his army.

Hermann Maurice, Comte de Saxe (1696–1750), son of Augustus II, Elector of Saxony and King of Poland, and of Countess Aurora of Königs-marck. Made his first campaign against Louis XIV; then, in 1720, entered the service of France. Became lieutenant-general in 1734 and Marshal of France in 1744. Was one of the heroes of the War of the Austrian Succession in virtue of the great victories of Fontenoy (1745), Rancoux (1746)—two Belgian villages—and Lawfeld (1747), in the Netherlands. Louis XV rewarded him with the gift of the Château de Chambord and an income of forty thousand *livres*, the grant of French nationality by letters of naturaliza-tion that were a veritable panegyric, and the rank of Marshal-General, which had previously been borne only by Turenne and Villars. On her father's side George Sand was descended from the Maréchal de Saxe, and we quote the song, dating from 1746, called " Les talents du Maréchal de Saxe ":

> Que tout dans ces lieux retentisse
> Pour célébrer le grand Maurice.
> Qu'un rouge-bord et souvent répété
> Marque nos vœux pour sa santé.
>
> Quelle santé pourrions-nous boire
> Qui fût plus chère à notre cœur ?
> Né pour l'amour, né pour la gloire,
> Maurice fut toujours vainqueur.

(Let everything resound in honour of the great Maurice. Let a bumper, oft replenished, be drained to his health.

What toast dearer to our hearts could we drink ? Born for love, born for glory, Maurice was ever a conqueror !)

such a weak state, " It is not a question of living, but of setting out." He had lost nothing of his activity and genius. After having kept the combined army of the allies in a state of uncertainty and misled them by marches and countermarches, he laid siege to Tournai. This was the strongest of the barrier fortresses, one of Vauban's masterpieces. As soon as the States General learned this place was in danger they put their wonted discretion aside and took a proud decision, ordering their generals to risk a battle. This was the situation when the King and the Dauphin set out. It was a moving sight to see the august father and his only son thus tear themselves from the comfort of their palace. Paris was in fear at seeing two such precious lives exposed at once. If they should be lost, the crown would fall to the Duc d'Orléans, who was ever consorting with the monks of Sainte Geneviève, lifting his hands to heaven while others fought. He was a saint—but it was a hero they needed.

The King reached Douai on 7th May and received a dispatch from the Marshal informing him that the enemy was approaching and that they would soon be at grips. " Gentlemen," said the King to his aides-de-camp and officers, " there is no time to lose ; I leave to-morrow morning at five o'clock. Let the Dauphin sleep on."

The Prince, who had been told, reached the camp before Tournai almost as soon as the King, whom he accompanied on his examination of the ground over which the battle was to be fought. The whole army welcomed them, in their military attire, with shouts of joy. The soldiers had not previously seen the Dauphin, who already possessed a manly figure and countenance, and was capable of bearing the fatigues of a campaign. He was endowed with pleasant features, a fresh complexion, and bright eyes ; the dignified simplicity that permeated his whole behaviour could not fail to commend him to the troops whose comrade he

MAURICE DE SAXE, MARÉCHAL DE FRANCE
From an engraving by Hopwood

sought to become. He won their affection at sight, and his presence in the King's company increased their enthusiasm ; they only asked to fight. Louis XV had never seemed so cheerful. On the eve of the conflict the conversation turned on battles at which kings had been present in person. His Majesty said that no French monarch accompanied by his son had fought and won a notable victory since Poitiers, and that he hoped to be the first to do so.

On Tuesday, 11th May, Louis XV woke very early and himself aroused the Comte d'Argenson, Minister of War. They soon learned that the enemy, who were camped in the neighbourhood, were advancing in order of battle. At this news the King and the Dauphin crossed the Scheldt by the bridge of Calonne, and appeared at the head of the army near Fontenoy. When they had inspected the dispositions made by the Marshal, he begged them to recross the river, but both refused, taking up a post near enough to the firing to share the risks of the action, while still observing the prudence demanded by their rank. Louis XV stood on the other side of Notre Dame aux Bois, keeping as an escort only a squadron of a hundred and twenty men of the company of Charost, one gendarme, one man of the light horse, and one musketeer. The Maréchal de Noailles talked to him and the Comte d'Argenson ; and the aides-de-camp were the same as in the previous year. The Duc de Villeroi was attached to the King as captain of his guard, and the Dauphin was accompanied by his gentlemen.

The somewhat numerous suite of the King and the Dauphin was accompanied by a crowd of people of all sorts who were attracted by the event, some of them even climbing trees the better to see the battle.

Although it does not come within our province to describe such events in detail, the importance of this battle, which settled the fate of the war and, by opening the way

to the conquest of the Netherlands, recompensed France
for all her losses, compels us to dwell upon it, but rather
in order to draw attention to the manifestations of ability,
courage, generosity, presence of mind, humanity, even
gaiety (for the French carry their gaiety everywhere), than
to discuss, as military or political critics, a day regarding
which eye-witnesses and even the most experienced parti-
cipants do not agree.

At about five o'clock the armies faced each other. The
French right reached the village of Antoing, the left resting
on the wood of Barry, while the centre was at Fontenoy.
The enemy were in three groups, the Count of Königseck
commanding the right wing, the Prince of Waldeck the
left, and the Duke of Cumberland leading the main body.
At six o'clock a cannon was fired as a signal for action. The
guns of both sides being equally well served, there was a
prolonged artillery duel which caused equal losses. Each
discharge thinned the ranks and strewed the ground with
dead. The Maréchal de Saxe, followed by his aides-de-
camp and attended by his staff, then visited all the posts ;
he and his suite endured a continuous fire from the Dutch.
He did not seek to hide the danger of their situation.
" Gentlemen," he said, " your lives are demanded to-day."

For some time he thought the enemy would persist
in this feint, and he said so to the Maréchal de Noailles.
He credited them with a cleverer intention than they really
possessed. He thought they would continue to hold the
French army in check and on tenterhooks, thus deferring
or perhaps even preventing the capture of Tournai. As
a matter of fact they occupied a position which was difficult
to attack and from which they could continually harass
the besieging force. This was the idea of the old General
Königseck, but the burning courage of the Duke of Cumberland and the confidence of the English would brook no
counsel.

After this murderous opening the allies were set in motion and advanced in perfect order. They made as though to attack the three opposing corps simultaneously, but, suddenly wheeling, they hurled themselves all together at the centre. The shock was terrible but not unexpected, and they were vigorously repulsed. Notwithstanding this fury, the conflict opened with much politeness and sang-froid. Officers saluted each other by raising their hats. Lord Charles Hay, captain of the English Guards, stepped forward; the Comte d'Auteroches, lieutenant of Grenadiers in the French Guards, advanced to meet him. "Gentlemen of the French Guards, fire!" cried the English captain. "No, my lord," replied the other, "we never fire first." [1]

The Duke of Cumberland, seeing how little progress was being made, altered his order of battle and, leaving the centre, attacked our left. Musketry fire was resumed and maintained long and steadily by the English, with a "rolling fire," or fire by divisions without interruption. They advanced slowly, as though on parade; the officers pressed down the soldiers' muskets with their canes, to make them fire low and straight. Our losses were heavy. It was at this juncture that a cannon-ball carried off the Duc de

---

[1] This saying is famous, through being so often quoted; but there was really nothing remarkable about it as it was a tradition, at least in the French army, to allow the enemy to fire first, as a matter of courtesy.

"This fight took place at such close quarters that the English officers, when they halted their troops, doffed their hats to us. We returned their salute, whereupon Lord Charles Hay, a captain in the English Guards, stepped forward from the ranks, and the Comte d'Auteroches, lieutenant of Grenadiers, advanced to meet him. 'Sir,' said the captain, 'let your men fire.' 'No, sir,' replied D'Auteroches, 'we never fire first.' And, having again saluted each other, they returned to their ranks. The fire of the English broke out at once, and with such intensity that we lost more than a thousand men forthwith, and were thrown into great disorder." *Souvenirs du Marquis de Valfons*, who was present at Fontenoy.

Quite apart from any question of courtesy, the French army was obeying its Marshal's orders. The tactics of Maurice were to be sparing of his musket-fire. He said that "troops should never be in a hurry to fire first, as if they fire in the presence of an enemy who reserves his reply they are bound to be defeated."

Grammont, who was only too well known for the disaster of Dettingen, but redeemed himself on this occasion. He was, indeed, greatly mourned, and deserved that a marshal's baton should be laid on his bier. In the morning the Maréchal de Noailles had said to him, " My nephew, let us embrace on this battle morn ; we may not see each other again." He died with calmness. "Take care," said the Comte de Lowendhal to him, " your horse is killed." " And so am I," was the reply.

The French had insensibly lost ground and found themselves only three hundred yards below Fontenoy. This position, as it turned out, was disastrous to the enemy, who were exposed to the fire of the redoubts in the wood of Barry and to the guns in Fontenoy. The Duke of Cumberland, who commanded the Anglo-Dutch, Austrian and Hanoverian troops, had recourse to that admirable manœuvre which makes him rank among the greatest captains. He turned about the rear ranks of his army, which, already contracted in front by the nature of the ground, thus formed an oblong, of which one side continued to press our left wing, while another covered the redoubts in the wood of Barry, and a third stood fast before the Fontenoy position. The success of this arrangement exceeded all expectation. It produced a solid formation almost unbreakable on account of its density and still more on account of its courage. His troops could bring a heavier fire to bear, and every shot told.

The Maréchal de Saxe, now on his horse, now on foot, now in his litter,[1] for he was still very ill, went wherever

---

[1] Specially in his litter, a great square basket on wheels. The Maréchal de Saxe was suffering at the time from a very bad attack of dropsy. " This battle decided the fortunes of the war, prepared the conquest of the Netherlands, and made up for all misfortunes. What makes the engagement for ever memorable, is that it was won when the suffering general, almost dying, was no longer able to act. The Marshal made the plans, and the French officers carried off the victory " (Voltaire).

the danger was greatest. It was at this juncture that
the Maréchal de Noailles, forgetting his own dignity for
a general who was a foreigner and junior to himself,
threw aside all jealousy in regard to the command for
the good of the State, and served as his aide-de-camp.
Everywhere the army performed prodigies of valour,
which only resulted in further losses; for if here and
there a soldier yielded before the heavy attack he returned to the charge without ever being discouraged,
but without ever succeeding. It would take an eternity
to recount all the great and heroic deeds of that day.
Monsieur de Luttaux, the senior lieutenant-general of
the army, on hearing of the dangerous situation of our
main force, rushed from Fontenoy, where he had been
seriously wounded. His aide-de-camp begged him first
to have his wound dressed. "The service of the King,"
he replied, "is dearer to me than life." He did not
retire till he had received two further wounds, which
proved fatal. He retained his presence of mind for the
command until the end, and, meeting some soldiers of the
Guard on the road, said to them, "My friends, go and
join those of your comrades who are defending the bridge
of Calonne."

This bridge of Calonne became of greater importance,
for the withdrawal of the King was in contemplation, and
he would have to cross that bridge. His suite begged
that he and the Dauphin would seek safety. At the
beginning of the battle they were on a little eminence at
which the enemy guns were firing freely. A ball fell at
the feet of the son. "Monsieur le Dauphin," cried the
King, "return it to the enemy, I wish to have nothing
from him!" The musket-fire reached them, and one of
the Comte d'Argenson's servants, standing far behind
the King, received a bullet in his head. All this is narrated
in a clever and interesting letter from D'Argenson to

Voltaire.[1] The letter from the Dauphin to his wife is not less remarkable for its gaiety and simplicity, and specially for its modest tone. The Prince only speaks of the King, saying nothing about himself.[2]

Louis XV watched everything carefully from this point, which was conveniently situated for communicating with all the forces. He made very wise comments, gave some necessary orders, and occasionally changed the disposition of the troops, but always with his wonted reserve and after seeking the advice of the General. He said he had come to the battle for the instruction of himself and his son. The same deference caused him to leave this position, which was too exposed, and withdraw to Antoing. There the Marquis de Meuse came on behalf of the Maréchal de Saxe to beg His Majesty to cross the bridge, adding that he would do his best to restore the situation. "Oh, I am quite sure of that," replied Louis, "but I will remain where I am." The burning zeal of the Dauphin could not be restrained. He wanted to charge at the head of the household troops. Sword in hand he cried, "Forward, Frenchmen, for the honour of the nation!" He was

[1] This most interesting letter is too long to be quoted as a note, but is printed at the end of the chapter.

[2] This letter from the Dauphin is not of special interest, as it only contains a somewhat long-winded account of the battle.

On the other hand, he wrote to his mother, with a drum as a desk, this affectionate letter :

"My dear Mamma, I congratulate you most heartily on the victory just gained by the King. He is well, thank God, and so am I, who had the honour to accompany him. I will write to you again this evening or to-morrow; and I finish by assuring you of my respect and love. I beg you to embrace my wife and my sisters. LOUIS."

To the Queen the King wrote (also on a drum-head) this laconic missive, dated "The Battlefield of Fontenoy, 11th May, half-past two":

"The enemy attacked us this morning at five o'clock, but has been beaten. I am well and so is my son. I have no time to tell you more, but am anxious to reassure Versailles and Paris. I will send you details as soon as possible."

restrained, and it was pointed out to him how precious was his life. "Ah," he replied, "on the day of a battle it is not my life but that of the General that is precious."

The bloodshed continued; the regiments advanced one after the other, only to be hacked to pieces. The Maréchal de Saxe noticed one in particular which gave no ground, though whole ranks were mown down. He asked who they were and was told it was the Vaisseaux Regiment, commanded by the Comte de Guerchi, the only officer who had been so fortunate as not to be killed or wounded. He cried, "That is really magnificent!"

Already the enemy, sure of victory, shouted with joy, their cries being heard in Tournai. The troops who were lining the ramparts as onlookers of the fight were preparing to make complete the defeat of the besiegers. The garrison even attempted a sortie, but some militia and raw recruits, who had been left in the trenches, behaved so well that they had to return with loss.

It was at this juncture that a supreme effort was decided upon, and it was determined to launch a triple attack on the front and both flanks of the English. It was hoped that such a move would change the aspect of things. The troops showed as much spirit as if they had been quite fresh, and the attack was resumed. Never did two armies, urged on by the desire for vengeance, hurl themselves at each other with such fury. The household troops, which had not been in action, covered themselves with glory. Adopting the plan recommended by the Chevalier Follard, of keeping away from the enemy those troops whose name inspired fear, the Maréchal de Saxe had kept the household troops and the carabiniers in reserve. The example of these fresh troops, whose ardour had grown in waiting, heartened the others, who were beginning to yield. All the regiments, French and foreign, cavalry and infantry, rushed forward with fresh impetuosity. The enemy formation, unbreakable, faced the triple attack and withstood it boldly. It was blasted with a terrible and continuous fire, but its own did not cease. The butchery on both sides was frightful. The Duke of Cumberland hid his losses; ours could not be hidden. The regiments " du Roi," " de la Couronne " and " d'Aubeterre " were seen to be sheltered behind piles of corpses. The army of the confederates gained fresh advantages to add to their previous successes. Our lines, crushed rather than broken, seemed to be in disorder here and there. Several detachments, however, inspired only by their own courage, dashed blindly at this invincible square, but nothing could shake it. All these separate assaults were delivered haphazard and were like false starts in which mere courage is useless against discipline and order.

More than ever the question of retreat was considered. Those around the King [1] regarded the battle as lost; there were no more cannon-balls in Fontenoy or in the redoubt of the wood of Barry. Most of the gunners had been killed. The Maréchal de Saxe had given the order to evacuate the post at Antoing, being only concerned to avoid a complete disaster. Panic began to spread among the French, and a large body of troopers were hustled in disorder to the place where the King was standing

[1] It is a fact that at a given moment we had actually lost the battle. The English were full of confidence, and already imagined themselves in Paris. Did not the Duke of Cumberland say, " I will get there or I will eat my boots," to which Maurice de Saxe retorted, " This Englishman is a bit of a Gascon; but if he likes to eat his boots, we will make it our business to prepare them for him." It was when we were thus defeated that the Marshal improvised another battle, gave his final orders as he hurried along in his litter, traversed the broken lines, restored the courage of all, reminding the troops that they were fighting under the eyes of the King. Thanks to their furious dash, France won the victory.

We are reminded of the saying of old Häsler (now, alas, Governor of the Ardennes), "If the Germans are not in Paris by 4th September, 1914, I will blow my brains out," and of Wilhelm's expectation of dining at a certain restaurant in the Faubourg St-Honoré, and finally of the retort to Häsler, " Marshal, the dinner is ready; only the dish of brains is missing."

with his son. The two were separated by the crowd that pressed upon them. His Majesty's face did not change; it was sad but revealed neither anger nor uneasiness. He noticed about two hundred troopers scattered behind him, in the direction of Notre Dame aux Bois, and said to a light-cavalryman, "Go on my behalf to rally these men and bring them back." The light-cavalryman was De Jouy, who obeyed and brought back the stragglers. He only thought he had done his duty, and had to be searched for after the victory, to receive thanks.

An excited discussion was in progress around the King, who was being urged, for the sake of the country, not to expose himself further. He resisted, feeling that his withdrawal would have a bad effect. The Maréchal de Saxe arrived at this moment, and the King told him about the discussion. "Who is the blackguard that offers such advice to Your Majesty?" he cried. "Before the fight commenced that was my view, but it is too late now. Things are not so bad as all that!" The Duc de Richelieu arrived soon after, and encouraged the timid. He learned that more cannon-balls had just arrived and that Fontenoy still held out. He assured them that he had reconnoitred the square, and that a few pieces of artillery would soon breach it, and that there would then be no difficulty in breaking it up. It was the scheme of an artillery subaltern that he was flaunting, and fortunately four guns, reserved to protect the retreat, were handy. The delighted King fastened on his favourite's advice, and told the Duc de Pecquigny to give the necessary orders to the four guns.

He ran to them, and was told for what purpose they were intended. "There is no retreat," he said, "the King orders these four guns to be used for victory!" They were at once trained on the enemy, who thought himself already master of our position and was only a few yards away. A few shots were immediately fired. The

certainty of being killed the next moment made a man
afraid to step into the place of his fallen comrade. The
square, hitherto unbreakable, at last showed a gap. The
household troops made for it and worked their way in.
The gendarmes and carabiniers widened the opening.
Other regiments followed, encouraged by success. The
forces dealing with the other attacks hurled themselves
against the troops in front of them, and effected several
breaches. Hand-to-hand fighting ensued, and the confusion was so great that the carabiniers for a moment
mistook the Irish for English, who were very similarly
dressed, and made them cry " *Vive France !* " but unfortunately only after several had been killed. Once the
square was broken there was a general collapse, and then
a rout. The enemy could no longer stand against the
French fury. The men, irritated by so long a struggle,
gave no quarter, but slew all that were within reach. Those
who escaped the steel of the foot-soldiers were crushed by
the cavalry. The horses, covered with blood to their
chests, laboured amid the piles of dead with which the
ground was covered. The remarkable thing was that the
total rout of an army so recently full of stubborn courage
was the work of a moment. The remainder took to flight
and escaped. It was like fighting against enchanted
legions which could be visible or invisible at will. All was
over in seven or eight minutes. The French, surprised
to meet everywhere none but French, were at last able
to take breath. They tasted the joy of a triumph that had
been so long disputed.

Each one offered his own explanation of the victory.
Some attributed it to the presence of the King and
the Dauphin, others to the skill of the Maréchal de
Saxe, others to the vigorous charge of the household
troops, others to the inspiration of the Duc de Richelieu,
and others again to the valour of our forces, whom nothing

could discourage. No doubt all these elements contributed to the victory, but the mistakes of the enemy had no less a share. Their first error was in leaving behind him the redoubts of the woods of Barry and Fontenoy, of which they might even have turned the guns against the French. Their second blunder was in advancing without cavalry. Their third was in not having seized the opportunity when the guns at Fontenoy were only firing blank to capture that position. The fourth, and no doubt the most important, was that of the Dutch who, alarmed at their first check, instead of forcing the Antoing position and the redoubts between them and Fontenoy and so coming to help and support the English, remained useless spectators of the battle.

As soon as the field was cleared, the King, with a view to inspiring the Dauphin with the horror he had always felt himself of even the most righteous wars, led him over it. The trembling young Prince saw with his own eyes what he had previously only met in books—humanity struck down by the hand of man, a vast plain soaked with blood, limbs severed from bodies and scattered everywhere, piles of corpses from which thousands of dying men vainly struggled to release themselves. He saw some who, forgetting their enmity, bandaged each other's wounds—the wounds they had themselves inflicted; others in their death agony rolling in their own blood and biting the dust. Some there were who raised their heads and summoned their last breath to cry " Long live the King and His Highness the Dauphin," and then died. A few, concerned for the salvation of their souls, in the absence of a priest, confessed themselves to God and implored His mercy. From every side his ear received the sound of pitiful groans or furious mutterings.

At this horrible spectacle, so affecting for a young prince with a very sensitive heart, he was deeply moved. The

King, who observed it, said : " Learn, my son, how costly
and sad a thing is victory." The monarch had already
given him a similar lesson early in the day when his chief
surgeon, La Peyronie, had presented himself to announce
the disaster to the Duc de Grammont. His Majesty had
said, with a sigh : " Ah, there will be many more to-day."
The Dauphin's only answer to his father had been a flood
of tears. At this moment the King was asked what was to
be done with the wounded English. " Treat them like
our own ; they are no longer our enemies." They were,
indeed, treated with the greatest attention, many of them
being sent to Lille, where all the convents and nunneries
were used as hospitals. The ladies of Lille forsook their
toilet and their amusements for several days, tearing up
their chemises to make lint.

At roll-call the enemy had fourteen thousand missing,
but six thousand returned at nightfall. They lost forty
pieces of artillery. The French paid dearly for their
victory ; every regiment mourned heavy losses, and some
were completely crushed, keeping only their names. The
losses in killed and wounded were proportionately heavier
among the officers than among the men, and, to do justice
to all it would be necessary to name almost the whole
nobility of the realm.[1]

---

[1] LA BATAILLE DE FONTENOY

J'ons vu ce poème fringant
Fait par monsieur Voltaire,
Quoiqu'il ait de l'esprit tant,
Est-ce que je devons nous taire ?
Pour briller tout comme lui,
Je n'avons qu'à chanter Louis.

Aux plaines de Fontenoi,
Si t'avais vu ce monarque,
Son air inspirant l'effroi
Semblait commander à la Parque ;
Ses ennemis criaient tous :
Le voilà, morbleu ! Sauvons-nous.

On voyait aussi partout
Le mari de la Dauphine;
De son père il a le goût,
La bonté, le cœur, la mine;
C'est grand bien d'être papa
Quand on a des enfants comme ça.

Et toi, brave maréchal,
Toi, de Saxe le grand comte,
Si l'on trouvait ton égal,
Je dirais : bon! queu chien de comte!
Car je n'y vois que le roi
Qui puisse l'emporter sur toi!

Vous aussi, braves guerriers,
Colonels et capitaines,
Et vous autres officiers
Cueillant lauriers par centaines,
Je dirai quoi vous convient.
Mais un moment v'la que ça vient.

Les Anglais, à leurs dépens,
Connaissent votre courage;
A tous vos coups foudroyants
En vain ils opposaient leur rage,
Ils expiraient glorieux
D'être terrassés par les Dieux.

Sous les yeux du grand Bourbon
Tous les Français se surpassent :
Dans les jambes de Biron
Trois ou quatre chevaux trépassent;
Chaque Anglais qui l'approchait
Sous son bras aussi trépassait.

Et toi, Richelieu, vraiment
Tu fis bien le diable à quatre,
Je crois que si Cumberland.
Contre toi seul voulait combattre,
Tu l'aurais plus tôt vaincu
Que tu n'aurais fait un cocu.

THE BATTLE OF FONTENOY

(I have seen the dashing poem written by Monsieur Voltaire;
although he has such a wit, must I keep silence? I can shine as
bright as he, if only I sing of Louis!

On the plains of Fontenoy if you had seen that awe-inspiring
monarch, seeming to command Fate; all his enemies cried:
" There he is ; 's death, let us fly ! "

Everywhere was also seen the Dauphine's mate ; he took after

12

his father—same kindness, same heart, same looks ; it's a fine thing to be a father if one has children like that.

And you, brave marshal, you, the great Comte de Saxe, if your equal were found, I should say, " What a devil of a count ! " for I see no one but the King who can take the prize from you.

You, too, brave warriors, colonels and captains and other officers, gathering laurels by thousands, I will say what you deserve. But a moment, here it comes.

The English to their cost know your courage ; in vain they oppose their fury to all your crushing blows. They count it glory to die struck down by the gods.

Beneath the eyes of great Bourbon all the French vie with each other. Three or four horses have fallen between the legs of Biron, and every Englishman who approached him went down beneath his hand.

And you, Richelieu, truly you played the very devil. I believe that if Cumberland had sought to fight you in single combat, you would have overcome him in less time than it takes you to deceive a husband !)

Even in war Richelieu is remembered as a lady-killer. As for Louis XV, the " great Bourbon," he is still the Well-Beloved, but not for much longer. Meanwhile he earns glory in Flanders with such good fortune as recalls the greatest days of Louis XIV.

Letter from the Marquis d'Argenson, Minister for Foreign Affairs, to M. de Voltaire, appointed Royal Historiographer.

" Monsieur Historian, You will have learned last Wednesday evening the news in respect of which you offer such congratulations. A messenger with letters left the battlefield on Tuesday at half-past two, and I learn that he reached Versailles at five o'clock on Wednesday afternoon. It was a fine sight to see the King and the Dauphin writing on a drum-head, surrounded by victors and vanquished, dead, dying and prisoners. Here are some incidents that I noted.

" I had the honour of meeting the King on Sunday near the battlefield. I came from Paris to the quarters at Chin and learned that the King was out for a ride. I

MARC PIERRE, COMTE D'ARGENSON
From an engraving by *Le Vasseur after Nattier*

borrowed a horse and joined His Majesty near a place from which the enemy's camp was visible. His Majesty was the first to tell me what was expected to happen ; and never have I seen a man so cheerful about an adventure as was the master. We discussed that very historical question, which you dispose of in four lines, which of our kings were the last to win battles. I assure you that courage did not get the better of judgment, nor judgment of memory. Then we went to sleep on straw. No ball-night was ever gayer, and never were there so many jokes. We slept soundly, except when disturbed by couriers, orderlies and aides-de-camp. The King sang a comical song with many verses. The Dauphin behaved at the battle as he would if he were coursing, and seemed to say : 'What ! is that all ?' A cannon-ball struck the ground and spattered with mud a man standing near the King. Our master laughed heartily at his dirty appearance. One of my brother's grooms who was well behind the King was wounded in the head by a musket bullet.

"What is really true, certain and without flattery is that the King won the battle himself by his will and determination. You will have learned that there was one terrible hour when we feared a second edition of Dettingen; our Frenchmen humbled before the English stubbornness, their rolling fire like a very inferno which I admit stupefied even the idlest spectator. At that moment we despaired of the republic. Some of our generals, less endowed with courage and spirit than with ideas, offered the most prudent of advice. They wanted to send orders to Lille, to double the King's escort, to pack up, and so on. But the King laughed at it all and, moving from the left to the centre, demanded the reserves and brave Lowendhal. They were not needed, however, for a sham reserve charged, consisting of the same cavalry that had charged originally without success, the household troops, the carabiniers, such of the

French Guards as were not already in action, and the Irish, who are specially good when they fight against the English and Hanoverians. Your friend Monsieur de Richelieu is a veritable Bayard. It was he who suggested (and carried the suggestion into effect) that the infantry should march like riflemen or foragers, pell-mell, full-tilt, masters, servants, officers, horse, foot, all together. Nothing could resist this French dash, of which so much has been said. It took only ten minutes to win the battle with this unexpected thrust. The huge English forces fled, and, to cut the story short, we killed fourteen thousand men.[1]

" It is true that this frightful butchery was due to the guns. Never was so numerous or so heavy an artillery used in a pitched battle as at Fontenoy. There were a hundred guns. Sir, it seems as though the doomed enemy took a delight in permitting the arrival of whatever was worst for him—guns from Douai, gendarmes, musketeers.

" In connection with this last charge of which I was speaking, one incident must not be forgotten. The Dauphin, with a natural impulse, drew his sword with the most perfect grace in the world, and insisted on charging, but was restrained. Afterwards, to tell you the ugly as well as the bright side, I observed the habit, too quickly acquired, of beholding unmoved stark corpses, dying enemies, reeking wounds. For my own part, I will admit that I wanted smelling salts. I watched our young heroes narrowly and found them too callous in this respect. I feared that for all the remainder of their lives the taste for such inhuman prey would grow.

" Victory is the finest thing in the world—' Long live the King,' hats lifted high on bayonet-points, congratulations from the master to his warriors, but, underneath it all are human blood and shreds of human flesh.

---

[1] Although fourteen thousand were missing at roll-call, about six thousand returned in the evening.

" After the triumph the King honoured me with a conversation regarding peace, and I dispatched couriers.

" The King thoroughly enjoyed himself yesterday in the trenches, where he remained for three hours under heavy fire. I was working in my office, which is my trench, for I will own that I am badly put out of my stride by all these distractions. The day before yesterday I went to see the trenches quite privately, but did not find them interesting in daylight. To-day we are to have a *Te Deum* in a marquee with a *feu de joie* from the whole army, which the King will witness from the hill of the Trinity. That will be fine ! " [1]

---

[1] It is also interesting to read (it is reprinted by Arsène Houssaye in *Galéries du XVIIIe siècle*, ii. pp. 36–37) the letter written by the groom of the Maréchal de Saxe, and to notice how this mere onlooker says " we " in connexion with every advance.

CHAPTER XIV

MADAME DE POMPADOUR IS RECOGNIZED—HER POSITION AT COURT—HER FATHER—HER BROTHER—SATIRICAL POEMS

THE winter of 1745–1746 passed in rejoicing and festivity. The Maréchal de Saxe enjoyed a fresh triumph on his return. The first time he appeared at the Opera he was in the balcony near the stage, and Mademoiselle de Metz, who was playing the part of Glory, came across to the hero and placed a laurel wreath on his head. This was not a piece of stage-play ; and the audience, by unanimous and prolonged applause, confirmed the award in most flattering fashion. It was a prelude to what his master was to experience at Versailles.

The glory with which Louis XV had covered himself at Fontenoy and throughout the campaign compensated for his weakness in taking his mistress with him. She did not, however, attract so much attention as had the Duchesse de Châteauroux. She remained quietly in the background, and many did not even know that she was with the army.[1] It was expedient to hide from the Dauphin an intercourse which would have offered him too bad an example at the beginning of his married life, and it would have been well if this secrecy had been preserved longer. The King's passion, however, so far from diminishing with indulgence, flamed up with such violence, and the ambition of the

---

[1] Their ignorance was well founded. Contrary to what our author says, Madame de Pompadour did not follow the King. She was at Étioles, whither, as to Versailles, came courier after courier from Flanders. The dispatches were addressed : " To Madame la Marquise de Pompadour," and were sealed with the motto, " Discreet and Faithful."

favourite soared to such heights, that she was the sole
topic of gossip from one end of the kingdom to the other.
She became the channel of all the favours that she could
not retain for herself or her family. She made and un-
made ministers and generals. She was arbitress of peace
and war. But above all she superintended the royal
pleasures, and for the time this was the one office that she
kept for herself, the only one that really appealed to her ;
and she filled it with the utmost taste and ability.

Madame d'Étioles had separated from her husband,
and it was not seemly for her to bear his name, particularly
as it was that of a mere assistant farmer-general. The
King made her Marquise de Pompadour, reviving in her
favour a title that had become extinct. In the early days
of this new dignity a very comical thing occurred in the
provinces. M. d'Étioles, banished from Paris, sought,
during his convalescence from a severe illness, to dissipate
his lingering melancholy by a change of scene. Accordingly,
he traversed all the remote parts of France, pending receipt
of permission to return to the centre. He was welcomed
and fêted by men, courted and caressed by women. The
former sought his protection, the latter his couch. They
had no doubt but that he would return to Paris and enjoy
great credit ; that, at any rate, his wife, learning of their
attentions to him, would regard them as constituting a
title to her patronage. In every province the most
distinguished personages wished to possess and entertain
him. At one of these banquets there was an old country
gentleman in happy ignorance of the Court, the King,
and his mistress, or even if there was a mistress. He was
struck by the respect with which the visitor seemed to
inspire all the guests, and, wishing to behave like the others,
he asked a neighbour the name of the stranger. He was
told that the gentleman was the husband of the Marquise
de Pompadour. He remembered the name and, the first

time he took a glass of wine, looked towards Monsieur
d'Étioles and cried, in accordance with usages and customs
that he supposed still to be in vogue : " Monsieur le Marquis
de Pompadour, will you permit me the honour of drinking
to your health ? " Every one laughed except the hero,
whose wound was cruelly reopened, and the speaker, who
was aghast at the general hilarity. He felt still more sheepish
when some one charitably explained the affront he had just
offered through his ignorance and indiscretion, an affront
which was the more grievous because it was one that could not
be mended by any excuse, but had to be left entirely alone.

Madame de Pompadour was by nature fond of the arts
and letters. When she was merely Madame d'Étioles she
had in her train authors and men of wit, among whom was
Voltaire. The favour enjoyed by the lady only served to
bind closer to her this great poet, who also was very ambitious. At first she utilized him in connexion with her
fêtes. On the occasion of the Dauphin's marriage he wrote
The Princess of Navarre, a comedy-ballet, with vocal music.
M. de la Popelinière,[1] farmer-general and author, added
some airs ; Rameau wrote the music,—and the whole was of

---

[1] Le Riche, known as de la Popelinière, one of the ostentatious financiers
of the day. " Endowed with much wit, taste for the arts and polite literature, and particularly for music," said one of his friends, " he had good
manners, and kept a splendid but refined table. He employed musicians
of the highest order, and was specially distinguished by his manners, which
were those of a monarch rather than of a private person. He was an indifferent financier, although really not devoid of skill and ability." He
was, like all the stock-jobbers of his day, rich and unscrupulous. " By
dishonest means he amassed several millions in paper," wrote a contemporary, and, when the storm had passed, " shook his clothes and reappeared
with more assurance than ever." " His love affairs," said Thirion, in his
Vie des Financiers au XVIIIe siècle, " are household words, particularly
that of the revolving fireplace." " Madame de la Popelinière," wrote
Maurepas, " had constructed in her bedroom a fireback moved by a spring,
and turning on pivots. It opened into the next house, which she
had rented for the purpose, and through it passed those admitted to her
good graces." Among these was, of course, Richelieu. " It was said,"
maliciously adds Barbier, " that he was lucky to be a farmer-general, as
otherwise he would have had to pay dues at the city gate as a horned

no great merit. All the same, the poet received as his reward
an appointment as gentleman-in-ordinary of the bedchamber,
without having to pay for it. This present was worth some
sixty thousand *livres,* and was the more welcome because,
shortly afterwards, he was granted the exceptional favour
of being allowed to sell the office while retaining its title,
privileges and duties. He joked about his work and the excessive price he received for it in a little-known impromptu :

> Mon *Henri Quatre* et ma *Zaïre,*
> Et mon Américaine *Alzire,*
> Ne m'ont jamais valu un seul regard du Roi ;
> J'avais mille ennemis, avec très peu de gloire ;
> Les honneurs et les biens pleuvent enfin sur moi,
> Pour une farce de la foire.

(My *Henri Quatre* and my *Zaïre,* and my American *Alzire,*
earned for me not a single glance from the King; I had a thousand
enemies and little glory. But, at last, honours and wealth rain on
me for a thing fit for a booth !)

---

animal." Marmontel relates this adventure wittily in his *Mémoires* ; and
there were also the inevitable songs :

> Voulez-vous apprendre l'histoire
> De monsieur de la Popelinière ;
> Sa moitié, pour voir son galant
> Traversait une cheminée
> Qui semblait close par devant,
> Et par derrière était percée.
>
> .   .   .   .   .
>
> Saxe, l'ami du militaire,
> Voulut accommoder l'affaire,
> Mais le mari lui répliqua,
> En faisant tirer la coulisse,
> Ma drôlesse, par ce trou-là,
> N'a que trop appris l'exercice.

(Would you know the story of M. de la Popelinière ? His better
half, to see her lover, went through a fireplace which seemed closed
in front, but was pierced behind. . . . Saxe, the soldier's friend,
wished to compose the trouble, but the husband replied, opening the
shutter : " My hussy, by means of this hole, has learned her drill
only too well.")

As a writer, he is best known by *Les Mœurs du siècle* ; at any rate, the
work is attributed to him, although there is no doubt it was written by
Crébillon, It consists of dialogues of extraordinary obscenity.

The want of success of *The Princess of Navarre* did not prevent the Marquise de Pompadour from employing Voltaire on the occasion of the King's return. It was desired to celebrate worthily the Monarch's victories, and to crown him as a hero.[1]

He wrote an opera called *The Temple of Glory*. In this " heroic ballet " Louis XV was represented as Trajan. He did not run after the goddess ; she came to him, associated him with herself, and placed him in her temple—the temple of public bliss. This spectacle, at first produced in the seclusion of the private apartments, was played by the lords and ladies of the Court, among whom the favourite was conspicuous. She took the leading part, and it can be imagined how gratified His Majesty was to see himself crowned by both Glory and Love. In connexion with this fête a curious anecdote was current to which it seems

[1] Voltaire, immediately after the victory of Fontenoy, hastened to send to Madame de Pompadour these flattering verses :

> Il sait aimer, il sait combattre,
> Il envoie en ce beau séjour
> Un brevet digne d'Henri quatre
> Signé Louis, Mars et l'Amour.

> Mais les ennemis ont leur tour,
> Et sa valeur et sa prudence.
> Donnent à Gand, le même jour,
> Un brevet de ville de France.

> Ces deux brevets si bien venus
> Vivront tous deux dans la mémoire ;
> Chez lui les autels de Vénus
> Sont dans le temple de la Gloire.

(Lover and warrior, he sends to this splendid home a patent worthy of Henry IV, signed " Louis, Mars and Cupid."

The enemy has his turn ; and his valour and discretion result the same day in the dispatch to Ghent of a patent creating it a city of France.

These two welcome patents will dwell in the memory ; for him the altar of Venus is in the temple of Glory.)

Voltaire refers to the patent of Marquise and to the capture of Ghent on 11th July, 1745. Not content to be the King's official historian, he also wants to be his official poet, and to sing of his victories as Malherbe celebrated

difficult to give credence, but which is narrated without qualification in the *Journal de M. le Président d'Ormoy*, published by his wife. Voltaire, all etiquette having been suspended for the moment, was in the royal box behind His Majesty. At the end of the play he could not contain his transports and, seizing the King in his arms, cried with ecstasy: "Ah, Trajan, you recognize yourself there!" The guards immediately came to punish this want of respect, and removed him; but the impulse was really so flattering to the King that the audacious enthusiast was forgiven.

To meet the heavy cost of these distractions, in connexion with which the favourite spared no expense as they were her only means of completing and perpetuating the spell she had cast over her royal slave, she needed, at the head of the finances, a man entirely amenable to her instructions. M. Orry,[1] who still practised the frugality those of Louis XIII. He had already made a commencement with "The Battle of Fontenoy," one of these cold, laborious poems that smell of the lamp.

He specially desired it to be thought that he was on the most friendly and intimate terms with Madame de Pompadour. He permitted, while affecting not to countenance it, the circulation of such verses as the following :

> Sincère, et tendre Pompadour,
> Car je peux vous donner d'avance
> Ce nom qui rime avec l'amour
> Et qui sera bientôt le plus beau nom de France,
> Ce tokaï dont Votre Excellence
> Dans Etioles me régala
> N'a-t-il pas quelque ressemblance
> Avec le Roi qui le donna ?
> Il est comme lui sans mélange ;
> Il unit comme lui la force à la douceur ;
> Plaît aux yeux, enchante le cœur,
> Fait du bien et jamais ne change.

(Sincere and tender Pompadour, for I may give you in advance this name which rhymes with "amour" and will soon be the greatest name in France ; was not the Tokay with which Your Excellency regaled me at Etioles in some way like the King ? Like him, it was unadulterated ; like him it combined strength with sweetness ; it was pleasing to the eye, attractive to the heart, beneficial and never changing.)

[1] Philibert Orry, Comte Vignory, Seigneur de la Chapelle, formerly

of the old cardinal, was unwilling to devote to these extravagances public funds that were required for the defence
of the State. Furthermore, he was not only Comptroller
General, but also Director of Public Works, which latter
office she coveted for her own family. She could scarcely
deprive the minister of it without a reason, whereas if he
fell into disgrace his successor would be well satisfied to
receive the first spoil. The temptation was too strong
for Madame de Pompadour to resist. Monsieur Orry was
dismissed and, like most men similarly situated, he could
not face the general desertion that followed upon such a
humiliation; he only lived for two years. He was succeeded by Monsieur de Machault d'Arnouville,[1] Intendant

Intendant of Soissons, Perpignan and Lille, was appointed Comptroller
General of the Finances in 1730, on the retirement of Le Pelletier Des
Forts. He was called "the useless Orry," and people asked: "What will
he do at Court? He will be as awkward as a bull in a china-shop."
He was the first to apply the system of the *corvée* to the construction and
maintenance of the roads. His portrait is well drawn in the *Mémoires secrets
pour servir à l'Histoire de Perse*:

"Rhédi (Orry) was a man of quite undistinguished birth who had served
in the Corps des Goulans and had been captain in the Dragoons, commanding
a troop of fifty men. When Ismaël Bey (Fleury) first noticed him, he was
already middle-aged. He was tall, with a rugged face, a stern eye, a frown-
ing expression, a harsh voice, a rough address, and an extremely brusque
manner; he was accused of loving presents, and even of allowing his closest
relatives to purchase his favour with money. He used his position to establish solidly his own fortune and that of his family. He was incapable of
granting any relief to the people, and did not appreciate that, by demanding
too much from them, he was exhausting the spring from which flowed the
Prince's revenues. He granted to commerce neither facilities nor advantages, and only maintained himself in office by extreme hardness. To flatter
Ismaël Bey by appearing to share his love for economy, he deferred making
even essential payments, and made deductions from the accounts of suppliers
and workmen without examination."

[1] J.-B. Machault d'Arnouville (1701-1794), Councillor of Parliament,
1721; Receiver of Petitions to the Council of State, 1728; President of the
Grand Council, 1728; Intendant of Hainaut, 1743; Comptroller General
of Finances, 1745-54. He was disgraced by Madame de Pompadour, because
he ceased to please her, at the time when he was organizing our fleet so
that it might be able to resist the English. In 1794 he was arrested on
suspicion at Rouen and taken to Paris to be interned in the prison of the
Madelonettes, where he died of chagrin.

of Hainaut. Although neither servile nor devoid of
strength of character, he yielded to circumstances and
agreed without a murmur to the separation of his offices.
M. le Normant de Tourneheim, the Marquise's uncle, was
appointed Director of Public Works until it should be
possible for Monsieur Poisson, her brother, to occupy the
post. He had just been made Marquis de Vandières; [1]

[1] This brother behaved in his delicate position with wonderful dignity,
which did not, however, protect him against epigrams. He had his verse
in the song "Les Bijoux" (The Jewels) :

> A la cour on vit, avant-hier,
> Zulmis orné d'un nouveau titre.
> Chacun glose sur son chapitre.
> Zulmis n'en est pas moins fier,
> Il pense que rien ne le blesse.
> Noble, mais comment et par où ?
> Ne sait-on pas que sa noblesse
> Est l'ouvrage d'un bijou ?

(At the Court the day before yesterday was seen Zulmis, decorated with a new title ; every one was talking about him. That
does not upset his pride in it, for he feels he is unassailable. A noble,
but how and by what means ? Do we not know that his nobility is
the work of a jewel ?)

As Director of Public Works he became Marquis de Marigny, and
offensive allusions still pursued him, such, for instance, as this satirical
"Placet," attributed to Voisenon :

> Protecteur des beaux-arts et de leur gloire antique,
> Daignez être le mien, dans ce triste moment ;
> Je vois tomber ma sœur dans le débordement
> Et, pour lors, adieu la boutique.
> Sa réputation dont le vernis est beau
> Est tout près d'aller à vau-l'eau ;
> Je ne puis soutenir cette cruelle idée.

(Protector of the fine arts and of their ancient glory, deign to
protect me in this sad hour ; I see my sister falling into dissolute
ways and, then, good-bye to the shop. Her reputation, at present
unscratched, is on the point of being swept away. I cannot bear this
cruel idea.)

It is, however, true that Abel François Poisson, brother of the Pompadour, showed himself worthy of the position he owed to favour. Coustou,
Vanloo, Boucher, Pigalle, Vernet, Cochin, among others, had nothing but
praise for the Marquis de Marigny and for his enlightened patronage. In
1773 he resigned, and made himself Marquis de Menars.
See later on the chapter that is almost wholly devoted to him.

the wits called him the " Marquis d'Avant-hier " (Marquis of the day before yesterday), and it was necessary to allow this gibe and many others to be forgotten before confiding to him an office which not ten years previously a Duc d'Antin, son of the Comtesse de Toulouse, had been proud to hold.

All these events led to a recrudescence of the verses attacking Madame de Pompadour. One day, at Marly, she found beneath her table-napkin this quatrain :

> La marquise a bien des appas,
> Ses traits sont vifs, ses grâces franches ;
> Et les fleurs naissent sous ses pas ;
> Mais, hélas ! ce sont des fleurs blanches.

(The Marquise is, indeed, attractive ; her face is bright, her graces are real, and flowers spring up beneath her feet—but, alas, they are white flowers !)

The insult was deadly, and no woman could have forgiven it. The attack was the more cruel in that it revealed to the whole world a secret disorder of which even her lover was ignorant. There was, however, no proof that the Comte was the culprit. Indeed, the wretched lines were scarcely worthy of him ; but the following song is more generally attributed to him :

> Cette petite bourgeoise,
> Élevée à la grivoise,
> Mesurant tout à sa toise
> Fait de la cour son taudis—dis.
>
> Louis malgré son scrupule
> Froidement pour elle brûle ;
> Et son amour ridicule
> A fait rire tout Paris—ris.
>
> On dit même que d'Estrade
> Si vilaine, si maussade,
> Aura bientôt la passade,
> Dont elle a l'air tout bouffi—fi !

(This nobody, brought up to be a merry wench, measuring everything by her own standard, makes of the Court her lodging.

MADAME LA MARQUISE DE POMPADOUR

Louis, despite his scruples, burns dispassionately for her; and his ridiculous passion makes all Paris laugh.

It is even said that D'Estrade, so ugly and disagreeable, will soon have the entry, and her pride is all puffed up.)

Suspicion was enough; Maurepas was ordered to resign all his offices forthwith. Monsieur de Rouillé, who was totally ignorant of the ports, received that department, which gave rise to the punning comment that they had given the control of the marine to a waggoner (*roulier*). The Comte d'Argenson received the Department of Paris and the direction of the royal stud.[1]

[1] All the songs, flattering and satirical, all the epigrams, all the madrigals, all the epitaphs—in short, all the verses for and against Madame de Pompadour would make a huge volume. It would be too long and very embarrassing to make a selection of them, for why choose this song in preference to that, this epigram rather than the other? There were also, of course, drawings and engravings.

Madame de Pompadour, kindly and gentle, was sometimes, as we see, to lose all her kindness and gentleness. The walls of the Bastille seemed scarcely thick enough to smother the voices of the pamphleteers.

One morning Madame de Pompadour herself, accompanied by Madame d'Estrades, called on Maurepas. This Madame d'Estrades was a spy of D'Argenson's, scheming, covetous, little, with fat cheeks; although a friend of the Pompadour's, she strove to rob her of Louis XV. See, in the *Mémoires de Madame du Hausset*, "The Amusing Reply to the King," which was sung as pitilessly as so many others:

> Si vous voulez faire,
> Dans le temps présent,
> La plus mince affaire,
> Il faut de l'argent.
> Parlez à d'Estrades, elle reçoit un écu,
> Lanturlu!
>
> Si vous voulez être
> Sûr de la trouver,
> Et la reconnaître
> Sans le demander,
> Cherchez le visage le plus semblable à un cul,
> Lanturlu!

(If, nowadays, you wish to arrange the least little business, you need money. Speak to D'Estrades, she receives an *écu*; fiddle-de-dee!

If you would be sure of finding and recognizing her without asking, seek the face that is most like a posterior; fiddle-de-dee!)

As we were saying, Madame de Pompadour and Madame d'Estrades called on Maurepas. " It shall not be said," said Madame de Pompadour, " that I send for ministers ; I come to them." Then she added, suddenly, " When will you know the authors of these songs ? " " When I know them, Madame, I shall inform the King." " You have little regard for the King's mistresses." " I have always respected them, Madame, of whatever sort they might chance to be." A few days later D'Argenson sent Maurepas this letter from the King :

" Your services are no longer agreeable to me. You will hand your resignation to Monsieur de Saint-Florentin. You will go to Bourges, seeing only your family. There is no reply."

The disgrace was notified in brutal fashion :

> On dit que maman Catin,
> Qui vous mène si beau train
> Et se plaît à la culbute,
> Vous procure cette chute.
>
> De quoi vous avisez-vous
> D'attirer son fier courroux ?
> Cette franche péronnelle
> Vous fait sauter l'échelle.
>
> Il fallait, en courtisan,
> Lui prodiguer votre encens ;
> Faire comme La Vallière
> Qui lui lèche le derrière.

(It is said that Mother Strumpet, who rushes you along at such speed and delights in upsets, has brought about your fall.

Whatever made you bring down upon yourself her fierce rage ? This brazen hussy has made you hop the twig !

As a good courtier you should have loaded her with flattery, like La Vallière, who licks her ——.)

CHAPTER XV

MADAME DE POMPADOUR AT COURT

VERSES and songs did not diminish the power of Madame de Pompadour; [1] but she was not the less conscious of the load she had assumed. King Louis XV, who was kept occupied with journeys, changes of scene, the uproar of camps, the movements of the army, relapsed into languor and depression, out of which he could only be stirred by all sorts of shaking. She was fond of the arts, which she called in aid; and she discovered new pleasures for her royal lover.

Some time previously the Government had ordered that attempts should be made to produce in France porce-

[1] All her contemporaries agree that these lampoons in no way decreased the influence of Madame de Pompadour or her power over Louis XV—see, for example, what D'Argenson, among many others, wrote in his *Journal* in January 1751 and August 1752: "She said to an ambassador, ' Continue, I am very pleased with you!' She arranges, she decides, she behaves as though the King's ministers were hers. . . . The Marquise settles everything. My brother said aloud in my presence that he could grant nothing according to merit, and that Madame de Pompadour took all posts into her own disposal. She said recently to the foreign ministers, ' For several Mondays it will not be possible for the King to see you, as I suppose you will not come to Crecy to visit us.' That ' us ' likened her to the Queen." Then there is the song, " Les Poissonnades," attributed to Maurepas, of which it will suffice to quote two verses :

> Cette Catin subalterne,
> Insolemment le gouverne,
> Et c'est elle qui décerne
> Les honneurs à prix d'argent ;
> Devant l'idole tout plie :
> Le courtisan s'humilie,
> Il subit cette infamie
> Et n'est que plus indigent, gent, gent, gent.

lain similar to that of Dresden. These attempts had been successful, and the Marquise prevailed on the King to

> Si dans les beautés choisies
> Elle était des plus jolies !
> On pardonne les folies
> Quand l'objet est un bijou.
> Mais pour si mince figure
> Et si sotte créature,
> S'attirer tant de murmure !
> Chacun pense le roi fou, fou, fou, fou.

(This second-rate strumpet insolently governs him and disposes of honours in exchange for money ; all bow before the idol ! The courtier demeans himself ; he puts up with this humiliation, but becomes only the more a pauper.

If only she were the loveliest of the chosen beauties ! Such follies might be pardoned if the object were a jewel, but fancy incurring so much grumbling for such hollow cheeks and so stupid a mind. Every one thinks the King is mad.)

And again, " Il faut plaire à la Pompadour " :

> Vous allez commander l'armée,
> Brave Clermont.
> Vous avez bonne renommée,
> Très grand nom ;
> Mais il faut plaire à la Pompadour,
> Vive l'amour !

> Vous gagnerez une bataille.
> En général ;
> Si vous ne faites rien qui vaille
> Tout est égal,
> Songez à plaire à Pompadour,
> Vive l'amour !

(One must please the Pompadour. You are going to command an army, brave Clermont. You are famous, and bear a great name ; but you must please the Pompadour. Long live love !

You, as general, will win a battle. But even if you do nothing worth while, it will matter nought so long as you remember to please the Pompadour. Long live love !)

The Prince de Clermont was taking his departure to succeed the Maréchal de Richelieu, who wanted to return, or rather whom it was desired to recall, as we shall see in a later chapter ; but was Clermont, half-priest, half-soldier, a better general than Richelieu ?

establish a factory for the purpose at the Château de Vincennes, and, later (in 1759), to transfer it to Sèvres, where a large and magnificent building was erected within reach of Versailles. The two lovers often visited this factory, encouraging the work by their presence, and causing the production of masterpieces, in a more vitrifiable paste than that of China, and far superior to it, as to all the European porcelains, in elegance of form, regularity of design and vividness of colour. In order to support this costly manufacture and to obtain custom for it, the King arranged that each year its productions should be brought and displayed in his palace, where he invited his courtiers to make purchases.

Louis XV continued this practice even after the death of the Marquise, and the following anecdote is familiar to all: The Abbé de Pernon, a young councillor of the Parliament, had come, like others, to admire the choicest pieces of Sèvres porcelain in the gallery at Versailles. The King, who was passing, said: " Well, Abbé, take that piece, it is very fine," pointing to a most magnificent object. " Sire," replied the Abbé, " I am not great enough or rich enough." " Take it," repeated the King, " a good abbey will pay for everything," and, having found the Grand Almoner, His Majesty instructed him to give the Abbé de Pernon the best living that was vacant.

We have already said that Madame de Pompadour was an excellent actress. Performances were often given in the private apartments,[1] in which the most exalted

---

[1] For the " private apartments," and the performances arranged by Madame de Pompadour, see the work we have already mentioned by Nolhac, pp. 182–200, where you will read an interesting passage. Madame de Pompadour burned to invite the Queen, but that was not an easy thing to do, and she did not know how an invitation would be received. The King risked it, at the same time granting his legitimate wife a favour she had much at heart. She was anxious that M. de la Mothe, " a deserving

and dignified personages of the Court devoted themselves to the histrionic art to amuse the King. It is to her that was due the taste for spectacle that spread throughout France, taking possession of princes, nobles and citizens, penetrating even into the convents and assailing the morals of the pupils who, in their childhood, so crave for spectacles, and saturated all classes with corruption.

She also granted to actors new credit and consideration, perhaps because she already foresaw the time when she would no longer excite the desires of her lover, but would, nevertheless, wish to direct them and to furnish new objects for his pleasures ; perhaps simply because she sought another method of amusing him with details of the intrigues, the revolutions, the lecheries of this public seraglio ; she secured control of the Opera, of which she charged the municipality with the management. This department was likened to the ædiles of Rome, who controlled the spectacles of the great city ; but it was a far cry from those magistrates to a shopkeeper of the Rue St.-Honoré, made alderman ! Furthermore, she got Berrier, the lieutenant of police, to furnish her with the *gazette scandaleuse* of the whole of Paris, and that huge and licentious capital furnished her daily with some incident suitable for her purpose.

Madame de Pompadour also inspired the King with a

and modest old soldier," should be made a general. Louis XV promised to do this, and Marie did not know how to show her gratitude. They embraced, and she accepted the invitation. It was arranged that a suitable piece, which she would enjoy, should be selected. The piece was the *Préjugé à la mode*, by La Chaussée. The prejudice in question was illustrated as follows : "A husband in love with his wife, but afraid to show his feelings because conjugal love had become a subject for ridicule, a ' prejudice ' in society. What a choice ! It was followed by an opera with three characters, *Erigone et Bacchus*. Madame de Pompadour played excellently. Her voice is not powerful, but it is sweet, and has a big range. She is a real musician, and sings with great taste. The dances are very beautiful, and no one equals Madame de Pompadour as a dancer."

mania for building. We have already seen that he had a leaning in that direction, but was restrained by fear of the cost.[1] She made him overcome this objection, and the Comptroller General had to forget the word "impossible" in connection with the King's fancies of this sort. There soon came into existence many costly kickshaws, less suited to display the magnificence than the folly of their owner. In addition to the usual Fontainebleau and Compiègne excursions, she thus furnished Louis with lodgings for his boredom, which he dragged ceaselessly from one place to another. She suggested to the King that he should go to Havre to visit the naval dockyard. Such an idea might have been useful by making him acquainted with, and leading him to encourage, that weak department of the administration, which was beginning to attract serious attention. But the journey was as frivolous as the woman who suggested it.

It was the same with the camp of Compiègne, which the King visited under the pretext of inspecting a new corps,

[1] Madame de Pompadour was extravagant, spending at least two million *livres* a year—see Le Roy, *Curiosités Historiques*; also Hervez, *Les Maîtresses de Louis XV*, pp. 149-151, for the names of the numerous châteaux and still more numerous princely mansions purchased by Madame de Pompadour, or built by her, and the fantastically enormous cost of their maintenance. They were scandalous extravagances. "No money is available for the fleet, which is being destroyed and diminished day by day, but the favourite's uncle, who superintends the public works, can spend large sums for trumpery buildings that cost as much as the splendours of Louis XIV, and are destroyed for the merest whim. For the Marquise alone, work is in progress on ten houses simultaneously. Pensions are scattered broadcast; enormous rewards are given for the smallest services. The expenses of the Court are increased without limit; the King's little journeys are ruinous—as much as a hundred thousand *livres* going in four days. That is for a little journey; what of his big ones?" These were the days of trinkets, of gewgaws and knick-knacks in the "Pompadour style." The mistress, to deliver her daily attack, and to win at any rate by surprise, and by stimulating a jaded imagination, had to heighten the attractions of her person with uncommon and original adornments, while her apartments were crowded with rare curiosities and charming fripperies which she never failed to acquire while they were novel, or to have made to her order, unless, indeed, they were presented to her.

called the Grenadiers of France.[1] This was an excellent idea of the Minister for War, who, in order not to lose the most precious material in each reconstructed regiment, namely the grenadiers, who were usually its life and soul, conceived the idea of retaining them and uniting them under a generic title. M. de Crémille, who had been Quartermaster-General of the Army in 1744 and 1745, and had contributed in his own sphere to the success of those two campaigns, and who, subsequently appointed inspector of cavalry, infantry and dragoons, sought to distinguish himself by innovations in tactics, had asked that they might have an opportunity of exercising before His Majesty. Madame de Pompadour saw an opportunity for an outing for the King and herself, and this inspection, like that at Havre, only amused the monarch for a moment, without instructing him. It cost much money, and revealed to France more than ever the power, luxury and prodigality of this woman, for whom the country's hatred was growing.

This hatred was already very real, for it was to Madame de Pompadour that the public imputed the fact that they had secured no advantage from the peace in the way of relief from taxation. On the grounds of effecting a prompt reduction in the public expenditure, and of relieving the people, the King had been induced to order certain army reforms. The scheme was important, and its execution redounded to the credit of the Comte d'Argenson, for it led to neither lawlessness nor disorder throughout the whole of the kingdom. On the other hand, by creating many malcontents, and robbing large numbers of men of their employment, their means of subsistence, and indeed all resource, it did not accomplish its prime object. At

---

[1] It was rather a reorganization, for the Grenadiers date from 1667. In the eighteenth century they no longer threw grenades, but were simply soldiers of the élite.

first there was a gleam of hope when an Order in Council was published suppressing several small imposts that had been instituted to help meet the expenses of the war. This gleam was soon extinguished by the edict that converted the tithe of August 1741 into an unlimited twentieth, and continued the two *sols* per *livre* of the tithe, in order to provide for the redemption of the national debt by creating an amortization fund. Then, for the first time, people began to regret Cardinal Fleury. The carrying out of this edict caused no trouble in the " election provinces," [1] where objection was limited to grumbling. It was different, however, with the clergy and the State lands ; Languedoc refused to submit, but its assembly was dismissed, and the taxes were collected by intendants.

The resistance of the clergy was not less vigorous and stubborn. In other days they would have threatened and,

[1] The name " State lands " (*pays d'État*) was given to those provinces that retained, until 1789, the right to assemble when summoned by the King, in order to regulate their affairs, voting the supplies such affairs demanded (fixed by themselves), for the needs of the State. The " election provinces " (*pays d'élection*) were the provinces that, in matters of finance, were controlled by their elected representatives ; but, since the time of Charles V, these elected representatives had been replaced by officials, so that the " elected " were men who, in fact, had not been elected. By this time Louis XV was no longer " the Well-Beloved "—see, in the *Recueil* Clairambault-Maurepas, vii. p. 140, the long poem *L'État de la France* (The State of France) :

Quel est le triste sort des malheureux Français ?

(What is the sad lot of the unhappy French ?)

and also, on p. 144, *Les Imprécations contre le Roi* (The Curses on the King) :

Lâche dissipateur des biens de tes sujets,
Toi qui comptes les jours par les maux que tu fais,
Si tu fus quelque temps l'objet de notre amour
Tes vices n'étaient pas encor dans tout leur jour.

(Base dissipator of thy subjects' goods, thou who numberest the days by thy evil deeds, if at one time thou wert the object of our love, it was because thy vices had not yet become known.)

perhaps, even used the thunderbolts of the Church. But the Comptroller General, Machault, imperturbable, firm and energetic, did not fear such ancient precedents. He inspired the King with his own courage. Moreover, he was supported by the favourite, who had need of him.

CHAPTER XVI

MADAME DE POMPADOUR ALL-POWERFUL—THE ARTS AND COMMERCE—KIDNAPPING FOR CANADA—RISINGS IN PARIS—DEATH OF THE MARÉCHAL DE SAXE

THE Marquise de Pompadour had pushed her brother on vigorously among the personages who governed the kingdom. To shield him from gibes his title of Marquis de Vandières was changed to Marquis de Marigny. But she quite understood that in the absence of any outstanding ability, unless such absence were redeemed by birth or by real or even apparent services, he would need support in his position. The death of M. le Normant de Tourneheim permitted of his appointment as Controller and Director-General of the royal buildings, gardens, arts and manufactures. It was a real ministry in its way, for, by virtue of his office, the Marquis transacted business directly with His Majesty, disposed of funds, awarded favours and pensions, had staffs, and made appointments. In the early days of his fortune this young man, fresh from college and still possessing the shyness of youth, blushed at an elevation for which he knew he was not born. He modestly admitted his embarrassment in the gallery at Versailles, where he could not appear without being surrounded by a crowd of great nobles. "I cannot drop my handkerchief," he said, in his simplicity, "but immediately knights wearing the blue ribbon quarrel for the honour of picking it up!" He was soon admitted to the private supper-parties, and the King called him "Little Brother." One day, when his sister was expecting him to dine alone with her, the King came in and, learning that she purposed putting off her guest, said : " No, your brother belongs to the household ; instead of removing his seat set another place and we will all three dine together." Was it possible for his head not to be turned ?

Be that as it may, he at first set himself the praiseworthy task of distinguishing himself in his department and of adding lustre to it. He availed himself of the advantages that resulted from the favour he enjoyed and from his sister's taste for the arts. He improved the status of the two academies, of which he was the patron under the King. The Academy of Architecture, which dated from 1671, had for several years met in the Louvre itself, but without authority, although it had received letters-patent of establishment in 1717 ; it stood in great need of encouragement. His sister helped by developing the King's taste for building. Monsieur de Marigny instituted prizes which stimulated the spirit of emulation among the younger men, and the winners were sent to Rome at the expense of His Majesty to see and study the ancient monuments. He conceived the great idea of completing the Louvre, that superb building which bore witness to the splendour of our sovereigns, to their bad taste in not occupying it, and to their lack of the power to finish it. It is difficult to imagine the rapid strides that architecture made under the influence of its new Mæcenas. The feature that distinguished our architects, a feature that not Egypt, nor Greece, nor Rome, nor Tuscany under the Medici, nor France under Louis XIV could display, although it is more essential than caryatids or colonnades, was the internal planning of the apartments. Hitherto, only long galleries and huge halls were known, and it is difficult to appreciate the vast improvement in the convenience of the apartments effected after 1722 when, for

ABEL FRANÇOIS POISSON, MARQUIS DE MARIGNY
From an engraving by J. G. Wille after L. Tocque

the first time, the happy inspirations in this direction were developed at the Palais Bourbon. We have already pointed out the surprise and admiration evoked by the efforts of the architects at Choisy for the benefit of the early mistresses of Louis XV, but the art was then only in its infancy. The arts of decoration, ornament and furniture, which also come within the province of the architect, originated to some extent under the Marquis de Marigny, whom Petronius would have called *elegantiarum arbiter*—the arbiter of elegance. What immense strides luxury made in such matters! Cote, who died in 1735, was the first to put mirrors over the fireplaces. To-day the humblest citizen would despise a room that was not so adorned. Since then, moving fireplaces, which turn on a pivot so as to heat two rooms, have been devised. Others have been contrived with sloping flues and with unsilvered glass through which the street or the country can be seen. The ingenious experiments of our architects resulted in the invention of heating-pipes which, without visible agency, radiate a genial glow, and make those who are not in the secret think that the weather has turned warmer.

The Academy of Painting and Sculpture was not less indebted to the Marquis de Marigny, and made no less progress under him in certain directions. Although men of genius may perhaps have been less numerous, artists in general were more plentiful and received more encouragement. The prizes and the maintenance of students in Italy so that they might form their tastes according to the best models perpetuated the idea of the beautiful even among those whom the fashion and frivolity of the times forced to give themselves over to depraved studies.

In 1740 the annual exhibitions in the great hall of the Louvre were instituted, at which were exposed to the inspection, praise and criticism of the public all the pictures, sculptures and engravings executed by the members of the Academy.[1] M. de Marigny encouraged this exhibition but, to make it more serious and important, arranged for it to take place only in alternate years. To stimulate the ambition of those artists who had not travelled, he opened to the public the magnificent Rubens gallery in the Luxembourg Palace, and obtained the King's orders for the immense royal collection also to be exhibited there— part at a time. It was there that, in 1751, was shown to the public the picture by Andrea del Sarto which, damaged by age, had been restored by the care of Monsieur Picot, the inventor of a method of transferring a painting without damage from one canvas to another and thus perpetuating its existence. He subsequently tried the same process with the St. Michael, painted on wood by Raphael, and was

[1] This is not quite accurate. In 1648 a Royal Edict recognized the Academy of Painting, forbidding "any disturbance or hindrance." Then, about 1653, were commenced the public exhibitions which for many years comprised only the work of academicians, who were compelled to exhibit under penalty of expulsion. In 1699 there were added the works sent by the students of the French Academy in Rome. From the end of the reign, and during the Regency, these exhibitions attracted no attention, but, in 1725, the Duc d'Antin gave them a new impulse, and even instituted a prize of fifty thousand *livres*. In 1737 the great Salon Carré of the Louvre was placed at the disposal of the painters and sculptors. From 1751 to 1791 exhibitions were held regularly every alternate year, but the number of works displayed was not great—something under two hundred each time.

> Il est au Louvre un galetas
> Où, dans un calme solitaire,
> Les chauve-souris et les rats
> Viennent tenir leur cour plénière.
> C'est là qu'Apollon, sur leurs pas,
> Des Beaux-Arts ouvrant la carrière,
> Tous les deux ans tient ses états
> Et vient placer son sanctuaire.

(There is in the Louvre a garret where, in the lonely silence, bats and rats hold high court. There it is that Apollo, following in their wake, opens the lists of the fine arts and, in alternate years, holds his assembly and sets up his altar.)

so successful that he excited general admiration, and the King and Court were delighted.[1]

Loriot invented the process of fixing pastels and giving them the same life as oil-paintings. Among the master-pieces of the most famous painters was to be seen a portrait in needlework, made at the Gobelins factory. The delicacy of the work and the truth of the colours deceived the spectator into taking it for a painting.

The art of enamelling on gold, which is regarded as a French invention, was brought to special perfection at this time, and was developed until important historical pictures were executed in this medium. There was a " Hercules spinning at the feet of Omphale," by Durand, cited by the Encyclopædia as a work worthy of the greatest masters.

The Savonnerie,[2] which copied the Gobelins in some respects, produced marvels of superb carpets to be trodden under foot by our sybarites.

Furthermore, while the brother of the favourite, under the auspices of this French Minerva, revived the arts and the royal manufactures committed to his care, there was a change not less marked in other parts of this side of the administration.

During the war that had just ended, the disadvantage had been recognized of going abroad, and even to enemies, for those enterprising speculators who, for a profit pro-portionate to the risk, guaranteed to property-owners their fortune against risks of weather and acts of war. In all these cases some part of the national wealth went abroad, and the country was gradually impoverished. To

---

[1] This is the process called *l'enlèvement* (the removal). The whole picture is removed from a panel or board that has been eaten by insects and transferred to a fresh canvas, a process devised in the eighteenth century by Haquin and Picault. The first picture to be thus treated was that by Andrea del Sarto.

[2] This was a place at Chaillot where soap was made and prepared. It was converted into a tapestry factory.

prevent the spread of this political evil and disastrous wastage several rich merchants, under the auspices of the Government, combined to establish in Paris a " Chamber of Insurance " with an initial capital of twelve millions.

Highways are essential links in commerce. Already under Louis XIV they had received some attention, but the science of road-making was then only outlined and in its infancy. It had made progress during the reign of Louis XV, and had attained, under the direction of Monsieur de Trudaine, Intendant of Finance, an astounding degree of perfection. He established the Department of Roads and Bridges on a first-rate basis, with an architect-engineer-in-chief, four inspectors-general, a director, geographers and twenty-five engineers. He soon endowed a school from which were drawn young men who wished to embark on such a career. Convenience, utility and ornament were combined. Those avenues, regular and majestic, that line and shade the public highways were designed later to form a reserve against the effects of an extravagance which would have swallowed up the mightiest forests. The only reproach that could be levelled against this splendid administrator was that he made the roads too broad, thus taking from agriculture precious land that could be much better employed in the raising of crops. There were still some abuses that called for reform, such as the cruel statute-labour with which an intendant afflicted the peasants, and the straight-cut cross-roads to which a man of influence or a great lord could make his vassals contribute for his mere convenience, to shorten his journey by a quarter of a league, giving no other advantage than saving a little fatigue to his horses and a little wearisomeness to himself. At the time of which we are speaking such a road was made for Louis XV of which the very name is exasperating. The story is worth preserving.

In May 1750 there took place some of those kidnappings [1]
that were effected from time to time in Paris which, as the
refuge of all the scum of the kingdom, needed constant
cleansing of this riff-raff, as otherwise, continually growing in numbers, it could not be controlled. It would
be remarkable if the silent and secret fashion in which they
were carried out by tools of the police, themselves the
scourings and dregs of the people, did not become unjust,
vexatious, and even tyrannical. These are characteristics
of all operations that are not subject to the law and carried
out under its control. A greedy police-officer, anticipating
immunity, carried off a child, thinking the mother would
pay ransom for its return. We know to what excitement
maternal love leads; the females of even the gentlest
animals become unrecognizable in their fury and ferocity
when under its sway. The woman in question, undeterred
by fear, shrieked till the whole neighbourhood heard;
other mothers, in fear for their own children, joined her.
Soon it had become not one nor two nor even several
children stolen, but thousands. Horrible rumours were
spread that Louis XV, a second Herod, was about to order

[1] For some time past, as the power began to decay, despotic measures
were taken, leading to popular outcry. When it was desired to populate
the Mississippi, the police seized the women of the streets. Manon Lescaut,
the heroine of the famous romance and play, was one of them. Then, at
nightfall, they laid hands on the servants, who no longer ventured abroad.
" It is even said that in this way the daughters of artisans and citizens were
taken. The great recruiting was effected by the nightly searches of the
officials in all quarters "—*Journal de Barbier*. In May 1750, for a whole
week, kidnappings of children by the archers of the *Écuelle* (so called because
they arrested the beggars and took them to the poorhouses), led to bloody
disturbances. Several archers were killed, and some houses were sacked.
The corpse of a " spy " was dragged to the house of Berryer, lieutenant-
general of police, while curses and insults were hurled at him. What was
the reason of these kidnappings? Boys and girls were shipped off to
America " to work in the silk-worm establishments that it was intended to
set up in Canada." Over-zealous police, or those who were greedy of gain,
instead of taking only children that had been abandoned, writes a contemporary, seized workpeople's children who were in the streets—on
their way to church or on some errand.

a new massacre of the innocents; that an illustrious invalid had been ordered by his doctors to bathe in human blood of the purest if he would escape death. Nothing more was needed to give the final impulse to this fury, which was not to be condemned, seeing that it sprang from the most beautiful and fundamental feeling in nature. The women started the rising in the Faubourg Saint-Antoine. It spread like wildfire; men joined in, and soon it reached the heart of the city. Woe to anyone who looked like a policeman! One of them was slain; an unfortunate man who looked like another had great difficulty in escaping. The lieutenant of police was M. Berryer. The favourite had wanted one of her own men in that position, and Berryer was entirely devoted to her, which had, from the outset, made him odious to the public. He was, moreover, insolent, hard and brutal. The mob made for his house, hurling the foulest insults at him and breaking his windows. As he was as cowardly as he was wicked he lost his head, and fled into his garden to escape from the rough handling with which he was threatened, and of which he felt himself already the victim. Some of his people, with more courage, opened the doors and, by their bold action, frightened the mob, who feared some trap if they entered. They fancied there might be a hole that would swallow them up; and they stood still. The French Guards, the Swiss Guards, the two companies of the Musketeers, the different corps of the household troops were called out, and soon got this undisciplined throng, in which there were more women than men, more spectators than fighters, under control. In a few hours everything was quiet. Those first arrested were hung as an example without any investigation as to their complicity in the rising; and, in order to give the people also some semblance of satisfaction, the Parliament summoned the lieutenant of police before it and told him to carry out his duties with more circumspection in future.

For this humiliation the Court soon repaid him by making
him a member of the Council of State. He was more than
ever in favour with the Marquise, who overwhelmed him
with rewards and honours.

With a view to avoiding the risk of other such assemblies,
which frightened the Court, the King issued an order
attributing all the trouble to beggars and vagrants, who
flowed from the provinces to Paris, and ordered them, under
various penalties, either to obtain employment or to return
to their native places. This regulation at any rate gave a
legal basis for the kidnappings, which continued under its
provisions. Tyranny also took the opportunity of seizing
other powers. The town-guard was a peaceful civic
force, controlled by the magistracy. Designed solely
for the protection of the populace and not for its oppression,
it was reproached for not having done its duty during the
rioting, whereas it was not within its province to arm
itself against its fellow-citizens and fire on them. The
Prefect of Paris, who hated the Parliament, was bold
enough to take this body out of their control and
place it under his own. Roquemont at that time commanded the *guet* (watch), as it was called. He was
ambitious and coveted the honours of war, being mortified
that he had not received the cross of Saint Louis which
had been worn by Duval, his father-in-law and predecessor,
although, it is true, as a reward for an evil deed, namely, an
assassination.[1] He it was who proposed to the Comte
d'Argenson that his force should be subjected to a severer
discipline and organized on a military basis. The minister
adopted his ideas, and the force was supplied with a uniform
and was drilled, so that an assemblage of artisans and work-

[1] It was persistently stated at the time that Duval had been charged by
the Regent to assassinate M. de la Grange-Chancel, the author of the
Philippiques, and that instead he shot the poet Vergier, Minister of Marine,
in the Rue du Bout-du-Monde. His goodwill was rewarded, notwithstanding his bungling.

14

men previously attired in all sorts of costumes was quickly changed into an orderly, well-trained body, deserving of respect and capable of making itself respected. Furthermore, the force was increased by a mounted day patrol which constantly perambulated the town, hastening to the least noise, and preventing assemblies, thus ensuring the constant safety and enslavement of the Parisians. The post of Chief Officer of the Watch has become so important that nowadays even generals have been known to seek it.

Monsieur d'Argenson also conceived the idea of erecting in the neighbourhood of Paris barracks for the French and Swiss Guards, so as to be able most readily to assemble those troops in case of need. These buildings were so many fortresses which might serve to command the town and control its inhabitants.

Some months after this rising the journey to Compiègne fell due. It was usual for the King to pass through Paris on his way, but he was advised that it would be as well for him not to honour a rebellious town with his presence. Accordingly, a way was cut from the Versailles road to Saint Denis, and was called the *Chemin de la Révolte*,[1] as though to perpetuate the memory of an imaginary crime and of the disgraceful weakness of the monarch. This was the disastrous period in which the bonds of love between the sovereign and his subjects began to relax. No longer did Louis XV come to Paris except with all the accompani-

[1] It was in this "Road of the Revolt" joining Neuilly-la-Garenne to Clichy, by the Boulevard Victor Hugo, that, on 31st July 1842, the Duc d'Orléans, eldest son of Louis Philippe, was killed. Before leaving for the camp of Saint Omer he went to Neuilly to take leave of the King, Queen and Royal Family. His horses bolted; he sprang from the carriage and fell so heavily, striking on the stones, that he died a few hours later, in a house hard by into which he had been carried. This death made the Comte de Paris head of the House of Orleans. The same day the Queen wrote to one of her sons, who was absent from Paris: "My poor friend, we have lost our Chartres. Reille will tell you the details of this frightful calamity. Victoire and Clémentine are leaving to meet the unhappy Hélène. Come to console your poor father, who needs comfort."

ment of severity and anger; no longer did the people bless him with those shouts of joy that are so gratifying to the ear and heart of good kings.

Not only did the arts, manufactures, commerce, municipal government, illumined by the as yet feeble and dull light of philosophy, make strides, but the administration of justice also emerged, at least in some particulars, from barbarism and prejudice. Among other happy and necessary reforms D'Aguesseau rounded off his career with his splendid ordinance of entail in primogeniture, as though to show to France and to the world that, notwithstanding the preoccupations of the war, he did not lose sight of his legislative duties.

About this time (November 1750) France sustained a great misfortune in the death of the Maréchal de Saxe, which took place at Chambord, when he was fifty-four years old. Many stories are current about the event, as about everything concerning great men; but the simple fact is he died in his bed as the result of his dissolute life. During his last two years he was a walking corpse, possessing nothing but a name. He fully deserves the reproach of not having been sufficiently discriminating in his pleasures, seeing that they brought him so early to his grave. His excessive fondness for women was indeed the chief element of his adventures and of his renown. Although his indulgences were detrimental to his health and impaired his faculties, they did not otherwise interfere with his life, and his mind retained all its wonted energy. He appreciated the danger of a too devoted passion. How many warriors had been lulled to inactivity in the arms of love! Besides, the excessive attachment of an actress for him was proof that these women are not incapable of the most generous efforts. Who does not know that Mademoiselle le Couvreur sold her diamonds to furnish him with his equipment when he was made Duc de Courlande? When her behaviour is compared with that of a great lady who, in the fever of her jealousy, stooped to the meanest, vilest and most atrocious crime against her rival, who would not have followed the Marshal's example in preferring the actress to the princess ? [1]

A man of extraordinary strength,[2] he was possessed of a temperament to match, although the two do not always go together. As, in his case, love was a necessity and not a passion, he only yielded to nature what was her due. He treated others just the same, and the satisfaction of physical

---

[1] We recall the story of the Duchesse de Bouillon who, having threatened Mademoiselle Lecouvreur with her fury if she did not relinquish the Comte de Saxe entirely to her, received an indignant glance from her one day when she witnessed her performance of *Phèdre*, at the moment when the actress pronounced these lines :

> Je ne suis point de ces femmes hardies,
> Qui goûtant dans le crime une tranquille paix,
> Ont su se faire un front qui ne rougit jamais.

(I am not one of those bold women who, finding in crime a perfect peace, have hardened themselves so that they never blush.)

Mademoiselle Lecouvreur died of poison soon after. The story of the poisoning is particularly well told in M. George Monval's preface to the *Lettres d'Adrienne Lecouvreur*, but nothing is proved beyond doubt.

" Lecouvreur was not pretty, but she possessed much wit, knowing everything and talking of everything. She had many lovers, the chief being the Maréchal de Saxe. She helped him greatly with money and advice in his dealings with his father, the King of Poland, regarding Courland " —*Journal de Barbier*. " She was of medium height, with well-poised head and shoulders, flashing eyes, a beautiful mouth, aquiline nose, attractive appearance and manners. Her features were well-marked and capable of expressing with facility all the feelings of the mind. Her voice was rather limited in range, but she possessed the art of using it with infinite variety and touching expressiveness "—Lemazurier, *Galeries des acteurs du Théâtre français*.

His love affair with Madame Favart, another famous actress of the day, is also well known. See the learned and interesting work by Maurice Dumoulin, *Favart et Madame Favart* (Paris : Michaud, 1911).

[2] " In his youth he was well known for his skill, strength and personal attractiveness ; but, later, he also displayed unusual talents in connexion with warfare. It was truly said that he represented our conception of the god Mars. He possessed courage of mind, correctness of judgment and coolness, of which he gave ample proof."

desire entered into his scheme of army discipline. In Brussels he set up bawdy-houses for the soldiers. A sentinel was posted at the door, with instructions to prevent officers from entering, so as to avoid the deplorable results that might result from promiscuity in debauch. He assumed that officers had other means of satisfying themselves.

The Maréchal de Saxe was not more particular in his choice of male friends. One of his intimates was a farmer-general called La Popelinière. Madame de Pompadour once asked him what qualities this farmer-general possessed that were so attractive. "Madame," replied the Marshal, "he possesses one that I regard as excellent, namely, that when I am in need of a hundred thousand *livres*, I always find them in his coffers, whereas if I go to the Comptroller General, he always replies that he has no money." [1]

He loved money; he was only great in war. In all

[1] See *ante*, the story of the fireplace. It was the Maréchal de Saxe and the Maréchal de Lowendhal who vainly tried to reconcile La Popelinière and his wife.

The Maréchal de Saxe died a Protestant. "What a pity we cannot say a *De Profundis* for a man who has caused so many *Te Deums*," was the sad remark of his niece, Marie Josèphe, the Dauphin's second wife. The Maréchal de Lowendhal, his comrade-in-arms, sought to catechize him, declaring that this was the most certain mark of friendship he could give him. "As you are my friend," said the dying man, "you will do me a kindness by not talking more of conversion." A priest who urged the Marshal to think of his salvation received no better answer. See vol. vii. of the *Recueil* Clairambault-Maurepas, pp. 174-178, "Le tombeau du Maréchal de Saxe."

> Il n'est plus ce guerrier ! . . .
> Il eut pour maître la Victoire.

(This warrior is no more ! . . . his master was Victory.)

And numberless epitaphs, among which was the following :

> Dans ce triste tombeau tout couvert de lauriers,
> Repose ce grand homme, admiré des guerriers ;
> A nos fiers ennemis son bras fut redoutable ;
> Il fut un autre Mars ; mais il perdit le jour
> Pour avoir trop souvent combattu pour l'Amour.

(In this sad tomb, all covered with laurels, lies the great man admired by soldiers ; his arm was feared by our proudest enemies.

other connexions he had the failings of vulgar minds and illustrated the truth of La Bruyère's saying that no man is a hero to his valet. He was very foul-mouthed and swore like a trooper. He had no taste for letters, and did not even know how to spell. In the *Mémoires de Noailles* is a letter from him to the old Marshal, consulting him about a vacancy in the Académie française that had just been offered to him. He had sense enough to decline it. The book known as his *Rêveries*, which was published after his death, was not by him, but was compiled from his ideas and what he had said to his comrades-in-arms. This work has wrought in our tactics a revolution which had already been sketched out by Chevalier Follard (translator and commentator of Polybius), who died shortly after the Marshal. Since then many soldiers have devoted themselves to their calling, and have put on record the results of their studies.

The death of the hero cast a gloom over the whole of France, who regarded him as her defence. Louis XV felt it more than any one else, saying: "I have no longer a general—only a few captains." On account of his being a Protestant, it was not possible to give him, like Turenne, a place in the royal crypt at Saint-Denis; but the King directed that the cost of taking him to Strasburg and burying him there should be borne by the royal purse, and that Pigalle, the celebrated sculptor, should be instructed to erect

He was another Mars, but he lost his life through fighting too often for Love.)

His *Rêveries*, to which our author refers, seem to have been compiled by the Abbé Piron—*Mes Rêveries ou Memoires sur l'art de la Guerre* (Paris, 1757).

With regard to the well-known saying that no man is a hero to his own valet, which our author erroneously attributes to La Bruyère, we owe it, if we are to believe Mademoiselle Cussé (*Letters*, Colin edition, p. 260), to Madame Cornuel, a lady famous for her wit in the time of Henri IV. Montaigne said earlier: "Few men have been admired by their servants." Villefré, an obscure poet, said: "No man is a hero to his valet"; and another poet said: "Rarely does a valet speak well of his master."

a marble mausoleum as a monument and last recognition of the Marshal's services. Monsieur d'Alembert, who was already well known as a great mathematician but had not yet been admitted to the Académie française, had never tried his hand at writing, and laid no claim to wit, made his début with an epitaph on the Maréchal de Saxe. Although it was poor enough it had a great vogue, and the mere name of its author was sufficient to preserve it. We can judge for ourselves :

> Rome eut dans Fabius un guerrier politique ;
> Dans Annibal, Carthage eut un chef héroïque ;
> La France, plus heureuse, eut, dans ce fier Saxon,
> La tête du premier et le bras du second.

(Rome had in Fabius a prudent warrior ; in Hannibal, Carthage had a heroic chief. France, more fortunate, had in this great Saxon the head of the former and the arm of the latter.)

The death of the Maréchal de Lowendhal [1] took place a few years later, robbing the country of its other defender,

---

[1] The Maréchal de Lowendhal (1700–1755) was, like Maurice de Saxe, a German ; born at Hamburg, descended from a natural son of Frederic III, King of Denmark. His greatest exploit was the capture, in 1747, of Berg-op-Zoom, which had been regarded as impregnable. Regarding *Les Troupes étrangères au XVIIIe siècle* and foreign commanders, see Rambaud, *Civilisation française*, ii. pp. 229–231 (Paris : Colin, 1887).

" This general made his début in the service of the Russian Empire. He distinguished himself in the attacks on Oczakof, when the Russians overcame the janissaries in that town. He spoke almost all the languages of Europe, was familiar with all the Courts, their ideas, the ideas of the people, and their manner of fighting ; and he had given the preference to France, where the friendship of the Maréchal de Saxe secured him an appointment as lieutenant-general "—Voltaire, *Siècle de Louis XV*.

Regarding the capture of Berg-op-Zoom, the virgin fortress that " valour alone could force," there was the usual " Song of the Siege," for in those days everything was made the subject of a song :

> Il va renverser ces murailles,
> Ecueil de tant d'autres guerriers,
> C'est dans les actions périlleuses
> Qu'on voit les âmes généreuses
> Se plaire à cueillir les lauriers.

. . . . . .

> Fiers Romains destructeurs du monde,

the only pupil of the Maréchal de Saxe worthy to succeed him, despite the gibe of a courtier who, after the death of Maurice, said : " Lowendhal will be no use at the war, for his adviser is dead."

The King awarded a pension of twenty thousand *livres* to his widow and a regiment of German infantry to his son. Such generous treatment must have encouraged foreigners to enter the King's service, but the jealousy of the nobles and ministers kept them away thereafter, which led to many disasters.

> Ne vantez plus tant vos Césars !
> La France, en miracles féconds,
> Vient d'effacer leurs étendards.

(He shall throw down these walls, the rock against which so many others had been wrecked. It is by daring actions that brave hearts delight to win their laurels. . . . Proud Romans, who overthrew the world, boast not of your Cæsars ! France, productive of so many miracles, has put their standards in the shade.)

And, as the King, feeling it was a disgrace that these victories should be won by foreign generals, complained that France did not produce great captains as in earlier days, the Prince de Conti, who was present, replied : " It is because nowadays our wives embrace their lackeys ! "

CHAPTER XVII

THE SECOND MARRIAGE OF THE DAUPHIN

THE outstanding event of the winter of 1747 was the Dauphin's second marriage.[1] The Prince had lost his august consort as a result of her confinement. The loss caused him the greatest grief, and, if it had been necessary to await an end to his sorrow before suggesting to him a second marriage, it would

[1] With Marie Josèphe of Saxony (daughter of Augustus III, King of Poland), born 4th November, 1731. The best authority is the well-authenticated and very attractive work of Stryienski, *La mère des trois derniers Bourbons* (Paris: Plon, 1902.)

The fishwives uttered their usual greeting:

> Ah ça ! v'la qu'est donc bâclé !
> V'la le Dauphin dans son ménage ;
> Le bon Guieu s'en est mêlé,
> Ça doit faire un bon mariage.
>
> . . . . .
>
> J'avons pris la liberté,
> Dauphaine, en fiolant l'rogome,
> De boire à votre santé
> Sans oublier monsieur votre homme ;
> Vous aimez c't'époux royal,
> Tout l'univers est votre rival.
>
> . . . . .
>
> Maurice vous est allié
> Par la gloire et la vaillance,
> Au gré de notre amiquié
> Le v'la, le parent de notre France !

(Ah, now, that's fixed up. There's the Dauphin settled down. As the good God has concerned Himself with it, it should turn out a happy marriage. . . . I have taken the liberty, Dauphine, when swallowing a dram, of drinking to your health, not forgetting that of your good man. You love your royal spouse, and the whole universe is your rival. . . . Maurice is related to you, in glory and bravery, and now to our delight, he is related to our dear France !)

have sorely tried the patience of France who saw with
regret that so far he had only a daughter. His feelings
had to yield to reasons of state, and he agreed to take a
second wife. All the powers were astounded at the choice,
which fell upon a princess of Saxony, the daughter of a
king who occupied the throne of Louis XV's father-in-law,
a king closely united to his enemy, one who had quite
recently seen the King of Prussia, the ally of France,
devastate his realm in concert with the French. But the
resentments of princes are not so deep or so enduring as
those of ordinary people. Policy, which makes them readily
forget benefits, also makes them forget injuries. Further,
she was the only princess that was at all acceptable at the
time. Spain had none to offer. Portugal had one of a
marriageable age, but that kingdom was so completely
under the sway of the English that such a marriage would
offer no advantage. A state of war existed with the King
of Sardinia whose daughter, although rather old, might
have been suitable. The alliance with Bavaria had just
proved too unfortunate for a renewal to be attractive.
Moreover, the Maréchal de Saxe, natural uncle of the
young princess, whose name was at the time famous
throughout France and, indeed, the whole of Europe,
contributed not a little by his suggestions to bringing
about this request which, as can readily be imagined,
was very welcome to the Polish Court. The future
Dauphine was by no means the least gratified of the
persons concerned.

The Duc de Richelieu, who grew in favour day by
day, now employed in the field, now in negotiations, now
in love affairs, now in ceremonials, and was adapted to all
these various functions, proceeded as the King's ambassador
extraordinary to Dresden to demand the hand of the
princess, to whom the news recalled an anecdote she had
herself related at Versailles to the Abbé Soldini, her

confessor.[1] When she was about thirteen years old, curiosity had led her into the convent of the Holy Sacrament at Warsaw. An aged nun approached her and took her hand, saying, " Madam, do you know me ? " " Yes, you are Mother Saint Jean." " No doubt ; but my name is also Dauphine, and I assure you (you will remember this some day) that one Dauphine is holding the hand of another." This flattering compliment, if it had not been made at the very moment of the Dauphin's first marriage, was outrageously improper. The great age of the prophetess caused it to be pardoned ; she was regarded as being in her dotage. Subsequently she lived in great repute as a saint !

However that may be, whether prophesied or not, the event was first celebrated at Dresden with the blessing of the Nuncio. The princess was delivered on a Rhine peninsula near the fort of La Pile, where Prince Lubomirski handed her over to the Maréchal de la Fare and the

[1] See *Vie du Dauphin, père de Louis XVI*, based on the *Mémoires de la Cour, présentés au roi et à la famille royale*, by M. l'Abbé Proyart. The formal official request was made at Warsaw by the Marquis des Issarts. This unexpected marriage caused as great an outburst of joy at the Polish Court, which, while magnificent, was terribly poor, as the union of his daughter to Louis XV had caused to the hard-up, dethroned King of Poland, Stanislas Leczinska. Richelieu only visited the Court as a splendid ambassador after all the terms had been settled. His arrival caused a certain amount of embarrassment. Richelieu spent without stint ; where could the money be found to entertain him and his suite ? Fortunately it was Richelieu's pocket that was concerned. At the end of the wonderful banquet he gave, guests and spectators carried off his silver without his appearing to notice it. In the public square, white and red wines flowed in streams. His palace was brilliantly illuminated, and in the middle of the lights was the device *Jamque puer tanti mensuram implet*, which meant that the Dauphin, although young, bore with honour so great a name. A mass of rock-work, on the top of which were bunches of lilies in flower and bud, was draped with a ribbon *Florent in amœno lilia saxo*—" lilies flourish on this charming rock " (*saxo*). This was a pleasing play of words in which *saxo* indicated the happy Saxon betrothed. See Stryienski, *op. cit.*, for the account of these unprecedented festivities. Louis XV was very anxious to finish with them, seeing that the Dauphin, who had been consulted very little, was still seriously mourning his loss.

Duchesse de Brancas, who had been charged by the King with her reception.

The courtiers did not regard her as at all pretty.[1] Two days before her arrival at Court the King and the Dauphin went to meet her, and the encounter took place near Brie-Comte Robert. The princess alighted first, and threw herself at the knees of the monarch, begging for his friendship. His Majesty raised her, embraced her, and presented her to the Dauphin.

The new bride would have needed many charms to make the Dauphin forget her whom he mourned. When on the first night he entered her room, the sight of its furniture awakened such tender memories that his grief overwhelmed him and he could not restrain his tears. On seeing them, the Dauphine seemed herself to be moved, and said, " Sir, give free course to your tears and do not think they will

---

[1] Richelieu made the presentations. After the ceremony, letters of welcome from the King, Queen and Dauphin were handed to her, as well as a diamond bracelet containing the Dauphin's portrait from Louis, which the Duchesse de Lauraguais clasped around the right arm of Marie Josèphe. The reception was enthusiastic, and the chroniclers of the day have preserved for us an account of magnificent fêtes. To Louis XV, who wanted to know in advance what his daughter-in-law was like, was sent this official description : " Princess Josèphe is of suitable height for her age (sixteen years) ; well built, with stately carriage ; a sweet and engaging manner ; she walks well and with grace. She is fair, with blue eyes that are large, bright and mild ; her expression is vivacious. She can scarcely be called beautiful, but is really rather pretty. She is generally pleasing, highly intelligent and very acute. She is upright and accomplished, possesses common sense, an excellent character, great sweetness, and has received the best education possible." Naturally this official portrait omitted any reference to her dull and rather ugly complexion, her red blotches, her rather coarse nose, her poor mouth and teeth, and her indifferent face. As to her character, the " excellence and sweetness," when all restraint was removed, occasionally became rather " difficult." The first impression she made was this : " While it was seen that she had an ugly nose and that her teeth had been neglected, her fresh colour, her fine hair, and especially her beautiful figure, were much admired." See *Mémoires de Luynes*, viii. 104–108.

The first meeting of the Princess with the King and the Dauphin took place at Cromazel on the Corbeil road—at cross-roads ; for details, see Stryienski, *op. cit.* pp. 53–57.

offend me. On the contrary, they only show what I may hope for myself if I am so happy as to deserve your esteem." She deserved it, but never won his heart to the same degree as her predecessor. On the other hand, she had far more in the way of mental equipment. Her education, like that of all the northern princesses, had received the most careful attention. Besides her own language she had been taught Latin, French and Italian ; history, drawing and various other subjects both useful and ornamental had been included in her curriculum, and her extraordinary thirst for knowledge had led to her making great progress in all. It was this that led Voltaire, that subtle courtier, so clever at using the tastes and passions of his masters as means to flatter them, to address to the Dauphine those philosophic verses that every one knows by heart in which he makes an ingenious contrast between the full, studious, active life of the Dauphine and the empty idle boredom of the Queen. His genius for satire led him astray on this occasion ; the princess was less flattered by the praises he showered on her than indignant at his thinking her capable of commending the ridicule he poured on Her Majesty. He was obliged to disown the poem, and later, when he printed it, he did not name the heroine, pretending it had been written for an anonymous princess.[1]

---

[1] Here are a few verses :

> Souvent la plus belle princesse
> Languit dans l'âge du bonheur ;
> L'étiquette de la grandeur,
> Quand rien n'occupe et n'intéresse,
> Laisse un vide affreux dans le cœur.
>
> . . . . .
>
> On croirait que le jeu console ;
> Mais l'ennui vient à pas comptés,
> A la table d'un cavagnole,
> S'asseoir entre des Majestés
>
> . . . .

The Dauphine's situation in relation to the Queen was very embarrassing. She trembled in the presence of a mother-in-law whose father had been dethroned by her own. Religion brought the Queen in time to stifle the aversion that arose in her heart, although forbidden by her head as a matter of policy. The young princess also helped as much as she could. The third day after her marriage, etiquette required her to wear her royal father's portrait set in a bracelet. Notwithstanding all the mutual and quite sincere protests of forgetting the past, it can readily be imagined how painful it would be to the daughter of

> Princesse, au-dessus de votre âge
> De deux cours auguste ornement,
> Vous employez utilement
> Ce temps qui si rapidement
> Trompe la jeunesse volage.
>
> Vous cultivez l'esprit charmant
> Que vous a donné la nature ;
> Les réflexions, la lecture
> En font le solide aliment,
> Le bon usage et la parure.
>
> S'occuper c'est savoir jouir :
> L'oisiveté pèse et tourmente
> L'âme est un feu qu'il faut nourrir
> Et qui s'éteint s'il ne s'augmente.

(It often happens that the most beautiful princess languishes even when she is at the age of happiness ; etiquette and exalted position leave a frightful void in the heart if she has no occupation or interests. . . .

Some may think that play will amuse, but boredom comes with measured tread and sits even among monarchs at the cavagnole* table. . . .

Princess, in advance of your age the august ornament of two Courts, you employ usefully the days that so rapidly deceive fleeting youth.

You cultivate the charming mind with which Nature has endowed you ; it is with reflection and reading that you feed it, utilize it, adorn it.

To be occupied is to be happy ; idleness weighs and wearies. The soul is a fire that needs fuel and will expire if not fed.)

---

* The Queen's favourite game.

Stanislas to see, shining triumphantly under her very eyes, in her own palace, the portrait of Augustus III. A part of the day had already elapsed without any one having the courage to examine this ornament, which outshone the others. At last the Queen ventured to speak of it and to look at it. " Is that, then, the portrait of your father ? " she asked. " Yes, mamma," replied the Dauphine, showing her arm to Her Majesty, " see what a good likeness it is ! " It was the portrait of Stanislas. From that moment both of them, struck with appreciation of this charming action, in which the heart counted for even more than the ready wit, adopted her as their daughter and lived in the happiest relations with her and all her family.

Of course the marriage of the Dauphin was the occasion of public rejoicings. The balls at Versailles attracted special attention, and several anecdotes regarding them are worth preserving. At the State ball only the most magnificent were admitted ; nobles in straits had to ruin themselves in order to make a brilliant show. The people of Paris, always eager to participate in the Court festivities, were very anxious to be present, but were only allowed to look on as spectators. The women were specially curious to be there. They were arranged on steps, the best-looking being carefully chosen for the positions in which they would catch the eyes of the Court ; the men were grouped beside them. A person having taken a position on a bench reserved for others, the officer of the bodyguard sought to remove him. The man objected, and, as the officer insisted, the other, no doubt having some good reason for remaining unknown, lost patience and burst out : " I don't care a damn, sir, and, if you don't like that, I am So-and-so, Colonel of the Regiment of Champagne ! " This altercation made a great stir and was the talk of the ballroom. A moment later a woman who was also being requested to change her place, resenting the bustling to which she was being subjected, cried, " I don't care, you can do what you like, but I belong to the Regiment of Champagne " ; and ever since that expression has been proverbial, being used to express in more polite terms, the strong language of the colonel.[1]

The masked ball was not so exclusive, any one possessing a ticket being admitted. The Marquise de Pompadour was afraid that the occasion might be seized to rob her of the King. She was on her guard, and was so well served by her emissaries that various attempts made by ladies who had designs on the King's heart came to nought or at any rate did not prejudice the position of the Marquise. An unusual and comical occurrence provided a diversion from gallant adventures, and greatly amused the King. A splendidly furnished buffet offered an abundance of refreshments to those taking part in the ball. A mask in a yellow domino constantly came to the buffet and made great inroads in the cool drinks, the exquisite wines, and the more substantial things. If he went away for a moment it was only to return hungrier and thirstier than ever. Several masks noticed him and pointed him out to others ; in fact, the yellow domino became the object of general curiosity. His Majesty went to look, and, anxious to know who he was, had him followed. It was then discovered that the yellow domino was a costume shared by the *cent-suisses* (Swiss Guard), who, donning it in turns, came one after the other to this most attractive position. It is well known that a *cent-suisse* is three or four times as heavy as an ordinary man, and eats as much as ten. Their

---

[1] Two or three years later, Frederic II was receiving a party of French officers at his Court. One of them was not in uniform, and wore white stockings. "What is your name ? " " The Marquis de Beaufort." "Your regiment ? " " The Regiment of Champagne." "Ah ! the regiment in which they don't care a damn for discipline." He passed on, and during the rest of the interview did not speak a word.

name indicates their number, so that it was as though a thousand appetites were satisfied at the buffet.

The most distinguished noble at the wedding of the Dauphin was the Maréchal de Saxe. The glory of this hero too greatly outweighed the illegitimacy of his birth for the princess to disown such a relative. All France regretted that he was not a Frenchman ; France grudged him to his own country, for she had adopted him. For his part, at heart a Frenchman, he desired to be regarded as such, and had sought and been granted letters of naturalization. After the battle of Raucoux, the King had given him six pieces of artillery, the number captured from the enemy, that being the way in which Louis XIV had rewarded Villars. Finally, he had made him Maréchal-Général of his camps and armies, the title formerly borne by Turenne. So many honours, however well deserved, could not fail to excite against this foreigner (for they always regarded him as such) the jealousy of the courtiers, and specially of the Ministers who beheld his constant progress in His Majesty's confidence. They resolved to work solidly for peace in order to put an end to his triumphs and the continuous increase of his authority.

CHAPTER XVIII

DEATH OF MADAME HENRIETTE—ILLNESS OF THE DAUPHIN—DEVOTION OF THE DAUPHINE—PORTRAIT OF THE DAUPHIN—MADAME DE POMPADOUR RECEIVES THE *TABOURET*

IN 1752 the Court was plunged into mourning by the death of Madame Henriette,[1] who carried to the grave the love, esteem and regrets of all who had the honour of approaching her. The King, whom she resembled more than did her sisters, was specially afflicted. Madame de Pompadour redoubled her zeal in order to distract His Majesty. The charming house that her august lover had built for her on the banks of the Seine, and of which the name Belle Vue [2] indicated

[1] Anne Henriette, born 14th August, 1727, died 2nd February, 1752; was the most sympathetic of the daughters of Louis XV, and twin-sister of the unfortunate Princesse de Parme, of whom we have already spoken. Sweet, shy, trembling in the King's presence, she hoped to marry the Regent's grandson, the Duc de Chartres, whom she loved. One day the Duc took Louis XV aside at a hunting party, and said, " Sire, I had a great hope which Your Majesty did not refuse to my father—to contribute to the happiness of Madame Henriette who has remained in France with Her Majesty. May I still hope ? " Louis XV leaned towards the young man and sadly pressed his hand twice; it was a refusal. Fleury opposed the marriage because he was afraid to see the influence of the Orléans family increased. After the Cardinal's death, the King still persisted in his refusal, and the Duc de Chartres then married Mademoiselle de Conti. " Be happy," said Madame Henriette to him, " your happiness will give me strength to live." She lived, in fact, as long as she knew he was happy; but when she learned that such was no longer the case, she fell ill, refused all remedies, and died.

[2] Concerning the Château de Bellevue, the name of which indicates its charming situation, see Nolhac, *op. cit.* pp. 250–260, and Georges Cain, *Les Environs de Paris*, pp. 149–169 (Paris: Flammarion). Struck by the beautiful view from the terrace overlooking the Seine above Bas Meudon,

the enchanting position, was the place she chose as the most suitable in which to calm his grief through its novelty, its freshness and its features more voluptuous than anything previously imagined. She had little plays performed in which she appeared herself. *Venus and Adonis* was presented, with the monarch figuring as the tenderest of mortals and his mistress as the queen of beauty. Then followed the *Impromptu de la Cour de marbre*, an allegorical play regarding the birth of a support to the throne. She wished to pay her court to the Dauphin and all the Royal Family, but succeeded no better than with the fête she gave in honour of the King's convalescence.

The Dauphin was seized with small-pox at a time when this disease, already very dangerous, threatened to become even more deadly. The horrible symptoms speedily revealed themselves. His august consort, knowing how nervous the Prince was of small-pox, had a special *Gazette de France* prepared to hide the nature of his illness. It described his condition as he himself appreciated it, but disguised its name and character. Her solicitude was not limited to this delicate attention; she remained by his bedside the whole day, and only left his room very late at night. She performed the most repugnant services in such fashion that Pousse, an eminent doctor of humble origin, took her for a paid nurse. " There," said he, as he pointed her out to some one, " there is a priceless nurse; what is her name ? " [1]

Madame de Pompadour decided to build a mansion " smaller and more intimate " than those she already possessed. Its cost was 2,528,000 *livres*! To enthusiasm succeeded lassitude, and she sold it to the King for a very handsome figure in hard cash. On his accession Louis XVI gave Bellevue to his aunts, the Princesses Adélaïde and Victoire. The former " Temple of Folly " then became a sort of country manor-house, recalling the patriarchal court of their grandfather, King Stanislas.

[1] In connection with this illness one or two pleasant little family stories are told. When, after a blood-letting, Dumoulin declared that the rash was coming out as he wanted it, the Queen flung her arms around his neck and kissed him. " Gentlemen," said the doctor, " you are witnesses that the Queen embraces me by force ! " Then there is the case of the other

When he was told it was Madame la Dauphine he apologized for not having shown her all the deference due to her position, and added, "Well, if your high and mighty ladies of Paris should refuse to see their husbands during illness I shall rebuke them worse than ever ; I shall send them to this school!" When it was represented to the princess that she was taking too many risks, she retorted, "What does it matter if I die, so long as he lives ? France can always get another Dauphine." The Dauphin felt more and more, during his convalescence, what he owed to his faithful wife, and forced himself to extinguish the memories of his first consort, whose picture still remained in his head. He had gone so far as to require the second to wear bracelets containing miniatures of her predecessor. But he suppressed all these mementoes of his first love, and entered into closer and closer intimacy with his present wife, his gratitude making up for what he lacked of affection.

The King could not, on this occasion, avoid breaking his resolve not to show himself to the Parisians, and went with the Queen, the Dauphin and the Royal Family to Notre Dame to render solemn thanks to God for having restored to health the heir to the throne, and to participate in a *Te Deum*.

During the illness and convalescence of the Dauphin, the Marquis de Paulmy inspected the fortresses and the troops in the south of France as representative of the Ministry for War, continuing the important work that had been started in Flanders by his uncle after the making of peace. A laudable rivalry animated the Ministers, for the Minister of Marine also went on a tour of inspection

doctor, Pousse, who asked Marie Josèphe, "What is your name, my girl ?" and who, taking Louis XV by a button, said, "Monsieur, Monsieur, I don't know how you are addressed, but you are a good papa, and you know we are all your children. We share your grief. But be of good cheer, your son will be restored to you." The royal family were highly amused at these breaches of etiquette.

to Dieppe and the other Channel ports. M. de Paulmy reported to the King on his return that, wherever he had been, the people had shown the liveliest interest in the Dauphin's illness and recovery, manifesting their feelings of grief and joy in turn. Specially he had been pleased that the Protestants in those cantons, although they had been defamed with the accusation of having contemplated revolt during the war, were to be found in their places of worship imploring Heaven for the preservation of the Dauphin.

That prince was little thought of by the nation.[1]

[1] We have reached 1749-1750, and here is the portrait of the Dauphin drawn by the Duc de Luynes, a conscientious and impartial writer : " He is still very childish. He lacks discretion, being capable of saying to a lady of high rank, 'You have a lover; I can tell you his name.' His judgment is not yet ripe enough to enable him to appreciate the consequences of such language. He has no pleasures ; hunting bores him, and he cannot bear the stage or play. He does not take after his father's family ; from his mother he inherits that tranquillity which degenerates into indifference and apathy. The Bourbon blood and the Slav blood have not blended. He makes locks (as later on did his son, Louis XVI) ; he plays the organ and the violin ; and he reads pious books. This indolent life induces stoutness. He is unknown to the people, who have for him nowadays neither love nor hatred. He is, indeed, of no account. His wife, Marie Josèphe, has lost many illusions, but does her best to be amiable and cheerful. All the same, there are many differences of temper between them which are known to their circle, and even beyond. The Dauphine bears her misfortune patiently ; satirical songs abound."

> Que monseigneur le gros Dauphin
> Ait l'esprit comme la figure,
> Que la Dauphine ait des enfants
> Ou qu'elle devienne stérile,
>
> .   .   .   .   .
> Ah ! le voilà ! Ah, le voici
> Celui qui n'en a nul souci !

(Let his Royal Highness the fat Dauphin have a mind like his face; let the Dauphine have children or be barren. . . . Ah ! there he is, here he is ! he who doesn't care !)

But soon the situation became easier. The Dauphin and Dauphine showed themselves more often to the Parisians, which pleased them, or, I should rather say, won them over. It became possible for the Maréchal de Saxe to write to Augustus III : " The Dauphine is getting stouter. She

During his childhood his cleverness was constantly mentioned, but after his education was finished, and particularly after his second marriage, he appeared to be a nobody. His conduct and morals won respect, but he was regarded as a bigot who spent a part of his time in chanting at the lectern, who was shocked by an uncovered neck and, like Tartuffe, required that a modest kerchief should hide so scandalous a spectacle. Many petty and childish acts were attributed to him. During his illness, however, the French, inspired solely by the blind love for their monarch, of whatever character, that always characterized the race, only saw in the Dauphin the hope of the kingdom and, on his recovery, gave vent to the liveliest transports. Among the princes the Duc d'Orléans, who would have gained the most by the death of the Dauphin, regarded it as politic to show his joy by the most magnificent entertainments ; and the favourite, who knew how much he hated her and in turn detested him whole-heartedly, affected to show her zeal by a new allegorical fête relating to the happy event. She told the King about it beforehand as being her own idea. The scene, which was presented at the Château de Bellevue, represented several caverns surrounding a lake, in the midst of which was an illuminated Dauphin. Many monsters, spitting out fire and flame, came to assail him, but Apollo descended from Olympus on a cloud (all the gods shared in the spectacle) and smote the monsters with his lightning, whereupon fireworks completed their destruction. This device was followed by the Palace of the Sun, all radiant with light, in which the

is very well, the Dauphin is very fond of her . but he is still a child, and makes her life rather hard." No doubt there were still some shadows to the picture, but, as the hero of Fontenoy goes on to say, " The Dauphine has sense and will gradually improve the situation." Enjoying the support of Louis XV she so succeeded in " improving the situation," that they had eight children, among whom were Louis XVI, Louis XVIII and Charles X, the last Bourbon to reign.

Dauphin reappeared in his pristine brilliance by means
of a rapid illumination. The King was too infatuated
with his mistress not to praise her. The tame courtiers
admitted to the fête found it all delightful, but when
they returned to Paris they agreed that nothing more
trivial, more dull, and more ridiculous had ever been
imagined.

The curious thing was that the hero of the entertainment was not present, nor any member of the Royal Family.
There was a feud between them and the Marquise. If the
gift had been a hundred times better it would not have
altered the Dauphin's opinion. He had, shortly before
being stricken down with small-pox, received an affront
which he had not forgotten. Monsieur Sylvestre, his
drawing-teacher, having solicited the post of keeper of the
drawings in the royal collection rendered vacant by the
death of Coypel, and Monsieur Cochin the younger, a
toady of the Marquis de Vandières, having received the
preference, the former, with the bitterness of wounded
pride, which is even more touchy in artists, if that is
possible, than in writers, wrote an insulting letter to the
Marquis reproaching him with his choice. The latter
was furious, and rushed with the letter to his sister,
who showed it to the King. His Majesty clapped
Monsieur Sylvestre into the For l'Evêque, and it needed
all the interest of his august pupil to get him out of
this scrape.[1]

Louis XV compensated the Marquise de Pompadour
for his son's contempt with new favours. As a token of
his pleasure with the fête we have just described, he granted
her, on the 18th October, 1752, the *tabouret* and the prerogatives of a duchess. It can readily be imagined how
furious was the Dauphin, who, on the occasion of her first

[1] Mademoiselle de Sylvestre was not the sister but the daughter of
Sylvestre, " the painter of the Saxon Court."

presentation to him, had made a gesture of insulting disgust [1] when he gave the beauty the embrace of ceremony.
The Marquise could not see this gesture, but all the onlookers appreciated how strongly it revealed his extreme
displeasure at the ceremony. His action resulted in his
being banished from the King's presence for some time.

[1] At that time the Marquise set an example of the most fervent piety.
She went to Mass daily, fasted, abstained from meat on Fridays, and even
abandoned the use of rouge on her permanently discoloured lips. It was
then, in February 1756, that she was appointed lady-in-waiting to the
Queen. Marie Leczynska was apprized of this by a letter from the King, to
which she replied : " Sire, I have a King in Heaven who gives me strength
to bear my troubles, and a king on earth whom I will always obey."
Madame de Pompadour performed her duties as if she had never done
anything else. The ill-feeling and vexation can be imagined. There were
at the Court a " Queen and Dauphin party " and a " Pompadour party."

CHAPTER XIX

MADAME DE POMPADOUR AND HER DAUGHTER—A GOOD
MOTHER—SHE LOSES HER DAUGHTER—HER SINCERE
REGRETS—M. POISSON AGAIN—THE PARC-AUX-CERFS

SINCE she had become a duchess, Madame de
Pompadour had flown even higher, and, to be
suitably housed, she had spent about six hundred
thousand *livres* on the purchase of the Hôtel
d'Évreux ; a knight of St. Louis served her as equerry,
and a young lady of condition as lady of the bedchamber.
She had appointed as her intendant a lawyer from the
Châtelet named Colin, whom also she enabled to wear the
Cross by getting him a post in the Order. Her vanity led
her to want to procure the blue ribbon [1] for her brother,
so that he might approach nearer to her as the King continually heaped new honours upon her. The monarch,
who refused her nothing, was disposed to agree, but a noble
whom he consulted replied wittily that the fish (Poisson)
was not big enough to be done in wine (*au bleu*). Louis XV,
who was very quick, understood the delicate significance
of this saying, and did nothing till several years later when
the Marquis de Vandières, having been changed into the
Marquis de Marigny, was appointed Secretary to the Order,
a post requiring no credentials. To pave the way for this
dignity the King had declared, in the patent of the mar-
quisate which he had created in his favour, that he required
that this newcomer should enjoy the honours attaching

---

[1] The insignia of the Order of the Holy Ghost, instituted by Henri III,
who was elected King of Poland on Whit-Sunday.

to the high nobility, to those of high rank. Then he was presented at Court under his new title.

But the person on whom the favourite lavished all her kindness was her only daughter, who was called Mademoiselle or Madame Alexandrine, like a lady of high quality or even a princess. She was charming, being possessed of all her mother's graces. She was at the Convent of the Assumption, where she was brought up like a princess, and was reaching an age to marry. Madame de Pompadour cast her eyes on the Duc de Fronsac,[1] the son of the Maréchal de Richelieu. She counted on the less objection as the father was paying her the most assiduous court, was smothered with royal favours, and had always shown the greatest deference to the tastes, caprices and fancies of his master. Not long before he had been competing with the Duc de la Vallière for a sort of servitude under the Marquise in connexion with the little entertainments she gave. The latter superintended them, as a man of letters and one in favour with the King. The Duc de Richelieu, in his capacity of Gentleman of the Bedchamber, claimed this honour, which some deemed unworthy of their rank, and obtained the preference. Furthermore, the Vignerot family was neither old enough nor distinguished enough

[1] Madame de Pompadour saw that her daughter Alexandrine received the most careful and refined education obtainable. Brought up like a princess, she was, like princesses, called only by her baptismal name. " She is as beautiful as an angel and possessed of an unusually precocious mind." It can be taken for granted that the Convent of the Assumption did not possess a pupil who was more pampered ; but when she was about ten years old she ceased to improve in appearance. " So long as she is not repulsive, I shall be content," wrote her mother, " for I am by no means anxious for her to possess exceptional beauty. That only makes enemies of the whole female sex who, with their husbands, make up two-thirds of society." We have said that Madame de Pompadour would gladly have married her daughter to the Comte du Luc, the son whom Louis XV had had by Madame de Vintimille. She caused the two children, the King and herself, to meet in the grounds of Bellevue. " They would make a lovely pair," she suggested to the King, who pretended not to hear. This incident, cleverly described, should be read in the *Mémoires de Madame du Hausset*.

to be very difficult. She knew of the compliment that a
sarcastic courtier had paid him when he succeeded the
Duc de Rochechouart, "I congratulate you, Monsieur le
Duc; at last you are a gentleman," a remark which, under
the appearance of a compliment on his new appointment,
and by means of a play of words, constituted a cruel insult
in respect of his birth. The Duc de Richelieu not having
sunk so low as to feel flattered by the proposal but, on the
other hand, valuing the favour of the Marquise too highly
to wish to offer a blank refusal, thought to get out of the
difficulty cleverly by replying that he appreciated her
choice and was grateful for it, but that, as his son had the
honour to be related through his mother to the princes of
the House of Lorraine, he could not dispose of him without
their approval, which he would seek forthwith if she adhered
to her suggestion. Madame de Pompadour saw what
would be the result, and feared the ridicule that would
fall on her if her wish became public, and the discredit
that would follow a refusal. She preferred to keep the
matter quiet, to wait, to negotiate, which was exactly
what the Marshal wanted, as he hoped as time went on
to find some way out of his embarrassment. He had the
good fortune to see a very certain means of escape, for
Alexandrine died soon after. Her mother was plunged in
grief; the weddings of her relatives, Mesdemoiselles de
Baschy and de Guitry, which were to take place with
much splendour at Bellevue, were put off, and were
celebrated without any ceremony. The young lady's
epitaph commenced in this remarkable fashion :

> Here lies ALEXANDRINE, daughter of Messire Joseph Le
> Normant and of Jeanne Poisson, Marquise de Pompadour, Dame de
> Crécy, etc. etc.

A few months later the body of this precious child
was transferred with great pomp from the Assumption to

one of M. de Créqui's chapels at the Capucines, which the
mother had purchased for the burial of her family, intending to have a magnificent mausoleum erected for them.[1]

Another death, which followed soon after, should,
according to natural feelings, have added to Madame de
Pompadour's grief, but really occasioned relief by ridding
her of a continual burden. She lost her father, Monsieur
Poisson, a person devoid of education, of manners, of
decency, of any regard for public opinion; he was a
constant anxiety, a source of perpetual humiliation. She
dared not have him near her because he was quite un-
presentable and could not be made decent. She could not
get rid of him because she could not bring herself to confine
the author of her days, and because a mere *lettre de cachet*
would not restrain him, and she feared that any more open
steps would draw further attention to his vileness.

His daughter had therefore adopted the attitude of
shutting her eyes to the disgrace he brought upon her
and of taking no notice of his failings and uncouthness.
She was afraid to refuse him anything, and humoured him
as much as possible. As soon as he appeared he was
admitted. One day a new footman who did not know
him and was not prepossessed by his vulgar appearance and
ridiculous garb, made some difficulty about showing him
in. " Rascal," he cried, " learn that I am the father of the
King's whore ! " He treated his son no better, regarding
him as a low fellow " of whom it would be hard work for
him to make anything."

---

[1] As a matter of fact, Madame de Pompadour loved only one person
with real sincerity—her daughter Alexandrine, who died suddenly on the
15th June, 1754, as the result of terrible convulsions. She was borne, in
great solemnity, to the splendid vault of the Church of the Capucines, in
the Place Vendôme, in the part of the Créqui chapel that the Duc de la
Trémoille had sold to Madame de Pompadour, and where Madame Poisson
had already been buried. The mother's grief was real and deep. " She
fell so ill as to cause serious anxiety to her circle."

One day, sitting at table with a lot of financial magnates after a splendid dinner, and with his head heated with wine, he roared out like a madman, " Gentlemen, do you know what makes me laugh ? It is to see us all sitting here surrounded by such pomp and splendour. A stranger coming in would take us for a gathering of princes, whereas you, Monsieur de Montmartel, are the son of an innkeeper ; you, Monsieur de Savalette, the son of a vinegar-maker ; you, Bouret, the son of a lackey. I—every one knows who I am ! " So long as he spoke thus of himself he felt entitled to say even more offensive things of the other guests ; and of them all not only did not one come even from a decent bourgeois family but many owed their fortune to the most unscrupulous and disgraceful means.

Some said that what made Madame de Pompadour feel her daughter's loss the more bitterly was to see herself cheated of the hope that she might succeed her in the King's favour. She knew that incest had no terrors for the monarch, but seemed rather to add a zest to his pleasures. The victim of an unpleasant complaint which had obliged her lover to forsake her couch, it would have been only a slight blow to her ambition if she could have seen herself thus maintain a position at Court. Fortunately such assistance was unnecessary, for she had acquired such an ascendancy over Louis that he remained her slave, notwithstanding her disability. It is true her situation demanded not only unrelaxing vigilance but also despicable abasement. She had unceasingly to keep away from the King's little suppers all the ladies of rank who made an impression on him, and even punish some, who had sought to be too successful, with banishment.[1] She had also, now that she had become superintendent of his pleasures,

[1] Regarding all these many passing fancies, rivals for a shorter or longer period of Madame de Pompadour, see the interesting *Louis XV intime et les petites maîtresses* by Comte Fleury (Paris : Plon, 1899).

to search the kingdom for new and unknown beauties with whom to recruit his harem, of which she was in absolute control. Such was the origin of the Parc-aux-Cerfs (Deer-park), that grave of innocence and simplicity in which were swallowed up so many victims who, when they eventually returned to the world, brought with them the corruption, the love of debauchery, and all the vices they naturally acquired from the infamous officials of such a place.

Quite apart from the damage to morals wrought by this abominable establishment, it is terrible to calculate the immense sums it cost the State. Indeed, who could arrive at the cost of that chain of procurers, principal and assistant, who busied themselves searching in all the corners of the country, of conveying to their destination the objects of the search, of polishing them up, dressing them, perfuming them, and furnishing them with all the means of seduction that art could contribute ? To this must be added the gratuities presented to those who were not successful in arousing the dulled passions of the sultan, but had nevertheless to be paid for their submission, for their discretion, and still more for eventually being despised. There were also the rewards for those nymphs who were more fortunate and received the monarch for a time in their arms and caused the fire of passion to burn in his veins. Finally, there were the sacred undertakings to these girls who bore in their womb the precious fruit of their fecundity. It can be seen that on the average each of these girls must have cost the public purse at least a million. If only two a week, that is to say a thousand in ten years, passed through this strange reservoir, we reach an expenditure of a milliard, and this does not include the maintenance of the children sprung from these clandestine unions. These expenses were accompanied by no compensating economies in those of the favourite, so that the Parc-aux-Cerfs may be regarded as one of the chief causes of the wastage of the national income. In this way the drafts became more and more exorbitant until the Parlement of Paris, in a protest addressed to the King, pointed out that in the time of Louis XIV they had never exceeded ten millions whereas now they exceeded a hundred millions.[1]

[1] With regard to the Parc-aux-Cerfs a whole volume is called for, but we must and will content ourselves with a short note. No doubt the Parc-aux-Cerfs existed, and M. le Roy, in his *Curiosités Historiques*, has definitely traced its location. " The secluded pavilion to which the King resorted without being recognized was in the quarter of the Parc-aux-Cerfs at Versailles. It was very small, and could only house one or, at most, two lodgers at a time." Although virtue might well be shocked, there was nothing monstrous about the place, nor indeed was there anything that greatly outraged the customs of the day, except that the King, who took no thought of cost, sometimes spent more than a financier. The fact is that everything concerning royal personages is liable to exaggeration, and the low pleasures of a licentious man become, in the public imagination, luxurious extravagances. The little one-storied building into which the King slipped secretly by a garden door became the infamous theatre of orgies worthy of Tiberius, and the pamphlets of the Revolution, embroidering the vague narratives of doubtful witnesses, immensely exaggerated the number of the " victims " and the " budget of infamy "—Nolhac, *Louis XV et Madame de Pompadour*, pp. 340–360.

Madame de Pompadour was very anxious during the period of the Parc-aux-Cerfs ; she did not know how she was to keep her hold on Louis. On 28th September, 1748, D'Argenson wrote : " It is said more persistently than ever that the King is about to dismiss the Marquise de Pompadour. He finds her quite repulsive, and has not touched her with his finger-tips for eight months past. Her methods of continuing to attract him are exhausted . . . already some courtiers are commencing to turn their backs on her."

The favourite specially feared his impetuous temperament, and she therefore sought to perfect herself in the art of gallantry. " Has she a rendezvous ? The King stumbles on her at the corner of a path sometimes dressed as a dairymaid, sometimes as a nun, sometimes as a cowherd offering milk still warm. Or she is dressed as a gardener, a shepherdess, a peasant, so difficult had it become to interest this King who was eaten up by melancholy "—*Mémoires de Soulavie*. She fought against her natural indifference to sensual pleasures. " Madame was vivacious and warm-hearted, but excessively cold in matters of physical love "—*Mémoires de Madame du Hausset*. In order to please the King she even took aphrodisiacs which merely warmed her and made her face blotchy, but had no other effect. " I am cold," she said to Madame de Brancas, weeping; " the King is about to give me up. Last night, on the plea that it was hot, he remained all the time on the couch ! "

But, because of that, must we say that, in order to retain the King, she was his procuress—the procuress of the Parc-aux-Cerfs ? The accusation is a grave one. Madame de Pompadour seems to have chosen the most discreet way with the master—that of shutting her eyes. Ticklish though this may have been, it was still very far from the scandalous participation attributed to her. People talk of vile complaisances that would profane the last scintilla of a woman's self-respect ; authentic accounts, which are all that count, do not warrant this addition to her faults.

With one exception the young girls who quitted the Parc-aux-Cerfs did so without knowing that their lover was the King. They were endowed. This did not cost hundreds of millions, not a milliard, which is the figure that has been mentioned, but simply some hundreds of thousands of francs. Many a lord has spent more on his secret pleasures, and we must not take too seriously the contemporary views of the period as reflected in the virtuous diatribe of our author.

CHAPTER XX

THE ATTEMPT OF DAMIENS

ON the eve of Epiphany, in January 1757, Louis XV was struck down in his own palace, surrounded by his guards and great officers, and in the presence of his son. He was getting into his carriage, to go to sup and sleep at Trianon, when he felt a sudden blow between his ribs on his right side. It was about six o'clock, and dark; under the shadow of the arch was the usual collection of courtiers and idlers anxious to see the monarch. The bitter cold made the onlookers button themselves up in their long coats. The assassin wore one and, after having struck his blow, he put the knife in his pocket and mixed with the crowd. Dressed like all the rest he would have escaped if he had held his hat in his hand like the others. The King felt by the flowing of his blood that he was wounded, and he turned. Seeing an unknown man with his hat on and with startled eyes, he said with the utmost coolness, " That is the man who stabbed me ; arrest him, but do him no harm."

The general terror communicated itself to the King, and those around him added to it. The wound might be fatal. Although slight it would be mortal if the knife were poisoned.[1] The King was put to bed, and surgeons

[1] Was the knife poisoned ? That was what Louis XV wondered when the bandage was removed. The doctors and surgeons reassured him, and he became calm. But he showed no more pleasure at being out of danger than he had shown fear when he thought himself doomed. He displayed great courage, and it appeared that death had no terrors for him. " The wound was not deep," he said to the courtiers around his bed, " but it went to my heart." " Oh," replied one of them, " still more it went to the heart of your subjects ! "

were fetched. The Queen and the Royal Family surrounded him and the surgeons. The King did not see his fond beloved and assumed she was being kept from him, that his danger was being hidden from her, that it was his last day. He wanted to confess. His confessor and the almoner were not available, and a simple chaplain was found and asked to perform the delicate duty. In vain he sought to excuse himself, pleading his ignorance and saying he did not know how to give absolution to kings. He was carried off and ushered into the presence of the King, who knelt before him as a penitent. Confusion, anxiety, terror reigned in the château till the next day when, on removing the dressings, the doctors found, instead of a nasty wound, merely a large cut which would not have prevented an ordinary person from going about his business.

In the meantime every effort had been made to ascertain from the assassin the reason for his crime ; imagination ran wild in conjecture. His first words, when he was seized, served to double the general alarm and to suggest a deeply laid plot against the whole Royal Family. He had cried, in the tone of a man seized with remorse and capable of revealing great secrets, " Take care of His Royal Highness the Dauphin ; do not let him go out." [1]

[1] Although there was no fear regarding the consequences of this scratch, the Dauphin was treated as King. The evening of the 5th January, he presided over the Council of Ministers. " He displayed," says D'Argenson, " intelligence, dignity and eloquence beyond anything that had been expected of him, so true is it that men must be put to the test before they can reveal their true worth." A few days later, the Council met again, and it was a cause of surprise that the Dauphin did not attend ; but the next day the King told his ministers to reserve a seat for a new colleague whom he purposed adding to their number, and the Maréchal de Richelieu went for the Dauphin. All the religious party promptly ranged themselves around the young heir to the throne. There was much talk of Louis' conversion. Arguing from the precedent of the King's illness at Metz, they hoped that if the King took the Sacrament, he would dismiss the Marquise. It was soon seen, however, that their hopes were vain, for on the 18th January, Madame de Pompadour, who had been kept away designedly, resumed her position with the King. Cf. Stryienski, *La mère des trois derniers Bourbons*, pp. 192–196

The escort of Bodyguards and Swiss Guards through whom the assassin had made his way to attack the King were furious. The Duc d'Ayen, who was the officer on duty charged with the safety of the King's person, was in despair that the attempt had been made under his very eyes, and issued the severest orders that the criminal should be put to the question and that his horrible secret should be torn from him. The blind and gloomy zeal of these soldiers led them to use the cruellest methods to make him speak. They burned his legs with red-hot pincers and might, as had been done in the case of Clément, have released him from the tortures and inquiries of the law by a prompt death if the Grand Provost, whose duty it was to deal with any crime committed in the King's palace, had not taken charge of the regicide. By this more regular procedure it was soon learned that there was no cause for anxiety as to the motive and consequences of the assassination. It was decided that the murderer, François Robert Damiens, born at Thieulloy, near Arras, in 1715, of a family of impoverished farmers, a servant of the Jesuits, had not been impelled by any reward, instigation or persuasion; that he was not a religious fanatic like Clément and Ravaillac; but a patriotic fanatic or rather maniac, a lunatic, a raging madman who, urged to his crime against his own will, had sought to avoid yielding to the impulse by applying the ordinary measures for calming his blood. He asserted that if he had been bled, as he had asked, he would never have committed the crime.

When the news of the attack on the King reached Paris a few hours later it caused a great hubbub. The princes of the blood, the great officers of State and the chief magistrates proceeded to Versailles; the Archbishop ordered forty hours of prayer, and the theatres were closed. But what a difference from the time of the King's illness at Metz! Of course there were detestation and execration of the monster who had dared to lay hands on the " Lord's Anointed," and people asked for news of the monarch and for details of the terrible occurrence ; but it was rather out of curiosity than concern. People were more scared than distressed. Their hearts were little moved by the event ; their eyes remained dry, and the churches were empty. What a lesson it was to Louis XV if only he could have perceived it, if flattery had not hidden the real feelings of the people ! Damiens at least did not hide those feelings. He had the audacity to dictate a letter to His Majesty in which, through all his rigmarole and uncouthness, is revealed a philosophy which reflects and disentangles the ideas that occupied the author's disordered mind, and would of itself explain quite simply how he came to conceive his horrible project.

Damiens had been a servant in various good houses ; he had been employed by Jesuits, by Jansenists, by magistrates. The luxury of our meals and the elaboration of their service call for far more servants than were necessary in our fathers' time. Consequently it was necessary to employ more, and particularly at meals, where there are as many servants as guests. Our luxuriousness has even led, for some time past, to the discontinuance of the prudent habit of sending them away at dessert, when, the tongue being loosened with wine, there is greater freedom of speech in the direction of violent diatribes against the authors of our national evils, or of pungent sallies of malicious wit. It is natural that in this capital, where despotism, always in arms against liberty, compels the greatest reserve in public places, people should, in the privacy of the home, seek compensation by giving vent to the most republican and extravagant sentiments. Damiens had been in the way of constantly hearing such remarks, sometimes in one direction, sometimes in the other. Guilty of theft, assassination and poisoning, he was by no means one of those men that are capable of such religious or political enthusiasms as sometimes lead astray the men they have inflamed, inducing both heroic virtues and atrocious crimes; but, possessed of an ardent and gloomy temperament, the leaven of their fermenting minds had passed into his own, and his blood, quickly excited, had heated his brain to the point of madness. As the charges he heard, whether from men of the Church or from men of the robe, or from plain citizens groaning under their troubles, were always against a vicious administration; as he was too thick-headed to appreciate that these complaints were really against the ministers, and thinking that, while reprobating a regicide people would no doubt glorify a patriot who was bold enough at the cost of his own life to make an example of one of the famous culprits who went scathless, he saw in his madness only the King as his object.

A curious feature of this attempt, which distinguishes it from its predecessors, was that Damiens had in his heart no hatred for the King, and that he maintained from the outset and throughout the inquiry that he had never intended to kill the King, but only to wound him in order to impress him and thus bring him back to God and the nation. An examination of the weapon he carried and the manner in which he struck seemed to support this plea. It was a spring knife, with a long pointed blade like a dagger, and a small blade about four inches long for cutting pens. It is obvious that if Damiens had wanted to strike a fatal blow he would have used the former.

During the night of 17th to 18th January, Damiens was transferred from the guards' lock-up to the prison of the Palais de Justice, where a cell had been prepared for him in the Tour de Montgomery. A tremendous fuss was made of this transfer, and undreamed-of precautions were taken. Here is an extract from a manuscript account of the ceremony, dated 18th January, 1757: " The wretched assassin left Versailles last night at 10.45. There were three four-horse carriages. The criminal was in one, accompanied by a royal surgeon and by two of the Provost's guards. In the two others were guards and a man who had been arrested in connexion with the matter. These carriages started off under the escort of a squadron of mounted police with drawn swords and of detachments who patrolled the route. Sixty grenadiers of the French Guard under four lieutenants and eight second-lieutenants, all mounted, accompanied the carriages, and six police officers, armed with muskets, marched at each door. Thus ordered, the procession reached Sèvres, where another company of grenadiers surrounded the carriages and the original sixty fell in behind. The route was by Issy and Vaugirard, entering Paris by the Sèvres gate and proceeding by the Croix, the Rue du Four, Rue de Bussy, Rue Dauphine, the Pont Neuf, Quai des Orfèvres and the Rue St-Louis. At Sèvres and Issy companies of Swiss Guards lined the route; at Vaugirard a company of grenadiers joined the escort. All the way from the Sèvres gate to the Palais de Justice squadrons of French Guards were stationed to keep the route. At three o'clock this morning the three carriages entered the Cour du Mai at the Palais de Justice, accompanied by all the detachments mentioned above. The criminal was taken down to the entrance of the Conciergerie. He was put in a sort of hammock made of a great blanket and thus carried up into the Tour de Montgomery, where he was guarded by four policemen who remained day and night in his room. Eight further policemen occupied the room above, and below was a bodyguard of ten French Guards. In the Cour du Mai at the entrance to the Conciergerie was stationed a body of French Guards consisting of seventy men under a lieutenant, a second-lieutenant, and two ensigns. This guard was relieved every twenty-four hours.

The officers who guarded the wretch never saw him, and no one could enter the prison without an order signed by the First President. Such precautions were taken that it was even forbidden to be in the street as he passed, or to look out of any windows or doors that commanded a view, under pain of being fired at. The night was chosen as the most suitable time for the removal."

Even after he was safely deposited in the Conciergerie the measures for keeping him securely were not relaxed. The cost to the public was more than six hundred *livres* a day. All Paris was sure, when it saw the culprit in the hands of the Parliament and the Princes and Peers summoned to give it greater importance, that there were to be startling disclosures. Curiosity was further excited by the remarkable and romantic gossip that was current. Sentence was pronounced on the 26th March. The hearing started at eight in the morning and did not finish till seven at night. Damiens was condemned to the same punishment as Ravaillac, it being ordered that he should first suffer the ordinary and extraordinary torture for two hours instead of the usual half-hour. The wretch maintained his character to the end ; through the five and a half hours of his questioning he replied with the same composure, the same boldness amounting to insolence, the same courage, as he had shown from the beginning, mingling his protests with irony, raillery and even gaiety. He stubbornly asserted that he was alone in his crime, that he had conceived his plan more than three years previously, that he had communicated it to nobody whatever, and that if he had thought that even his hat suspected it, he would have thrown it in the fire. As for motives for such a horrible outrage he stated that he had been grieved to see the royal authority degraded and compromised by the disputes between the clergy and the Parliament, and the small heed the King had paid to the remonstrances addressed to him,

At a quarter to five in the afternoon of the 28th March the horror of his torture commenced. His right hand was burned; then he was wrenched with red-hot pincers. Molten lead was poured into the wounds, and afterwards he was quartered. He remained alive and firm during the whole of this torture, which lasted an hour and a quarter, evincing only the suffering of his physical self. For the last item of his punishment a little platform had been erected at the height of horses' traces, to which he was attached so that his arms and legs might be dragged out. The executioner had bought six horses, at a cost of three thousand six hundred *livres*, so that if one of the first four should fail it could be replaced without delay. Although these horses were very powerful and the two spare ones were used, they did not succeed in severing the limbs even after many attempts, and the job had to be finished with an axe. The arms, legs and body were assembled, a fire was lit, and they were reduced to ashes which were scattered to the winds.

The same fuss was made of Damiens' execution as had been made of his detention. The whole town and its suburbs were occupied by French Guards with drawn swords. The crowd was so enormous, indeed, that it really needed a large force to maintain order. It is impossible to describe the influx of people to Paris. People from the surrounding villages, from the provinces, even from abroad, flocked as though to the most brilliant festivities. The windows looking on the Place de Grève and even the openings of lofts were let at fabulous prices. The roofs were black with spectators. What was specially noticeable was the eagerness of the women, the sensitive, pitying women, to witness the spectacle. They gloated over it, watched every horrible detail with dry eyes, unmoved, while men shuddered and turned away.

In accordance with a barbarous custom, which is condemned by reason, justice and humanity, the father, wife and daughter of Damiens, although recognized to be quite innocent, were banished from the realm and forbidden to return under pain of death. As though it were not enough to belong to such a monster, they received a punishment worse than death.

In the general confusion and trouble that followed the first announcement of the King's danger all foreign and domestic business was suspended, but only for a moment until His Majesty's fate was known. Then the French people mingled with their grief a certain consolation in thinking of the event as a salutary lesson from Providence. They believed that Louis XV would appreciate it and alter. The fact that Madame de Pompadour was kept away from him, and the presence of the Dauphin at the Council, seemed to augur a gratifying change. But the mistress soon returned, and the young Prince no longer enjoyed the confidence of his august father. She was too much interested in depriving him of it and in fomenting doubt, mistrust and jealousy in the King's heart. So things were worse than ever, and the King, more and more dejected by reverses, had no will but that of his mistress and no strength but to carry out her plans.[1]

---

[1] This narrative is, on the whole, reliable, and it scarcely seems worth while to discuss certain petty and quite unimportant details. The complete records of the Damiens affair are to be found in the Arsenel library, as well as a large collection of printed papers, engravings and manuscript records, among which is a long and horrible account of the torture signed by Bouton, one of the executioner's assistants. This shocking death remains one of the disgraces of the monarchy, particularly in that eighteenth century when the philosophers were preparing the minds of the people for the French Revolution. At that time, when the King was not content to reign, but wanted to govern, he could easily have exercised his prerogative of mercy, the more so, as he had said, " Do the man no harm." He contented himself with regrets, if we are to believe an interesting page in the *Mémoires de Madame du Hausset*. " Many women," she said (we condense the passage), " were savage enough to be present at the execution, among others the very beautiful wife of a farmer-general. This was recounted to the King, who

said, 'Ugh! the wretch!' I was assured that she and others thought they might win the King's favour by being present."

The monarchy was so firmly rooted in the French mind that, because of the scratch, Louis XV, of whom violent criticisms were beginning to be heard, almost became again " the Well-Beloved," as is shown by the following song about Damiens :

L'ATTENTAT DE DAMIENS

C'est en vain qu'un monstre exécrable
Vomi par l'enfer en courroux
Frappe des rois le plus aimable,
Et l'assassine aux yeux de tous.
Du haut des cieux, Dieu qui protège
Ce Roi, chéri de ses sujets,
Retient le bras d'un sacrilège
Et rompt le plus noir des projets.
Pour éprouver un Roi qu'il aime
Il laisse attenter à ses jours ;
Mais sa bonté, dans l'instant même,
S'éveille et vole à son secours.
Tendres sujets, séchez vos larmes,
Louis ne perdra pas le jour ;
Un Dieu n'a permis vos alarmes
Que pour augmenter vos amours.
Non, non ! le traitre, le parjure
N'a ni complice, ni parti ;
Il est le seul, dans la nature,
Dont Louis ne soit pas chéri.

The Attempt of Damiens

(Vain is it for a hateful monster, spewed out by a wrathful hell, to strike the most amiable of kings and slay him before the eyes of all. From the heavens above, God, who protects this monarch, beloved of his subjects, restrains the sacrilegious hand and foils the darkest plan. To prove a king whom He loves, He permits the attempt on his life ; but immediately His goodness is aroused and hastens to his aid. Loving subjects, dry your tears, Louis will not die ; God has only permitted your fright in order to increase your love. No, no, the traitor, the felon, has no accomplice or supporters ; he is the only one in all nature by whom Louis is not beloved.)

This rhymed drivel, which possesses heaven knows what rhythm, is a mass of hyperbolical and insincere platitude.

CHAPTER XXI

INCAPABLE GENERALS—NUMEROUS DEFEATS—UNPOPU-
LARITY OF LOUIS XV AND MADAME DE POMPADOUR
—THE CHEVALIER D'ASSAS — SOUBISE — SATIRICAL
VERSES

THIS is not the place to narrate all the military details, all the fights and battles that took place in our unhappy country. We will content ourselves with saying that in five years the French were never able to regain the advantage that a single campaign had given them; that it was often the fault of the generals; and that merely to maintain some sort of position, with alternate success and failure, cost infinitely more in blood and treasure than had been spent on the brilliant victories of the Maréchal de Saxe.

The Comte de Clermont,[1] who succeeded the Maréchal

---

[1] Louis de Bourbon Condé, Comte de Clermont, prince of the blood, son of Louis III, Prince de Condé (1709-1771). He at first took orders, but subsequently obtained from Pope Clement XII permission to bear arms, and made the campaigns of Alsace and the Netherlands. This appointment to be practically generalissimo is one of the most notable examples of the favour and omnipotence of the Marquise de Pompadour. Clermont was one of those generals of whom General de Fontenay, the Saxon Ambassador said, "If you raise an army the women are all excitement until those in whom they are interested are appointed. If the campaign lasts three months, they make just as big a fuss to get them released again." He was fifty-one years old and was Abbot of Saint-Germain-des-Prés. This did not, however, prevent his enjoying himself with Mesdemoiselles Leduc and Camargo of the Opera. He was witty, with the somewhat vulgar wit of a street-urchin, and high-spirited. His officers and troops said he was easy to get on with. The command for which he applied, and which thanks to Madame de Pompadour he received, was far above his military capacity. It is one thing to be an officer able to carry out intelligently orders received from a superior; it is a quite different thing to be commander-in-chief,

de Richelieu, possessed beyond question the qualities that earned the esteem both of his army and of the enemy. Humane, gentle, affable, popular, he commenced by seeing that great attention ought to be paid to the troops, who had fallen into a lamentable state. The spirit of pillage, all too common in war, instead of being repressed had been encouraged by the example of his predecessor in the command, and had reached an incredible pitch. His Highness condemned to the pillory a storekeeper who, instead of receiving in kind the supplies of forage that the country should have delivered to him, accepted money, and as he had been authorized to do so by the Director General, a man named Milin de Grand Maison, His Highness ordered the latter to be hung. He anticipated the penalty by flight.

After dealing with the commissariat, the Prince found it necessary to punish other culprits. He reported to the King that his army could not be maintained unless discipline was restored by the dismissal from their regiments of a large number of officers who had absented themselves, but that he was afraid His Majesty's clemency might lead him to pardon the majority. The King assured him of his determination to spare no one, whereupon the commander sent in a list of fifty-two officers, who were cashiered.

He was exasperated at the way in which Minden [1] had surrendered after only six days of siege, although it had a garrison of eight battalions and eight squadrons, all of whom were made prisoners of war. It was of the utmost

Richelieu had just been recalled to Versailles, as his incapacity became more and more evident, and his lordly plundering and unscrupulousness became more and more unbearable. He was, moreover, weary of the business himself, and had asked to be relieved of his command. His haste to get back was so great that he could not even await the arrival of his successor. He returned to France, head erect, confident of indulgence and of the King's favour. But he was astounded at the reception given to him by the Dauphin, to whom people were grateful for his courage in speaking the truth of this perfumed warrior. Cf. Stryienski, *La mère des trois derniers Bourbons.*

[1] Minden, a town in Westphalia. The French captured it in 1757 and lost it the following year, after being defeated by Prince Ferdinand of Brunswick.

importance to retain this position, which covered the
army in that region and prevented the advance of Prince
Ferdinand, who was too prudent to leave it in his rear.
The behaviour of a corporal of the Lyons Regiment, named
La Jeunesse, threw this shameful surrender into higher
relief. Furious at learning that he and his comrades were
to be sent as prisoners to Magdeburg, he stirred up their
courage till he collected a troop of fifteen hundred, at the
head of which he overcame the enemy force opposed to
him, fought his way through and rejoined the army of the
Comte de Clermont. We regret we cannot say what
reward was given for this brave action, which was worthy of
the heroic days ; but all the officers who signed the surrender were dismissed. M. de Morangiés, lieutenant-
general in command, was exiled to a distance of fifty leagues
from Paris ; M. de Maisoncelle, lieutenant-colonel of
Clermont Prince, was sent to the Fort of la Petite Pierre
in Alsace. Only the Comte de Guiche, who was not
included in the surrender, which he refused to sign, was
permitted to present himself to the King.

Unfortunately this prince, Abbot of Saint-Germain-des-
Près, did not succeed better with his army than with his
monks.[1] He had not sufficient genius to command, and he
was confronted by an opponent who was too clever for
him to stand against for long, even if he had been as resourceful as he was the reverse. It was no doubt this
knowledge of His Highness's incapacity that gave rise to
the cynical but very true gibe of the Comte de Saint-
Germain. That general, always watchful, always seeking
the enemy, having received a visit from an aide-de-camp
of the Prince de Condé, who came to ask where the enemy
was, handed him a telescope and pointed it to Headquarters
saying, " Look there, that is where you will find the

---

[1] See the various epigrams collected by our author, which will be found
at the end of the chapter.

enemy." This was only too true a prophecy of the ills that befell the French army shortly after in the loss of the battle of Crefeld,[1] and the capture of Düsseldorf.

[1] Crefeld, a town in Rhenish Prussia. The battle was lost in June 1758 by the Comte de Clermont, whose opponent was the Duke of Brunswick. After this defeat, the incompetent general abandoned the army, leaving the command to M. de Contades, the senior of his generals. The following song was current :

Le general des Benedictins

D'où venez-vous, Monsieur l'abbé ?
Vous avez l'air tout essoufflé ?
Je reviens de la guerre. . . . Eh bien
Eh ! qu'alliez-vous y faire ?
Vous m'entendez bien ?

Je suis arrivé, j'ai juré,
J'ai sacré, me suis enivré ;
J'ai fait le diable à quatre,
Je me suis laissé battre.

On a pourtant bien combattu,
Brunswick montrait déjà le cul ;
Mais j'ai laissé pour boire
L'honneur de la victoire.

L'ennemi s'en est aperçu,
Tout de suite il est revenu,
J'ai battu la retraite
Et ma campagne est faite.

Je reprendrai mon ancien train,
Mon vin, mes amis, ma catin,
Nous boirons à Mortagne, eh bien !

The General of the Benedictines

(Whence come you, abbé, all out of breath like that ?—I return from the war.—Well, and what did you go there for ? Do you hear me ?

I went, I swore, I cursed, I got drunk, I played the very devil ; but I was beaten.

Still, we fought well ; Brunswick had already turned tail, and I went to drink a glass in honour of the victory.

The enemy noticed this, and suddenly returned. I retreated, and so my campaign was ended.

I shall take up my old life—my wine, my friends, my wench ; we will drink to Mortagne, lackaday !)

The little prestige that still clung to the house of Clermont disappeared on the battlefield of Crefeld.

This defeat caused consternation at Versailles. The Dauphin, knowing well the French genius and the discouragement that would fall upon the troops, was specially dismayed at such a blot on the name of Bourbon, and nobly determined to wipe it out without a moment's delay. He wrote to the King for permission to go and place himself at the head of the defeated army. He used the most pressing and persuasive arguments, foreseeing all the difficulties that might be urged against his going, and promising to do nothing without the advice of the generals. " No," he said in conclusion, " I am sure there is not a single Frenchman whose courage would not be restored and who would not become invincible at the sight of your only son leading him to the fray." His august father made this reply : " Your letter, my son, moved me to tears. We must not yield before misfortune. Great ills call for great remedies, but this is only a scuffle. I am delighted to see in you the spirit of our fathers, but the time has not yet come for us to part."

This precious missive shows how the King was hoodwinked. What had been represented to him as a mere scuffle was in fact a complete rout by which in one day were lost more than eighty leagues of ground and all the advantages that had been won since the beginning of the war. On the other hand, if he did not accede to the Dauphin's request, he determined to take the command from the Comte de Clermont, who returned to Paris with the burlesque title of " General of the Benedictines." His Highness had handed the command over to the Marquis de Contades, the senior lieutenant-general, to whom the favourite procured the award of the baton of a Marshal of France, not as a reward for what he had done, but in anticipation of what he might do, or rather in order to help the Prince de Soubise, his junior, for whom she desired to obtain the same honour. The battle of Lutzelberg, in

Cassel, which the latter won against an army of Hanoverians, Hessians and English, provided a favourable opportunity. Voltaire remarks that Paris, which had growled so loudly at the general who was defeated at Rosbach,[1] scarcely concerned themselves with this victory. This was because his defeat had had the most disastrous consequences, whereas he had not known how to reap advantage from his

[1] Rosbach, a village in Saxony, one of the most resounding and disastrous defeats in these years of unsuccessful warfare, inflicted on us by Frederic II, King of Prussia. In his *History of the Seven Years' War*, he said of this battle : " 5th November, 1757.—Soubise, a favourite of Madame de Pompadour's, wrote to the King : ' I write to Your Majesty full of despair. The defeat of your army is complete.' "
Then came the *Soubisades*. Some of them will be found at the end of the chapter, but here are three more, missed by our author :

> Sur sa déroute, à tort, on brocarde Soubise,
> Quoiqu'il ait été bien battu,
> Il a plus gagné que perdu,
> Puisqu'il lui reste sa marquise.

(It is wrong to jeer at Soubise over his defeat ; although he may have been beaten, he has gained more than he lost, for he still retains his marquise.)

> Soubise vient d'être battu.
> Il s'est de désespoir, la tête la première,
> Précipité dans la rivière,
> Mais les poissons l'ont soutenu.

(Soubise has just been defeated. In his despair he plunged head first in the river ; but the fish [Poissons] saved him.)

> Entrez, entrez ! s'écriait un fripier,
> J'ai des habits à la Soubise !
> Au diable ! dit un officier.
> Qui voudrait donner un denier
> De si chétive marchandise ?
> Le fripier, qui l'entend, aussitôt lui répond :
> " Monsieur, vous vous trompez, j'en connais la facture,
> Je vous garantis que ce sont
> Des habits à plate-couture."

(" Walk in, walk in !" cried an old clothes-man. " I have clothes " à la Soubise." " Be damned," says an officer, " who would give a copper for such wretched goods ? " The man forthwith replied, " Sir, you are wrong. I know the make, and I guarantee that they are sound.")

victory, which the superior ability of the enemy rendered nugatory. Indeed, throughout this war we see the French on the whole winning as many actions through their valour and dauntlessness, and gaining almost as much ground as the enemy. The latter, however, if defeated, immediately rallied and showed themselves as redoubtable as ever, whereas the smallest defeat overwhelmed the former, putting them to flight and shattering them for the rest of the campaign. The generals' ignorance of the principles of war, their faulty dispositions, their neglect of measures in case of check or total defeat, their troops' lack of confidence in them,— all these things, combined with the national temperament, quickly elated by success and even more quickly discouraged by failure, contributed to explain this difference.

The frequent changes in the command added materially to the disadvantages. M. de Contades was soon succeeded by the Duc de Broglie, who was made a Marshal of France. The short period of his command was only marked by the battles of Bergen and Minden. The former was won by the Duc de Broglie ; [1] the latter was lost under his orders and in his presence. It was even more disastrous and shameful than the defeat of Crefeld. The remarkable thing is that it might have been a glorious success, that the dispositions had been well planned, and that M. de Contades complained that only the Duc de Broglie's inaction had robbed him of the happiest results. Be that as it may, these reproaches did not prevent the disgrace of

[1] Victor François, Duc de Broglie (1718–1804), lieutenant-general in 1748, after his campaigns in Alsace, Bavaria and Flanders. In 1757 was at the defeat of Rosbach, but was victorious the following year at Sondershausen, Bergen and Lutzelberg; defeated at Minden. Commanded in chief the Army of Germany and made Marshal of France in 1750. Victor of Corbach, but, as he had to share with Soubise the defeat of Billinghausen, he was disgraced and exiled. He was recalled and became Minister of War in 1789. He was one of the chiefs of the *émigrés* in 1792 ; entered the service of England and Russia, and died at Munster.

He was no worse a general than many others of his day and, indeed, was,

17

the one and the promotion of the other, who passed over more than a hundred of his seniors. When he received the baton his friends announced the fact in the Press in these terms : " The Duc de Broglie, Lieutenant-General of the King's armies, has just been made a Marshal of France. This dignity has been awarded to him in advance of his seniority, but not in advance of proofs of his exceptional ability, of the brilliancy of his services, or of public opinion. If it had been the immediate reward of the brilliant victory of Bergen, the enemy would certainly not have been able to urge against it the disastrous day of Minden." All that is true enough, but he had a brother, the Comte de Broglie, his adviser and mentor, with whom he could not dispense, and who did him much injury. Jealous, envious, unruly, a bungler, haughty, devoid of feeling, he was as much detested by the troops as the other was beloved, and the bondage of the older to the younger constantly led to his losing the fruits of his good qualities.

The Marshal signalized his arrival by the victory of Corbach over a body of thirty thousand Hanoverians. on the whole, a good deal better. Consequently the rhymesters deal kindly with him.

> Soubise est un fanfaron,
> De Broglie, un vrai Gascon,
>   Voilà la ressemblance.
> L'un tourne le cul au feu.
> L'autre se jette au milieu ;
>   Voilà la différence.
>
> Soubise a quarante-cinq ans,
> De Broglie à peu près autant,
>   Voilà la ressemblance.
> L'un sait battre l'ennemi,
> L'autre toujours s'est enfui.
>   Voilà la différence.

(Soubise is a swaggerer, De Broglie a true Gascon ; and that is the resemblance. The former turns his back to the fire, the latter plunges into the midst of it ; and that is the difference.

Soubise is forty-five, De Broglie about the same ; and that is the resemblance. The latter knows how to fight, the former always bolts ; and that is the difference.)

They were commanded by the Crown Prince of Brunswick, and this young hero with his fearless courage, having provoked the combat before Prince Ferdinand was at hand to support him, was obliged to fall back, leaving the road to Hesse open, and to carry away as the sole reward for his bravery a shot in the loins. The defection of the Comte de Saint-Germain was, in the view of the best judges, too high a price to pay for these advantages. He returned his red ribbon and his patents to the King, and entered the service of Denmark. He was an excellent officer, whose loss was attributed to the irritations of the Comte de Broglie. He could have worked with the Marshal, whose accomplishments and ability he appreciated, but could not tolerate the latter's being only a sort of agent and satellite of his younger brother.

The battle of Rhinberg, on the Lower Rhine, deserves mention not so much on account of its importance, although that was considerable enough seeing that the Marquis de Castries, who fought it, forced that same Crown Prince to cross the river and raise the siege of Wasel, through a personal exploit which was almost overlooked at the time but should be remembered for ever. The Chevalier d'Assas, of the Auvergne Regiment, was sent out by night to reconnoitre and was surprised by an enemy patrol. He was told to keep silent, and threatened with death if he uttered a word. He cried all the more loudly, " Help, Auvergne, here is the enemy ! " This brave Curtius, at whose feet the barbarians should have fallen in admiration, was slain without pity.[1]

[1] The Chevalier d'Assas was not killed outright, but only expired several hours later. Did he really utter the famous words concerning which (like many other historic sayings, true and false) enormous quantities of ink have been spilt, as their authenticity was contested ? They were attributed to Dubois, a sergeant of his company, who accompanied him on a reconnaissance. But would Dubois have merely cried "Help" ? This is not the place to recommence the duel—a duel of the pen. We refer those who are interested to Edouard Fournier, *L'esprit dans l'Histoire*, pp. 351–360 (Paris : Dentu, 1883).

Other personal successes consoled the French to some extent for the losses they had sustained elsewhere and made them applaud the Marshal. The stout defence of Fritzlar by M. de Narbonne was highly thought of at the time and earned for him his honourable name. The Crown Prince, who reaped as much advantage from a defeat as from a victory, was routed at Althenhayn, near Grunberg, an affair leading to the raising of the siege of Cassel and the evacuation of Hesse which the enemy had suddenly invaded, and giving the Parisians an opportunity for a *Te Deum*, a thanksgiving to the Almighty for which there had been no occasion for long enough. The French thus secured the mastery over the Landgraviate, of the town of Minden, of Göttingen, and a free passage into the Electorate of Hanover. Things were going well. The skill of Prince Ferdinand had only enabled him to retard the success of our arms and the junction of the army of Soubise with that of Broglie, which gave the French such a superiority that he ought to have been crushed. An unfortunate misunderstanding saved him.

There was jealousy between the two commands. It had been agreed to attack, but when and how? That was the problem. The Prince de Soubise said that the Duc de Broglie, in order to secure all the credit of the victory, attacked too soon. The latter said that the Prince, fearing his success, supported him too late, or rather not at all. Such was the dispute between the two generals over the action of Filingshaufen, which took its name from a village that was at first captured by the Maréchal de Broglie but was recaptured the following day by Duke Ferdinand. We have questioned many officers who were present, and they have all replied according to their own personal predilections. For our own part, we think that even the evidence of Broglie's partisans shows him to have been at fault. It is probable that he allowed himself to be carried away by the Count, with his ill-considered rash and ambitious plans ; but that was no comfort to France.

As these rivals could not work together, they seemed to abandon all idea of activity for the rest of the year. The two armies separated, the Maréchal de Broglie retiring towards Cassel and the Maréchal de Soubise crossing the Roer. More concerned with their own quarrel than with that of the State they sent to the Court their respective reports. Soubise had too good a friend in Madame de Pompadour ; his rival was recalled, and received an order of banishment to his own estates. The public, with its usual tendency to sympathize with the unfortunate and knowing little of the rights and wrongs of the matter, swayed too by its liking for the accused and its contempt for the accuser, gave Broglie a reception which was calculated to temper his disgrace. The day after his exile *Tancrède* was played at the Comédie française with Mademoiselle Clairon as Aménaïde. When she came to the lines :

On dépouille Tancrède, on l'exile, on l'outrage.

. . . . .

C'est le sort d'un héros d'être persécuté.

. . . . .

Tout son parti se tait ; qui sera son appui ?
Sa gloire. . . .

. . . . .

Un héros qu'on opprime attendrit tous les cœurs.[1]

(Tancred is being robbed, exiled, outraged. . . . It is the lot of a hero to be persecuted. . . . All his adherents are silent ; who will support him ? His glory. . . . A hero oppressed softens every heart.)

---

[1] Claire Josèphe Hippolyte Legris de Latude, called Clairon (1723–1803), born at St. Warnon de Condé. At the age of thirteen she appeared in soubrette parts at the Comédie italienne, in opera. She found her real calling, however, at the Théâtre français, where she appeared in 1743 with brilliant success. She was one of the most justly famous actresses of the eighteenth century, and one of those whose love affairs made the greatest stir. Her best parts were in Saurin's *Iphigénie en Tauride* ; Du Belloy's *Le Siège de Calais* ; Châteaubrun's *Les Troyennes* ; but specially in Voltaire's

the sublime actress gave such exalted and striking tones to her voice that all present, with their minds full of the events of the day, felt how appropriate they were. Broglie's name was in every mouth, and the play was interrupted several times by constantly renewed applause.

The same public who had so greatly regretted the loss of the Maréchal d'Estrées, in its enthusiasm for his pre-

tragedies, of which she was one of the favourite interpreters—*Zulime*, *Sémiramis*, *Olympie*, *Tancrède*, *Oreste*, *L'Orphelin de la Chine*. . . . In her old age she write her *Memoirs*, which are full of interest and curious anecdotes. Even after she had passed her best, Bachaumont was able to write of her, in January 1762, " Mademoiselle Clairon is still the favourite, and whenever she is announced, the house is filled. As soon as she appears, she is applauded to the echo. She is the consummation of art."

She was the most good-natured creature imaginable and an easy conquest—see, for example, in Marmontel's charming *Memoirs*, how their love affair began. They were supping together. " Are you sad ? " asked Clairon. " Yes, I am sad," replied Marmontel, " because I am in love ! " " Silly child ! " " Yes, I love you." " Well, then, fall at my knees ; I will lift you up, and we will love each other as much as ever God wills ! " And this is the way the breach came : The Bailli de Fleury was accusing her of being cruel. " I cruel ? It is the first time that has ever been said of me ! " Marmontel protested. " Oh, that will be all right," she replied. " You will be my lover in verse, and he will be my lover in prose." But we are not writing her life, and will merely mention the pleasing pages that Arsène Houssaye devotes to her in his *Galeries du XVIIIᵉ siècle*, iv. pp. 303-330.

During her lifetime a large pamphlet of gross licentiousness appeared regarding Clairon, and a whole volume could be compiled of the lampoons and songs of which she was the heroine.

Cette actrice immortelle enchaîne tous les cœurs,
Ses grâces, ses talents, lui gagnent les suffrages
Du critique sévère, et des vrais connaisseurs.
Et de nos jours, bien des auteurs
Lui doivent le succès qui suivit leurs ouvrages.

(This immortal actress captivates all hearts ; her charm, her talents win the suffrages of the severest critic and of the real connoisseurs. In our days it is to her that many authors owe the success of their works.)

Sans modèle au théâtre et sans rivale à craindre,
Clairon sait " tour à tour " attendrir, effrayer ;
Sublime dans un art qu'elle semble créer,
On pourra l'imiter, mais qui pourra l'atteindre ?

(Without pattern as an actress and without a rival to fear, Clairon

decessor, seemed scarcely to appreciate the choice of this
old man to replace the young hero, a choice which, indeed,
had no brilliant or striking consequences. The evil star
of France even insisted that the joy attending the making
of peace should be clouded with the bitter news of the
capture of Cassel, almost at the moment when the treaty
was being signed. It made no practical difference, but it
was draining the cup to the dregs.

moves us by turns to pity and to terror; sublime in the art that she
seems to originate, she may be copied, but who can equal her ?)

> Quoi ! mille francs pour ma vérole,
> Disait Dubois à son frater !
> Frétillon, pour beaucoup moins cher
> A fait cent tours de casserole.

(What, pay a thousand francs for my pox, said Dubois to his
comrade ! Frétillon has served a hundred times for much less !)

> Eh ! donc, répliqua le Keiser,
> Sandis ! c'est un exemple unique,
> La belle alors de tout Paris
> Etait la meilleure pratique.
> J'aurais dû la traiter gratis !
> C'était l'espoir de ma boutique.

(By Jove ! replied Keiser, the belle of all Paris was my best
customer. I ought to have treated her free, for she was the main-
stay of my business.)

Dubois was one of her comrades at the Comédie française. He accused
Clairon, as these lines show; and Keiser was a quack well known for his
anti-venereal tablets.

> De la fameuse Frétillon
> A bon marché se vend le médaillon,
> Mais à quelque prix qu'on le donne,
> Fût-ce pour douze sous, fût-ce même pour un,
> On ne pourra jamais le rendre aussi commun
> Que le fut jadis sa personne.

(The medallion of the celebrated Frétillon was sold cheaply;
but whatever the price, whether twelve sous or only one, it could
never have so great a circulation as did her person.)

"A medal was struck in honour of Mademoiselle Clairon. M. de
Sainte Foix, who did not appreciate this tribute to the actress's glory, has
spoiled her pleasure in it by a bad and malicious epigram. It was as an act
of revenge, and in consequence of quarrels between authors and actors
that he did so "—*Journal de Collé*.

Regarding the Prince de Clermont and the Maréchal de Soubise many verses were written, of which some are given below :

On M. de Clermont

Au lieu du comte de Clermont
L'on devait cette année,
Nommer Christophe de Beaumont
Pour commander l'armée.
Plus brave qu'un Carcassien
Qui jamais ne recule,
Il eût fait à l'Hanovrien
Comme-il fit à la Bulle.

(Instead of the Comte de Clermont, Christophe de Beaumont [the Archbishop of Paris] should have been appointed this year to command the army. Braver than a Carcassian [Doctor of the Sorbonne ; the Sorbonne was then called Carcassia], who never falls back, he would have treated the Hanoverian as he treated the Papal Bull.)

On M. de Clermont

Est-ce un Abbé ? L'Église le renie.
Un général ? Mars l'a bien maltraité :
Mais il lui reste au moins l'Académie ;
N'y fut-il pas muet par dignité !
Qu'est-il enfin ? Que son mérite est mince !
Hélas ! j'ai beau lui chercher un talent ;
Un titre auguste éclaire son néant,
Pour son malheur le pauvre homme est un prince.

(Is he an Abbé ? The Church repudiates him. A general ? Mars has behaved ill to him. But there remains the Academy, where he preserved a dignified silence ! Really what is he ? His merit is slender. I look in vain for talent ; his dignified title only lights up his nothingness. To his misfortune this poor man is a prince.)

On M. de Clermont

Moitié casque, moitié rabat,
Clermont en vaut bien un autre ;
Il prêche comme un soldat,
Et se bat comme un apôtre.

(Half helmet, half stole, Clermont is as good as another ; he preaches like a soldier and fights like an apostle.)

On M. de Clermont

Savez vous pourquoi l'on nous bat ?
Le général porte un rabat,
Le ministre a ses ordinaires,
Laire la lire lanlaire,
Laire la lire lanla.

(Do you know why we are beaten ? Our general wears a stole,
the minister has his courses. Fa la, la, la, la !)

On Soubise

Soubise dit, la lanterne à la main :
J'ai beau chercher ou diable est mon armée ?
Elle était là pourtant hier matin :
Me l'a-t-on prise, ou l'aurais-je égarée ?
Ah ! je perds tout, je suis un étourdi ;
Mais attendons au grand jour, à midi ?
Que vois-je, ô ciel ! que mon âme est ravie !
Prodige heureux, la voilà, la voilà.
Ah ! ventrebleu, qu'est-ce donc que cela ?
Je me trompais, c'est l'armée ennemie.

(Soubise, lantern in hand, says, " I am looking to see where the
devil my army can be. It was here yesterday morning. Has some
one stolen it, or can I have lost it ? Ah, I lose everything, I am so
heedless ; but wait till it is really light—at noon. What do I see ?
Great Heavens, what delight ! What a happy miracle ! there it
is, there it is. Ah, damnation ! What is it really ? I have made
a mistake ; it is the enemy.")

On Soubise

Soubise après ses grands exploits
Peut bâtir un palais qui ne lui coûte guère ;
Sa femme en fournirait le bois
Et chacun lui jette la pierre.

(Soubise after his great adventures can build a palace for next
to nothing ; his wife will provide the wood, and every one else
will throw a stone at him.)

On Soubise

Frédéric combattant et d'estoc et de taille,
Quelqu'un au fort de la bataille,
Vint lui dire nous avons pris . . .
Qui donc ? Le général Soubise.
Ah ! morbleu, dit le roi, tant pis,
Qu'on le relâche sans remise.
Je connais du sujet, l'importance et le prix
Et sa présence ici me deviendrait contraire.

(While Frederic fought with point and edge, in the heat of the battle, some one came and said, "We have captured . . ." "Whom ? " " General Soubise." " Oh, damnation ! " said the King, " so much the worse ; let him go at once. I know the fellow's importance and value, and his presence here would only be a nuisance.")

On Soubise

En vain vous vous flattez, obligeante marquise,
De mettre en beaux draps blancs le général Soubise ;
Vous ne pouvez laver à force de crédit
La tache qu'à son front imprime sa disgrâce ;
Et quoique votre faveur fasse,
En tout temps on dira ce qu'à présent on dit,
Que si Pompadour le blanchit,
Le roi de Prusse le repasse.

(It is vain, kind Marquise, for you to imagine you can whitewash General Soubise ; even your influence cannot remove the blot that disgrace has impressed on his brow ; and, whatever your favour may do, be sure that people will always say, as they say now, that if Pompadour washed him,[1] the King of Prussia ironed him.)

---

[1] " Never was the public more bitter against Madame de Pompadour than after receiving news of the Battle of Rosbach. Every day there were anonymous letters containing gross insults, outrageous verses, threats of poison and assassination. For long she was plunged in the deepest woe, and could only sleep with the aid of sedatives. Her protection of the Prince de Soubise aroused general displeasure, and the Lieutenant of Police had the greatest difficulty in preserving order "—*Mémoires de Madame du Hausset.*

On Soubise

Soubise agira prudemment,
En vendant son hôtel, dont il n'a plus que faire ;
Le roi lui donne un logement
A son école militaire.

(Soubise will be wise if he sells his mansion, for which he has no
further use ; the King is providing him with accommodation at the
Military Academy.)

On M. de Clermont

Moitié plumet, moitié rabat,
Aussi propre à l'un comme à l'autre,
Clermont se bat comme un apôtre,
Il sert son Dieu comme il se bat.

(Half plume, half stole, as well suited by one as by the other,
Clermont fights like an apostle and serves God as he fights.)

On MM. d'Estrees and de Richelieu

Nous avons deux généraux,
Qui tous deux sont maréchaux ;
    Voilà la ressemblance.
L'un de Mars est le favori,
Et l'autre l'est de Louis,
    Voilà la différence.

Dans la guerre ils ont tous deux,
Fait divers exploits fameux,
    Voilà la ressemblance.
A l'un Mahon s'est soumis,
Par l'autre il eût été pris,
    Voilà la différence.

Que pour eux dans les combats,
La gloire eut toujours d'appas,
    Voilà la ressemblance.
L'un contre les ennemis
L'autre contre les maris,
    Voilà la différence.

D'être utile à notre roi,
Tous deux se font une loi,
   Voilà la ressemblance.
A Cythère l'un le sert,
Et l'autre sur le Weser,
   Voilà la différence.

Cumberland les craint tous deux,
Et cherche à s'éloigner d'eux,
   Voilà la ressemblance.
De l'un il fuit la valeur,
De l'autre il fuit l'odeur,
   Voilà la différence.

Dans un beau champ de lauriers,
On aperçoit ces guerriers,
   Voilà la ressemblance.
L'un a su les entasser,
L'autre vient les ramasser,
   Voilà la différence.

(We have two generals who are both marshals; that is the re-semblance. One is the favourite of Mars, the other of Louis; that is the difference.

During the war both performed great deeds; that is the resemblance. To one Mahon surrendered, by the other it should have been captured; that is the difference.

Both were always attracted by glory in fighting; that is the resemblance. One against the enemy, the other against husbands; that is the difference.

Both were ever at the King's service; that is the resemblance. One served in Cythera, the other on the Weser; that is the difference.

Cumberland feared and avoided them both; that is the resemblance. He fled before the valour of the one, before the perfume [1] of the other; that is the difference.

In a fine laurel grove both warriors are seen; that is the re-semblance. One accumulates them, the other gathers them; that is the difference.)

---

[1] Richelieu was always extravagantly scented.

CHAPTER XXII

CHOISEUL AND MADAME DE POMPADOUR

IN 1757–58 power passed to the Comte de Stainville, who was at the same time created Duc de Choiseul.[1] This noble, born to no exalted position, was early prompted by overwhelming ambition. Agitated by the noble desire to cover with fresh glory a name already famous, he embraced a military career, but,

[1] Étienne François, Comte de Stainville, later Duc de Choiseul (1719–1785). He started in a military career, and had risen to be a lieutenant-general when the favour of the Marquise made him successively Ambassador to Vienna, to Rome, Minister of Foreign Affairs, of War, of Marine. When he took office, the resounding defeats of our armies, the crumbling away of our colonies, and the mutterings at home presaging the rapidly approaching Revolution constituted a situation that was far from brilliant. A statue of Louis XV was unveiled in front of the swing-bridge of the Tuileries. The ceremony was a dull affair, not so much through the bad weather, as on account of the mocking jests levelled at a monarch who was at that time little deserving of such an apotheosis. His administration was excellent for the period. France annexed Corsica and Lorraine. Choiseul, a genius and a patriot according to some, a boudoir diplomat, a worn-out ambitious man according to others, fell, either through becoming involved in the intrigues of the parliaments, or through running the risk of war with England over the affair of the Falkland Islands ; or perhaps he was overthrown by the religious party of the Dauphin because he had looked with too favourable an eye on the *Encyclopédie* and the philosophers. Nor must it be forgotten that the Dauphin had taken an active part in the defence of the Jesuits, who were expelled during Choiseul's administration. But what could he do against a minister, then all-powerful, who was irritated by his pertinacity ? Did not Choiseul, in the heat of the discussion, say, " Perhaps, Sir, I shall some day be so unfortunate as to be your subject, but it is certain I shall never be at your service." His disgrace and his exile to Chanteloup were a sort of triumphant apotheosis.

A great noble, immensely rich, he married the daughter of the financier Crozat, a charming and refined lady ; he lived in great state, sumptuous to the pettiest detail. He was witty and possessed of exceptional intellect. " Choiseul," says Sénac de Meilhan, " was of medium height and might have been called ugly, but his face was relieved by bright eyes and his noble,

as his natural genius was rather for politics, he soon turned to diplomacy. He first became ambassador at Rome, polite and bold manners gave his whole person a character which distinguished him among his fellows and outweighed its defects."

A song of the times, attributed by some to the Abbé de l'Attaignant (not that it matters), wittily sums up Choiseul.

Quand Choiseul
D'un coup d'œil
Considère
Le plan entier de l'Etat
Et seul, comme un Sénat,
Agit et délibère ;
Quand je vois
Qu'à la fois
Il arrange
Le dedans et le dehors,
Je soupçonne en son corps
Un ange.
Serait-ce un Dieu tutélaire ?
Dans la paix et dans la guerre,
Ses traités,
Sont dictés
Par Minerve.
J'admire en lui les talents
Que d'elle il obtient sans
Réserve.
A l'Amour
Tour à tour ;
A la table.
Quand il trouve des loisirs,
Qu'il se livre aux plaisirs
Il est inconcevable.
Du travail
Au sérail,
Vif, aimable,
A tout, il est toujours prêt.
Pour moi, je crois que c'est
Un diable !

(When Choiseul at a glance takes in the whole situation of the State, and deliberates and acts alone, as though he were a Senate ; when I see him settling everything at home and abroad simultaneously, I fancy an angel must lodge in his body. Is he a tutelary deity ? In peace and in war his treaties are dictated by Minerva. I admire his possession of talents he receives from her without stint. Love, the table, both have their turn. It is inconceivable that he should find time for pleasures. At work, in the seraglio, ever vivacious, ever amiable, ever ready for everything. Really, I believe, he is a demon !)

ETIENNE FRANÇOIS, DUC DE CHOISEUL
From an engraving by Delpech after Belliard

and a study of that Court enabled him to develop his
natural talent for intrigue. Proceeding thence to Vienna,
the House of Austria, to which he had the honour of being
related, imagined it had found in him a zealous friend at
the French Court, and furnished him with a powerful
backing. It was thus that he laid the foundations of his
progress. All the same, he might not have succeeded so
quickly if he had not been willing to do violence to his
natural frankness and high-mindedness by being guilty
of a base deed which he no doubt hoped would be buried
in the darkness where it was planned. A lady of the Court,
who was related to him, commenced to attract the King ;
their intimacy ripened and she reached the stage of receiving
letters and rendezvous. A courtier less subtle than the
Duc de Choiseul would have regarded this as a fortunate
opportunity for getting on and reaching his goal. He
would not have neglected to stimulate the passion of the
august lover and to seek to replace the official mistress
by the new one, who seemed to possess means of triumphing
that were real and irresistible. Choiseul reasoned differently and took the safer line. He preferred to sacrifice
his relative, whose reign might be short, rather than Madame
de Pompadour, whose power seemed to grow as time went
on. He was in the confidence of the former, who indeed
consulted him regarding her behaviour. One day, when
the passion of Louis XV had reached such a pitch that
he solicited a decisive interview by means of an urgent
letter, the Duc de Choiseul, who helped the lady to draft
her replies, affected to desire to think over the King's
missive. He bore it away and, with it in his hand, went
to the Marquise, to whom he said : " Madame, you think
of me as your enemy ; you are so unjust as to believe I
enter into conspiracies to rob you of the King's favour.
Now read this, and judge." He showed her the King's
tender and impassioned letter, and told her how it came

into his possession, and what risks he was running to serve
her. But he preferred the welfare of the State and the
happiness of his master to his own advancement, and he
regarded her as more essential to these two great objects
than any one. Madame de Pompadour knew Louis XV
too well not to be sure of winning him back on this occasion
so long as she was warned in time. Advised of this intrigue,
she quickly exploded it and made her rival experience all
the disgrace of discovery and the punishment that her
treacherous confidant really deserved. Thereafter he
became the favourite's creature. He was young, ardent and
bold ; and he sealed his reconciliation with the Marquise
in such a way as to flatter her that her charms had lost
nothing of their attractiveness. So he made his way to the
supreme power to which he succeeded.[1]

[1] All this is by no means to Choiseul's credit. The lady in question was
his cousin, Madame de Choiseul-Romanet. He alleged, in justification
of his treachery, that she was not worthy to be the King's mistress, as she
would certainly have abused her influence ! Choiseul's first reward for
this unscrupulous action was the receipt of one of the most coveted honours,
that of being admitted to the King's "little suppers" after the play. As
to the pretty, credulous and stupid Madame de Choiseul-Romanet, who had
dreamed of playing a brilliant rôle in the front of the stage, she had no option
but to leave it entirely.

This episode is very minutely recorded in *Mélanges d'Histoire et de
Littérature* by Sénac de Meilhan who concludes : " The Comte de Stainville, from this moment a protégé of Madame de Pompadour, was appointed
ambassador at Rome and afterwards at Vienna, but distance did not prevent
his cultivating her favour. Disgusted with the Abbé de Bernis, who was
minister, she caused him to be exiled, and recalled the Comte de Stainville
from Vienna to succeed him. Immediately after this appointment he was
made Duke and Peer, in 1759, and his influence with the favourite naturally
increased his power."

CHAPTER XXIII

A MYSTERIOUS AFFAIR

ON the 6th January (Epiphany) Louis XV, while supping in State, received a fright almost like that caused by Damiens in 1757, but fortunately not having the same effect. The King was at table, surrounded by all the family and a considerable number of spectators ; his heart, free from care, was given up entirely to family pleasures, when suddenly a great noise was heard outside the room. People asked each other what it was, found out, told each other, and alarm spread over every countenance. His Majesty noticed it, and asked what was the cause of the hubbub. They tried to calm him, but in vain. He read in the eyes of the onlookers an uneasiness that was not in conformity with the anticipated festivities, and he feared another attempt on his life. He asked the princes nearest to him, but their agitated appearance and vague answers only led him to think that his suspicion was justified. " What have I done ? " he said as he got up hastily from the table and tore away his napkin, " what have I done to possess such enemies ? " With these words, which struck the whole assembly with consternation, the monarch retired to his own rooms. When he was going to bed he asked for a proper account of the startling uproar. " Do not deceive me," he said to Monsieur L., " explain the mystery." " Sire," replied Monsieur L., " I tremble to tell you the story but, as you insist, here are the real facts. M. Truche de Lachaux, one of your guards, has just been stabbed by two wretches who sought to attack you. They have escaped, and your guard is on the point of death." At these words the King turned pale and his heart, which did not deserve to be betrayed, was greatly stirred. "See that great care is taken of my poor guard," he said ; " if he recovers I will reward his devotion." Although the monarch was far from imagining at the moment that this uproar was the result of an infamous trick conceived by Truche, he was overwhelmed with uneasiness.

All Paris, who soon learned of this disagreeable incident, sought to discover its authors and, as one of the alleged assassins was supposed to have been dressed as a priest, it was at once said that the Jesuits were responsible for the attack and must certainly be banished from the realm in whatever habit they were found. Prejudice does not stop to think ; only proof can destroy it. The people persisted in this idea till the next day, when the truth came to light, and it appeared that the guard who said he had been the victim of his devotion to the King, was only a deliberate and cowardly impostor.

Lachaux' trick was not the work of a moment. At any price he desired a pension from the King. He sought a pretext. He conceived this idea in October 1761, carefully elaborated it during three months, and put it into operation when he thought it could not fail to succeed.

As a matter of fact, on the 6th January, Lachaux, being on duty in the château, hid himself between nine and ten o'clock in the evening on one of the staircases, extinguished the light that might have revealed his proceedings, broke his sword, took off his coat, pierced it and his vest in several places, then stabbed his body also in several places with a knife which he had had sharpened a month previously by a Versailles cutler. Finally he put on his coat again, lay down, and called for help in despairing tones. At his cries two guards came. "My friends," he said to them,

" I have just been assassinated. See that the guard take good care of the King ; the two wretches who stabbed me are after His Majesty ; one is dressed as a priest, the other has a green coat. They asked me to admit them to the banquet, or to permit them to stand where the King would pass, offering me a great reward. The bait did not tempt me and I refused. Then they flung themselves on me with their knives, declaring their intention of delivering an oppressed nation and of giving renewed strength to a religion that had almost vanished." Truche said all this with such feeling as could not fail to deceive honest folk. He was borne away and treated with the attention due to a man really devoted to the King.

In spite of all his precautions an impostor usually leaves something that will reveal the truth. The next day he shrieked loudly when his wounds were dressed, and this showed the surgeon how deceitful he was. The surgeon said, with contemptuous coldness : " Sir, you are making a great fuss about very little ; you scream as though you were very ill, but instead of wounds I see only scratches." This completely disconcerted the soldier.

The surgeon did not leave the matter there, but determined to investigate it thoroughly. He examined Truche's coat and, from what he discovered, reported that the guardsman must have been his own assailant, as the holes in the coat and vest did not correspond with the wounds. Thereupon Truche was questioned. The inquiry did not last long ; the coward's tears foretold his conviction, and in a few minutes he confessed his shameful behaviour.

Such a confession could not long remain secret. It was necessary to undeceive the King, and a report was made to him. His Majesty was astounded and said : " I did not believe there existed in France a single soldier capable of so base an action." The King was so indignant that he washed his hands of all concern with the sort of death the wretch was to suffer. It was in vain that Madame de G. threw herself at the King's feet to beg mercy for Lachaux. His Majesty, notwithstanding his attachment to the Duchess, merely raised her and said : "Madame, I don't want to hear a word about that man ; justice must take its course."

Lachaux' torture was as humiliating as his crime had been base. The Parliament, by order dated 1st February, condemned him to be placed in a tumbril, clad in his shirt, a cord around his neck, a candle in his hand, with placards before and behind him bearing these words : "Fabricator of impostures against the safety of the King and the integrity of the Nation," and thus drawn through the various districts of Paris as a public penance. During this journey to the Place de Grève, where the wretch was hung, he seemed so repentant and his tears appeared to be so real that the spectators were moved, and their own tears seemed to express regret at the sad scene they were witnessing. Thus ended the career of a man whom birth and position had intended for a more glorious death.

CHAPTER XXIV

DEATH OF MADAME DE POMPADOUR—EPIGRAMS

THE Marquise de Pompadour was seized with a serious illness [1] during a pleasure trip to Choisy, an illness which speedily brought her so low that death seemed the only possible end. The spectacle was terrible for a lover, and even for a friend. Louis XV, who from the outset urged the doctors to hide nothing from him, received the fatal verdict without emotion. It should be added, however, that he behaved to the favourite as though he held the contrary belief, for not only did he treat her with all the kindness, attention and devotion that could comfort a sick person, but he continued to consult her on public affairs. [2] The minister,

---

[1] Madame de Pompadour died " by piecework," if one may so express it. Her whole system was disordered since she had abandoned her milk diet. To please Louis XV she resumed normal conditions and the usual heating food. She grew thin, she coughed, she had terrible palpitations during which her heart seemed to jump. She wept and groaned, " My life is a fight." She coloured her cheeks, masked her thinness (for she had fallen away to a skeleton), hid her wrinkles with rouge. The whole system was failing ; and the change of life came to put her at the mercy of the slightest trouble. She did not know whom to trust ; she dismissed her doctor, Quesnoy, and gave herself over to the quacks. On the 28th February, 1764, she had a hæmorrhage of the lungs which she survived, and a Mass of thanksgiving was celebrated. But on the 7th April she collapsed and was carried to Versailles, to her apartments on the ground floor of the right wing, " although, according to etiquette, only a prince might be permitted to die in a royal palace ; but had not the same privilege been granted to Madame de Vintimille ? "—Lacretelle, *Histoire du XVIIIe siècle.*

[2] The King, who, in the early stages of the illness, showed the greatest anxiety, seemed less afflicted than one would have expected. Every day, however, he went to see her, but, " as the illness was long and hopeless, he affected a callousness regarding it and appeared not to trouble." Cf. Fleury, *Louis XV et les petites maîtresses.*

the kingdom, everything was subject to her as before. She died, so to speak, with the reins of government still in her hands. Shortly before she breathed her last, Monsieur Janet came to make his usual report on the secrets of the post. Every morning the Duc de Fleury, gentleman of the bedchamber on duty, brought to His Majesty the medical bulletin regarding Madame de Pompadour's condition and she, transported from Choisy to Versailles, had the privilege, reserved exclusively to the royal family, of being ill and dying in the château whence was ordinarily banished, with the utmost care, everything that could remind the King of suffering and death. It is true that the very moment she expired (on the 15th April) her body was taken on a stretcher to her private mansion in the town, and Louis XV was observed to look out of his window as it passed without the least emotion, evincing complete apathy. Beyond question the King's love for her was quite dead.[1]

[1] Tradition has it that, on the day of her funeral, the King was quite unmoved. "A heartless word said as the cortège passed," wrote the Goncourts, like other historians before and after them, was all the funeral oration the King, "weary of his servitude" uttered over Madame de Pompadour. Gazing out of the window at the funeral procession, which started off in a flood of rain, and looking at his watch to see when it would reach Paris, he is stated to have said, cynically: "The Marquise will not have it fine for her journey." This has been proved untrue. Louis XV was as much affected as so selfish a monarch could be, and we prefer the more reliable evidence of Cheverny.

"At last the day of the Marquise's funeral arrived. The King, who had ordered all the arrangements, knew the hour. It was six o'clock on a winter evening, in a veritable hurricane. The will of the Marquise contained a request that she should be buried in the Church of the Capucines, Place Vendôme, where she had prepared a magnificent mausoleum. The King took the arm of Champlost, his principal valet, and, when he reached the door of his room, made him close it behind them as they stood outside on the balcony. He maintained a religious silence as the procession passed along the avenue. Despite the bad weather and the bitter air, of which he seemed insensible, he followed it with his eyes till the last bit of the funeral cortège vanished from sight. Then I entered the room. Two great tears rolled down his cheeks, and he said to Champlost these few words: ' That is the only respect I can pay her,' words more eloquent than any others he could have uttered at such a moment "—*Mémoires du Comte Dufort de Cheverny*, i. p. 324 (Paris: Plon, 1909).

But what man could have seen a union broken after twenty years without a tear ? Furthermore, this bereavement left him practically alone, in the midst of his family, from whom the Marquise had tended to separate him more and more. Sick of his wife, afraid of the austerity of his son and the Dauphine, he could no longer reconcile himself to the straightlaced Mesdames and their life of scrupulous religious observances. He had long lost the affection of his subjects, but at least he shared their dislike with his mistress,—and now it fell on him alone. Finally, his very indolence made him unwilling to assume the burden of public business, of which the Marquise de Pompadour had relieved him and of which her death left him to bear the whole weight. The ministers, and particularly the Duc de Choiseul, became more despotic in their respective spheres and thus relieved the King of his trouble—the only one that really worried him.

The Marquise, who was quite properly hated by the people,[1] truly deserved the devotion or affection of her august lover. Very different from Madame de Mailly, she never loved the King for himself. She was dazzled by the splendour of the throne, like the Duchesse de Châteauroux, and, while devoured by a noble ambition, did not seek to imitate her in inspiring the King to win glory that might reflect on her and palliate her dishonour. She was intelligent, but in a petty fashion ; and all her affections bore the imprint of this pettiness. She loved money, and saw in her exalted position only a greater facility for acquiring wealth and for satisfying her overwhelming appetite for luxury and amusement. Her

[1] Contrary to this ill-natured assertion " many of those whom she had benefited had good reason to mourn her death ; she was specially esteemed by all the poor of Paris, of Versailles, of her own estates, and, indeed, of everywhere she went "—*Report of General de Fontenay, Polish Ambassador.*

interest in and encouragement of the arts were only from this point of view, and only concerned those branches that were specially associated with her feminine tastes. She governed because she was dealing with a prince who wished to be governed, and consequently she felt obliged to seize the reins so that they should not fall into other hands. Possessing no energy herself, she could impart none to Louis XV, and so she was the most dangerous and baneful of mistresses for him and for his people. It was this that led to anarchy, disorder and all the ills of France.

If we want an accurate description of this woman let us listen to Voltaire,[1] who, in ten lines has described her birth, her life, her mind and her face. They occur in " La Pucelle," a rare poem suppressed in the later editions :

> Telle plutôt cette heureuse grisette
> Que la nature ainsi que l'art forma
> Pour le b . . . ou bien pour l'Opéra ;
> Qu'une maman avisée et discrète,
> Au noble lit d'un fermier éleva,
> Et que l'amour, d'une main droite
> Sous un monarque entre deux draps plaça.
> Sa vive allure est un vrai port de reine,
> Ses yeux fripons s'arment de majesté,
> Sa voix a pris le ton de souveraine
> Et sur son rang son esprit s'est monté.

(Such now is this charming lass, whom nature and art intended for the bawdy-house or for the Opera ; whom a cunning and discreet mother brought up in the splendid bed of a farmer-general, and the strong hand of passion placed between the sheets of a king. Her lively gait has become a regal carriage, her roguish glance has become majestic, her voice has acquired royal dignity, and her mind has risen with her rank.)

---

[1] The reference is doubtful, for if, as our author states, we want " an accurate description of this woman," we can also find it in the flattering madrigals, verses and lines with which this same Voltaire, who hated her, overwhelmed the Marquise. She was too good-natured and too secure in her power to hate the toady in turn. She contented herself with distrusting him, and often there were petty quarrels between them.

FRANÇOIS MARIE AROUET DE VOLTAIRE
From an engraving by B. L. Henriquez after Barat

Considering the character attributed to her it could scarcely have been expected that Madame de Pompadour would have watched the gradual approach of death without a murmur, with heroic fortitude. The place where she was and the attitude of the King's mind demanded that she should observe her final religious duties, which she did without fuss and without cowardice. She publicly asked pardon of all her household and of all the courtiers present for the offence she had caused them. The most curious thing was that the priests did not demand of this woman, who lived in double adultery, what they would have demanded in a case of simple fornication, namely, that the concubine should depart from the scene of her immorality, making this atonement in the place that for twenty years had beheld her sin. But Court confessors are accommodating, and it was decided that she was too ill to be moved. On the day that she felt would be her last, the curé of the Madeleine, in whose parish her Paris mansion was situated, was taking his leave of her when she said, "One moment, Monsieur le Curé, we will depart together."[1] Madame du Hausset, her chief attendant, closed her eyes. She was the widow of a gentleman, and

---

[1] Her death was very peaceful, as had been foretold by a fortune-teller. We read in the *Mémoires de Madame du Hausset* (pp. 203–208 of the edition of Baudoin Frères, Paris, 1824) a very interesting passage. The fortune-teller Bontemps, who had already made wonderful predictions to Bernis and Choiseul, was summoned to Madame de Pompadour. She prepared (as is done nowadays) two cups of coffee, and poured each into a glass, to examine the grounds. Madame de Pompadour asked, "When shall I die, and of what ailment?" The fortune-teller said, "I never speak of that, or rather fate will not let me. Look, he jumbles everything up!" And she pointed to several confused patches of the coffee-grounds. Madame de Pompadour went on, "Very well, then, regarding the date; but what will be the nature of my death?" The Bontemps woman looked at her and said, "You will have plenty of time for reflection." She reflected so well that she showed not the least sign of impatience. Two hours before she passed away, her women wished to change her clothes. She said, "I know you are very skilful, but I am so weak that you would be bound to distress me, and it is not worth while for the short time I have to live."

necessity had driven her to attach herself to the favourite ; grave, discreet, upright, even devout, she served her for twenty years and retired with very modest means. Of the epitaphs engendered in flattery or satire we will quote the following, brief, forcible and very true :

> Ci-gît qui fut quinze ans pucelle,
> Vingt ans catin, puis huit ans maquerelle.

(Here lies one who was for fifteen years a virgin, for twenty years a harlot, then for eight years a procuress.)

There was another in Latin, which was quaint and, while turning on a play of words, contained a truth which rendered it invaluable.

D. D. JOANNIS POISSON EPITAPHIUM

> Hic piscis regina jacet, quæ lillia succit
> Per nimis ; an mirum si floribus occubat albis,
> Obiit die 15 aprilis, anno 1764.

(Here lies Queen Poisson who drained too greedily the royal lilies. It is therefore not to be wondered at if she died of " white flowers " [leucorrhœa]. She died the 15th April 1764.

Here is another of the many epitaphs :

> Ci-gît la fille d'un laquais
> Qui vint à bout, par ses attraits,
> D'être marquise et pas duchesse.
> A cette âme noire et traîtresse
> Louis remit aveuglément
> Les rênes du gouvernement.
> On en murmura hautement.
> Mais un sot qui se préoccupe
> Ne change pas facilement ;
> Le roi crut être son amant
> Et ne fut jamais que sa dupe.

(Here lies the daughter of a lackey who succeeded by her attractions in becoming a marquise, not a duchess. To this evil and treacherous soul, Louis blindly handed the reins of government. There were loud complaints, but an absent-minded fool is not easily moved ; the King thought he was her lover, but he was only her dupe.) [1]

---

[1] We must not dwell too much on all these invectives, which smell of the times, or take them too seriously. The following seem to us more sober, more accurate, and more in conformity with the truth : " Madame de Pompadour had enemies, who delighted in misrepresenting everything concerning her. In the first place, during her lifetime, there were the great nobles and courtiers who, notwithstanding the deference they paid in public, could not forget her humble birth and that she had been chosen from the commons." Then there were the Jesuits, who were against her because she was the friend of the philosophers and a great admirer of the Encyclopædists ; and, again, the ultra-revolutionary pamphleteers who based violent diatribes against the monarchy on the royal mistresses. To-day we see things in truer perspective. Successful efforts have been made to trace her origin, humble enough it is true, but not low. The many plots of those who envied the favourite, their endeavours to procure her overthrow or, failing that, to cloud her triumph, have been unravelled. It has been proved superabundantly that, if the Marquise squandered money on sumptuous or elegant buildings, she nearly always built them on royal estates, so that these luxurious dwellings became Crown property. The truth has been established regarding the legendary Parc-aux-Cerfs which our author, like his contemporaries, depicts as " an abyss of innocence and simplicity in which a host of victims was engulfed." This palace, costing more than a milliard, " one of the principal causes of the exhaustion of the finances," was smaller than the retreats of the nobles and financiers. It could accommodate at most one girl and an attendant, and the King sold it eventually for 16,000 francs. The conclusion is that, while Louis XV was the reverse of virtuous, he was not the shameless monster, the luxurious Sardanapalus, the sumptuous pasha of the novelettes ; and that Madame de Pompadour was not the superintendent of his pleasures, scouring the kingdom for fresh and unknown beauties suitable for " replenishing the seraglio of which she had the entire direction." It has been recognized that her choice of Bernis and Choiseul was not bad, but that all the defeats sustained by inadequate and inefficient Court generals were skilfully utilized against her. Gradually, in the light of the evidence of authors possessed of more impartiality or more knowledge, in the light of unpublished letters, of documents in the archives, of notarial acts, of business records, the fantastic tales so ingeniously originated in the eighteenth century and so readily enlarged upon in our own times, have been dissipated. It was all natural enough at the time, but the farther we get away the more clearly we see things, and the more does the truth come to light. Even the truth may not be very attractive, but it does not warrant extravagant rant and outrageous imprecations. See Roustan in chap. ii., " Les philosophes et les favorites," pp. 73–110 of the volume *Les Philosophes et la Société française au XVIIIe siècle* (Paris : Hachette, 1911). Our readers have seen the charges

against the royal mistresses; here is the defence. They can judge Mme du Barry for themselves after reading her defence as presented by the Marquis de Ségur. But, bearing in mind the historians' axiom that the same deeds must not be judged in the same way in all times, will they deny at least a little indulgence to Madame de Pompadour, "who was an enlightened friend of the arts, and a generous patron of painters, sculptors and authors? On these grounds she deserved well of posterity, who will not refuse to give the benefit of sympathetic indulgence to this charming woman whose refined tastes, whose extravagances at times foolish, whose very vices, so truly represent French society in the middle of the eighteenth century?"—Raunié, in the Introduction to vol. vii of the *Recueil* Clairambault-Maurepas.

CHAPTER XXV

DEATH OF THE DAUPHIN, OF KING STANISLAS, OF THE DAUPHINE AND OF THE QUEEN—A NEW FAVOURITE : MADAMOISELLE ROMANS—HER SON AND MADAME DE POMPADOUR

SOON after the death of Madame de Pompadour it was observed that the Dauphin, who had always enjoyed excellent health, was beginning to fail. He gradually lost weight, and his high colour gave way to pallor. It could not be concealed that he was the victim of some internal trouble. The cause was sought, and every one had his own theory. It is said that the Prince had a rash [1] from which the pus had been carelessly squeezed and had affected his chest. As the Dauphine did not tell this story to the compiler of her august husband's life it should be taken as apocryphal. It is more likely, from what she led the historian to say, that chagrin concerning the religious troubles, and particularly the expulsion of the Jesuits, was the chief cause of his illness. Be that as it may, after raising hopes by the use of grapes as his sole food, the Prince overtired himself, at Compiègne, with the drill of which he was so fond, and caught a bad cold. It soon became evident that his chest

[1] "This rash, or rather this ailment, was probably a ' barber's rash ' on the upper lip, which not unfrequently attacks tuberculous people. It is usually amenable to treatment, particularly in the case of a sharp attack "— Dr. Balzer of the Academy of Medicine. Cf. Sénac de Meilhan, pp. 272 et seq. of *Mélanges d'Histoire et de Littérature*, in which he says : " To cure this rash he secretly used a quack remedy. The Dauphine came to know of it, and as she knew the risk, she got hold of the drug and threw it away. The Dauphin was angry, procured a fresh supply, and continued to use it. The rash disappeared, but the poison was driven into the system."

was affected.[1] He would not consent to any change in regard to his return from this journey or his journey to Fontainebleau, whence he never came back. The King behaved in the same way as he had with regard to Madame de Pompadour and left nothing lacking so far as appearance went. He even remained at that extremely dull and unhealthy place until his son died ; but the very moments were counted and, in consequence, the dying Prince witnessed a spectacle so horrible that only religion could mitigate it. From his bed he could see everything that happened in the courtyard, which sometimes served to distract him from his suffering. As he was nearing his end, and it had been decided that the Court should depart immediately he expired, every one was busy making preparations so as to be in advance of the general confusion. The dying prince saw packages being thrown out of the windows and loaded on carts, and said to La Breuil, his doctor, who was trying in every way to keep from him any idea of his approaching end and to encourage his hopes : " It is best to die, for I am only wearying every one." [2]

---

[1] "The Dauphin commenced to cough, and his depression made him reject all advice. It was in this condition that, in July 1765, he went to Compiègne. The Dauphin's Regiment of Dragoons arrived, and he busied himself with exercising them, both mounted and dismounted. One day when he had made himself very hot, he witnessed some dismounted drill in a very wet meadow. He got damp feet and, as he was in a hurry to attend the Council, he went off in his carriage without stopping to change. The next day he had a bad chill, which he took no steps to cure. Rather he continued to tire himself, in all weathers, throughout the stay of his regiment at Compiègne. When he returned to Versailles, his lungs appeared to be affected."—Sénac de Meilhan.

[2] He was extremely good and kind to all who attended him. He said to Lassonne, the Queen's principal doctor, who was watching him : " My poor Lassonne, I am very sorry to have caused you to pass such a bad night ; go to bed, you must be very tired." To the Duc d'Orléans he said, with a gaiety which must have been forced, " I must be a nuisance to you, for every now and then I favour you with a minor death-struggle." He caused all the ambassadors to come into his room, and asked their pardon for the inconvenience he was causing them by preventing their departure from Fontainebleau.

The King had instructed the Grand Almoner not to leave his son while he was dying, but to receive his soul. When he saw the Prelate reappear in his presence on the 20th December he assumed that all was over. He immediately decided to send for the Duc de Berry, the oldest of the royal children, and, after having spoken to him as befitted the occasion, took him to his mother's room. He told the usher to announce " The King and His Highness the Dauphin." The Princess comprehended the meaning of this new ceremonial. She threw herself at the King's feet and begged his goodwill for her and her children.

In accordance with the Dauphin's last wishes only his heart was taken to Saint-Denis, his body being transported to Sens. His funeral was solemnized throughout the kingdom with a fervour and earnestness for which no precedent could be recalled even in honour of a king. Among the countless funeral orations regarding the Prince none was so good as this couplet, which Voltaire wrote for inscription beneath his portrait :

> Connu par ses vertus, plus que par ses travaux,
> Il sçut penser en sage, et mourut en héros !

(Known for his virtues rather than his works, he thought like a sage and died like a hero.)

The death of a virtuous prince is a general calamity. Even foreigners mourned his death, and Dr. Maty, an English man of letters who was in a position to know and appreciate the feelings of his compatriots, wrote to the Duc de Nivernais :

" Permit a foreigner to mingle his tears with yours and those of all France. Germanicus, who was mourned by the Romans, was also mourned by his neighbours— even by the enemies of the Empire. If the Dauphin should look down at this world now, he would see only French hearts." [1]

If Louis XV bore with his usual indifference the death of his only son, on the other hand he did everything he could to console the Dauphine for her irreparable loss. He did not want her to feel any change in her position. He increased the number of her guards ; he gave her a suite of rooms beneath his own which she seemed to desire, and ordered the construction of a communicating staircase. He thought of every possible courtesy, and, to save the princess the fatigue of the stairs, he had a bell placed in his own room communicating with hers. When he was asked about her rank at Court he replied : " Only the Crown can give absolute precedence. Nature gives a mother precedence over her children, and Her Highness will have precedence over her son until he becomes King."

All these attentions, privileges and favours did not, however, have the result the King so earnestly desired of softening the Dauphine's grief and improving her health. The fatal blow had been struck. Before the Dauphin's final illness she had always slept with him. During the illness she had watched him, often spending hours together under his curtains breathing the disease-laden air that the dying man exhaled. Her lungs thus became affected, and her unceasing sorrow, so calculated to aggravate the slightest illness, soon rendered hers incurable. After fifteen months she joined her husband, and on the 13th

---

[1] The Dauphin, judged according to his times and circumstances, was what we should call nowadays a good fellow. It is true he supported the Jesuits through thick and thin, but he did not oppose the " philosophers " (we know what that word signified in the eighteenth century), and openly condemned the banishment of Rousseau, saying that " if Rousseau was to be pitied, he certainly was not to be persecuted." Voltaire was pleased to say that, during his last illness, the Dauphin read Locke, and that he knew the tragedy of *Mahomet* by heart. " If this age," he concluded, " is not that of great talents, at least it is that of cultivated minds." His motto was " Let us persecute no one "—Cf. Stryienski, *Le XVIII* siècle*, chap. xiv.

March was buried beside him, in accordance with the wish she had expressed to the King. It was a remarkable example of conjugal love, so rare in this world of ours and specially at Court. The Princess's maternal love was not less marked. She had always regarded it as her first as well as her most important and most sacred duty to watch over the education of her children. During the Dauphin's lifetime she shared this duty with him ; after his death she performed it alone. Latin and French, sacred and profane history, the duties of their position and of religion, all came within the scope of this scholarly and virtuous woman, and, despite her feebleness and exhaustion, she did not cease to fulfil her duties till the eve of her death.

This sad event had been preceded by another of the same kind, which occurred without warning, although in extreme old age, and in striking circumstances. King Stanislas, whom the love of the Lorrainers would have made immortal had their desires been granted, was sitting alone by the fire, in perfect health, when a corner of his dressing-gown caught light. Help came too late, and he died as a result of this sad accident in February 1766.

Finally, by a conjuncture of notable fatalities, the Queen was taken ill with an unknown lingering disease which the doctors called by the new or revived name of *coma vigil*, by which they sought to describe Her Majesty's condition as one in which she was unconscious although her senses had not entirely ceased to function. For several months she lingered, sometimes better, sometimes worse, but without hope. She passed away on the 25th June, following her father after a short interval of time about equal to that which elapsed between the death of the Dauphin and that of his wife.[1]

[1] Poor Queen ! " a great innocent married to a vicious child." Unhappy as a girl, she was still more unhappy as a wife, her dignity sorely wounded when she saw herself supplanted by mistresses. Always good and kind, although not quite devoid of malice, always ready to forgive, she lived

19

We are not ignorant of the gossip regarding most of these deaths, which succeeded each other so rapidly, all remarkable, all different, all slow, all foreseen, all fixed at certain dates, almost systematically and evenly spaced; but we believe it to be the mere outcome of the disordered imagination of politicians eager for sensational tales, and believing that the most risky crimes are as easy to commit as they are to imagine. These rumours are all founded on the premise that Damiens' attempt was the result of a deep-laid plot, and, as an untraced crime is always attributed to him who profits most by it, people were so horrible as to fasten suspicion on the heir-presumptive to the throne. Unfortunately, or rather fortunately, the thing that made the first breach in the calculations of these sinister investigators was the fact that Madame de Pompadour was the first in the succession of victims, and it is difficult to imagine that the same hand that poisoned her would have

modestly in the background, seeking forgetfulness in extreme devotion or passing her evenings with a few old friends around the fire. By no means pretty, she had nevertheless an attractive figure. Quite suddenly this insignificant Queen would become imposing. "Sometimes this simple princess assumes a dignity that inspires respect and even embarrassment if she does not take steps to reassure you. Between one room and the next she becomes the very Queen, and maintains that same idea of grandeur that we associate with Louis XIV"—*Mémoires du Président Hénault.* Was it not strange that this little Polish princess should be the one to recall at Versailles the majesty of the great reign ? Let us say, with her contemporary the Duc de Croy : "The goodness of her character was depicted on her most gracious countenance. This estimable princess, who had done nothing but good, deserved the regrets of the nation." Here we recognize the model of La Tour, whose delightful portrait in the Louvre perpetuates her calm smile and reveals the resignation she showed both as woman and as wife. Yes, again we say, "Poor Queen Marie Leczinska !"

One person alone loved her sincerely—her father. His letters to his daughter, less "touched up" than those of Madame de Sévigné, are masterpieces of paternal love, and come straight from the heart. "You are my *alter ego*, and my thoughts are as near yours as my heart, since I live only for you." And again : "I am not young, yet I would fain be three months older to make myself younger by the pleasure of seeing you. I kiss the tears that you are shedding, those little pearls which are jewels of infinite value to me." To quote one letter is to quote them all. Cf. Stryienski, *op. cit.* pp. 210–212.

STANISLAS LECZINSKI, KING OF POLAND

poisoned the Dauphin,[1] the Dauphine, and the Queen. To do so would be to recognize two sets of poisoners at the Court, who, fighting against each other, vied with each other in committing their atrocities, and reaped no other reward than impunity, while the King who, by his silence, acquiesced in these abominable affairs, enjoyed the savage pleasure of witnessing the sacrifice of those most dear to him. Unless we attribute to Louis XV the heart of a Nero, or the hypocrisy of a Tiberius, such a prolonged and frightful spectacle must have been a continuous torture for him, a torture that not even the most abandoned wretch could have borne. Such are the contradictions, the absurdities, the abominable consequences that would follow from the admission of a fact without which the others are untenable and fade away. It would appear that if there were assassins they must have been the doctors !

An act of kindness performed by the King when the Queen died suggests that hers was the death he felt the most. Monsieur de Lassonne, Her Majesty's principal medical attendant, came, in accordance with custom, to announce the sad news to the King, who followed him

---

[1] We will not spend time on all these untenable and ridiculous theories of poison. We have already spoken about them in connexion with the Duchesse de Châteauroux and Madame de Vintimille. The Dauphin, to speak only of him, died quite simply of pulmonary tuberculosis. All the same, it is not without interest to quote the following lines from Sénac de Meilhan : " A person worthy of credence, who was so placed as to be a close eye-witness of these things, assured me that he had often seen the Prince during his illness, and heard the theories of the doctors ; that he had seen the progress of the disease ; and that there could not be a calumny not merely more false but more absurd than the suggestion that the Duc de Choiseul had caused him to be poisoned." This rumour was widely spread, and it was even alleged that it was the cause of Louis XVI's dislike for that minister, a dislike which was simply due to a discussion in which he showed disrespect to the Dauphin. Louis XVI once said, when speaking of M. de Choiseul : " I owe it to the memory of my father never to let approach me a man who lacked respect for him and insolently declared himself the enemy of his sovereign's son." Choiseul's words, which we have already quoted, may be mentioned again : " Perhaps, Sir, I shall some day be so unfortunate as to be your subject, but it is certain I shall never be at your service."

back to her room. He went to the death-bed and kissed
her for the last time. Then he asked M. de Lassonne for
the fullest details of the Queen's last moments. The
doctor, while reporting to His Majesty, turned pale,
staggered, and collapsed. The King supported him in his
own arms and carried him to an arm-chair, giving a notable
example both of conjugal tenderness and of humanity.

The more deeply we study the life of this Prince, the
more unaccountable we find it. We see by his will that in
1766, when first he thought of it, he recognized his failings
and the imperfections of his reign. He had suppressed
the Parc-aux-Cerfs and sought at least to avoid the scandal
of a life too openly dissolute. It was after the death of
the Queen, who evidently strengthened him in his good
resolves, that he fell again into gross irregularities, giving
himself up to all his weaknesses and allowing his kingdom
to become the prey of the crowd of adventurers that
surrounded him.

This caused the more dismay because in the meantime
Louis XV had performed an act of unwonted vigour which
seemed to indicate a sincere resolve to live better and to
remove from the public gaze everything that might remind
the people of his dissipations. Among the countless
beauties who were submitted for his choice he had remarked a Mademoiselle de Romans, an artless girl of fairly
good birth and education who, at first resisting him, would
only consent to submit to his caresses on condition of not
having to enter that disgraceful seraglio where others were
herded. His Majesty agreed, and purchased for her a
house at Passy, where she gave birth to a son. The delighted
King permitted her to have the child baptized in his name,
and promised to recognize him in due course, demanding
silence regarding his promise until he should decide otherwise. Mademoiselle de Romans fed the baby at her own
breast and regarded him not so much as her child as the

King's. She was so stupid as to pay the baby respect in anticipation of his recognition. She always addressed him as " Your Highness." She sat him on the back seat of her carriage, herself taking the front seat like a governess. She demanded similar homage not only from the servants and household, but also from every one that visited her. For some time the King, gratified by this childishness, tolerated it, for, as it took place within the house, it did not become public. Moreover, this lesser sultana lived in complete retirement, behaved very modestly, and even, so far as her condition would permit, pleased her neighbours and her priest, making herself generally liked by her benevolence and charities. Above all, she did not concern herself with public affairs, which prevented Madame de Pompadour, and later the ministers, from being jealous of her. But what retreat is proof against a schemer ? What quiet will he not disturb if his plans so demand ? A certain Abbé de Lustrac, a man of some position, when he saw that the dead official mistress was not replaced, thought the opportunity propitious and procured a footing in Mademoiselle de Romans' house on the pretext of helping with the education of her son. She was rather dull, and he soon obtained her confidence. She was very glad to find in him a counsellor and a man who could write letters for her to the King. Although she was not burning with ambition to become the official mistress, he worked on her weakness for her son and induced her to press His Majesty to fulfil his royal promise regarding this precious pledge of his love. The more the monarch avoided satisfying her, the more the priest urged the need of reawakening his love, persuading her that the King could not give a position to the young prince without consolidating her own and rendering it unassailable. He so flattered her pride that she began to go about more and to affect airs of importance, not concealing the grounds on which they were based. She thought she would thus force her august lover to hasten the desired moment, but it turned out otherwise. Louis XV took offence; and his ministers, who greatly appreciated being relieved of the yoke of an imperious mistress and had no wish to see a second, fanned the monarch's displeasure. One fine morning she was roughly seized and carried to a convent under the King's warrant. She was separated from her son, who was put in a school without her knowing where he was, and her confidant was closely confined in a fortress. Thus was the scheme shattered, and the public, who were ignorant of the inner reason for such an event, attributed it to the repentance of the erring monarch. We have seen how different was the real explanation. Since his death, Madame Adélaïde has even said, in connexion with the will already mentioned, that her august father was at that time really converted and resolved to live as a good Christian, but that the Maréchal de Richelieu, on the plea of distracting him from his grief, had led him again into dissipation. Soon after there appeared on the scene Madame Dubarry, who was the heroine of the last of the Prince's love affairs and crowned the infamies with which his life was already crowded. But the time has not yet come to tell that vile tale, which we would prefer that our readers should not ask us to narrate. Let us at least postpone it, although, in whichever direction we look, we see nothing but horrible things to record.[1]

---

[1] There is a very interesting chapter in *Casanova's Memoirs* regarding Mademoiselle de Romans. Without going through the eight large volumes of those *Memoirs* the particular chapter will be found at pp. 253–275 of *La Cour et la Ville sous Louis XV*. (Paris : Albin Michel). After leaving Switzerland Casanova stopped at Chambéry to change horses, and then went to Grenoble, where he stayed for some time in the household of her who was to be one of the most famous of Louis' temporary mistresses. Anne was the daughter of M. Jean Joseph Romans Couppier, a respectable citizen, and Madame Arman, his wife. Casanova relates at length, but in very interesting fashion, how he came to foretell that she would be the King's mistress, a prediction

which appears, however, to have been recorded long after the event. Then followed the journey to Paris and the presentation. This presentation is described by Madame de Campan, but in too much detail to be quoted here. The King, on his way to the Tuileries, saw a young girl whose beauty struck him : it was Mademoiselle de Romans. He sent for her, and she was brought to him by Lebel. "Mademoiselle de Romans found the King awaiting her with all the desires of a prince who had arranged the moment for him to possess her."

This tale of Madame de Campan's is pure imagination ; it is really the story of another of the King's mistresses, Mademoiselle Tiercelin, at the time when the Pompadour's sway was tottering. Mademoiselle de Romans was not fifteen years old, as Madame de Campan says, nor seventeen as Casanova says, but fully twenty-one ; and she was not so artless as our author suggests. Her beauty was somewhat exaggerated by Casanova, " a skin of satin, its dazzling whiteness enhanced by her magnificent black hair. Her features were perfect. Her large, black eyes were both extremely bright and extremely soft ; she had arched brows, a small mouth, regular teeth, a smile full of charm and sweetness." In fact, according to him, nothing was missing in this ideal beauty. Sophie Arnould describes her as " well formed, but much bigger than those around her, like the nymph Calypso—so much so that the King himself, although a very fine man, looked like a student or a princeling beside her."

Louis XV loved her for some time. Her baby was born in a secluded house at Passy, and was baptized Louis Aimé de Bourbon. She nursed him herself, and always called him "Your Highness." See the *Mémoires de Madame du Hausset* for the meeting between Mademoiselle de Romans, who was taking her baby out, and Madame de Pompadour, whom she did not know. The conversation was most interesting ! Tired of her morganatic posing, Louis XV had her shut up in a convent from which she eventually emerged, and married the Marquis de Cavanac. Cf. Fleury, *Louis XV intime et les petites maîtresses.*

The child was entrusted to a clerk who received a thousand *écus* a year to bring him up. In the reign of Louis XVI, Mademoiselle de Romans at last traced the boy, and caused him to be recognized, a recognition which was the easier because of his marked likeness to Louis XV, which, according to contemporaries, was seen in his morals as well as in his appearance. He took orders, and became the Abbé de Bourbon, " indolent, voluptuous, libertine." At Rome, where he was ambassador in 1785, Cardinal de Bernis " gave him a welcome such as he might have expected from the former favourite of Louis XV." He hoped for an abbey or a fat bishopric, but died of small-pox on 27th February, 1787, without receiving anything, at Naples, on his way back to France, where he wished to go to Versailles " to defend himself against those who had attacked him."

We have already said what we think of the phraseology of Mouffle d'Angerville !

CHAPTER XXVI

THE CHEVALIER D'ÉON—GROWING UNPOPULARITY OF LOUIS XV—HIS SADNESS—POVERTY IN FRANCE—THE KING OF DENMARK—WITTY AND SATIRICAL SAYINGS

HAVE people forgotten the strange lawsuit that was instituted after the peace of 1763 between the Comte de Guerchy, French Ambassador in England, and the Chevalier d'Éon, who had meanwhile been appointed Minister Plenipotentiary ? [1] Every one was astounded at the way in which the latter flouted and insulted the Comte and still more at the impunity with which he remained living in London and disseminating

[1] Charles Geneviève Louis Auguste André Timothée de Beaumont d'Éon, French diplomat and publicist, born at Tonnerre, 1728 ; died in London, 1810. Éon, who was not without distinction as a writer, as a diplomat, and even as a soldier, and who sometimes dressed as a man, and sometimes as a woman, owes his fame specially to the doubt in which his contemporaries remained throughout his life as to his sex. To-day we know that he was a man. For particulars of his adventurous career, see specially *Mémoires du chevalier d'Éon*, Paris, 1836 ; *Vie politique, militaire et privée de demoiselle C. G. L. A. A. d'Éon* ; *Correspondance de Grimm* ; *Mémoires de Madame de Campan* ; and in *L'Espion anglais*, three chapters which are reproduced on pp. 151–179 of Pol André's *Les Petits boudoirs sous Louis XV*. (Paris : Albin Michel).

Song on the Chevalier d'Éon

Du chevalier d'Éon,
Le sexe est un mystère ;
L'on sait qu'il est garçon ,
Cependant l'Angleterre
Le fait déclarer fille,
Et prétend qu'il n'a pas
De trace de béquille
Du père Barnabas.

LE CHEVALIER D'ÉON
J. Condé Delint. et Sculpt.

the most outrageous pamphlets attacking his antagonist.
The quarto *Lettres, Mémoires et Négociations particulières,*
etc., was not only offensive to the latter, but incriminated
the most powerful personages of the day—the Duc de

Jadis il fut garçon,
Très brave capitaine ;
Pour un oui, pour un non,
Chacun sait qu'il dégaîne ;
Quel malheur !   S'il est fille !
Que ne serait-il pas
S'il avait la béquille,
Du père Barnabas ?

Il est des francs maçons
Un très réel confrère,
Sachant de leurs leçons
Les plus secrets mystères ;
Pour le coup s'il est fille
Plus on n'en recevra,
Qu'on n'ait vu la béquille
Du père Barnabas.

Il fut chargé ; dit-on,
D'ordres du ministère ;
On lui donna le nom
D'un extraordinaire ;
Ah ! parbleu, s'il est fille,
Que lui va mieux que ça,
Si ce n'est la béquille
Du père Barnabas ?

Pour ses amusements
Il a fait vingt volumes,
Touchant le droit de gens
Dont il sait les coutumes.
Quoique avocat habile
Il ne fait pourtant pas,
Le droit de la béquille
Du père Barnabas.

Qu'il soit fille ou garçon,
C'est un grand personnage
Dont on verra le nom
Se citer d'âge en âge ;
Mais pourtant, s'il est fille,
Qui de nous osera
Lui prêter la béquille
Du père Barnabas !

Choiseul, the Duc de Praslin, the Duc de Nivernois, even the Marquise de Pompadour. Their pettiness of mind was revealed by their own despatches, and we know how touchy people can be in such a case! It has since become known that there was talk of kidnapping the Chevalier d'Éon; that the King had concurred, and had asked for details of the scheme; that His Majesty, who had long

> Quoiqu'il ait le renom
> D'être une chevalière,
> Il paya la façon
> Aux yeux d'Angleterre,
> D'une petite fille,
> Ce qui ne serait pas
> Sans avoir la béquille
> Du père Barnabas.

(The sex of the Chevalier d'Éon is a mystery. We know he is a male; but England says he is a female, and has no trace of the crutch of Father Barnabas.

Formerly he was a male, a brave captain ready at a word to unsheath his sword. What a pity if he is a girl! What would he not have done if he had had the crutch of Father Barnabas?

He is a sincere comrade of the Freemasons, knowing the most secret mysteries of their craft; but if he is a girl he will receive no more, as they have not seen the crutch of Father Barnabas.

It is said he was entrusted with orders from the minister and was appointed "Extraordinary." By Jove! what could suit him better than that if he is a girl—unless it be the crutch of Father Barnabas?

He amused himself by compiling twenty volumes on the law of nations, with whose customs he was well acquainted. Although a clever lawyer, he did not do justice to the crutch of Father Barnabas.

Whether man or woman, he was a great personage, whose name will be handed down to posterity. But if he was a woman, which of us would venture to offer him the crutch of Father Barnabas?

Although reputed to be a dame, he complied with the fashion in England with a little girl, which could not have come about without his possessing the crutch of Father Barnabas.)

This famous crutch served in those days to round off many a verse. Father Barnabas was a lame monk who left his crutch behind—in a brothel!

carried on a secret correspondence with the Chevalier, disclosed the whole thing to him, and told him what steps to take in order to baffle the kidnappers. Moreover, a little while after Louis XV granted him a secret allowance of twelve thousand *livres* per annum, the warrant for which, as follows, was written and signed with his own hand : " In recognition of the services that Monsieur Éon has rendered in Russia, in the army, and in connexion with other matters that I have committed to him, I am anxious to assure him an annual allowance of twelve thousand *livres* which I will cause to be paid to him punctually every half-year, in whatever country he may be (except in enemy territory in time of war), until I find an occasion to appoint him to some post, the salary of which is greater than this allowance.—Versailles, 1st April, 1766. LOUIS."

Apparently the Chevalier remained in London until the death of the King, as a spy not so much on the English as on his ambassador, an arrangement from which another would have derived more benefit in connexion with high policy, whereas he only instituted it to amuse himself and to enable him to laugh at the expense of his ministers.

The Chevalier d'Éon, who has since been turned into a woman, and who probably partook of both sexes, deserves to be better known. Here is what he says of himself. Born at Tonnerre, Mademoiselle d'Éon (for he speaks of himself as a girl) was endowed in her earliest youth with discretion that well suited the political ideas of her parents, who made her pass as a boy. She was sent to the Collège Mazarin at Paris, and it is easy to imagine how wearisome she must have found it to engage in the various exercises of body and mind without betraying her sex, which was never suspected. After literature she studied law, and became doctor of civil law, and then a barrister. Already known by several works, she had occasion to reveal herself to the Prince de Conti, who honoured her family with his special patronage. Russia had quarrelled with France and it was necessary to effect a reconciliation between the two Courts. Search was made for a secret agent, not too scrupulous, but yet capable of insinuating himself and of carrying out the delicate mission that would be entrusted to him. The Prince de Conti thought that Mademoiselle d'Éon possessed all the necessary qualities, and suggested her to Louis XV, who was very fond of such mysteries. He gladly approved of this female negotiator, who, when nearing St. Petersburg, put on woman's clothing, and played her part so well that His Majesty sent her to Russia again with the Chevalier de Douglas. On this occasion she was dressed as a man, and her performance was even more skilful than before, as it is asserted that the Empress quite failed to recognize her. The result of these negotiations was that Russia decided to ally herself with Vienna and Versailles rather than with Prussia. When the treaty was signed, Mademoiselle d'Éon was sent with the news to the King. She broke her leg *en route* ; but she did not allow the accident to stop her, and arrived at Versailles thirty-six hours before the courier sent by the Court of Vienna at the same time as she left. The delighted King ordered his surgeon to give her every attention, and granted her a lieutenancy in the dragoons, which she greatly coveted. She served in the later campaigns, and then resumed her political career, receiving an appointment as Secretary to the Embassy in London. She made herself so agreeable to the English Court that His Britannic Majesty, contrary to all custom, chose her to carry to Versailles and to the Duke of Bedford, his ambassador in Paris, the ratification of the peace that had been negotiated between the two countries. It was on this occasion that the King gave her the Cross of St. Louis. He had already granted her two pensions. It must, indeed, be admitted that she was the most remarkable person of her time. There have been several cases of women disguising themselves as men and fighting as soldiers, but there was no other who combined such military, political and literary ability.

An incident related by the Comte de Broglie proves more than ever the truth of what we have said regarding the character of the late King. He relates [1] that on the occasion of his appointment as Ambassador to Poland in 1752, His Majesty sent him, by the late Prince de Conti, an order signed with his own hand to correspond secretly with him and to give preference to the orders he should receive through that Prince over those that should reach him from the Council. He adds that, in 1757, when the Prince de Conti had lost the King's favour, His Majesty corresponded with him direct, and continued the practice till his death. His double-dealing went so far that he punished him twice, at the same time intimating privately that the exile was not justified; and he still shows the documents. In the affair of the Bastille he insisted that the Comte de Broglie, who was inculpated, should, without complaining or seeking to defend himself, permit his liberty and honour to be compromised, permit the gravest accusations to be levelled at him, and allow himself to be branded, in the eyes of the country and of foreign Courts, as a political incendiary, a contriver of intrigues and of abominable plots.

We do not know when the King formed his secret intimacy with the Duc d'Aiguillon, but it is beyond question that it developed and began to be known just when that officer was becoming more odious in Brittany and that, when the King felt compelled by public opinion to dismiss him, he brought him nearer to his own person by appointing him to the command of the Light Horse of his Guard.

---

[1] In a memorandum, produced as evidence in court, and printed in 1779, under the title of *Exposé des motifs qui ont nécessité la plainte du comte de Broglio*.

Finally, when he formally recognized the innocence of M. de la Chalotais, who had been unjustly calumniated, he harboured the calumniator in his own palace and persistently shielded him from all proceedings.[1]

After these striking examples of the way in which Louis XV distinguished the private person in himself from the head of the State, it is not surprising that he behaved similarly in respect of his interests. He had a private purse, quite separate from the public purse. He left the superintendence of the receipts and expenditure of the latter to the Comptroller General; but for his private affairs he had a confidential servant, a minister *ad hoc*, M. Bertin. Not only did he not permit any of his money to be taken for the State treasury, but, if he saw a chance of benefiting his private fortune at the public expense, he regarded it as a lucky speculation. He held all sorts of securities and, whenever a decision was reached at the Council that could damage any of them, he gave orders for their immediate sale before the fall took place. When the present King of Sweden, then Crown Prince, came to France to effect a settlement regarding the subsidies due to his father, the Treasury was empty, and Louis XV made a great difficulty of advancing the sum from his private

---

[1] Louis René de Caradeuc de la Chalotais, attorney-general of the Parliament of Brittany, was among the first magistrates to move for the expulsion of the Jesuits from France by his *Comptes rendus des Constitutions des Jésuites*. His sarcasms earned for him the enmity of the governor of the province, and he was regarded as one of the chief instigators of the resistance offered by the Parliament at Rennes to the fiscal decrees with which the Duc d'Aiguillon annoyed that body. Consequently the Duc sought an opportunity to overthrow him, and fastening on a suspicion that certain anonymous letters to the King regarding the troubles in Brittany were in his handwriting, he procured his arrest with those of his son (also attorney-general) and four councillors of the Parliament, on 11th November, 1765. The King, however, soon put an end to the matter, saying that the past must be forgotten; but he banished to Saintes the father, son and four councillors. They were recalled from exile by Louis XVI, and reinstated in their offices. When the Revolution broke out, la Chalotais retired to Dinant, but was arrested and guillotined " as a conspirator " in 1794.

funds, and then only on condition that it should be promptly repaid.

What was at first only laughable childishness became, at the period of Louis' reign at which we have arrived, incredible hard-heartedness. The evil - minded people around him excited his cupidity, dazzled him with immensely profitable speculations (by cornering wheat) which they could carry out the more effectively under His Majesty as the system of so-called freedom helped them. He was advised to build royal storehouses, under the pretence of supplying the people. This caused a scarcity of the commodity and kept up the price, which rose in consequence of the poorness of the harvest. We will not go into the manipulations of the lesser monopolists, which are very clearly depicted in a host of works by the economists, but will content ourselves with saying that Louis XV gave such serious attention to this speculation that those admitted to his private rooms saw on his desk accurate records of the prices of wheat, day by day, on the different markets of the kingdom. This explains why the courts, which were ostensibly authorized to trace abuses to their source, were thwarted when they discovered the thread and still more so if they sought to punish the authors. It also explains the uselessness of the famous assembly of notables which was held in Paris in 1768 under the title of Assembly of the General Safety. It might have been very important if the Parliament had been courageous and had not been presided over by a creature of the Court. We read that President Choart, of the Court of Excise, invited his colleagues to confer as to the steps that should be taken, subject to the King's good pleasure, regarding the excessive dearness of corn and bread, and had to admit that the conference fulfilled its mission but imperfectly. He tells us that the object of the invitation and of the conference was only known shortly before the meeting, notwith-

standing the importance of the subjects it had to discuss ;
that he could not procure its postponement, nor that it
should last long enough to take a vote. He finished by
signifying to his colleagues his regret at being forced to
decide too quickly on matters that demanded fuller
consideration, in an assembly hastily summoned and
comprising many members who were as badly situated as
himself. It followed that this assembly was a veritable
laughing-stock, a snare to deceive the people into thinking
that the King was concerning himself with their troubles,
whereas he really had a share in bringing them about.
Collectors carefully preserve the Royal Almanac of 1774,
in which the compilers had the effrontery to include in the
list of financial officers entrusted with the royal purse
Monsieur Marivaud, treasurer of wheat for account of
His Majesty.

It has been said that, during the latter part of his reign,
Louis XV, worn out with the troubles and misfortunes of
his kingdom, hankered after abdicating. While he was
incapable of imposing his own authority, he was too jealous
to entrust authority to others. If he could have passed
on the whole burden of government, retaining all that was
honorary, all that could contribute to his own security
and well-being, he would gladly have done so. It will be
seen from what we have said that he had long ago abdicated
in fact in respect of what concerned his people and even
his own connexions, whom he treated as outsiders in
regard to everything that he thought was the concern of
the State. We will select one further episode out of a
thousand as a final illustration of this deliberate apathy of
the King's.

The curé of St. Louis at Versailles, the parish of the
château, attended the King's levée one morning in accordance with his privilege. His Majesty, with his usual
appearance of humanity, asked after the priest's flock—

whether there were many sick, dead, poor. To this last question the curé replied, with a deep sigh, that there were many. "But," said the King with interest, "are there not abundant alms, are they not sufficient ; has the number of the poor increased ?" "Yes, sire." "How is that ? Where do they come from ?" "Sire, even the lackeys of your own household ask me for charity." "I can believe that, they are not paid," said the King crossly. He turned on his heel and broke off the conversation as though he were grieved to learn of evils that he could not relieve. Anyone who had heard the answer but not the question would have thought he was talking of the servants of some noble, or of the Emperor of China !

It was in this state of callousness that the King of Denmark [1] found him when he visited Paris. The first meeting of the two monarchs took place at Fontainebleau, on the 21st October, 1768. The King returned from the hunt and kept his guest waiting a quarter of an hour while

---

[1] "The Prince," said Collé, "who is only twenty years old, carries away the respect of the nations he visits ; a thousand sensible and witty things are narrated of him."

"It is not the King of Denmark who has just landed in our island, but the king of the fairies. He is not bad-looking; he is polite, grave and very considerate. He is accompanied by a whole chivalry of white sashes, which makes this travelling court look like a crusade "—Letter from Horace Walpole to Madame du Deffand.

This King, Christian VI (1749–1808), had reigned two years when he came to France, and naturally he had his song :

> Enfin, j'lons vu d'nos yeux
> Ce roi qui n'cherche qu'à plaire.
> Louis est, dit-on, fort joyeux
> D'avoir un si charmant confrère,
> A son air doux, affable et bon
> Vous l'prendriez pour un Bourbon !
>
> Quoiqu'il soit depuis longtemps
> Accoutumé qu'on le fête,
> L'hommage qu'ici on lui rend
> De plaisir lui tourne la tête.
> Dam ! C'est qu'il voit bien qu'à Paris,
> C'est de bon cœur qu'on reçoit ses amis.

he dressed. He apologized, saying that at his age he had need of a little sprucing up. At first he made a good impression on the prince by a remark which unfortunately only came from the lips. The visitor, after seeing the royal children and the princes, returned to the King and expressed his gratification with the august persons he had just visited and congratulated His Majesty on having such a circle. This gave Louis occasion to recall his recent losses, whereupon the Danish king observed that the large family that still remained must be a valued compensation. Louis said, with a sigh, " I have an infinitely larger one whose happiness would make me really happy." This was an expression of tender feeling which touched the inexperienced heart of the young monarch ; but he soon saw

> Ce fut vendredi dernier
> Que chez lui j'allâmes nous-même ;
> Ce roi-là fait bien son métier,
> Car il veut que tout l'monde l'aime.
> En fréquentant souvent Louis
> Il n'changera pas sitôt d'avis.
>
> On peut bien dire sans l'flatter
> Que pu fin qu'lui n'est pas bête,
> Car partout on n'fait qu'raconter
> Ce qu'à chacun il dit d'honnête.
> S'il a tant d'esprit à present
> Jugez ce que s'ra en veillissant.

(At last I have seen him with my own eyes, this king who only seeks to please. Louis is, so they say, very pleased to have such a charming comrade ; from his sweet affable and kindly air, you would take him for a Bourbon.

Although he has long been used to being fêted, the honour done to him here is turning his head with pleasure. To be sure, he sees that here in Paris we receive our friends most heartily.

It was last Friday that I went to see him ; he knows his job, for he wants every one to love him ; and familiarity with Louis will not quickly change his views.

It is no flattery to say that anyone who is wiser than he is, is no fool, for wherever you go you hear of nothing but the nice things he says to every one. If he is like that now, think what he will be when he is older !)

how empty it was when, on the roads, his coach was surrounded by peasants craving bread, when he received petitions begging him to draw the King's attention to the deplorable condition of the country ; when, in fact, he saw the same things constantly taking place around Louis' own carriage with but little effect.

At the State banquet that night it was remarked that all the wit and sallies came from the visitor. Speaking of the difference between their ages Louis XV said, " I might be your grandfather," to which the Danish king gallantly replied, " That is the one thing lacking in my good fortune."

Another repartee, not less clever, was his reply to the King who, noticing that he seemed to be attracted by Madame de Flavacourt, whose neighbour he was, asked him, with apparent malice (which, however, was as far from his mind as the reverse would have been), " Would you believe that the charming lady to whom you are talking is over fifty ? " " That shows, Sire, that people never grow old at your Court."

To prove our statement that Louis XV was as insincere when he said malicious things as when he said kindly things, a remarkable trait in his character, we cannot omit an anecdote of the Abbé de Broglie, one of the most convincing we could quote.

At a banquet the King asked after one of his guests and was told he had died. " I told him so," he said. Then, looking around the circle of courtiers until he came to the Abbé, he said, " Your turn next ! " The Abbé, who was cross-grained, harsh and passionate, could hardly contain himself. " Sire," he replied, " yesterday you went hunting ; a storm came and Your Majesty got as wet as the others," and he flung out, boiling with rage. " That's like the Abbé de Broglie," exclaimed the King, " he always gets angry " ; and he took no further notice.

If, however, Louis XV did not trouble to display, in the society of the Danish king, the amiability he reserved for his intimates, if from the throne he did not reveal to him any royal aptitude for government, he received him with a magnificence that did honour to both. The Duc de Duras, First Gentleman of the Bedchamber, was appointed to accompany the visitor wherever he went. He heaped him up with costly presents. He desired each of the princes of the blood to entertain the Danish king in turn, and the fêtes occasioned by this visit to some extent relieved the sadness and boredom of the Court. As a matter of fact, the King really longed to be relieved of this unwelcome visitor so that he might give himself up wholeheartedly to a fresh caprice, the baseness of which he appreciated.

CHAPTER XXVII

MADAME DU BARRY

AFTER the death of the Marquise and the disgrace of Mademoiselle de Romans, Louis XV had not had an official or even a known mistress.[1] There was a succession of passing fancies—ladies of the Court, middle-class women, work-girls. They were chosen from all ranks, for his insatiable lust found all acceptable but tired of all. It was the task of the vicious wretches who had plunged him again into the dissipation that he had at one time been disposed to give up, to furnish him constantly with the pleasures that would gratify him. Among the panders was Monsieur Le Bel,[2] first valet to the King, whose special duty it was to discover these women. In the course of his searches he met a certain Comte Dubarry, who was performing the same function for several gentlemen of the Court, and told him of his difficulties. " Is that all your trouble," replied Dubarry, " I have the very thing for you, a dish literally fit for a king." He took him to his own home and showed him a Mademoiselle Lange who had been his mistress and whom

---

[1] After the death of the Queen, Louis XV thought of marrying again. If he had done so, his second wife would have been the Archduchess Marie Elisabeth, sister of Marie Antoinette, and the King seriously considered the matter. Durand, who was going to Vienna, was told to procure the most detailed information regarding this princess. " Let him examine her figure from head to foot, omitting nothing that he can see ; let him find out about her character, and all with the utmost secrecy, and without arousing any suspicion in Vienna, and let him report in due course."

[2] The reference is to Lebel, the King's " caterer " ; but we have reached 1769, and Lebel died in 1768.

he now lent to others.[1] He assured Monsieur Le Bel that
she was a wonderful find, and that when the King had once
tried her he would stick to her for a long while.   She made

[1] The baptism certificate of the Comtesse du Barry runs as follows :
" Jeanne, natural daughter of Anne Bécu, called Quantigny, was born
19th April, 1743, and baptized the same day, her godfather being Joseph
Demange and her godmother Jeanne Birabin, both of whom have signed
with us."   According to a tradition, her father was really a monk of the
Convent of Picpus, where Anne Bécu, " the beautiful dressmaker," went to
work.   His name was J.-B. Gomard de Vaubernier, or, in religion, " Frère
Ange."   This explains why the Comtesse du Barry was sometimes known
as Mademoiselle de Vaubernier, sometimes as Mademoiselle Lange, and also as
Mademoiselle Rançon after her mother was married, in 1749, to Nicholas
Rançon, for whom Dumonceau got an appointment from the Syndicate of
Farmers-General as storekeeper.   The cynical proposal of Jean du Barry is
perhaps open to doubt, but is not devoid of probability.   At that time
Jeanne was the mistress of Jean, whose brother Guillaume she married a little
later.   She had various lovers, among whom are reputed to have been the
two Lagardes, M. de Monville, several others, and the inevitable Richelieu.
" Before me she had only had Richelieu," wrote (seriously or not) Louis XV
to the Duc de Choiseul.   She was at this time engaged in the shop of Madame
Lametz, dressmaker, whose son was a good-looking hairdresser.   For five months
he taught her the complicated art of hairdressing *à la maréchale* and the
harmonious arrangement of flowers and ribbons.   In her fifteenth year she
was ravishingly beautiful, with her long, fair hair and her snow-white complexion.   But it is a false calumny to state that about that time she was
one of the most sought-after inmates of the notorious Madame Gourdan's
establishment.   No reliance should be placed on the scandalous suggestion
of *L'Espion anglais*, by Maurepas, or the obscene pamphlet, *Anecdotes sur
la Comtesse du Barry*.

In reference to this sojourn with the hairdresser's mother, the satirists
said :

> Je sais qu'autrefois les laquais
> Ont fêté ses jeunes attraits,
> Que les cochers, les perruquiers
> L'aimaient, l'aimaient d'amour extrême.

(I know that formerly lackeys did honour to her youthful
charms, that coachmen and hairdressers loved her, yes, loved to
extremes.)

Again, regarding her alleged stay in the celebrated Gourdan house of
ill-fame :

> Quelle merveille
> Une fille de rien,
> Une fille de rien
> Donne au roi de l'amour,
> Est à la Cour !

MADAME DU BARRY

From an engraving by J. Condé after a miniature by Cosway

such a good impression that it was decided to introduce
her to the monarch's bed. We will not go farther into the
dark mysteries of the interview, but will simply observe
that His Majesty was so delighted that he announced his
satisfaction to the Duc de Noailles, saying that she had
given him pleasures he had not previously known of.

> Elle est gentille,
> Elle a les yeux fripons,
> Elle excite avec art
>   Un vieux paillard !
>
> En bonne maison
> Elle a pris des leçons,
> Chez Gourdan, chez Brissot ;
>   Elle en sait long !
>
> Que de postures !
> Elle a lu l'Arétin,
> Elle sait, en tous sens,
>   Prendre les sens !
>
> Le roi s'écrie :
> Lange, le beau talent !
> Encore aurais-je cru
>   Faire un cocu !

(What a wonder, a common wench, a common wench inspires
the King with love and comes to Court.

She is pretty, she has roguish eyes, and she knows how to excite
an old rake.

She has studied in a good school, at Gourdan's, at Brissot's ; and
she knows her job !

What postures ! She has read Aretino and knows every way of
capturing the senses.

The King cries, " Lange, what a clever girl ! I might have
thought I was again deceiving some husband ! ")

As for the du Barrys, they claimed to be descendants from the Barry-
mores, who went to England after the Norman Conquest ; and d'Hozier
supports this claim. Jean and Guillaume assumed, without justification,
the title of Comte and re-established the silver shield with three double-
bars *gules* with, as crest, a crown surmounted by a castle *argent*, and, issuing
from it a wolf's head *sable* ; supporters two wolves *sable* with a ducal crown
and golden chains, with the war-cry, *Boutez en Avant*. It is a long way from
this magnificence to the obscurity of " sons of a vine-tender," as one lam-
pooner calls them. Cf. Claude Saint-André, *Madame du Barry* (Paris :
Émile Paul, 1909).

"Sire," replied the courtier, "that is because you have never been to a brothel." [1] This should have opened the eyes of his master if he had been capable of overcoming so unworthy an attachment. The spell was too strong, and he could not do without this licentious creature. He had her taken privately to Compiègne and to Fontainebleau, and, the excess of his passion blinding him more and more, he wanted her to be married and so obtain a name that would render her presentable. The Comte Dubarry had a brother quite ready to play the part, and Mademoiselle Lange was thenceforth known as the Comtesse Dubarry. We will not stop to inquire who she was, what was her origin, whether she was legitimate or illegitimate ; we are sufficiently enlightened on all these points by the anecdotes related of the fair one. Suffice it to say that her origin was very humble, that from her early days she was destined, by both taste and condition, to a life of debauchery, and that despite her youth and the brilliant charms she still possessed, she could only offer to her august lover what was left from a life of most degraded prostitution ; that he could hardly fail to be aware of all this, and that he had sunk so low in vice and abandonment that he treated her like a member of his family, forced his children to meet her, almost set her on the throne beside him, poured out the public treasure to keep up her regal state, increased the

---

[1] We quote for mere purposes of reference this libellous (we insist on the word " libellous ") phrase of Maurepas, commenting on one of the songs he collected : " The girl Lange, a public prostitute in Paris," and this extract from *Anecdotes sur Madame la Comtesse du Barry*, London, 1778 : " It was in these circumstances that a celebrated procuress, Madame Gourdan, the recognized purveyor of pleasure to the town and the Court, learned through her touts that a new person had appeared. She seemed to be about sixteen, had a ravishing figure, smart and imposing, a perfectly chiselled oval face, large ogling seductive eyes, a dazzlingly white skin, a pretty mouth, small feet, hair that I could not hold in my two hands. . . . She replied that this calling suited her better than any other, that she was not fond of work, but would much rather always be laughing and frolicking. . . . Then I kissed her warmly, took her to my rooms, and showed her my boudoirs of gallantry."

taxes to satisfy her childish whims and made the fate of his people depend on the caprices of such folly.

The promotion of Madame Dubarry naturally caused much cavilling at Court, but opposition only made Louis XV the more stubborn in his passion. This was, perhaps, the one occasion when he kept a stiff back against difficulties, and evinced a pertinacious firmness which was lacking in more important matters.[1]

The first opposition came from a woman who was jealous not of the King's heart but of his sceptre, which she wished to share—the Duchesse de Grammont,[2] sister of the Duc de Choiseul. Haughty, imperious, excessively greedy of power, she had gained such a mastery over her

[1] See (next chapter) the note regarding the relations between the Dauphine and du Barry after her presentation.

[2] It can readily be imagined that, after Mme de Pompadour's death, " every woman in society would strive to pick up the glove if the King should throw it down." Among these women was Béatrix de Choiseul Stainville, sister of the Minister, born at Lunéville in 1730, canoness of Remiremont, who had made a good match when, in 1739, she married the Duc de Grammont, sovereign of Bidache, governor of Béarn. He was a widower, and a " sorry fellow who lived a dissolute life." Almost immediately after the marriage they separated. Urged on by her brother, and emboldened by her friends, Madame de Grammont " wanted to go too fast." She offered her services to the King even before she was invited. She failed because she " surrendered with too good a grace." The King quietly avoided private interviews with her, regarding them as risky. Here is a reference in a poem called " Les Pompadouriques " :

> Des jeux d'un amour impudique
> Il instruit sa coupable sœur,
> Déjà cette femme lubrique
> De son maître attaque le cœur ;
> Et tandis que son lâche frère
> Etend les voiles du mystère
> Dont il veut les envelopper,
>   Oh ! comble de perfidie,
> Ce monstre à son tour sacrifie
> Sur l'autel qu'il veut renverser.

(He taught his guilty sister tricks of shameless love. Already this lewd creature attacks the heart of her master ; and, while her dastardly brother spreads the veil of mystery in which he seeks to enshroud them, oh, height of perfidy ! this monster in his turn sacrifices on the altar he endeavours to overthrow.)

brother that that proud and autocratic minister allowed himself to be entirely governed by her. To account for this remarkable ascendancy the malevolence of the courtiers led them to discover the explanation in a more than fraternal intimacy between the two, both of whom were sufficiently independent of appearances not to be restrained by religion or public decency. Be that as it may, this story, fully believed at Court (where everything is readily believed because the courtiers know they are capable of everything), was cleverly and ingeniously recorded in the following quatrain relative to the principal events of the day, namely, the expulsion of the Jesuits and the death of the Marquise :

> Aprés avoir détruit l'autel de Ganimède
> Vénus a quitté l'horizon ;
> A tes malheurs encor, France, il faut un remède ;
> Chasse Jupiter et Junon.

> (After having destroyed the altar of Ganymede, Venus has disappeared ; but thy misfortunes, oh, France ! still call for a remedy —the banishment of Jupiter and Juno).

The Duchesse de Grammont, no doubt in agreement with her brother who wanted to consolidate and retain power in the family, conceived the idea of becoming the King's mistress. Although she was neither young nor pretty, the knowledge they both had of the monarch's past and of his character led them to hope for success. The precedent of Madame de Mailly, who possessed neither charm nor youth, but had succeeded through boldness and shamelessness, greatly encouraged them ; and the Duchess already saw herself victorious when she was displaced by a newcomer. She was the more furious when she learned what sort of woman had been preferred to her. She poured out her anger to her brother, whose aristocratic mind naturally made him revolt against the approaches of this party, for the Dubarrys, not daring at the outset to enter into direct competition with the all-powerful Minister, sought to conciliate him. It is even asserted that the Comtesse made eyes at him, and was ready to go farther if he had so desired. His haughtiness, the favourite's incredible progress with the King, and the support of the Choiseuls' rivals, led them to open warfare, which eventually resulted in a disgrace which the Duke, lulled by ten years of prosperity, regarded as out of the question.

It was thus less out of fear for himself than to satisfy his sister's resentment, that he decided to open his master's eyes to the disgrace that his choice would bring upon him, not directly, for he knew too well the dangers, but indirectly, by the most obscure bypaths. First of all he got his spies to trace out the whole of the Comtesse's scandalous life and adventures, which he caused to be referred to in the farces, the pamphlets and the little stories that went the round of the clubs. On his orders the police, so far from contriving to throw a veil over the sovereign's disgraceful behaviour, were the first to noise it abroad by those popular songs with which they amuse the capital—allegorical songs it is true, but no one was long without the key. The Court became full of them, and the story of the "Bourbonnaise" [1]

[1] The name by which Madame du Barry was called in the songs

LA BOURBONNAISE

La Bourbonnaise
Arrivant à Paris
A gagné des louis.
La Bourbonnaise
A gagné des louis
Chez un marquis.

Pour apanage
Elle avait la beauté,
Mais ce petit trésor
Lui vaut de l'or.

Étant servante
Chez un riche seigneur,
Elle fit son bonheur,
Par son humeur.

even reached the Princesses and made them very stubborn about the presentation. Louis XV, fully alive to

> Toujours facile
> Aux discours d'un amant,
> Ce seigneur la voyant,
> Prodiguait des présents.
>
> De bonnes rentes
> Il lui fit un contrat;
> Elle est, dans la maison,
> Sur le bon ton.
>
> De paysanne
> Elle est dame, à présent,
> Porte les falbalas
> De haut on bas.
>
> En équipage
> Elle roule grand train,
> Et préfère Paris,
> A son pays.
>
> Elle est allée
> Se faire voir en cour,
> On dit qu'elle a, ma foi!
> Plu même au roi!
>
> Filles gentilles
> Ne désespérez pas;
> Quand on a des appas,
> Filles gentilles,
> On trouve, tôt ou tard,
> Pareil hasard!

(The woman of Bourbonnais on arriving in Paris earned some louis. The woman of Bourbonnais earned some louis in the house of a marquis.

Her sole possession was beauty, but that little treasure was worth much gold.

As a servant in a rich lord's house she made him happy by her amiability.

When the lord found her always ready to listen to words of love, he showered presents upon her.

He settled a handsome income on her and gave her a good establishment.

From a peasant she has become a lady, and now wears finery from head to foot.

She dashes along in her carriage, and prefers Paris to her native province.

She went to show herself at Court, and, my word, they say she even attracted the King.

Pretty ones, do not despair; pretty ones, those who possess charms will find similar luck come their way, sooner or later.)

his folly, did not wish to cause an upset by hastening the event before he had prepared the minds of the royal family. There were long negotiations which kept the Court in suspense for several months, and led to bets for and against. The Choiseuls secretly encouraged the Princesses to resist, whilst redoubling their efforts to enlighten His Majesty, to open his eyes and make him ashamed of his choice. It is even alleged that Le Bel foresaw the consequences that might result from the deception he had practised towards his master, and, in fear of his anger, unsuccessfully strove to warn him ; and that, frightened and disappointed at his failure, in his despair he died suddenly and tragically, either voluntarily or involuntarily.

Whatever may be the facts, the agents employed by their august father could only bring Mesdames to consent by causing them to fear for his health, which would be affected by the chagrin their refusal would cause. They yielded to this irresistible argument. The next difficulty was to find a woman who would undertake the ceremony. They were obliged to hunt out a Madame de Béarn,[1] an old

---

[1] For the interesting but lengthy details of this presentation, read Claude Saint-André, *op. cit.* pp. 37–50. Very briefly the *Gazette de France* recorded : " On the 22nd of this month of April, 1769, the Comtesse du Barry had the honour of being presented to the King and the royal family by the Comtesse de Béarn."

It was only after this that " the despairing Princesses ceased to believe in the second marriage of their father. For the King's daughters, convinced that there was no other way of snatching him ' from his evil courses,' had combined in most urgent persuasion to induce the monarch to give them a queen, and to allow his choice to fall on the Archduchess. He agreed in principle, but as soon as he saw Madame du Barry again he forgot all his promises. It was not without difficulty that some one was found to present her at Court. The Comtesse de Béarn was almost ruined. Louis XV promised to pay her debts and to ' protect her two sons, who were officers in the Navy.' The opposition of the anti-Barry party can be imagined." The Comtesse de Béarn was so upset by the black looks all around her that in January an opportune sprain glued her to her couch. Fortunately in April she was better ! Her poverty was her excuse.

petitioner to whom was paid the sum of a hundred thousand
livres for her trouble in the matter and for accompanying
Madame du Barry in the early steps of the path that no
one wished to take with her. The advent of favour did not
fail to bring her a court. The King supped every evening
with his mistress. She issued invitations and, to prevent
the grandees from declining, put at the foot, " His Majesty
will honour me with his presence." Gradually certain
ladies attached themselves to her—the Comtesse de
l'Hôpital, Madame de Valentinois and the Maréchale de
Mirepoix being among the first; and the Comte de la
Marche joined her band of admirers. The Prince de
Condé, having been successful in getting the King to come
and visit him at Chantilly, showed his gratitude by having
the Comtesse as well.

CHAPTER XXVIII

MARRIAGE OF THE DAUPHIN (LOUIS XVI) AND MARIE ANTOINETTE

ONE of the most important events in the reign was the alliance with the House of Austria. This alliance [1] was due to the Duc de Choiseul, who, apparently thinking as much about his own greatness as that of France, overcame all difficulties and succeeded in arranging the marriage. Nothing could have been better for him, for he who had disdained the aid of petty intrigues acquired the support of the Dauphine herself. It seemed impossible that he could maintain himself so long ; but when they saw his success his friends had more hope, particularly on account of his share in this happy event. He received the King's permission to go to Compiègne to meet the Princess and to be the first of the Ministers to pay his respects. The Dauphine received him with remarkable favour and granted him a personal interview, at which, after saying how much she had desired to see him, she thanked him for all he had done to contribute to her happiness. She added that she hoped he would continue to interest himself in her, and help her youth and inexperience with his advice.

Notwithstanding the poverty of the kingdom, the preparations, the ceremony and the celebration of the

---

[1] The alliance was the marriage of him who was to become Louis XVI (the oldest son of the Dauphin) with Marie Antoinette, daughter of Maria Theresa. This King and Queen, both of whom were guillotined, are too well known to need even the briefest of biographies here.

marriage of the heir-presumptive were necessarily very costly, but the expense was excessive because the master was prodigal, thinking of nothing but himself, allowing everything else to drift, and shutting his eyes to all the depredations for which such heavy outlays gave opportunities. For example, it is stated that thirty thousand horses were used, that a whole detachment of upholsterers posted from town to town to decorate the various places where the Princess was to lodge, that sixty new carriages were included in the procession that went to bring her from Strasburg.

This was only the prelude. Eyes had never beheld anything like the costumes of the King and the Princes, which the people crowded to see at the tailors' and embroiderers'. His Majesty's was one that had already been made for him to wear at the marriage of the Duc de Chartres. He had then asked whether anything more splendid could be imagined, and, on receiving a reply in the negative, had ordered it to be put aside for the marriage of his grandson. There were six as fine as this, and those of the royal children were in keeping. All were adorned with countless precious stones. Not less attention was attracted by the State coaches. They were as rich as they were elegant, as can readily be believed seeing that they were ordered by the Duc de Choiseul.

As to the spectacles, the fêtes of Louis XIV, so famous throughout Europe and in history, could not compare with them. The crowning piece of the firework display was said to comprise thirty thousand rockets, which, at an *écu* apiece, would cost four thousand *louis*—and all to vanish in the twinkling of an eye !

The preparation of all these prodigalities contrasted violently with the risings caused by the scarcity of bread, which continued and even grew worse at this time in some districts, such as Besançon and Tours. In the latter city the position was so desperate that the Intendant had to escape by a back door, and the Archbishop deemed it his duty to come to Court to show his care for his flock. In La Marche and Le Limousin more than four thousand people died of hunger, and many more would have died in the former province but for the charity of Monsieur de Persan, Master of Petitions, who, as lord of part of the province, caused substantial aid to be given to his vassals.

These troubles gave rise to a little pamphlet called *The Peculiar Idea of a Good Citizen regarding the Public Fêtes it is proposed to give in Paris and at Court on the Occasion of the Marriage of His Highness the Dauphin.* After enumerating the expenses, the banquets, spectacles, fireworks, illuminations, balls, all designed on the most magnificent scale at a cost of twenty millions, the writer terminated his really original brochure as follows :

" I propose to do nothing of all this, but to remit these twenty millions from the year's taxation, and particularly from the poll-tax. Thus, instead of furnishing amusement for the idlers of the Court and the capital by empty and passing entertainments, I shall cause the soul of the sorrowing peasant to be filled with joy, the whole nation to have its share in the happy event, and the cry to arise in the remotest corners of the realm, ' Long live Louis the Well-Beloved ! ' This new sort of celebration would cover the King with glory more real and more enduring than all the pomp and ceremony of Asiatic fêtes, and history would hand down this trait to posterity with more gratification than the frivolous details of a splendour that is burdensome to the people and far removed from the true greatness of a monarch who is a father to his subjects."

There were too many influential people interested in seeing that this idea should come to nought for it to receive attention ; they merely took steps to see that the cries of the wretched should not reach the throne. They pretended, in an announcement in the *Gazette de France*,[1] that there was plenty of corn at Nantes, the transport of which was prevented by the bad weather, floods and other obstacles.

It was in these depressing circumstances that the Dauphine arrived at Compiègne. The King was very anxious to see her and to learn whether she was pretty. It is said that, when the Prince de Poix came to announce the arrival of the Archduchess at Strasburg, Monsieur Bouret, secretary of the Cabinet, presented at the same time the deed of exchange which had been executed at the frontier. His Majesty, who was very free with this official, asked him what he thought of the Dauphine and whether she had a good bust. He replied that she had a charming face, fine eyes, and so on. " That is not what I am talking about," said His Majesty laughingly ; " I am asking whether she has a good bust." " Sire, I did not take the liberty of looking," answered the ingenious courtier. " You are a booby," continued the monarch, " that is the first thing one looks at in a woman."

It is easy to imagine from this story how eagerly Louis XV inspected his granddaughter-in-law as he approached her. He advanced towards her until the moment when, in accordance with the usual ceremonial, the princess alighted from her coach, threw herself at the feet of His Majesty, who raised her and embraced her. The night was spent at Compiègne, and the next day, as they passed through Saint-Denis, they called on Madame Louise, one of the royal princesses, who had recently taken

---

[1] See the *Gazette de France* of Monday, 14th May, 1770. Regarding the terrible want of the people and peasantry at this time (rarely did France pass through so grave an economic crisis as during these years preceding the Revolution) see, with reference to all these significant outbursts in town and country, the Preface (pp. 1-17) and chapter viii. (pp. 282-375), which we wish we could quote in full, of the profound, powerful and characteristic work, already mentioned, by Roustan, *Les philosophes et la Société française au XVIII⁰ siècle* (Hachette).

MARIE ANTOINETTE AS DAUPHINE

the veil in the Carmelite convent there. All Paris had taken up its position on the route, and both sides of the road from Saint-Denis to the Porte Maillot were lined with carriages. The royal family supped at the Château de La Muette, where Louis XV unblushingly presented the Comtesse Dubarry to the Dauphine and made her sit at the same table.

The Dauphine did not know the position of Madame Dubarry, of whom she had often heard before she left her own home. One day, weary of the continual repetition of the name, she had asked what this woman did to cause so much stir. The answer was that she amused the King. "If that is so," replied the Archduchess innocently, "I declare myself her rival." She was no longer tempted to be her rival now that she knew more, but, wishing to flatter the monarch's taste, she delighted him by replying "Charming" when he asked her what she thought of the lady. Beyond all question she was at the time the most remarkable woman at Court by her natural beauty and grace. Not only was she very beautiful in herself, but externally her behaviour and speech were in perfect taste.

The King, the Dauphin, and the royal family went to sleep at Versailles, leaving the Dauphine alone at La Muette, in conformity with the laws of the Church which forbade her sleeping under the same roof as her future husband. She went to the palace the following day, and, after putting on her wedding-dress, proceeded to the chapel to receive the nuptial blessing. The Princess was much admired. Although surrounded by strangers and strange conditions, she did not appear at all nervous, but performed her part of the ceremony with complete ease and unusual grace.

In the afternoon an enormous crowd thronged the gardens, where they could see the arrangements for the evening's fireworks and illuminations. The preparations for a magnificent fête obscured the fact that the park was very dilapidated and in places looked like the gardens of a mansion in the occupation of bailiffs. In the first place, the fountains, so essential for such a day, were not playing and, indeed, could not play. Several basins were empty, and even the canal was dirty and full of filth. There were broken and fallen statues which no one had troubled to set up again or remove. The very staircases were in a wretched state. There were no violins, no dancing, no refreshments for the crowd, who were not in the mood that is the first essential to a public festival. It is true a few mountebanks were preparing to give some performance in the evening. The very sky seemed to be antagonistic to the earth, for two heavy storms compelled the crowd to disperse without seeing the fireworks and illuminations, which were postponed. Another piece of neglect, which was unworthy of so majestic a place, resulted in the court-yards, at nine in the evening, being not so well lighted as those of a private mansion. The corridors and passages were in complete darkness, and there was not a single lamp or lantern on either façade of the palace. The town of Versailles appeared to take no part in this great event, and Paris was reproached with having done things in a very niggardly fashion. Beggars were in the streets that day as on other days—there were no polonies or bread or wine for them. The great nobles made no better show, and the magnificent palace of the Minister of Paris, the Comte de Saint-Florentin, was only lit by two low triangles of lamps.[1]

[1] The song, " The Marriage of the Dauphin," ran very differently ; but it was written before the event.

A la villa l'on fera
Grand gala,
Le bon vin y coulera,
L'on y verra abondance
Et des gueuletons d'importance !

(There will be great doings in town ; good wine will flow, there will be plenty, and great feasting !)

On the other hand, those who entered the State apartments on the wedding-day, and specially those who were present at the royal banquet, agreed that they had never seen such a wonderful sight, that any description must fall short of the facts, and that not even what was said in fairy tales could give more than an imperfect idea of the splendour. The richness and luxury of the costumes, the flashing of the diamonds, the magnificence of the apartments dazzled the spectators and made it impossible for them to appreciate details. The Dauphine was the cynosure of all eyes, and, if they were withdrawn out of respect, they soon returned. Here is a description of her, written at the time : " This princess, tall for her age, is slim without being gaunt, like a young lady not yet fully developed. She is well built, and her whole body is well proportioned. She has splendid, graceful, fair hair, which will probably turn chestnut. Her brow is already majestic, and her face is a rather long oval. Her eyebrows are as heavy as can be expected in a fair person. Her eyes are blue without being insipid, and are full of life and expression. Her nose is aquiline, rather pointed at the tip. Her Highness has a small mouth, with thick lips—specially the lower one, which is the famous ' Austrian lip ' ; [1] her

---

[1] " Austrian lip " is a common expression which has perhaps no very sound ethnological justification. Charles the Bold (1433–1477), a true Frenchman, the redoubtable adversary of Louis XI, great-grandson of Philippe VI of France, had a very drooping lip. His daughter, Mary of Burgundy, who had a drooping lip like her father, married Maximilian of Austria. Of this marriage was born Philippe le Beau, with lips like his mother's, who married Jeanne the Foolish, daughter of Isabella and Ferdinand the Catholic ; they were the father and mother of Charles Quint, from whom sprang the present Spanish kings with their pendent lower lips. Brantôme, in his *Dames Galantes* (seventh discourse), says : " Now, to return to our queen, Mary of Hungary, her large protruding mouth of the Austrian type does not come from the House of Austria but from Burgundy. I have heard it told to a lady of the Court of those times that Queen Eleanor was once passing through Dijon and went to pay her devotions at the monastery of the Carthusians in that place, and to visit the ancient tombs of her ancestors the Dukes of Burgundy ; and she was curious to have them opened as several kings had

complexion is dazzling, her natural colour enabling her to dispense with rouge. Her carriage is that of an archduchess, but her dignity is tempered with sweetness, and it is difficult, when one looks at this princess, to withhold respect mingled with affection."

The State ball, the most wearisome of the festivities because of its strict etiquette, also gave rise to much vexation. His Majesty fixed the procedure in advance. It was arranged, at the urgent request of the Ambassador of the Emperor and Empress-Queen, to pay special respect to Mademoiselle de Lorraine, who had the honour to belong to their august house. Consequently she was to dance before all the duchesses, immediately after the princesses of the blood, just as the Prince de Lambesc was to come immediately after the princes. The dukes and peers met at the house of M. de Broglie, Bishop and Count of Noyon, the doyen of the peers then in Paris and, despite the Church's horror of dancing, they discussed, drew up, and read a memorial which the prelate was entrusted with presenting to the King. To make it the more impressive they asked on this occasion for the support of the high nobility, of whom a large number signed. The King, very awkward as usual, avoided coming to a decision and fell back on the plea that the dancing at the ball was the one thing that could not be of consequence, that the choice of dancers was his personal concern.[1] He appealed

caused to be done. She beheld some so well preserved and complete that she recognized certain features, including the mouth. Upon which she cried suddenly : " Ah, I thought we inherited our mouths from Austria, but from what I now see we inherit them from Mary of Burgundy, our ancestress, and other Dukes of Burgundy, our ancestors." It is from his mother, Maria Christina, that Alfonso XIII, the present King of Spain, derives his characteristic lip.

[1] These expressions are taken from the remarkable " Letter from the King to the Dukes," date 17th May, 1770, which we quote in full : " The Ambassador of the Emperor and Empress-Queen, at an audience he had of me, asked on behalf of his master (and I am bound to believe all he says) that I would show some distinction to Mademoiselle de Lorraine on the

to their fidelity, attachment, submission and even friendship. This reply, unworthy of a great monarch, merely evoked ridicule, and only those attended the ceremony who were obliged to do so.

We shall never finish detailing the fêtes, entertainments and rejoicings, which continued for more than a month; but we cannot omit to mention the frightful catastrophe of the 30th May, that terrible night when, in the midst of delirious joy, more people perished than is often the case in a bloody battle! It was the occasion of the city's firework display. No better site could have been chosen than around the statue of Louis XV in that vast area that is more like a plain than a public square. After the fireworks there were illuminations on the boulevards, which led to a great crowd pouring through a broad street opening from the fortifications. It was, however, in this broad street that occurred carnage without precedent. Three circumstances combined to increase it, namely :

1. A plot, arranged by thieves, to cause a congestion, a crowd, a great confusion, so that they might be able in the disorder to rob and steal with impunity. The discovery of the bodies of several well-known thieves goes to establish their crime.

2. The neglect of the city architect to clear this site, where some six hundred thousand spectators were

occasion of the marriage of my grandson to the Archduchess Antoinette. The dancing at the ball being the only thing of no consequence, seeing that the choice of dancers is entirely my affair, without distinction of precedence, rank or dignity, except in regard to the princess and princesses of my blood who cannot be compared with or put on the same level as any other French people, and not desiring, moreover, to make any innovation in the practice of my Court, I rely on the grandees and nobles of my realm, in virtue of the fidelity, submission, attachment and even friendship which they have ever shown to me and to my predecessors, not to cause me any displeasure, particularly on the present occasion when I desire to show to the Empress my gratitude for the present which I, like you, hope will make me happy for the rest of my days.

"A true copy.   SAINT-FLORENTIN."

to congregate, by filling in the ditches in the gangways and removing all obstacles that might restrict or hamper the traffic.

3. The inadequacy of the guard and the meanness of the municipal authorities who would not pay the bonus of a thousand *écus* demanded by the Maréchal Duc de Biron to have the Gardes Françaises to supplement the weakness and inefficiency of the archers of the Town Guard.

Be that as it may, one hundred and thirty-three corpses were picked up and taken to the cemetery of the parish of the Madeleine (Ville l'Évêque) for identification, and subsequently buried with solemn ceremony by order of the Lieutenant of Police, issued on the representations of the Public Prosecutor. If we add the wounded, disabled and suffocated who were taken to neighbouring houses or to hospitals and died soon afterwards, those who thought at first that they were all right, but, commencing to spit blood, in the course of six weeks also fell victims to their curiosity, the total must be some eleven or twelve hundred. General indignation was aroused by the appearance, three days after the disaster, of M. Bignon, the Provost of the Merchants, who was regarded as chiefly responsible, in his box at the Opera.[1]

On the other hand, the Dauphin was greatly upset at having been the indirect cause of this calamity. He sent to the Lieutenant of Police his month's income of two thousand *écus*, the only money he had at his disposal, for the help of the most needy cases. The Dauphine, Mesdames and the princes of the blood followed his example. Various corps did the same. The Parliament, one of whose members had narrowly escaped death, wished to take cognizance of

[1] Regarding these fêtes of unheard-of magnificence and this catastrophe, the facts and details will be found in chapter ii. of *Le Mariage de Marie-Antoinette*, by P. de Nolhac, pp. 73–132 : "Marie Antoinette Dauphine."

the matter and inquire into its cause. A precedent was cited, though a much less serious one, from the reign of Louis XII, in which the Provost of the Merchants and the two senior aldermen were fined for not having properly examined a bridge that had given way, causing the death of four or five citizens. This was enough to frighten M. Bignon,[1] but the report of Seguier, the Solicitor-General, exculpated him. Everything was attributed to fate and, as the magistrates were distracted by other things which interested them more nearly, he got off with a fright and with a regulation restricting the jurisdiction of the municipal authorities in such matters.

When this sad event was exhausted and people were tired of talking about it and of cursing the Provost of the Merchants, they turned to more agreeable things. They were full of the Dauphine, of her vivacity, her pleasant ways, the frankness with which she eluded those around her. But she did nothing without the King's approval. She gave the name of " Madame l'Étiquette " to the Comtesse de Noailles, her lady-in-waiting, very grave and austere, who told her every minute that she was not conforming with the usages of her position ; and she did not the less obey her whims, particularly in regard to matters that concerned the brightness of her temperament and her health.

[1] In one of the verses of the song we have already quoted, *Le Mariage du Dauphin*, it was said, *in advance*, concerning Bignon, the Provost of the Merchants (the equivalent of the Mayor of Paris) :

> Les arbres en guéridons
> Les balcons,
> Seront chargés de lampions,
> Partout le bon goût décide,
> C'est un Bignon qui préside.

(Trees turned into stands, balconies, all will be hung with lamps. Everywhere good taste will prevail, for it is a Bignon who superintends.)

We have just seen what came of the festivities organized and superintended by Bignon.

She rode alone, without a groom; she went out as and when she pleased; she walked on foot; and so she formed her bodily faculties and cultivated the powers that her age was developing. She invited her brothers, sisters and aunts to dinner or supper whenever the idea struck her, and went to dine with them in the same free-and-easy fashion. In short, she recalled as much as possible the intimacy to which she had been accustomed in the inner life of the Court of Vienna, where the strictest etiquette was observed in public but freedom and simplicity prevailed in private.

This behaviour, which was fundamentally consistent with the character of Louis XV, would have suited him much better in those happy days when he was as innocent as his little granddaughter-in-law; but at a certain age it is impossible to alter. Moreover, his ministers, his favourites, his mistress were all concerned that he should not give himself up too much to his family, and, if his friendliness and kindness to the Dauphine did not allow him to restrain her as much as they would have liked, at least they succeeded in keeping the King away from her instead of bringing them together, which would have been the natural consequence of her unrestrained attitude towards His Majesty.

CHAPTER XXIX

MADAME DU BARRY AGAIN—PUBLIC DISASTERS—DEATH OF LOUIS XV

WHAT could be more outrageous than the things that occurred at the Court, during the last years of the reign, between the two lovers, things that became public property because indiscreet witnesses revealed them ? To hear the countless tales with which Paris enlivened its supper-parties it might be thought that the follies of Caligula's empire were being repeated in another setting. Now it was Madame Dubarry who, in the presence of the King and his notary, rose naked from her bed and took one slipper from the Papal Nuncio and the other from the Grand Almoner, which two prelates regarded themselves as fully compensated for their humiliation by their good fortune in getting a glimpse of the secret charms of such a beauty. Again there was the talk of the Marquise de Roses, companion to the Comtesse de Provence, being whipped by the favourite's women in her presence on the grounds that the King, rebuking her because of her youth in respect of some want of deference, had said laughingly, "Ah, she is a naughty child who ought to be spanked ! " The two mad creatures embraced and were more inseparable than ever. It was a more contemptible sycophancy that made the Duc de Tresmes, who found the favourite not at home, leave a note : " The monkey of the Comtesse Dubarry has called to pay his respects and make her laugh," for she found his hunch amusing and he regarded himself as very fortunate to be her plaything. Another story was of M. de Boisnes granting the Cross of St. Louis to a ship's paymaster in return for a parakeet which he had presented to the Countess. How vulgar it was, too, to see Madame Dubarry digging the Duc d'Orléans in the ribs when he came to beg her support of his marriage with Madame de Montesson and the exercise of her influence with the King to recognize her as Duchesse d'Orléans, her reply being, " All right, fatty, go ahead and get married ; we will see what can be done afterwards. You know how interested I am," as if she did not despair of seeing herself later on following in the footsteps of Madame de Maintenon.

Nothing could equal the degradation of Louis XV who, sharing the lady's favours with her negro boy,[1] made Zamora governor of the Château de Lucienne at a salary of six hundred *livres*, by a warrant sealed by the Chancellor. He allowed himself to be treated by his mistress like one of her servants, and to be called " France " (which amused him) in the private apartments where he liked to prepare his own breakfast. Who was there in the whole country that did not hear of Madame Dubarry, while in bed, saying to the King who was making coffee but allowed his attention to be distracted, calling to him, " Look out, France, your coffee's doing a bolt ! "[2]

---

[1] This negro was one of her affections without there being any question of his being a rival of Louis XV. She had him baptized, with herself as godmother, the godfather being the Comte de la Marche, son of the Prince de Conti,—a prince of the blood ! Zamora wore, on the day of his baptism (he was ten years old) a wonderful hussar's dress which appears in the accounts of the tailor, Carlier, as follows : " White costume, striped with silver ; coat, breeches, boots in heavy silk ; buttons, belt and sabre of silver ; hat plume of jasmine."

[2] This story has, however, been strongly contested. With regard to all these attacks on Madame du Barry, we repeat what we said about similar attacks on Madame de Pompadour. Without feeling called upon to attempt a rehabilitation, which would be no easy task, we would say that in all these gross pamphlets, these improper and cynical poems, politics often constituted the prime and only inspiration. In the case of Madame du Barry they would proceed from the friends of the disgraced Choiseul, and the supporters

It was this same woman, so shameless, coarse and disgusting in private, who gave audiences to ambassadors, who was surrounded by the representatives of the allies, of all the little German principalities that trembled for their lot at the time of the partition of Poland, and begged her interest with the King on their behalf. It was this same woman whom Louis XV led in triumph to the inauguration of the Bridge of Neuilly, a ceremony from which even the

of the dismissed Parliament, because, rightly or wrongly, they regarded the royal decisions as largely due to the favourite.

"A shameless, coarse, disgusting woman," says our author. What evidence there is against such insults ! " She is kind and generous, gentle in company, an excellent friend, charitable, obliging. She behaves with the greatest propriety both in her own home and abroad," says the Comte d'Espinchal. "Her speech was not common, much less vulgar ; although not brilliant, she was not so totally devoid of mind as has been said " (Marquis de Bouillé). " There is no record by reliable contemporaries of that alleged coarseness of language with which it is sought to pollute her pretty mouth. As to her manners, they are perfect " (Prince de Talleyrand). " I was astounded to see how she had adopted the speech and behaviour of the ladies of the Court. . . . She was kindly, anxious to oblige, bore no ill will, and was the first to laugh at the many songs that were aimed at her " (De Belleval). " She had a dignified air " (Inspectors of M. de Sartines). "When I recall her smile, so full of kindness, I become more indulgent towards the favourite " (Brissot).

And how many testimonies still remain ! Let us record just one more : " In the Revolution—(we know that she was guillotined on suspicion of helping the *émigrés* and forwarding Royalist intrigues, but could she have done otherwise ?)—in the Revolution she distinguished herself by her devotion and her singular goodness to those who were threatened. This woman, who had not been warned against vice in her youth, who had been dragged down by poverty and evil counsels, hurt no one when she came to possess so much power to hurt. Such moderation, remarkable in one placed as she was, entitles her to the indulgence of the most severe " (Sénac de Meilhan). We conclude with this : " No one would seek to deny that Madame du Barry was a sinner, and that her long reign was a scandal. But this sinner, all things considered, was no worse than others who, during their lifetime, or after their death, have been treated with more consideration. And the scandal, if the last, was not the greatest nor the most disastrous of the reign. Above all, Madame du Barry was not so silly, so vile, so coarse, so badly brought up as is made out by these absurd stories, including the remark so frequently quoted as revealing the royal degradation : " France, your coffee's doing a bolt ! " In the first place nobody, not even the mistress, ever called Louis XV ' France' "—Marquis de Ségur, *Silhouettes Historiques*, pp. 188–189 (Paris : Calmann Lévy).

Princesses and the Dauphine were excluded so that none should rival her. It was this woman who made him take it amiss that the heir-presumptive to the throne should keep her away from his wife at a supper of reconciliation arranged by a Court intriguer, to the point that he cried, " It is clear that none of my children love me ! " It was this same woman for whom a golden toilet set was made, although the Dauphine did not possess one and the Queen had never had one. Specially noticeable was the mirror, which was surmounted by two little cupids holding a crown which was suspended over her head every time she looked at herself—an allegory of what was in store for her. It was this same woman who, deeming herself inadequately housed in the palace of a princess of the blood, caused to be built the Pavillon de Lucienne, a trinket of which the cost was incalculable because everything was fanciful and the price depended only on the greed of the artist and the folly of the proprietor. Finally, it was this same woman who, against scraps of paper signed by herself, dipped into the public purse for herself and her family, costing more than all Louis' previous mistresses put together, and, notwithstanding the poverty of the people and the public calamities, went on increasing her prodigalities and inroads to such an extent that a few years would have seen the complete ruin of the kingdom if the death of Louis XV had not put an end to them.

Since the marriage of the Comte d'Artois [1] the King had become more depressed than before, and felt his strength beginning to fail. Nature gave him warning that

[1] Charles Philippe, Comte d'Artois, later Charles X, was born at Versailles in October 1757, died at Gorritz, in Illyria, the 6th November 1837. He married Maria Theresa of Savoy, daughter of the King of Sardinia. Their children were the Duc d'Angoulême (1775-1844), who renounced his rights to the throne; the Duc de Berry (1778-1820), who was the father of Henri V ; and Mademoiselle d'Angoulême, who was born and died in 1783. The scandal-mongers say he was the lover of his sister-in-law, Marie

he ought no longer to indulge in sexual pleasures. He himself said to his surgeon, " I can see that I must put on the brake," to which the latter replied, very frankly, " Sire, you would do better to stop altogether." The sudden death of Chauvelin, one of his favourites, who was in the best of health, a companion in his parties of debauchery, at one of which he succumbed under the King's very eyes, affected him greatly and was constantly in his thoughts. The very similar death of the Maréchal d'Armentières, who was about the same age as the monarch, added to his depression. Finally, a sermon preached before him on the Thursday in Holy Week by the famous Bishop de Senez brought remorse to his heart. This eloquent prelate recalled the period of his illness at Metz, the most glorious time of his life, when the love of his subjects had been shown in the highest degree. He did not disguise the fact that this love was diminishing, that the nation, burdened with taxes, could only groan under its own misfortunes ; he showed the monarch that, although on the throne, he no doubt had, and deserved to have, personal friends, but that his best friends ought to be his people. He finished by urging him not to trust blindly, in regard to the administration of the realm, to the advice of his ministers, who were only too often concerned to deceive him, but to rely on himself, on his own feelings, on his experience of more than half a century.

This evangelical boldness did not displease Louis XV, who received the preacher in very friendly fashion. He reminded him of the engagement to preach before him in

Antoinette, concerning which allegation there were filthy pamphlets, songs and satirical pieces which can be glanced at (quotation, or their obscene reproduction, is impossible) in H. d'Almeiras, *Les Amoureux de Marie Antoinette* (Paris : Albin Michel) ; Fleischmann, *Pamphlets Libertins contre Marie Antoinette* (Librairie des Publications Modernes) ; Fleischmann, *Madame de Polignac* (Bibliothèque des Curieux) ; Hervez, *Les Galanteries à la Cour de Louis XVI* (Bibliothèque des Curieux).

Lent, 1776, an engagement which, he said with a laugh, he had now called on him to fulfil, although he was a bishop. After this the King redoubled his visits to Madame Louise who, it was known, used every endeavour to bring him to God. The evil-minded courtiers feared lest the same weakness that had made him their slave should now make him the slave of the priests. At a meeting held in the favourite's room, it was decided that His Majesty must be aroused from this condition by some special orgy capable of distracting him and of reviving his taste for pleasure. They prevailed on him to arrange a visit to Trianon, where he should find a young creature possessing the most seductive charms ; for Madame Dubarry had for some time past followed the example of Madame de Pompadour and, both to secure rest for herself and to excite her worn-out lover, constantly furnished him with fresh delights. As a consequence of the blind fate that mocks at the vain hopes of men and often upsets the greatest efforts of their minds, the very steps taken by these corrupters to perpetuate their dominion were their undoing, and France was saved.[1]

The new beauty who had been placed in the King's bed already bore in her bosom the germ of small-pox which, commencing to develop, rendered her insensible and unresponsive even to the King's embraces. They had given

---

[1] This story is quite improbable, although several reliable historians, such as Lacratelle, Jobez, and Henri Martin, have given it credence. The *bon mot* of the Superior of St. Sulpice, " There is nothing little about the great," may be witty, but it cost him his place.
" Towards the end of April 1774, Louis XV on his way to the hunt met a funeral procession. His natural curiosity regarding such matters led him to approach the coffin and ask who was to be buried. They told him it was a young girl who had died of small-pox. At that moment he received his death-blow, although he did not know it "—Voltaire, *Précis du Règne de Louis XV*. " It is a frightful story, which my pen refuses to tell. The King's small-pox simply came from excessive indulgence at a party of debauchery at Trianon with an extremely pretty girl of sixteen, provided by Madame du Barry. This girl already had the germ, although she was not aware of it, and she communicated it to the King, whom it carried off

the King, as aids to jaded nature, all the resources that
art could devise to stimulate the most violent lust, so that,
while he was pumping his blood-vessels full of the poison
of that fell disease, his exertions were robbing him of the
strength to withstand it.   He took to his bed the next day,
and the first idea of the favourite's advisers was to keep
him at Trianon in ignorance of what was the matter.   The
doctors decided differently, however, and the King was
removed in his dressing-gown to Versailles.

It soon became known that Louis XV was suffering
from small-pox, and the news rapidly spread to the utter-
most ends of the kingdom.   Many rejoiced, but some
trembled at the prospect of a king who was not yet twenty
years old.

The Dauphin behaved with a prudence far beyond his
years.   His first step was to present himself at his grandfather's door.   Without disclosing to the invalid the nature
of his illness, he was told that he must not allow any of the
royal children to enter his room.   The Duc de la Vrillière
informed the Prince, on His Majesty's behalf, that his
health was too precious to the State and was not merely
his own concern ;   and that he must not prejudice it by
entering the room of his august grandparent who forbade
him to do so.   He withdrew, shut himself up with the

---

in three days," wrote Hardy.   The Abbé Baudeau speaks of " a good story
regarding the King's illness ; a little dairymaid, who it was thought would
please Louis, had been washed, combed, perfumed and put in the King's
bed, while her brother was dying of small-pox, which also carried her off.
And that is the story that is going the round of Paris, and you can guess the
talk it is making "—*Chronique indiscrète*.

Sometimes it is a miller's daughter, sometimes a baker's ; sometimes it is
a cow-herd, sometimes the daughter of Montvallier, Madame du Barry's
intendant and secretary ; sometimes it is the daughter of the gardener at
Lucienne, whom the favourite, as his procuress, had prostituted to the King.
There is nothing reliable, merely old women's gossip and tales.   No
substantial evidence is available.   At the time there was a serious epidemic
of small-pox at Versailles, and the worn-out body of Louis XV was receptive
soil.   The King died of the black pox, so specially fatal to a patient of his age.

22

Dauphine, and refused to see the crowd of courtiers who already sought the rays of the rising sun.

The whole medical faculty was summoned except Dr. Bouvard, a personal enemy of Dr. Bordeu, Madame Dubarry's medical attendant, to whom she had asked her royal lover to give his confidence. The full effects of etiquette were revealed, and it was manifest how a monarch, possessed of absolute power to injure his people, finds difficulty in arranging for his own preservation. At the very beginning of the King's attack an English doctor named Sutton, who was celebrated for a special system of inoculation and for a remedy against small-pox, was in Paris and came with an offer to treat and save the patient. The faculty drove him away, and only recalled him when the King's condition had become desperate ; he then replied that it was too late.

As soon as the King was struck down, the question of administering the sacrament was considered. Dr. Bordeu, knowing how such a thing would distress the mistress, put it off as long as possible, and strongly opposed any mention of it to the King. He asserted that there was no immediate danger, and that three-quarters of the people were killed by such steps. Madame Dubarry took advantage of this respite to spend every moment at her lover's bedside.[1] During the first days he, in ignorance of his condition, made her stroke his running sores with her white, delicate hands. It is related that, lustful even on his death-bed,

---

[1] Careless of contagion and with the admirable devotion of which women are capable, the daughters of Louis XV remained with the King during the day, and at night, Madame du Barry, not less courageous, took their place. There is no need to deal with our author's coarse suggestion ; but this vigil at the bedside was, as between the party of du Barry and that of her enemies, a matter of life and death in connexion with the approaching " palace revolution." As at Metz, the question of dismissal preceded the administration of extreme unction.

" Between the two parties stood the Princesses, whose austere piety so strangely consorted with the most remarkable indulgence, and whose filial

he caressed her from time to time, kissed her breast, and allowed himself such other liberties as his weakness would permit.

The clergy, fearing that the august invalid would escape them, were furious. They loudly blamed the Archbishop of Paris, who had repaired to Court immediately on receiving the grave news, but had made no effort to obtain possession of the King's conscience and had even allowed himself to be excluded from the royal presence in the most humiliating fashion. The prelate was suffering at the time with bladder trouble, regarding which the irreverent, who did not know how serious things were, made facetious remarks to the effect that His Reverence passed blood in Paris and only got his water clear when he was at Versailles. It was the sick man himself who, when Monsieur de la Martinière with his usual frankness told him he had small-pox, was impressed and, on the fifth night of his illness, said to those around him, " I have no desire for a repetition here of what happened at Metz. Please tell the Duchesse d'Aiguillon that she will do me a favour by taking away the Comtesse Dubarry." Once this painful separation was effected the priests had no difficulty with regard to the rest, and two days later Louis XV received the last sacrament after listening to this declaration by the Grand Almoner :

" Although the King owes no account of his actions to any one but God, he regrets the scandal he has given to his

love, singularly unenlightened, led them to defer the moment when the favourite should be sent away, and the King learn of his danger. Frightened, but forcing themselves to remain standing at the foot of the sick man's camp bed whenever Madame du Barry was not there, the King's three daughters braved contagion, but had not the courage to come to any decision "—Comte Fleury, *Louis XV intime.* See also the whole chapter, " The Death of the King ".

See specially in the Appendix, " The Death of Louis XV," an honest and remarkable account of the death and of the unseemly intrigues around the death-bed.

subjects, and declares that henceforth he only desires to
live in order to uphold religion and to promote the happiness of his people."

The speaker wished by his words to maintain his
master's dignity, but had uttered an absurdity, something
actually contrary to the teachings of the clergy. Even if
it is admitted that a king is not accountable to his subjects
for his conduct of public affairs, he none the less owes them
the example of a good Christian in religious matters, and
this obligation is the greater because of his exalted position
which lays upon him stricter and more striking duties.
These principles are preached daily from the pulpits,
but Monsieur de la Roche Aymon, one of the most ignorant
and shallow prelates in France (which is saying a lot), spoke
with the zeal of a courtier and not with that of an apostle ;
he praised better than he reasoned. If he had done his
duty he would no doubt have persuaded His Majesty to
recall the Prince de Conti, who was still in disgrace, and to
be reconciled with him, reconciliation being the first step
religion demands from the dying.

Louis XV only survived three days after he had taken the
sacrament. The next day there was a temporary improvement, which was reflected by the behaviour of the courtiers.
They had howled at the Dubarrys till they had obliged them
all to leave Versailles except the young marquis of that
name, who had to remain on duty with the Comtesse
d'Artois, and even he was compelled to doff his uniform
so as to attract less attention. Now there was a constant
procession of carriages from Versailles to Rueil, where
the favourite was, exceeding that between Paris and
Versailles—but it diminished as the bulletins became less
favourable.

The King died at twenty minutes past three on the 10th
of May. The whole Court immediately moved to Choisy,
only those remaining with the dead body whose duty

obliged them to do so. There was a great hurry to remove
it from the château. The usual formalities were neglected
in order to shorten the delay, and because it was difficult
to find experienced people with the necessary courage.
Within forty-eight hours the body was transferred to
Saint-Denis, escorted by forty men of the bodyguard and a
few pages carrying torches. The coffins (there were two
leaden coffins because of the stench) were transported in
a hunting-coach, into which it had been put through
the front, and the escort convoyed the corpse at the same
speed as they had often maintained when escorting him
alive. Never was a monarch so rushed off. The same lack
of decency was shown by the spectators along the road and
at Saint-Denis. The dramshops were filled with drunken
people singing, and, if it is through wine that one hears
the truth, the feelings of the people could be learned from
what one of them said. In order to get rid of him the
wine-seller told him that the funeral procession of Louis XV
was about to pass. " What," said he, with a freedom of
speech which betrayed his condition, " that blackguard
made us die of starvation when he was alive, and now that
he is dead he wants to make us die of thirst ! " [1]

[1] They sang, " There is the ladies' delight, there he is," and cried, " Tally
ho ! " in the somewhat affected way that the King had been accustomed to
utter the cry at the hunt. " The philosophy of the people had made great
progress," wrote the Duc de Liancourt—a bitter thought from a great
noble who saw the approach of the Revolution. The night of the funeral,
Madame du Barry was escorted by the constabulary, " as a prisoner of
State," from Rueil to the Abbey of Pont-aux-Dames. " All the way she
cried like a child. As she crossed the threshold of the dilapidated monastery,
she looked at the high, gloomy walls and said : " What a wretched place
to which to send me." The severe, haughty abbess, Madame de la Roche
Fontenilles, surrounded by the sisters, awaited the prisoner in the parlour.
The young nuns did not at first dare to look directly at her, but examined
her in a mirror, and were all surprised to find in her, not the features of a
devil, as they had anticipated, but the most beautiful and distressed of
women. There were thirty ladies of the choir, and twenty lay sisters ;
they wore the white robe with stomacher of the Bernardines, and a black
veil and long scapular reaching to the feet. The Countess was taken to the

A *bon mot* of a different kind, attributed to the Abbé of Sainte-Geneviève, confirms the desire of the lower classes by that of the more thoughtful citizens. This priest was being teased about the Saint and the want of any good resulting from the discovery of her shrine, which had in earlier days been so efficacious. His retort was, " Why gentlemen, what are you grumbling at ? Is he not dead ? "

Again, the name of " Louis the Longed-for," given to his successor, was the cruellest reflection that could have been cast on the reign of " Louis the Well-Beloved." Modesty did not permit Louis XVI to adopt this appellation of flattery in advance. He rejected it indignantly, no doubt wishing to obtain it more deservedly from posterity through his actions. *O utinam!*

FUNERAL ORATION ON LOUIS XV

Te voilà donc, pauvre Louis,
Dans un cercueil à Saint-Denis ;
C'est là que la grandeur expire !
Depuis longtemps, s'il faut le dire,
Inhabile à donner la loi
Tu portais le vain nom de roi
Sous la tutelle et sous l'empire
Des tyrans, qui régnaient pour toi.

---

most remote corner of the convent and kept in absolute privacy. For a time she thus suffered, on the plea of political necessity, the closest imprisonment. Marie Antoinette wrote to her mother, " The creature has been put in a convent, and every one whose name was associated with the scandal has been driven from Court." The Empress regarded this as so violent that she thought it her duty to suggest to the young Queen, her daughter, the need for " more Christian charity "—Claude Saint-André, *Madame du Barry*, pp. 278–280 (Paris : Emile Paul). Marie Antoinette was less entitled than anyone else to speak like this. The heroine of the affair of the diamond necklace, the friend of the Princesse de Lamballe and of Madame de Polignac, was soon to have levelled at her, rightly or wrongly, so many filthy books, obscene plays and licentious poems that, as we have already said, a mere bibliography would occupy a large volume !

Etais-tu bon ? C'est un problème
Qu'on peut résoudre à peu de frais ;
Un bon prince ne fit jamais
Le malheur d'un peuple qui l'aime ;
Car on ne peut appeler bon
Un roi sans frein et sans raison
Qui ne vécut que pour lui-même.

Voluptueux, peu délicat,
Inappliqué par habitude,
On sait qu'étranger à l'État,
Le plaisir fit ta seule étude.
Un intérêt vil en tout point
Maîtrisait ton âme apathique,
Et le pur sang d'un peuple étique
Entretenait ton embonpoint.

On te vit souvent à l'école
De plus d'un fourbe accrédité,
Au mépris de ta Majesté
Te faire un jeu de ta parole ;
Au milieu même de la paix,
Sur l'art de tromper tes sujets
Fonder ton unique ressource,
Et préférer dans tes projets
A l'amour de tous les Français
Le plaisir de vider leur bourse.

Tu riais de leur triste sort,
Et, riche par leur indigence,
Pour mieux remplir ton coffre-fort
Tu vendais le pain de la France.
Tes serviteurs mourant de faim
A ta pitié s'offraient en vain ;
Leurs plaintes n'étaient pas admises.
L'infortune avait beau crier :
Prendre tout et ne rien payer
Fut ta véritable devise.

Docile élève des cagots,
En pillant de toutes manières,
Quoique parmi les indévôts
Tu disais pourtant tes prières,

Des sages ennemi secret,
Sans goût, sans mœurs, et sans lumières,
En trois mots voilà ton portrait.

Faible, timide, peu sincère
Et caressant plus que jamais
Quiconque avait pu te déplaire,
Au moment que de ta colère
Il allait ressentir les traits,
Voilà je crois ton caractère.

Ami des propos libertins,
Buveur fameux et roi célèbre
Par la chasse et par les catins,
Voilà ton oraison funèbre !

(There you are then, poor Louis, in a coffin at Saint-Denis ; that is where splendour finishes ! For long enough, if truth be told, incapable of ruling, you have borne the empty name of king under the control and domination of tyrants who reigned in your stead.

Were you good ? That is a riddle easily answered. A good prince never yet brought unhappiness to a nation who loved him ; and you cannot call good a king devoid of restraint and reason, who only lived for himself.

Voluptuous, coarse, indolent in habit, it is well known that, ignoring the State, you thought only of pleasure. An interest that was low in every way dominated your apathetic mind, and the pure blood of an emaciated people nourished your fatness.

Oft were you seen taking lessons from an accredited rogue, and, to your disgrace, making light of your word ; even in times of peace using as your sole resource your skill in deceiving your subjects ; and, in your plans, subordinating love for the French to your delight in emptying their pockets.

You mocked at their sad lot, and, profiting by their poverty, filled your coffers by selling the bread of France. Your servants, dying of hunger,[1] appealed in vain to your compassion ; their

---

[1] Let us recall what has already been said about the misery of the times of Louis XV. He was hunting in the Forest of Sénart, during one of the periods when bread was excessively dear, and met a man on horseback carrying a coffin. " Where are you taking that coffin ? " asked Louis XV. " To the next village," replied the peasant. " For a man or for a woman ? " " For a man." " And what caused his death ? " " Sire, he died of hunger." The King immediately spurred on his horse.

murmurs were unheard. Misfortune might well cry that " Take all and pay nothing " was your real motto.

Apt pupil of the bigots, you robbed in all directions; although among the unbelievers, you still said your prayers. The secret enemy of the wise, devoid of taste, devoid of morals, devoid of enlightenment; there is your portrait in a word.

Weak, timid, insincere, favouring more than ever him who has offended you just when he should feel the force of your anger; that, I think is your character.[1]

Fond of licentious talk, a great drinker, a king famous for hunting and whoring; there is your funeral oration.)

---

[1] These verses are very characteristic. We have seen that on the very day when he decided to dismiss Madame de Mailly and replace her by her sister, Madame de Vintimille, he was more amiable than usual to the poor lady, and made an appointment with her, so that she might, presumably, witness her sister's triumph. The more amiable the King was, the more he was to be distrusted !

" This poem contains truths that are strong and harsh, but they are truths," wrote Hardy in his *Journal*.

APPENDIX

THE DEATH OF LOUIS XV

IN the *Revue Rétrospective* for the year 1885, M. Paul Collin publishes an interesting narrative taken from a manuscript preserved in the Library of the Arsenal: "The last illness of Louis XV," by the Duc de Liancourt, reversionary Grand Master of the Wardrobe. Its style is bad and its spelling worse. It is a terrible but very interesting picture of the Court at the time of the King's death, particularly with respect to the rivalry between the enemies and the friends of Madame du Barry:

All Paris was told that the King had remained in bed till four o'clock and had then been slowly carried in his dressing-gown to Trianon,[1] where he had at once gone to bed. All the princes and high officials came, I among others, but without great haste. On my arrival I found the King in bed. Le Monnier, whom I saw, told me that he, like every one else, hoped that the fever would leave the King during the night, but that his weak conditon made him fear that such might not be the case, in which event he would ask for assistance and more doctors the next morning. I also learned that the royal family who had come to see him on his arrival, had only stayed a minute and that the King had promised to send when he wanted to see them. This was all due to the precautions of Madame du Barry who, furious at the King's return to Versailles,

---

[1] This should manifestly be Versailles.—*Trans.*

wanted to shut herself up with him as much as possible, to the exclusion of his children. The King had submitted, and told his children not to return till he sent for them.

The fever continued all night, even increasing in intensity. His headache became worse, and at eight in the morning we were told that the King was to be bled, a step which was decided upon by Le Monnier in consultation with La Martinière. We also learned that Lorry and Bordeu had been sent for from Paris. Le Monnier, in accordance with the decision he had come to the previous night, had asked the King for help and had begged him to name the doctors he would like to have called in consultation. He said he had not chosen either, which was quite true. The King had chosen them both after asking Madame du Barry. One was her own doctor and the other the doctor of M. d'Aiguillon, who had persuaded the mistress to induce the King to make this choice, hoping to derive some advantage himself as occasion arose during the illness. The news of the bleeding attracted the courtiers ; those who had official duties and those who had not all assembled, and the cabinet was soon thronged with people eager for news of the King, but without any means of getting it. Hardly anyone left the sick-room, and those who did said nothing.

But the proposed bleeding of the King, the existence of the fever, the summoning of the doctors, all proclaimed that a real illness was feared, and gave free course to the conjectures of the whole Court. Madame du Barry persisted in believing firmly that the fever would not last another twenty-four hours. She saw what M. d'Aiguillon wanted her to see and, following his advice, contented herself with delaying the calling of the officials and with monopolizing the King's attention herself. Her supporters similarly refused to believe that the King could be ill, and regarded the slight indisposition as an occasion for increasing their credit, seeking what advantage they could derive from it. . . . It was midday. The doctors had just arrived. At last the Wardrobe were summoned, and we found the King surrounded by a host of doctors and surgeons, asking them with inexpressible weakness and anxiety about the progress of his illness, about their views regarding his condition, and the remedies they would administer in such and such circumstances. The doctors reassured him, characterizing his illness as a catarrhal fever ; but their treatment revealed more anxiety than their words. They had already told him that they would bleed him again in three hours and a half, and even a third time during the night or the next day if the second did not give him relief from his headache. The King, whose questions had driven Lorry to make this statement, showed great dissatisfaction. " A third bleeding ! " he said. " Then I am really ill ? A third bleeding would make me very weak. I hope most sincerely I shall not be bled a third time." Everything that kings say is repeated, and even construed. His remarks concerning the third bleeding soon went all round Versailles. They made a great impression on us when we heard them, and similarly affected others when they learned of them. The general impression was that a third bleeding would convince the King of his serious condition and decide him to dismiss Madame du Barry. Here it had always been said that a third bleeding was followed by the last sacrament and, according to each one's favourable or unfavourable feeling towards the mistress, he feared or hoped to see it ordered. As the party that desired the dismissal of Madame du Barry and her vile satellites was for the most part composed of decent folk, it confined itself to hoping for anything that would hasten that event, without intriguing to bring it about. It was far different with her wretched supporters. Accustomed to clandestine schemes, to low secret intrigues, they were determined to

use them in such important circumstances. They surrounded the doctors ; they buttonholed them and sought
to persuade them (or those of them they regarded as
upright) how seriously the King had taken the idea of
this third bleeding, how ill he would think himself if it
took place, and how great an effect fear might have on
so weak and apprehensive a man. They spoke more clearly
to those whom they regarded as less scrupulous, pointing
out that a third bleeding would be followed by the sacrament, by the dismissal of Madame du Barry, with the consequence that, if they carried it out, they would make of
her their irreconcilable enemy, for there could be no doubt
of her speedy return.

The surgeons, as usual, agreed with the opinion of the
doctors, and preparations were made for the bleeding
ordered for midday. The party who desired everything
that might result in the dismissal of Madame du Barry and
all the base courtiers, of which party I was one of the most
active, knew all that was going on among their opponents ;
but stopped at that, prudence forbidding any active step,
for in view of the risk to the King that would result from
the woman's banishment, it would have been dangerous
to show how greatly they longed for it. The cowardice
of the doctors, which had made them abandon the idea
of a third bleeding if the second did not give sufficient
relief, did not prevent their thinking that it would really
be essential. They had, however, given their word, and
to satisfy both that word and their consciences they
decided to make the second bleeding so heavy that it
would take the place of a third. Consequently they drew
from the King four large basinfuls. Kings must grow
accustomed to seeing their glory and their health at the
mercy of the intrigues and interests of those around
them.

The King was quite true to himself during and after

this bleeding. His fear and cowardice were inconceivable. He sent for smelling salts, saying that the mere sight of the surgeon would make him feel bad ; he had himself held up by four people, having his pulse felt and asking the doctors the same questions about his illness, the treatment, and his condition, every moment. " You say I am not ill and that I shall soon be cured," he said to them, " but you don't believe a word of it, and you ought to tell me so." The doctors protested that they were speaking the truth, but the King did not moderate his complaints, his whines, his cries. His fear and complaints were not those of anxious concern, but of cowardly and repulsive weakness. His headache, which had not yielded to the first bleeding, did not yield to the second, and the news was spread at Versailles, to the great satisfaction of some and the great grief of others, that the King was seriously ill. The agitated and suffering King spoke of nothing but himself on the rare occasions that he spoke at all. About five o'clock he sent for his children, who came and passed half an hour by his bedside without hearing or speaking a word. He would not have thought of this visit had not Laborde, who wished to arrange another, suggested that he should go for the King's family.

Laborde, the King's first valet, was, like M. d'Aumont, devoted to Madame du Barry, and fell in with her plans whenever they promised common advantage ; in this way he had great ideas for the present juncture. Although Laborde was low and quite devoid of honour, his baseness must not be confounded with that of M. d'Aumont ; it was more elevated, or rather less unblushing. The King, however, lying in his bed, had no desire to see her whom M. d'Aumont was so anxious to bring, only opening his mouth to groan and talk of himself to his medical advisers. The number of doctors by whom he was surrounded had already, earlier in the day, made me sorry for him ; fourteen people, all entitled to approach and examine an invalid seemed to me a real torture. The King, however, did not think so, and, over and above his being accustomed to a degree of solicitude that would be intolerable to others, his anxiety and fear made him really welcome it. The group comprised six doctors, five surgeons, and three apothecaries, and he would willingly have seen the number increased. He had his pulse felt six times an hour by all the fourteen, and when the whole crowd was not in his room he called for those that were missing so that he should constantly be surrounded, as if he hoped that so many attendants would prevent disease from daring to attack His Majesty. I shall never forget that, when Le Monnier had said he must see his tongue (the bed being open only enough to allow one to approach at a time) he put his tongue out a foot and, covering his eyes with his hands to screen them from the light, which bothered him, he left it out for more than five minutes, only drawing it in to say, after Le Monnier had looked at it, " Now you, La Sone," then " Now you, Lorry," and so on, until he had called in turn all the doctors, who manifested, each in his own way, the satisfaction they found in the beauty and colour of this precious and royal morsel. It was the same a moment later with his stomach, and he called each doctor, each surgeon, each apothecary in turn, and gladly submitted to their examination. During all these inspections great care was taken to keep the light, which bothered him and of which he had already complained, out of the King's eyes, the rays being allowed only to shine on the part it was desired to illuminate. A servant had been told off to see to this, and he never bungled. He was, indeed, more than exact, and I must describe, in passing, a ridiculous and laughable scene that resulted. They were going to give the King an enema. With difficulty they drew him to the edge of his bed and placed him in a convenient position with his head in his pillows and his hinder part bare and suitably disposed. The doctors stood around the bed, but made way for the chief apothecary, who came with the tube in his hand, and followed by his assistant bearing the rest of the syringe and the servant carrying the light with which the scene was to be illuminated. M. Fargeau, the chief apothecary, having taken up the correct position, was just about to direct and insert the tube when suddenly the servant, seeing that the light he held was shining full on the royal posterior and apparently thinking it might be dangerous to the health, or at least to the comfort, of His Majesty, snatched a hat from beneath the arm of a doctor and held it between the light and the place to which M. Fargeau was devoting his attention. I really cannot describe the wretched, scornful anger of the apothecary whose action had been spoiled by this eclipse, the indignation of the little assistant apothecary, and the general desire to laugh of those who were fortunate enough to witness the scene. This ridiculous incident will illustrate the unreflecting zeal and mechanical punctilio of underlings who never lose their deep veneration.

The doctors were not satisfied with the effect of their treatment ; and the continued weakness of the King and other symptoms made them fear a malignant fever. They still gave it out that the illness was a humoral fever, but they were constantly conferring with each other and manifesting their anxiety. Bordeu had been to see Madame du Barry and tell her that the King was seriously ill. Lorry had told M. d'Aiguillon that the King's condition might cause anxiety ; but both mistress and favourite did not yet believe it, and did not want to believe it. All Versailles, however, began to get nervous ; every one began to make his plan of conduct for the period of the illness. My own was to watch over the King and to help him with my presence as long as it should last. It had often been said, and with considerable truth, that I served him in accordance with my own convenience, and people had sought to make this a matter of reproach in the eyes of the King; but his apathy, which made him so indifferent, prevented his taking offence, and I had taken more advantage than others of his freedom with those around him, which earned so much approbation but was really only the result of complete indifference. All the same I did not wish, now that he was ill, not to serve him as well as and even better than others. I regarded it as my duty not to leave him any longer than was absolutely necessary for rest and meals. I also regarded that as my interest, for by such assiduous attention during his illness and by spending nights at his bedside, I should earn the right to resume my ordinary manner of living after his recovery. Moreover, I also wanted, and intended, to be a close spectator of so interesting an event, and to unravel the many intrigues to which it would certainly give rise.

It was already ten o'clock at night. The King had been moved from his State bed to a small one for greater convenience in attending to him. His feebleness, pain and dulness increased, and even allowing for his weakness and fear, it became abundantly evident that he was seriously ill. All Versailles was convinced of this except those who did not want to be. The doctors saw it like every one else, and announced it by their silence. They spoke to nobody outside their own circle, and deferred till the next day any announcement as to the nature of the illness. The royal family were very anxious, and had come after supper to see the King; they were preparing to take a little rest in the next room to see how he passed the first part of the night, when suddenly as some one carried an unshaded light near the King's face and illuminated his forehead and cheeks, a rash was seen. When the doctors around the bed perceived this rash, which had already developed into

23

pustules standing well above the skin, they looked at each other with a unanimity and an astonishment that testified to their ignorance. Le Monnier had seen the King for two days suffering with pains in his loins, with weakness and heart trouble; the other four had seen the symptoms develop since noon, but not one of them, even when feeling the pulse, had imagined that the disease might be small-pox. Every one now saw it in a flash, and one did not need to be a doctor to have no doubt about it. The doctors left the King's room to make the announcement to the royal family, saying that at last they knew what the matter really was, that there was no room for doubt, that the King was prepared for it and that all would go well. The first care of all concerned was to get the Dauphin, who had not had small-pox, away from the King's apartments. The Dauphine took him away; and the Comte de Provence and the Comte d'Artois, with their wives, also withdrew. Only the princesses remained. They had not had small-pox any more than the Dauphin and they were afraid of it; but they would not yield to our representations, being unshakeable in their determination not to abandon their father. It is difficult to understand why this act of filial piety excited so little public notice.

The manner in which the doctors had announced to the princesses that the King had small-pox seemed to them to convey not merely the hope but the assurance of a cure. They repeated that he was prepared for it, and mentioned five or six cases of people of even seventy having small-pox; and the ladies went to bed satisfied that all was well with the King as it was small-pox. Several other people of the household shared this gladness, and almost every one said at first, " Ah, that's all right! it is only an affair of nine days and a little patience." I did not share this general impression and, without expressing my own views, said to Bordeu, " Listen to these gentlemen who are delighted because the King has small-pox!" "By Jove," replied Bordeu, "apparently they have expectations. Small-pox at the age of sixty-four and with a body like the King's is a terrible disease!" He left me to go and impart the sad news to Madame du Barry, who had not seen the King all day, and he frightened her terribly when he told her practically what he had told me. Perhaps he minimized the danger a little, but he always assured me that at this first visit he told her that preparation had nothing to do with it and that there was cause for the gravest anxiety. While Bordeu was with Madame du Barry, there was a great discussion in a room close by the King's as to whether or not he should be told that he had small-pox. The princesses, when they retired, had referred the matter to our discretion and relied on our judgment and that of the doctors.

I was called, like the others, to this conference, which comprised all the medical men except Bordeu, with M. de Bouillon, M. d'Aumont and M. de Villequier. Opinions were divided.

I was asked my view, and replied that I had no doubt whatever that if the King learned that he had small-pox that knowledge would be his death-blow. I adduced his fear and weakness as reasons for my opinion, and finished by advising most positively that he should not be told. This advice was not in accordance with my desires, but it conformed with my conscience. I should have been culpable had I supported M. de Bouillon's recommendation, which I wished to see put into operation, for if the King knew definitely that his illness was really serious, he would resolve to take the sacrament and to dismiss all this troop, this infamous and shameful gang. Moreover, I had a feeling within me that it was meet for the King, who had never in his life enjoyed greater pleasure than in worrying those about him regarding their health and promising them an early death, to be concerned about his own and torture himself with anxiety.

The news that it was small-pox spread throughout Paris and at once everybody took it for granted that the King would die. The people took it very differently from the news of his illness at Metz thirty years earlier. Then there could have been found in the capital a million men foolish enough to be willing to sacrifice their own lives to save his ; and all his people, with one accord, had given him (goodness know why) the splendid title of " the Well-Beloved," a title of which he never appreciated the sweetness and value. They had learned much since then, and the disgraceful conduct of the King, the infamies that had been perpetrated in his name and to which his apathetic weakness had been accessory, had contributed greatly to their education. Paris was not now full of anxious people running, hurrying, stopping to get news ; everything seemed quiet and calm, happy and contented. Although the feeling was the same at Versailles there was a more anxious air, for Versailles is the home of hypocrisy. If hypocrisy is ever permissible it is in a case where, if it is possible without outraging honour to hide one's feelings, it would be a blunder to reveal them, and would incur almost certain risk of everlasting degradation.

INDEX